Water CFRs
Made Easy

André R. Cooper, Sr.

Government Institutes
Rockville, Maryland

 Government Institutes, a Division of ABS Group Inc.
4 Research Place, Rockville, Maryland 20850, USA
Phone: (301) 921-2300
Fax: (301) 921-0373
Email: giinfo@govinst.com
Internet: http://www.govinst.com

ISBN: 0-86587-631-2

Printed in the United States of America

Water CFRs Made Easy

Introduction

Appendices

Table of Contents

CWA & CFR Overview

Determination of Reportable Quantities for Hazardous Substances

Effluent Limitations General Provisions

Hazardous Waste Injection Restrictions

Marine Sanitation Device Standard

National Primary Drinking Water Regulations

NPDES Permit Program

State and Federal 404 Programs

State Permit Program (SPDES) Requirements

State UIC Program Requirements

State Underground Injection Control Programs

Toxic Pollutant Effluent Standards

Underground Injection Control Programs

Water Quality Planning and Management

Water Quality Guidance for the Great Lakes System

Water Quality Standards (WQS)

Appendices

Laws and Regulations

The difference between laws and regulations are sometimes misunderstood. Congress, and only Congress, enacts laws. Federal executive departments and administrative agencies write regulations to implement the authority of laws. Regulations (and Executive Orders and Proclamations) are ancillary or subordinate to laws but both laws and regulations are enforceable.

1.1 Statutes

The U.S. Statutes-at-Large is the official chronological compilation of all laws. United States Statutes-at-Large contains all laws, concurrent resolutions, and joint resolutions enacted during a session of Congress. It also includes reorganization plans, proposed and ratified amendments to the Constitution, and proclamations by the President, and legislative histories. It also contains laws that apply to the general populace. These are known as public laws, and are referred to as PL. in this guide. Arrangement is chronological by approval date in each category. The U.S. Statutes serve as the official legal source (1 U.S.C. 112) and must be considered when proposing a variance to a section of the U.S. Code.

1.1.1 U.S. Code

The U.S. Code is the official compilation of codified laws by subject. The U.S. Code (U.S.C.) is published every six years with annual supplements. The U.S. Code codifies, by category, public laws of general and permanent nature in effect on the date of publication. The vast quantity of expired and repealed laws since 1789 are not included in the U.S.C. The U.S. Code is most often used to find the current "laws of the land." Besides compiling laws by subject matter, the U.S. C. contains the history of recent amendments, cross-references and other notes of pertinence to aid the researcher. The U.S. Code also contains the Index of Acts by Popular Name, General Index and several tables.

1.2 The Federal Register System

The Federal Register consists of two publications, the annually revised Code of Federal Regulations (CFR) and the daily Federal Register (FR). These two publications should be used together to find the latest version of a regulation.

1.2.1 The Code of Federal Regulations (CFR)

The Code of Federal Regulations is the official compilation of regulations. The CFR codifies the general and permanent rules of executive departments and agencies that have been published in the Federal Register. The CFR is divided into 50 titles that represent broad areas subject to federal regulation. Each title is divided into chapters that usually bear the name of the issuing agency. Each chapter is further subdivided into parts covering specific regulatory areas. Throughout this guide, the CFR is cited by title and part, followed by the part's name and then the agency promulgating the regulation.

1.2.2 The Federal Register (FR)

The Federal Register is the daily supplement to the CFR. It serves as the mechanism to provide official notification to the public about federal documents or proposals having general applicability, such as: Presidential proclamations and Executive Orders, and federal agency rules, regulations, and notices. The FR also serves to notify the public and interested parties about an agency's intent to prepare an environmental impact statement, or about proposed changes to an agency's rules and regulations. It also provides the mechanism for obtaining comments from affected parties regarding the proposed action by the agency.

History of the Clean Water Act (CWA)

> *The CWA's stated goals were to make the nation's waterways "fishable and swimmable" by 1983, to ban toxic pollution, and to eliminate the discharge of all pollution into the nation's "navigable waters" by 1985.*

2.1 Brief History

The discharge goal is still far out of reach and toxics are still being released into the environment, but substantial progress has been made in many river basins toward the "fishable and swimmable" standards. The primary elements of the CWA include:

- ❏ a system of minimum national effluent standards based upon specific industries;
- ❏ a system of water quality standards;
- ❏ a discharge permit program (NPDES) providing enforceable limitations on dischargers;
- ❏ a set of provisions for special problems such as toxic chemicals and oil discharges; and
- ❏ a construction grant/loan program for Publicly Owned Treatment Systems (POTWs).

The Clean Water Act is the legislative basis for water pollution control regulations. Originally passed in 1972 as the Federal Water Pollution Control Act, the primary stated objective of the CWA is to "restore and maintain the chemical, physical and biological integrity of the nation's waters." To achieve this, several goals and policies were declared. One goal was to reach zero discharge of pollutants by 1985. Others include providing funding for the construction of publicly owned treatment works (POTWs), creating a nonpoint source pollution program, and generally, making the waters of the U.S. "fishable and swimmable."

These goals are achieved by the establishment of effluent limitations for industrial discharges based on what is technologically and economically achievable for particular industries. More stringent requirements may also be established when it is necessary to achieve water quality objectives for particular water bodies into which the facility discharges. Although not specifically stated in the above goals, the CWA contains most of the nation's wetlands legislation.

2.1.1 Priority Pollutants

The CWA originally focused on conventional and high volume pollutants. These included Biochemical Oxygen Demand (BOD), Suspended Solids (SS), pH, Chemical Oxygen Demand (COD), oil and grease and fecal coliform. Subsequently, 129 "priority pollutants" were added to the list of target compounds.

These additional "priority pollutants" come with toxic water quality standards that require controls above those required by the standard technology-based water quality standards. The statute requires each state to identify waters where the applicable technology-based standards will not result in the achievement of water quality standards for toxic pollutants. Individual control strategies are then developed which focus on the affected point sources to bring the water body into compliance.

While the USEPA has issued guidance documents on how this is done, assessments of impaired water bodies are typically made on the basis of existing water quality data. The water quality data and related standards come together as a National Pollutant Discharge Elimination System (NPDES) permit, and the primary level of control is based on a "point source" which refers to the end of the discharge pipe. Individual point source discharge limitations are imposed based upon the nature and source of these discharges. Typical examples of regulated effluents include:

- ☐ oil/water separators,
- ☐ sewerage treatment plants,
- ☐ stormwater collection systems,
- ☐ industrial treatment processes, and
- ☐ thermal discharges resulting from the generation of electricity and cooling needs.

See NPDES Permit.

2.1.2 1977 Amendments

The Clean Water Act is a 1977 amendment to the Federal Water Pollution Control Act of 1972, which set the basic structure for regulating discharges of pollutants to waters of the United States. The law gave EPA the authority to set effluent standards on an industry basis (technology-based) and continued the requirements to set water quality standards for all contaminants in surface waters. The CWA makes it unlawful for any person to discharge any pollutant from a point source into navigable waters unless a permit (NPDES) is obtained under the Act. The 1977 amendments focused on toxic pollutants.

2.1.3 1987 Amendments

In 1987, the CWA was reauthorized and again focused on toxic substances, authorized citizen suit provisions, and funded sewage treatment plants (POTWs) under the Construction Grants Program. The CWA has provisions for the delegation by EPA of many permitting, administrative, and enforcement aspects of the law to state governments. In states with the authority to carry out CWA programs, EPA retains oversight responsibilities.

The CWA Amendments of 1987 signaled a national effort to strengthen the control of Nonpoint Source (NPS) pollution. Section 319 called upon states and territories to develop NPS pollution assessments and management programs. Additional amendments to the CWA in 1987 established a program that required NPDES permitting of point source discharges of storm water associated with industrial facilities. A facility may choose one of three options to obtain coverage under this permit. These include applying for a group, individual, or general permit, and complying with the conditions of the permit issued. Again, the conditions can include periodic sampling, analysis, and development of a Storm Water Pollution Prevention Plan (SWPPP).

2.1.4 1990 Amendments

The Coastal Zone Act Reauthorization Amendments of 1990 (CZARA, section 6217 of P.L. 101–508) requires coastal states to develop nonpoint source control programs that emphasize impacts of land use practices on coastal water quality and directs federal agencies to provide specific guidance on measures or practices to limit nonpoint pollution. Coastal state groups have sought more flexibility to target CZARA control programs, more implementation time, and more funding; recent efforts by federal agencies to address these issues through program changes have satisfied some sates' concerns, but not all of them. Much of the objection to CZARA relates to its requirement that state programs will include enforceable elements to control coastal nonpoint pollution. H.R. 961 as reported would have repealed section 6217. During debate on the bill, the House adopted two amendments in this area. The first, a Boehlert amendment, deleted the repeal and modified section 6217 to give states additional compliance time and allow conditional approval of state programs (to avoid possible funding sanctions). The House also adopted a Petri amendment giving EPA the lead role in administering the CZARA program (now shared by EPA and NOAA) and allowing coastal states the option to choose participation in the CZARA or CWA section 319 nonpoint program. (Also see discussion of title X of the bill, below.) The bill would reverse a 1994 federal circuit court ruling that land application of livestock manure from a concentrated animal feeding operation is a point source that is subject to permit and enforcement provisions of the CWA (Concerned Area Residents for the Environment v. Southview Farm, No 93–9229 [(2 Cir. Sept. 2, 1994)]. The Supreme Court recently declined review of the Southview Farm case.

The amendments in this title give EPA the lead role in administering the CZARA program (now shared by EPA and NOAA) and allow coastal states the option to choose participation in the CZARA or CWA section 319 nonpoint program. However, the state's choice would be subject to EPA review, and EPA could determine, in consultation with the state, that a state's choice of the voluntary nonpoint source plan under section 319 (as modified by H.R. 961) is not sufficient to address coastal nonpoint source pollution. EPA could then require the state to submit an enforceable CZARA plan instead.

2.1.5 1995 Clean Water Act Amendments (CWAA)

HR 961, a bill to reauthorize and amend this law, reflects efforts to make the Clean Water Act more flexible and address several regulatory reform issues. The reform efforts are most evident in titles III and VIII of the bill, amendments to the standards and regulatory requirements and wetlands provisions of current law.

The House of Representatives passed H.R. 961 in May of 1995 by a vote of 240-185. The measure had the strong support of a coalition of House Republicans and conservative Democrats. The fate of the bill is uncertain since Senator John Chafee (R-R.I.), Chair of the Senate Environment and Public Works Committee that has jurisdiction over the legislation, has put Clean Water low on his committee's legislative priority list. There are also strong possibilities of a Democratic filibuster should the legislation come to a vote on the Senate floor, and a Presidential veto should the bill pass both houses.

2.2 Nonpoint Source Pollution Management

Title III contains several amendments to section 319 of the Act, concerning management of nonpoint sources of pollution. Runoff from nonpoint sources such as farm fields, city streets, and constructions sites, is believed to account for more than one-half of all remaining pollution nationwide.

In 1987 Congress established the first comprehensive program in the CWA to address nonpoint source pollution through state management programs using technical and financial assistance from EPA. Section 323 of the bill largely retains the current structure of section 319, while requiring that state management programs be updated and revised periodically. It modifies current language concerning management programs to clarify that voluntary or incentive-based approaches, and regulatory programs, enforceable policies and mechanisms, are allowable. The goal of a state management program under the bill's language is to:

❑ provide for "reasonable further progress toward the goal of attaining water quality standards within 15 years of program approval."

It requires states to resubmit management programs every five years, including documentation of the degree to which the state has achieved interim goals and milestones (taking into account adequacy of federal funding under 319). The bill adds new language directing EPA, in the event a state fails to submit a management program, to prepare and implement one for the state. In the initial implementation of section 319, all states eventually submitted the required management program; this new provision would give EPA fallback authority, if states did not do so in the future. Title III would allow section 319 grants to be used for preparing reports and management programs as well as implementing approved programs (current law only addresses grants for implementation). It increases the share of a project that may be funded by grants from 60 to 75 percent. EPA is authorized to withhold grants if a state has not made satisfactory progress in its schedule. The bill mandates an EPA study on allocation of 319 funds. H.R. 961 amends section 319 to provide that an agricultural producer who is implementing an approved voluntary whole farm or ranch natural resource management plan will be deemed in compliance with a state nonpoint source management program.

The intent of this provision is to avoid duplicative requirements where producers are carrying out approved plans that consolidate numerous separate conservation and similar planning requirements.

Federal agencies that own or manage lands or license activities that cause nonpoint source pollution are directed to coordinate their nonpoint source control measures with states. Section 319 grants funds would be increased (FY 1991 funds, the last authorized year, were $130 million) to $100 million in FY 1996 up to $300 million in FY 2000 (a total of $1 billion). Authorizations for groundwater projects would be increased from $7.5 million to $25 million per year.

EPA is directed to issue guidance to identify economically achievable measures for controlling nonpoint source pollution which reflect application of best available practices, technologies, processes, siting criteria, operating methods or other alternatives.

2.3 Watershed Management

Title III adds watershed management program language to the Act, new section 321. Watershed planning has recently been advocated by varied groups and the Administration as a new water quality management tool to supplement existing regulatory tools in the Act. It centers on the idea of using a broader, systems approach that considers all sources of pollution in a watershed in order to focus on the most important problems. Watershed planning is implicit in several existing planning and management provisions of the Act, but new section 321 would make the concept explicit.

In simple terms, a watershed is a land area in which all of the rainfall or snowmelt drains toward a common point or waterbody such as a lake or stream. The bill authorizes and encourages states to participate in voluntary watershed management programs. Approved state programs would be eligible for certain CWA assistance for activities such as planning, developing and implementing water quality standards, and implementing practices to meet identified goals. No deadlines are specified. Several incentives for approved state watershed programs are provided. The bill would allow:

- ❑ trading or transfer of pollution control requirements between sources or dischargers in a watershed;

- ❑ issuance of modified permits with limitations that exceed water quality standards if the plan for the watershed includes assurance that standards will be met by a specified date;

- ❑ extension of permit terms for sources in a watershed management unit to synchronize permits with others; and

- ❑ application by states to EPA for multipurpose grants under several sections of CWA, thus giving the state flexibility to focus on priority activities within the watershed.

2.4 Stormwater Management

In 1987 Congress directed EPA to implement a specific permit program for stormwater discharges from industrial sources and municipalities. Many have criticized implementation of the permit program, particularly concerning applicability to small cities that have yet to be covered by regulations.

H.R. 961 adds new section 322 to the Act that would essentially convert the current stormwater permit program (section 402(p)) into a nonpoint source management-type program. It would define stormwater as a nonpoint source pollutant (because stormwater results from intermittent precipitation events and is thus more typical of nonpoint source pollution), repeal current CWA section 402(p), and call for states to assess stormwater discharges and to prepare and submit a management program "for controlling pollution added from stormwater discharges to the navigable waters within the boundaries of the State."

The goal is to attain water quality standards not later than 15 years after program approval. Critics objected to the stormwater provisions of H.R. 961, saying that while it would be appropriate to give states more flexibility in dealing with stormwater discharges, the bill would reduce water quality protection by relaxing stormwater pollution controls. Efforts to modify the stormwater provisions during House debate were rejected. The state program in H.R. 961 is intended to include industrial and commercial as well as municipal stormwater sources and construction activities.

For industrial, commercial, oil, gas, and mining discharges, a state program is to provide incentives for implementing pollution prevention practices and eliminating exposure of stormwater to pollutants. The bill details a hierarchical framework, beginning with voluntary plans and proceeding to permits (general and site specific) and enforceable measures, depending on whether stormwater at the facility does or does not have contact with equipment, raw materials, or waste products. Permits already issued under section 402(p) would remain in effect until the effective date of a state program.

Under H.R. 961, states would have full discretion to identify categories of industrial and commercial facilities, as well as municipalities, which would be subject to stormwater management programs. However, if a state fails to submit a report or program, EPA will implement a program for the state. For stormwater runoff from construction activities, states are to develop management programs consistent with current pollution prevention practice (many states have erosion and sediment control programs in pact), but are not required to duplicate the program for industrial and commercial discharges.

If part of a state's navigable waters is not meeting standards due to stormwater pollution from another state, the downstream state may petition EPA to convene a management conference for developing an agreement among the states to reduce the pollution from stormwater and to improve water quality.

The bill authorizes $20 million per year for state and local demonstration and research programs concerning stormwater. However, it includes no general grant funds to develop and implement state management programs. States may use title VI (State

Revolving Fund) moneys to implement a stormwater program. The legislation directs EPA to develop stormwater criteria that:

- ☐ will be technologically and financially feasible

- ☐ includes performance standards, guidelines, guidance, and

- ☐ includes model management practices and measures and treatment requirements.

2.5 Risk Assessment and Cost-Benefit Analysis

Title III adds new provisions to the CWA concerning risk assessment (new section 323) and cost-benefit analysis (new section 324). These provisions would significantly expand attention to these factors in the CWA, which currently does not specifically address risk assessment but does provide for consideration of costs in several parts of the law, notably in EPA's issuance of effluent limitations for categories of industrial point sources and limited opportunities to modify permit requirements where costs bear no reasonable relations to benefits. The Act's standards provisions require EPA to evaluate a range of factors including cost, production process and process changes, and non-water quality environmental impact (including energy requirements). Section 323 would require EPA to prepare risk assessments before issuing:

- ☐ standards,

- ☐ effluent limitations,

- ☐ water quality criteria,

- ☐ CWA guidance, and

- ☐ other regulatory requirements under the Act.

Permits or other procedural requirements would not be covered. The contents of such risk assessments are specified to include, among other things:

- ☐ all readily obtainable data and information;

- ☐ discussion of significant assumptions or models used in the risk;

- ☐ measurement of the sensitivity of results;

- ☐ consideration and discussion of alternatives to the maximum extent possible;

- ☐ descriptions of the risk and quantitative estimates of uncertainty; and

- ☐ comparison to other risks to human health and the environment.

When establishing a margin of safety as part of a regulatory requirement, EPA is to provide an explicit and quantitative description of the margin of safety relative to an unbiased estimate of the risk being addressed.

Section 324 would prohibit EPA from issuing any standard, effluent limitation, other regulatory requirement, or guidance under the CWA without a certification that it maximizes net benefits to society. This requirement is to supplement and, if there is conflict, supersede decision criteria otherwise applicable to such CWA actions.

EPA is to issue guidance on conducting benefit and cost analyses including:

- ☐ identification of policy alternatives;

- ☐ estimates of the incremental benefits and costs;

- ☐ estimates of the nature and extent of the incremental risk avoided by the EPA action; and

- ☐ estimates of the total social, environmental and economic costs of implementing the action.

Certain actions are exempted from the cost-benefit requirement, including permit issuance, implementation of purely procedural requirements, and issuance of water quality criteria and water quality-based standards (sections 304 and 303 of the CWA, respectively). Risk assessment provisions and cost-benefit requirements under these two new sections would apply to EPA actions under the CWA as follows: between Feb. 15, 1995, and the first year after enactment of H.R. 961, they would apply to any of the covered standards or other requirements, or guidance issued under the CWA likely to result in an annual increase in cost of $100 million or more. After that, they would apply to any of the covered standards or other requirements regardless of cost and any guidance issued under the CWA likely to result in an increase in cost of $25 million or more. The bill also provides program authority and funding for Fiscal Years 1996 through 2000.

2.6 1996 Safe Drinking Water Act Reauthorization

One of the most significant programmatic environmental laws passed by the 104th Congress was the reauthorization of the Safe Drinking Water Act (SDWA). Because of the severe criticism received about proposed regulatory reform efforts and the controversy over the Clean Water reauthorization, the Republican leadership in both houses made SDWA reauthorization a high priority in 1996.

In the Senate, the lead on SDWA reform was taken by Senator Chafee, Chairman of the Senate Environment and Public Works Committee, and Senator Dirk Kempthorne (R-ID), Chairman of the Drinking Water, Fisheries, and Wildlife Subcommittee. Their bill (S. 1316) proposed to replace the requirement that EPA issue drinking water standards for 25 new contaminants every three years with a requirement that EPA prepare a list of unregulated contaminants for study and, beginning in 2001, determine every five years whether five of those contaminants merit regulation. S. 1316 further required EPA to conduct cost-benefit analyses when promulgating a new standard. The bill also proposed a state revolving loan fund program to help localities finance projects necessary to meet SDWA requirements. The Senate Environment Committee approved S. 1316 unanimously on October 24, 1995, and the full Senate unanimously passed it in November.

After months of bipartisan negotiations, the House Commerce Committee unanimously approved its bill (H.R. 3604) on June 11. The bill received broad, if qualified, support from the Clinton Administration and environment and public health groups. On June 25, 1996 it passed the House, after being merged with legislation reported by the House Transportation and Infrastructure Committee (authorizing additional assistance for public water systems and watershed projects). The final, conference committee version of SDWA:

- ❏ revoked the requirement that EPA regulate 25 contaminants every three years;

- ❏ added flexibility to the Act s standard setting process;

- ❏ directed EPA to conduct risk reduction and cost analyses for new standards; and

- ❏ authorized a state revolving loan fund program.

The law also increased health effects research funding, expanded consumer information programs, and included new source water protection programs. Both houses approved the conference report on August 2, and on August 6, 1996, President Clinton signed the long-awaited Safe Drinking Water Act Amendments into law.

The most significant change is the requirement that in future standards, EPA must make a determination whether the benefits of an M.C.L. justify the costs. The new cost-benefit analysis may not be used to relax any preexisting standards. The Amendments also require public water utilities to notify consumers within twenty-four hours about violations that may present a risk to public health. EPA will no longer promulgate MCLs for trace contaminants that do not occur nationwide at levels of public health concern.

2.7 H.R. 961 Program Authority for Fiscal Years 1996-2000

H.R. 961 was an effort to make the CWA more flexible and to address several regulatory reform issues of concern to many of those regulated by the law industries, states, and cities, in particular. These efforts are most notable in titles III and VIII of the bill, amendments to the standards and regulatory requirements and wetlands permit provisions of current law. The legislation was designed in large part to provide relief to businesses, states, local governments, and individual landowners from what many perceived to be excessive clean water regulation. It accomplishes this task by incorporating risk assessment and elevating cost considerations in the implementation of CWA programs. H.R. 961 consists of ten titles:

- ❏ Title I, Research and Related Programs (CWA title I)

- ❏ Title II, Construction Grants (CWA title II)

- ❏ Title III, Standards and Enforcement (CWA title III)

- ❏ Title IV, Permits and Licenses (CWA title IV)

- ❏ Title V, General Provisions (CWA title V)

- ❏ Title VI, State Water Pollution Control Revolving Funds (CWA title VI)

- ❏ Title VII, Miscellaneous Provisions

- ❏ Title VIII, Wetlands Conservation and Management (CWA section 404)

❏ Title IX, Navigational Dredging (amending the Marine Protection, Research, and Sanctuaries Act)

❏ Title X, Additional Provisions

2.7.1 Title I, Research and Related Programs

Title I concerns research and related programs and authorizations for some core programs in the Act. H.R. 961 adds goal and policy statements concerning support for state water pollution prevention and control efforts, and support for wastewater reclamation, beneficial reuse of wastewater, and water use efficiency. A new policy statement provides that implementation of CWA programs should produce benefits that justify their costs and should be based on scientifically objective and unbiased information concerning risk. Grants under section 106 of the Act, assistance to state water quality management programs, are reauthorized through FY 2000 at $150 million per year. (Authorized funding in current law is $75 million; recent appropriated funding has been $80 million per year.)

2.7.2 Title II, Construction Grants

Title II provides certain technical amendments to the construction grants provisions of the Act, concerning assistance for construction of municipal wastewater treatment plants. In 1987 amendments, the direct grant assistance provisions of CWA title II were superseded by revolving loan fund provisions of CWA title VI, but many of the regulatory requirements and project eligibility definitions of CWA title II continue to apply to projects funded under title VI. Current limitations on the use of federal funds are modified by H.R. 961 to remove limits on eligible project categories, allow use of funds for control of nonpoint sources of pollution, and remove restriction on the use of title VI funds for collector sewer and combined sewer overflow projects.

A new requirement for consideration of water use efficiency options in wastewater projects is added. EPA is authorized to negotiate an annual budget with a state for administering the close-out of projects funded under CWA title II. Current language regarding sewage collections systems is modified to update "existing collection system" to mean a system existing upon enactment of this legislation. The definition of "treatment works" is amended to include acquisition of lands and interest in lands which are necessary for construction of a treatment works. (Current law does not permit use of federal funds for land acquisition, unless the land is integral to the treatment process.)

2.7.3 Title III, Standards and Enforcement

Title III amends CWA title III, concerning standards, regulation, and enforcement. This title and title VIII reflect the most substantive and controversial amendments contained in H.R. 961. Several sections in this title would allow for modification of industrial point source discharge requirements or permit limitations. For example, the bill provides new authority for discharge permits to be modified if the facility undertakes pollution prevention programs which will achieve an overall reduction in environmental releases (to air and land, as well as water). Another provision authorizes modification of permit requirements concerning conventional or toxic pollutants to allow for trading of pollution reduction requirements between sources. Permit modifications would not be allowed if the action would result in water quality standards violations or failure to attain water quality standards, or would interfere with the operation of a publicly owned sewage treatment works. Further, where the modified discharge would affect waters within the jurisdiction of two or more states, notice to neighboring states is required, and the neighboring state may modify or veto the permit.

Section 301(k) of current law authorizes EPA to modify regulatory requirements for industrial facilities which utilize innovative technologies. H.R. 961 expands the factors for considering a 301(k) waiver and extends compliance for such facilities from two years to three years. The bill includes potential for modifying CWA requirements imposed on industrial facilities whose wastes are treated by municipal wastewater treatment plants. These facilities are required by current law to pretreat wastes before discharging to the municipal system.

H.R. 961 would permit the locality to impose local requirements, instead of national pretreatment standards, to eliminate unnecessary or redundant mandates. Both the treatment works and the industrial facility must be in compliance with other applicable standards before local limits may be substituted. In addition, the bill would allow for modified requirements and permit extensions for industrial facilities proposing to use innovative pretreatment processes. The bill would allow industrial facilities such as photo processing companies which discharge silver wastes to municipal plants to utilize a code of management practices instead of pretreatment requirements and would allow for related modification of the treatment works' discharge permit. Title III provides some modifications for municipal dischargers, as well.

2.7.4 Title IV, Permits and Licenses

Title IV contains amendments to permit provisions of CWA title IV (not including CWA section 404, which would be amended by title VIII of H.R. 961). Several proposed amendments would modify section 402 of the Act, the National Pollutant Discharge Elimination System, which is the principal permit section of the law. Under current law, section 402 permits are issued for terms no longer than five years. H.R. 961 would extend permits to 10 years. Ten-year permits have been proposed on several occasions in the past; at issue has been how to craft statutory language that would provide for some reopening of 10-year permits in the event of changed circumstances. The bill as passed authorizes permits to be modified in order to address a significant threat to human health and the environment. The bill amends section 402 to clarify the scope of EPA's existing exemption for permitting certain waste treatment systems involving concentrated animal feeding operations and impoundments. (This provision relates to an amendment in title III to reverse a 1994 court decision concerning land application of livestock manure, discussed above.) Other clarifying amendments provide that when enforcing effluent limitations, authorities shall take into account the statistical basis on which the effluent limitation is based (for example, if the technology can only achieve 95 percent compliance, the permittee need only achieve 95 percent compliance).

2.7.5 Title V, General Provisions

Title V of H.R. 961 provides miscellaneous amendments to definitions and general provisions of the Act. It amends the definition of "publicly owned treatment works" to include privately owned facilities which, if they treat industrial wastes, are carrying out a pretreatment program which meets requirements of the Act.

Title V provides language clarifying that the federal government may not use the CWA to supersede or otherwise impair the allocation of water quantity rights by states. This provision arises from persistent tensions and questions about controlling water quality under the CWA and allocating water quantity (generally reserved to the states). Separately, this title of the bill requires EPA to consult and substantively involve state and local governments in CWA decision making and implementation. Language would be added to the Act to establish an independent Board of Audit Appeals to review and decide contested audit determinations related to grants and contract awards.

2.7.6 Title VI, State Water Pollution Control Revolving Funds

Title VI of H.R. 961 extends authorization for the SRF grants, providing $2.25 billion in FY 1996 and $2.3 billion annually in FY 1997-2000 (compared with FY 1995 SRF appropriations of $1.235 billion) and provides a new state-by-state allotment formula for SRF grant distribution based on population and recently estimated needs.

The allotment formula in H.R. 961 as passed was included in H.R. 961 when it was introduced in February. During subcommittee markups a modified version was adopted which moderated some of the large percentage changes in allotment that several states would experience. However, during floor debate the House adopted a Lipinski amendment which replaced the subcommittee-approved formula with the version in the bill as introduced.

2.7.7 Title VII, Miscellaneous Provisions

Title VII provides technical amendments to the text of the CWA. It designates the EPA laboratory and research facility in Duluth, MN as the John A. Blatnik National Fresh Water Quality Research Laboratory. Title VII authorizes $50 million for grants to help states along the U.S.–Mexico border with planning and constructing treatment works in border communities known as *colonias.*

EPA is directed to conduct a study on the savings to cities in the construction, operation and maintenance of drinking water facilities resulting from CWA actions. It is widely recognized that wastes which are not discharged into the Nation's waters will not increase the demands on drinking water treatment facilities for water delivered to consumers, but there has been little attempt to quantify such savings.

2.7.8 Title VIII, Wetlands Conservation and Management

Title VIII concerns wetlands regulatory programs, conservation and management. It incorporates language based on a wetlands proposal that Rep. Jimmy Hayes has introduced as H.R. 1330 in several recent Congresses. Its statutory purpose is to establish a new federal wetlands regulatory program, and it does so by revising section 404 of the CWA, the dredge and fill permit program in the CWA.

Section 404 is the principal federal program that provides regulatory protection for wetlands. In recent years it has become a source of conflict between those who view it as a critical tool in wetland protection and others who see it as intruding on private landuse decisions, imposing an excessive economic burden. The changes contained in title VIII are among the most controversial provisions of H.R. 961 and were opposed by environmentalists and the Administration; efforts to amend this title in committee and during House debate were unsuccessful.

2.7.9 Title IX, Navigational Dredging

Title IX amends portions of title I of the Marine Protection, Research and Sanctuaries Act (the Ocean Dumping Act) to streamline regulatory requirements applicable to navigational dredging. Under current law, the Corps issues permits for ocean dumping of dredged material, while EPA issues permits for ocean dumping of other material and designates sites for ocean dumping. Corps permits for dredged material are to be based on the same criteria used by EPA under other provisions of the Act, and to the extent possible, EPA recommended dumping sites are used. EPA is authorized to impose permit conditions or even deny a permit, if necessary to prevent environmental problems.

H.R. 961 modifies these provisions by designating the Corps as the lead federal agency for issuing ocean dumping permits for dredged and nondredged material, designating dumping sites, and establishing permit criteria. The Corps would carry out this authority in consultation with EPA, but EPA's prior concurrence on transportation or disposal of dredged material would not be required. Other substantive criteria of the Ocean Dumping Act, including consultation with states, development of site management plans, and general permit conditions, are not altered by the bill.

2.7.10 Title X, Additional Provisions

This title of the bill contains amendments to section 6217 of the Coastal Zone Act Reauthorization Amendments (see discussion of CZARA in the "Nonpoint Source Pollution Management" portion of this report, above). The amendments in this title give EPA the lead role in administering the CZARA program (now shared by EPA and NOAA) and allow coastal states the option to choose participation in the CZARA or the CWA section 319 nonpoint program. However, the state's choice would be subject to EPA review, and EPA could determine, in consultation with the state, that a state's choice of the voluntary nonpoint source plan under section 319 (as modified by H.R. 961) is not sufficient to address coastal nonpoint source pollution. EPA could then require the state to submit an enforceable CZARA plan instead.

*Note: The H.R. 961 information above is attributed to "Clean Water: Summary of H.R. 961, As Passed" a report by Claudia Copeland, Specialist in Environmental Policy, Environment and Natural Resources Policy Division.

CWA & CFR Overview

During the 1970s, Congress passed or amended a number of environmental protection statutes, beginning with the Clean Air Act (CAA) in 1970 and the Federal Water Pollution Control Act [renamed the Clean Water Act (CWA)] in 1972. For the protection of groundwater, Congress enacted the Safe Drinking Water Act (SDWA) in 1975. With the passage of the Resource Conservation and Recovery Act (RCRA) in 1976, the federal government had, for the first time, a complete suite of statutes intended to reverse the degradation of the environment caused by discharges to air, water, and soil.

3.1 Overview

Each of the statutes relating to water quality relies heavily on permitting programs to establish minimum national standards for the control of air and water effluents, as well as to govern the treatment, storage, and disposal of solid and hazardous waste. In order to avoid redundant permitting and regulatory programs (many states had environmental programs preceding federal involvement), the U.S. Environmental Protection Agency (EPA) has delegated the administration of the CAA, CWA, SDWA, and RCRA regulatory programs to states that adopt, at a minimum, the technical and administrative requirements found in federal regulations. The timeline below presents twenty-four years of the major regulatory events affecting water quality in the U.S.

3.1.1 Statutory Timeline

1972	Federal Water Pollution Control Act
1974	Spill Prevention, Control and Countermeasures (SPCC) Plan Regulations
1974	Safe Drinking Water Act (SDWA)
1976	Resource Conservation and Recovery Act (RCRA)
1977	Clean Water Act (CWA)
1980	"Superfund" Comprehensive Environmental Response Compensation and Liability Act (CERCLA)
1984	Hazardous and Solid Waste Amendments (HSWA) to RCRA
1986	"Superfund" Amendment and Reauthorization Act (SARA) & Safe Drinking Water Amendments
1987	Water Quality Act (WQA)
1990	Publicly Owned Treatment Works (POTW) Pretreatment Rules

1990	National Pollution Discharge Elimination System (NPDES) Stormwater Regulations
1990	Oil Pollution Act (OPA) & Pollution Prevention Act
1994	SPCC II Plan Regulation Revisions
1995	Clean Water Act Amendments
1996	Safe Drinking Water Act Reauthorization

3.2 Environmental Permits

It is common for facilities to have environmental permits covering emissions from air pollution sources, water discharges to streams and municipal Publicly Owned Treatment Works (POTWs), and the treatment, storage, or disposal of solid and hazardous waste. Environmental permits must be managed according to applicable federal and state regulations and some of these regulations vary in detail, depending on the environmental program (air, water, or solid and hazardous waste) and issuing authority (state or federal). The following categories represent the federally mandated water quality permit requirements a facility may have:

- ❑ CWA National Pollutant Discharge Elimination System (NPDES) permits for discharges to surface water.

- ❑ CWA Section 404 permits for the management of dredge and fill materials.

- ❑ CWA Section 405 permits for the use and disposal of domestic sewage sludge.

- ❑ SDWA Underground Injection Control (UIC) permits for discharges to groundwater.

- ❑ RCRA treatment, storage, and disposal (TSD) facility permits for the management of hazardous waste.

3.3 The Suite of Environmental Statutes for Water Quality

Following is a brief overview of the federal government's suite of environmental statutes that are the primary source of water related compliance issues:

3.3.1 Federal Water Pollution Control Act of 1972

The Federal Water Pollution Control Act, originally enacted in 1972 and last amended in 1987 consists of two major parts: regulatory provisions that impose progressively more stringent requirements on industries and cities in order to abate pollution and meet the statutory goal of zero discharge of pollutants, and provisions that authorize federal financial assistance for municipal wastewater treatment construction.

The Federal Water Pollution Control Act (FWPCA) established the legislative authority for the United States Environmental Protection Agency (USEPA) to adopt regulations concerning discharges of oil (40 CFR 110) and oil pollution prevention (40 CFR 112). The FWPCA further provides the USEPA with authority to adopt regulations which designate hazardous substances (40 CFR 116) and notification requirements for reportable quantities (RQ) of spills of hazardous substances (40 CFR 117).

3.3.2 Safe Drinking Water Act (SDWA), 40 CFR Parts 141-149

In 1974, the Safe Drinking Water Act (SDWA) was enacted with the general intent to protect the quality of drinking water the public receives from public water systems. To accomplish this, the SDWA focuses on two approaches. The first is to assure the quality of drinking water coming from the tap. The other approach is to prevent the contamination of groundwater that may be a source for drinking water. To implement the first approach EPA established maximum contaminant levels (MCLs) for a wide variety of chemicals present in drinking water. These MCLs are based upon health and economic considerations. In addition, for each of these substances, EPA publishes maximum contaminant level goals (MCLGs), which are based solely upon public health. MCL requirements apply to public water systems, which include the traditional suppliers of water to communities as well as those manufacturing plants that provide their own source of drinking water to employees and visitors. For the second objective this statute authorizes EPA to establish a regulatory program to prevent contamination of underground sources of drinking water. All underground injection control (UIC) wells are subject to special regulatory controls under this statute. The law now also contains certain provisions for the protection of ground water quality near drinking water wells.

3.3.3 Resource Conservation and Recovery Act (RCRA) of 1976

RCRA addresses the management of municipal and industrial solid waste and hazardous wastes. The primary objectives of RCRA are promoting the protection of human health and the environment from potential adverse effects of improper waste management; conserving material and energy resources through waste recycling and recovery; and reducing or eliminating the generation of hazardous waste as expeditiously as possible. Under various provisions of RCRA, EPA and states implement three major regulatory programs for waste management.

3.3.4 Clean Water Act (CWA) of 1977

CWA is the federal statute under which EPA establishes national water quality goals and addresses water pollution from industrial and municipal facilities and other sources. Under CWA, EPA and approved state programs implement five primary elements: a system of national effluent standards for each industry; water quality standards; a discharge permit program that applies the standards as enforceable limits (that is, permit conditions); provisions for special problems, such as toxic chemicals or oil spills; and a revolving construction loan program for publicly owned treatment works (POTW).

3.3.5 Water Quality Act (WQA) of 1987- Water Pollution Control Act

Congress addressed the need to control the discharge of toxics into the nation's waters via the Clean Water Act (CWA). The CWA established nationwide minimum discharge standards. Since each water body has differing capacities to handle wastewater, the CWA recognizes this and accommodates it through a system of variable standards designed to protect the integrity of the water body for its normal or preferred uses. The establishment of goals within the CWA aids in establishing these various water quality targets and discharge limitations. The CWA has as its roots the Refuse Act of 1899 which prohibited discharges into navigable waters or tributaries without a permit from the US Army Corps of Engineers (USACOE).

3.3.6 "Superfund" Comprehensive Environmental Response Compensation and Liability Act (CERCLA) of 1980

CERCLA established a comprehensive federal program to respond to the release of hazardous substances to the environment. CERCLA establishes a trust fund, commonly referred to as Superfund, that EPA may use to fund the cleanup of hazardous waste disposal sites. Under CERCLA, EPA also may take enforcement action against potentially responsible parties to compel the cleanup of hazardous waste sites. All cleanup activities under CERCLA are governed by the National Contingency Plan (NCP) that established comprehensive regulations for conducting cleanup activities.

3.3.7 "Superfund" Amendment and Reauthorization Act (SARA) & Safe Drinking Water Amendments (SDWA)(1986)

SDWA establishes requirements for the protection of public drinking water supply systems. Under the SDWA, EPA sets standards for the quality of water provided by public water supply systems (known as maximum contaminant levels [MCL] for specific contaminants). Public water supply systems must monitor for compliance with the MCLs. EPA and authorized states enforce the requirements of the SDWA. Under the SDWA, EPA and states also regulate the disposal of wastes and other substances by underground injection wells.

3.3.8 National Pollution Discharge Elimination System (NPDES) Stormwater Regulations (1990)

In the Clean Water Act of 1972, Congress established the basic framework for current programs to control water pollution. The statute's main emphasis was on controlling pollutant discharges from both industrial and municipal sources through the National Pollutant Discharge Elimination System (NPDES) permit program. The NPDES permit program requires that every industrial or municipal "point source" discharging into public waters obtain a NPDES permit. NPDES permits are issued for five-year periods.

The NPDES permit performs two distinct functions within the CWA regulatory process:

☐ establishes a level of performance the discharger must maintain, and

☐ requires the discharger to self report any failures to maintain those levels of performance.

3.3.9 The Pollution Prevention Act of 1990

In Section 302 under Title III of the CWAA, the legislation authorizes EPA or the states to modify permit conditions to implement innovative P2 technologies, P2 measures or pollution reduction agreements. It allows permit requirements regarding total maximum daily loads and water quality standards to be modified based on an overall reduction in emissions (including emissions to water, air and disposal of solid wastes) which result in a "net environmental benefit." The legislation also exempts P2 technologies, pollution reduction agreements and P2 or water conservation measures from antibacksliding provisions. This means that the new permits can relax standards that the current law requires when an overall net benefit to the environment is achieved. The 1990 Pollution Prevention Act defines P2 as source reduction, which includes the following: equipment or technology modifications, process or procedure modifications, reformulation or redesign of products, substitution of raw materials, and improvements in housekeeping, maintenance, training or inventory control.

3.3.10 SPCC II Plan Regulation Revisions (1994)

Besides permitting of discharges, the CWA also provides regulations governing the preparation of Spill Prevention, Control and Countermeasure Plans (SPCC) and Facility Response Plans. Oil pollution prevention regulations apply to non-transportation-related onshore and offshore facilities that handle oil which could reasonably be expected to reach the navigable waters of the United States or adjoining shorelines in case of a spill. As required by 40 CFR 112.3, a Spill, Prevention, Control, and Countermeasure (SPCC) Plan must be developed for certain facilities detailing the implementation of various aspects of spill prevention and control.

3.4 Water Quality Enforcement and Regulatory Overview

During this project it has become evident to me that regulations concerning water quality are spread throughout the CFRs. While 40 CFR Parts 104 through 149 contain the largest body of information on the subject, and as such, provide the emphasis for this book; other sections of the CFRs play a major role in water quality in the U.S.

Along with the 40 CFR Parts, many other CFR parts come into play, but special attention must be given to the Army Corps of Engineers (ACOE) water quality regulations contained in 33 CFR Parts 320 through 330. This is where you will find the ACOE's general regulatory policies, Section 404 permit, permit processing, public hearing procedures, and the nationwide permit program implemented by the CORP. A brief overview of ACOE specific functions in the area of water quality follows.

3.4.1 ACOE General Regulatory Policies (33 CFR Part 320)

The Corps issues permits under several different acts, the CWA being only one of them. The Corps must issue permits for discharges to insure that they comply with the applicable limitations and Water Quality Standards (WQS). Section 320.4 describes the general policies that the Corps follows when reviewing permits. Such permits must consider public interest, affect on wetlands, fish and wildlife, water quality, property ownership, energy conservation, navigation, environmental benefits, and economics, among other things. Their focus pertains particularly to dredge and fill permits covered under 404 of the CWA.

3.4.2 ACOE Section 404 Dredge and Fill Permits (33 CFR Part 323)

A permit must be obtained from the Corps of Engineers under section 404 of the Clean Water Act for many types of construction activities in waterways and wetlands. Section 404 is the principal federal program that provides regulatory protection for wetlands. Section 404 permits are subject to review under NEPA and may trigger a requirement to complete a full blown Environmental Impact Statement. State 404 programs are contained in 40 CFR Parts 232 and 233.

3.5 H.R. 961 and Section 404

Title VIII of H.R. 961 concerns wetlands regulatory programs, conservation and management. Its statutory purpose is to establish a new federal wetlands regulatory program, and it does so by revising section 404 of the CWA, the dredge and fill permit program in the CWA. The changes contained in title VIII are among the most controversial provisions of H.R. 961 and were opposed by environmentalists and the Administration; efforts to amend this title in committee and during House debate were unsuccessful.

3.5.1 Agency Action Under Section 404

H.R. 961 provides that if a federal agency action under section 404 diminishes the fair market value of any portion of a property by 20 percent or more, the federal government shall compensate the owner for an amount equivalent to the diminution in value. If the diminution is more than 50 percent, the federal government is to buy the affected portion of the property. The bill sets some limitations (no compensation will be made for uses which are a nuisance, or for agency actions whose primary purpose is to prevent a hazard to public health or safety). It also establishes procedures for the property owner to seek compensation, for negotiations and for arbitration, if necessary. States which operate delegated 404 programs would not be required to pay compensation.

3.5.2 Wetlands Classification

The revised section 404 separates wetlands into three categories according to ecological significance, ranging from type A (the most ecologically valuable) to type C (the least valuable). The bill details procedures for permit issuance, following determination that an area is a wetland and following resolution of compensation, if applicable. The definitions of the wetland classifications are:

- ❑ Type A Wetlands — wetlands of critical significance to the long-term conservation of the aquatic environment of which they are a part;

- ❑ Type B Wetlands — areas which provide habitat for a significant population of wetland dependent wildlife or provide other significant wetlands functions; and

- ❑ Type C Wetlands — those areas which serve limited wetlands functions or marginal functions but exist in such abundance that regulation is deemed not necessary.

For type A wetlands, permits would be issued following a sequential analysis seeking to avoid adverse impact on wetlands, minimize adverse impacts, and compensate for loss of wetland functions. Type B wetlands would not be subject to the same sequential analysis as type A wetlands, but the bill details factors to be considered for a type B wetland permit. These include quality and quantity of wetlands functions affected, costs of mitigation and benefits of the proposed activity, the environmental benefit of mitigation, and whether the impact on wetlands is temporary or permanent. Final decisions on all permit applications are to be made in 90 days. If a final decision is not made within that time, the permit is deemed approved. For type C wetlands federal permits are not required.

The ACOE issues regulations governing mitigation for activities occurring in wetlands, allowing for minimization of impacts, enhancement or restoration of degraded wetlands as compensation, offsite compensatory mitigation, and other measures including contribution to a wetlands mitigation bank. In issuing permits, the Corps may require mitigation to prevent the unacceptable loss or degradation of type A wetlands or, for type B wetlands, if the proposed activity will result in the loss or degradation of wetlands functions which are not temporary or incidental. The Corps also is directed to issue regulations for the establishment, use, and oversight of mitigation banks.

3.5.3 ACOE Responsibility

The revised section 404 gives the Corps sole responsibility to administer the Act's wetlands programs and would thus eliminate EPA's role of providing environmental guidelines and its current authority to veto a proposed 404 permit. The opportunity for other federal agencies such as the Fish and Wildlife Service (FWS) to review and comment on permit applications also would be eliminated. A state's request to be delegated permitting authority would be reviewed by the Corps; under current law, this is EPA's responsibility. The Secretary of Agriculture would have sole responsibility to delineate wetlands on agricultural lands, including rangelands and lands used for livestock production.

As under current law, the Corps could issue general permits for activities that are similar in nature and that will not, separately and cumulatively, result in significant loss of ecologically valuable wetlands. The revised section 404 would direct the Corps to establish standards governing the delineation of lands as wetlands, based on clear evidence of wetlands hydrology, hydrophytic vegetation, and hydric soils. In addition, the bill specifies that wetlands delineations are to be done during the growing season and that the hydrology criterion must require that water be present at the surface of the soil for 21 consecutive days in the growing season. This hydrology criterion is more restrictive than the criterion under current administrative practice, and critics argue that it will result in the loss of regulatory protection for many wetland areas.

The bill directs that wetlands regulated under section 404 are to be identified and classified within 10 years in a project to be conducted by the Secretary of Agriculture (for agricultural and associated nonagricultural lands) and the Secretary of the Army. (The FWS has been conducting a national wetlands inventory for several years, for identifying wetlands, but not for regulatory purposes.) Any classification of wetlands is to be recorded on local property records.

3.5.4 ACOE Permit Processing (33 CFR Part 325)

This section contains general processing procedures for all Department of the Army permits. Attention is given to dredge and fill activities in 325.1(d)(3) & (4). Federal agencies that initiate or authorize proposed actions that include dredge or fill discharge operations must ensure that the appropriate permits are obtained. In states with approved programs, permit application is done through the appropriate state agency. See State 404 Programs. For ACOE Public Hearings procedures see 33 CFR Part 327, and for details on the ACOE Nationwide Permits see 33 CFR Part 330.

3.6 Other Provisions

Under prior law, violations of section 404 are subject to the same civil, criminal and administrative penalty sanctions as are violations of other provisions of the CWA. The revised 404 provides new, less stringent penalties for violations of these provisions and specify in the case of civil penalties that the amount of the penalty should be proportional to the scope of the project. Authorized enforcement actions include issuance of a compliance order, a civil action and penalties, and/or criminal penalties. Title VIII also amends the federal enforcement provisions of the CWA, section 309, to delete authority to use that section in connection with section 404 violations, relying instead on the revised section 404 enforcement authority.

The revised state program language is largely the same as prior law, but it eliminates language limiting state permits to five years in length. Prior law authorized EPA to review permits which delegated states propose to issue; the bill deletes this permit-by-permit review and replaces it with a review every five years by the Secretary of the Army to determine adequacy of the state's program. See State 404 Programs.

Determination of Reportable Quantities
for Hazardous Substances

> *This regulation sets forth a determination of the reportable quantity for each substance designated as hazardous in 40 CFR Part 116. See Appendix F for the full list.*

4.1 Overview

The regulation applies to quantities of designated substances equal to or greater than the reportable quantities, when discharged into or upon the navigable waters of the United States, adjoining shorelines, into or upon the contiguous zone, or beyond the contiguous zone as provided in section 311(b)(3) of the Act, except to the extent that the owner or operator can show such that discharges are made:

- ❏ in compliance with a permit issued under the Marine Protection, Research and Sanctuaries Act of 1972 (33 U.S.C. 1401 et seq.);

- ❏ in compliance with approved water treatment plant operations as specified by local or state regulations concerning safe drinking water;

- ❏ pursuant to the label directions for application of a pesticide product registered under section 3 or section 24 of the Federal Insecticide, Fungicide, and Rodenticide Act (FIFRA), as amended (7 U.S.C. 136 et seq.), or pursuant to the terms and conditions of an experimental use permit issued under section 5 of FIFRA, or pursuant to an exemption granted under section 18 of FIFRA;

- ❏ in compliance with the regulations issued under section 3004 or with permit conditions issued pursuant to section 3005 of the Resource Conservation and Recovery Act (90 Stat. 2795; 42 U.S.C. 6901);

- ❏ in compliance with instructions of the on scene coordinator pursuant to 40 CFR Part 1510 (the National Oil and Hazardous Substances Pollution Plan) or 33 CFR 153.10(e) (Pollution by Oil and Hazardous Substances) or in accordance with applicable removal regulations as required by section 311(j)(1)(A);

- ❏ in compliance with a permit issued under 165.7 of Title 14 of the State of California Administrative Code;

- ❏ from a properly functioning inert gas system when used to provide inert gas to the cargo tanks of a vessel;

- ❏ from a permitted source and are excluded by 117.12 of this regulation;

- ❏ to a POTW and are specifically excluded or reserved in 117.13; or

❑ in compliance with a permit issued under section 404(a) of the Clean Water Act or when the discharges are exempt from such requirements by section 404(f) or 404(r) of the Act (33 U.S.C. 1344(a), (f), (r)).

4.1.1 Applicability to Discharges from Facilities with NPDES Permits

This regulation does not apply to:

❑ discharges in compliance with a permit under section 402 of this Act;

❑ discharges resulting from circumstances identified, reviewed and made a part of the public record with respect to a permit issued or modified under section 402 of this Act, and subject to a condition in such permit;

❑ continuous or anticipated intermittent discharges from a point source, identified in a permit or permit application under section 402 of this Act, which are caused by events occurring within the scope of the relevant operating or treatment systems; or

❑ a discharge is "in compliance with a permit issued under section 402 of this Act" if the permit contains an effluent limitation specifically applicable to the substance discharged or an effluent limitation applicable to another waste parameter which has been specifically identified in the permit as intended to limit such substance, and the discharge meets the effluent limitation.

A discharge results "from circumstances identified, reviewed and made a part of the public record with respect to a permit issued or modified under section 402 of the Act, and subject to a condition in such permit," whether or not the discharge is in compliance with the permit, where the permit application, the permit, or another portion of the public record contains documents that specifically identify: the substance and the amount of the substance; the origin and source of the substance; and the treatment which is to be provided for the discharge either by:

❑ an on-site treatment system separate from any treatment system treating the permittee's normal discharge; or

❑ a treatment system designed to treat the permittee's normal discharge and which can treat the identified amount of the identified substance; or

❑ any combination of the above.

The permit must also contain a requirement that the substance and amounts of the substance, as identified in 117.12(c)(1)(i) and 117.12(c)(1)(ii) be treated pursuant to 117.12(c)(1)(iii) if there is an on-site release; and the treatment to be provided is in place.

A discharge is a "continuous or anticipated intermittent discharge from a point source, identified in a permit or permit application under section 402 of this Act, and caused by events occurring within the scope of the relevant operating or treatment systems," whether or not the discharge is in compliance with the permit, if the hazardous substance is discharged from a point source for which a valid permit exists or for which a permit application has been submitted; and the discharge of the hazardous substance results from:

❑ the contamination of noncontact cooling water or storm water, if such cooling water or storm water is not contaminated by an on-site spill of a hazardous substance; or

❑ a continuous or anticipated intermittent discharge of process waste water, and the discharge originates within the manufacturing or treatment systems; or

❑ an upset or failure of a treatment system or of a process producing a continuous or anticipated intermittent discharge where the upset or failure results from a control problem, an operator error, a system failure or malfunction, an equipment or system startup or shutdown, an equipment wash, or a production schedule change, if such upset or failure is not caused by an on-site spill of a hazardous substance.

4.1.2 Applicability to Discharges from Publicly Owned Treatment Works

These regulations apply to all discharges of reportable quantities to a POTW, where the discharge originates from a mobile source, except where such source has contracted with, or otherwise received written permission from the owners or operators of the POTW to discharge that quantity, and the mobile source can show that before accepting the substance from an industrial discharger, the substance had been treated to comply with any effluent limitation under sections 301, 302 or 306 or pretreatment standard under section 307 applicable to that facility.

4.1.3 Demonstration Projects

Despite any other provision of this part, the Administrator of the Environmental Protection Agency may, on a case-by-case basis, allow the discharge of designated hazardous substances in connection with research or demonstration projects relating to the prevention, control, or abatement of hazardous substance pollution. The Administrator will allow such a discharge only where he determines that the expected environmental benefit from such a discharge will outweigh the potential hazard associated with the discharge.

4.2 Notice of Discharge of a Reportable Quantity

Any person in charge of a vessel or an onshore or an offshore facility shall, as soon as he has knowledge of any discharge of a designated hazardous substance from such vessel or facility in quantities equal to or exceeding in any 24-hour period the reportable quantity determined by this part, immediately notify the appropriate agency of the United States Government of such discharge. Notice must be given in accordance with such procedures as the Secretary of Transportation has set forth in 33 CFR 153.203. This provision applies to all discharges not specifically excluded or reserved by another section of these regulations.

4.2.1 Liabilities for Removal

In any case where a substance designated as hazardous in 40 CFR Part 116 is discharged from any vessel or onshore or offshore facility in a quantity equal to or exceeding the reportable quantity determined by this part, the owner, operator or person in charge will be liable, pursuant to section 311 (f) and (g) of the Act, to the United States Government for the actual costs incurred in the removal of such substance, subject only to the defenses and monetary limitations enumerated in section 311 (f) and (g) of the Act.

The Administrator may act to mitigate the damage to the public health or welfare caused by a discharge and the cost of such mitigation must be considered a cost incurred under section 311(c) for the removal of that substance by the United States Government.

Effluent Limitations General Provisions

Regulations promulgated or proposed under parts 402 through 699 of this subchapter prescribe effluent limitations guidelines for existing sources, standards of performance for new sources and pretreatment standards for new and existing sources pursuant to sections 301, 304 (b) and (c), 306 (b) and (c), 307 (b) and (c) and 316(b) of the Federal Water Pollution Control Act, as amended (the "Act"), 33 U.S.C. 1251, 1311, 1314 (b) and (c), 1316 (b) and (c), 1317 (b) and (c) and 1326(b); 86 Stat. 816; Pub. L. 92–500.

5.1 Overview

Point sources of discharges of pollutants are required to comply with these regulations, where applicable, and permits issued by states or the Environmental Protection Agency (EPA) under the National Pollutant Discharge Elimination System (NPDES) established pursuant to section 402 of the Act must be conditioned upon compliance with applicable requirements of sections 301 and 306 (as well as certain other requirements). This part 401 sets forth the legal authority and general definitions which will apply to all regulations issued concerning specific classes and categories of point sources under parts 402 through 699 of this subchapter which follow. In certain instances the regulations applicable to a particular point source category or subcategory will contain more specialized definitions. Except as provided in 401.17, in the case of any conflict between regulations issued under this part 401 and regulations issued under parts 402 through 499 of this subchapter, the latter more specific regulations shall apply.

5.1.1 Law Authorizing Establishment of Effluent Limitations Guidelines

Section 301(a) of the Act provides that "except as in compliance with this section and sections 302, 306, 307, 318, 402 and 404 of this Act, the discharge of any pollutant by any person shall be unlawful."

Section 301(b) of the Act requires the achievement of effluent limitations for point sources, other than publicly owned treatment works, which require the application of the best practicable control technology currently available as determined by the Administrator pursuant to section 304(b)(1) of the Act. Section 301(b) also requires the achievement by not later than July 1, 1983, of effluent limitations for point sources, other than publicly owned treatment works, which require the application of the best available technology economically achievable which will result in reasonable further progress toward the national goal of eliminating the discharge of all pollutants, as determined in accordance with regulations issued by the Administrator pursuant to section 304(b)(2) of the Act.

Section 304(b) of the Act requires the Administrator to publish regulations providing guidelines for effluent limitations setting forth the degree of effluent reduction attainable through the application of the best practicable control technology currently available and the degree of effluent reduction attainable through the application of the best control measures and practices achievable including treatment techniques, process and procedure innovations, operating methods and other alternatives.

Section 304(c) of the Act requires the Administrator, after consultation with appropriate federal and state agencies and other interested persons to issue information on the process, procedures, or operating methods which result in the elimination or reduction of the discharge of pollutants to implement standards of performance under section 306 of the Act.

Section 306(b)(1)(B) of the Act requires the Administrator, after a category of sources is included in a list published pursuant to section 306(b)(1)(A) of the Act, to propose regulations establishing federal standards of performances for new sources within such category. Standards of performance are to provide for the control of the discharge of pollutants which reflect the greatest degree of effluent reduction which the Administrator determines to be achievable through application of the best available demonstrated control technology, processes, operating methods, or other alternatives, including, where practicable, a standard permitting no discharge of pollutants.

Section 307(b) provides that the Administrator shall establish pretreatment standards which shall prevent the discharge of any pollutant into publicly owned treatment works which pollutant interferes with, passes through untreated, or otherwise is incompatible with such works.

Section 307(c) of the Act provides that the Administrator shall promulgate pretreatment standards for sources which would be "new sources" under section 306 (if they were to discharge pollutants directly to navigable waters) at the same time standards of performance for the equivalent category of new sources are promulgated.

Section 316(b) of the Act provides that any standard established pursuant to section 301 or section 306 of the Act and applicable to a point source shall require that the location, design, construction, and capacity of cooling water intake structures reflect the best technology available for minimizing adverse environmental impact.

Section 402(a)(1) of the Act provides that the Administrator may issue permits for the discharge of any pollutant upon condition that such discharge will meet all applicable requirements under sections 301, 302, 306, 307, 308 and 403 of this Act. In addition, section 402(b)(1)(A) of the Act requires that permits issued by states under the National Pollutant Discharge Elimination System (NPDES) established by the Act must apply, and insure compliance with any applicable requirements of sections 301, 302, 306, 307 and 403 of the Act.

5.2 Test Procedures for Measurement

The test procedures for measurement which are prescribed at part 136 of this chapter shall apply to expressions of pollutant amounts, characteristics or properties in effluent limitations guidelines and standards of performance and pretreatment standards as set forth at parts 402 through 699 of this subchapter, unless otherwise specifically noted or defined in said parts.

5.2.1 Toxic Pollutants

The following comprise the list of toxic pollutants designated pursuant to section 307(a)(1) of the Act:

- ❑ 1. Acenaphthene
- ❑ 2. Acrolein
- ❑ 3. Acrylonitrile
- ❑ 4. Aldrin/Dieldrin. Effluent standard promulgated (40 CFR Part 129).
- ❑ 5. Antimony and compounds. The term compounds shall include organic and inorganic compounds.
- ❑ 6. Arsenic and compounds
- ❑ 7. Asbestos
- ❑ 8. Benzene
- ❑ 9. Benzidine
- ❑ 10. Beryllium and compounds
- ❑ 11. Cadmium and compounds
- ❑ 12. Carbon tetrachloride
- ❑ 13. Chlordane (technical mixture and metabolites)
- ❑ 14. Chlorinated benzenes (other than di–chlorobenzenes)
- ❑ 15. Chlorinated ethanes (including 1,2–di–chloroethane, 1,1,1–trichloroethane, and hexachloroethane)
- ❑ 16. Chloroalkyl ethers (chloroethyl and mixed ethers)
- ❑ 17. Chlorinated naphthalene
- ❑ 18. Chlorinated phenols (other than those listed elsewhere; includes trichlorophenols and chlorinated cresols)
- ❑ 19. Chloroform
- ❑ 20. 2–chlorophenol
- ❑ 21. Chromium and compounds
- ❑ 22. Copper and compounds
- ❑ 23. Cyanides
- ❑ 24. DDT and metabolites

❏ 25. Dichlorobenzenes (1,2–, 1,3–, and 1,4–di–chlorobenzenes)

❏ 26. Dichlorobenzidine

❏ 27. Dichloroethylenes (1,1–, and 1,2–dichloroethylene)

❏ 28. 2,4–dichlorophenol

❏ 29. Dichloropropane and dichloropropene

❏ 30. 2,4–dimethylphenol

❏ 31. Dinitrotoluene

❏ 32. Diphenylhydrazine

❏ 33. Endosulfan and metabolites

❏ 34. Endrin and metabolites

❏ 35. Ethylbenzene

❏ 36. Fluoranthene

❏ 37. Haloethers (other than those listed elsewhere; includes chlorophenylphenyl ethers, bromophenylphenyl ether, bis(dichloroisopropyl) ether, bis–(chloroethoxy) methane and polychlorinated diphenyl ethers)

❏ 38. Halomethanes (other than those listed elsewhere; includes methylene chloride, methylchloride, methylbromide, bromoform, dichlorobromomethane

❏ 39. Heptachlor and metabolites

❏ 40. Hexachlorobutadiene

❏ 41. Hexachlorocyclohexane

❏ 42. Hexachlorocyclopentadiene

❏ 43. Isophorone

❏ 44. Lead and compounds

❏ 45. Mercury and compounds

❏ 46. Naphthalene

❏ 47. Nickel and compounds

❏ 48. Nitrobenzene

❏ 49. Nitrophenols (including 2,4–dinitrophenol, dinitrocresol)

❏ 50. Nitrosamines

❏ 51. Pentachlorophenol

❏ 52. Phenol

❏ 53. Phthalate esters

❏ 54. Polychlorinated biphenyls (PCBs)

☐ 55. Polynuclear aromatic hydrocarbons (including benzanthracenes, benzopyrenes, benzofluoranthene, chrysenes, dibenz–anthracenes, and indenopyrenes)

☐ 56. Selenium and compounds

☐ 57. Silver and compounds

☐ 58. 2,3,7,8–tetrachlorodibenzo–p–dioxin (TCDD)

☐ 59. Tetrachloroethylene

☐ 60. Thallium and compounds

☐ 61. Toluene

☐ 62. Toxaphene

☐ 63. Trichloroethylene

☐ 64. Vinyl chloride

☐ 65. Zinc and compounds

5.2.2 Conventional Pollutants

The following comprise the list of conventional pollutants designated pursuant to section 304(a)(4) of the Act:

☐ Biochemical oxygen demand (BOD)

☐ Total suspended solids (nonfilterable) (TSS)

☐ Fecal coliform

☐ Oil and grease

5.2.3 pH Effluent Limitations Under Continuous Monitoring

Where a permittee continuously measures the pH of wastewater pursuant to a requirement or option in a National Pollutant Discharge Elimination System (NPDES) permit issued pursuant to section 402 of the Act, the permittee shall maintain the pH of such wastewater within the range set forth in the applicable effluent limitations guidelines, except excursions from the range are permitted subject to the following limitations:

☐ the total time during which the pH values are outside the required range of pH values shall not exceed 7 hours and 26 minutes in any calendar month; and

☐ no individual excursion from the range of pH values shall exceed 60 minutes.

The Director may adjust the requirements set forth in this section with respect to the length of individual excursions from the range of pH values, if a different period of time is appropriate based upon the treatment system, plant configuration or other technical factors.

Hazardous Waste Injection Restrictions

This part identifies wastes that are restricted from disposal into Class I wells and defines those circumstances under which a waste, otherwise prohibited from injection, may be injected.

6.1 Overview

The requirements of this part apply to owners or operators of Class I hazardous waste injection wells used to inject hazardous waste. Wastes otherwise prohibited from injection may continue to be injected if:

☐ an extension from the effective date of a prohibition has been granted pursuant to 148.4 with respect to such wastes; or

☐ an exemption from a prohibition has been granted in response to a petition filed under 148.20 to allow injection of restricted wastes with respect to those wastes and wells covered by the exemption; or

☐ the waste is generated by a conditionally exempt small quantity generator, as defined in 261.5. Or the following applies—

Wastes that are hazardous only because they exhibit a hazardous characteristic, and which are otherwise prohibited under this part, or part 268 of this chapter, are not prohibited if the wastes:

☐ are disposed into a nonhazardous or hazardous injection well as defined under 40 CFR 146.6(a); and

☐ do not exhibit any prohibited characteristic of hazardous waste identified in 40 CFR Part 261, subpart C at the point of injection.

6.1.1 Waste Analysis

Generators of hazardous wastes that are disposed of into Class I injection wells must comply with the applicable requirements of 268.7 (a) and (b). Owners or operators of Class I hazardous waste injection wells must comply with the applicable requirements of 268.7(c).

☐ Prohibitions on injection

☐ Waste specific prohibitions–solvent wastes

☐ Waste specific prohibitions–dioxin containing wastes

- ❏ Waste specific prohibitions–California list wastes
- ❏ Waste specific prohibitions–first third wastes
- ❏ Waste specific prohibitions–second third wastes
- ❏ Waste specific prohibitions–third third wastes
- ❏ Waste specific prohibitions–newly listed wastes
- ❏ Waste specific prohibitions–newly listed and identified wastes
- ❏ Petitions to allow injection of a waste prohibited under subpart B.

Any person seeking an exemption from a prohibition under subpart B of this part for the injection of a restricted hazardous waste into an injection well or wells shall submit a petition to the Director demonstrating that, to a reasonable degree of certainty, there will be no migration of hazardous constituents from the injection zone for as long as the waste remains hazardous. The specific requirements for this demonstration are included in this section of the CFRs.

6.2 Review of Exemptions Granted Pursuant to a Petition

When considering whether to reissue a permit for the operation of a Class I hazardous waste injection well, the Director shall review any petition filed pursuant to 148.20 and require a new demonstration if information shows that the basis for granting the exemption may no longer be valid.

Whenever the Director determines that the basis for approval of a petition may no longer be valid, the Director shall require a new demonstration in accordance with 148.20.

6.3 Termination of Approved Petition

The Director may terminate an exemption granted under 148.20 for the following causes:

- ❏ noncompliance by the petitioner with any condition of the exemption;
- ❏ the petitioner's failure in the petition or during the review and approval to disclose fully all relevant facts, or the petitioner's misrepresentation of any relevant facts at any time; or
- ❏ a determination that new information shows that the basis for approval of the petition is no longer valid.

The Director shall terminate an exemption granted under 148.20 for the following causes:

- ❏ the petitioner's willful withholding during the review and approval of the petition of facts directly and materially relevant to the Director's decision on the petition;
- ❏ a determination that there has been migration from the injection zone or the well that is not in accordance with the terms of the exemption.

However, the Director may at his discretion decide not to terminate where:

❑ the migration resulted from a mechanical failure of the well that can be corrected promptly through a repair to the injection well itself or from an undetected well or conduit that can be plugged promptly; and

❑ the requirements of 146.67(i) are satisfied.

The Director shall follow the procedures in 124.5 in terminating any exemption under this section.

Marine Sanitation Device Standard

The standard adopted herein applies only to vessels on which a marine sanitation device has been installed. The standard does not require the installation of a marine sanitation device on any vessel that is not so equipped. The standard applies to vessels owned and operated by the United States unless the Secretary of Defense finds that compliance would not be in the interest of national security.

7.1 Overview

In freshwater lakes, freshwater reservoirs or other freshwater impoundments whose inlets or outlets are such as to prevent the ingress or egress by vessel traffic subject to this regulation, or in rivers not capable of navigation by interstate vessel traffic subject to this regulation, marine sanitation devices certified by the U.S. Coast Guard (see 33 CFR Part 159), installed on all vessels shall be designed and operated to prevent the overboard discharge of sewage, treated or untreated, or of any waste derived from sewage. This shall not be construed to prohibit the carriage of Coast Guard certified flow-through treatment devices which have been secured to prevent such discharges.

In all other waters, Coast Guard certified marine sanitation devices installed on all vessels shall be designed and operated to either retain, dispose of, or discharge sewage. If the device has a discharge, subject to this section of the CFRs, the effluent shall not have a fecal coliform bacterial count of greater than 1,000 per 100 milliliters nor visible floating solids. Waters where a Coast Guard certified marine sanitation device permitting discharge is allowed include coastal waters and estuaries, the Great Lakes and interconnected waterways, freshwater lakes and impoundments accessible through locks, and other flowing waters that are navigable interstate by vessels subject to this regulation.

Any vessel which is equipped as of the date of promulgation of this regulation with a Coast Guard certified flow-through marine sanitation device meeting the requirements of this section of the CFRs, shall not be required to comply with the provisions designed to prevent the overboard discharge of sewage, treated or untreated, in this section of the CFRs, for the operable life of that device.

Marine sanitation devices on all vessels on waters that are not subject to a prohibition of the overboard discharge of sewage, treated or untreated, as specified in this section, shall be designed and operated to either retain, dispose of, or discharge sewage, and shall be certified by the U.S. Coast Guard. If the device has a discharge, the effluent shall not have a fecal coliform bacterial count of greater than 200 per 100 milliliters, nor suspended solids greater than 150 mg/1.

The degrees of treatment described in this section are considered "appropriate standards" for purposes of Coast Guard and Department of Defense certification pursuant to section 312(g)(2) of the Act.

7.2 Prohibitions

7.2.1 Prohibition Pursuant to CWA Section 312(f)(3)

A state may completely prohibit the discharge from all vessels of any sewage, whether treated or not, into some or all of the waters within such state by making a written application to the Administrator, Environmental Protection Agency, and by receiving the Administrator's affirmative determination pursuant to section 312(f)(3) of the Act. Upon receipt of an application under section 312(f)(3) of the Act, the Administrator will determine within 90 days whether adequate facilities for the safe and sanitary removal and treatment of sewage from all vessels using such waters are reasonably available. Applications made by states pursuant to section 312(f)(3) of the Act shall include:

- ☐ a certification that the protection and enhancement of the waters described in the petition require greater environmental protection than the applicable federal standard;

- ☐ a map showing the location of commercial and recreational pump-out facilities;

- ☐ a description of the location of pump-out facilities within waters designated for no discharge;

- ☐ the general schedule of operating hours of the pump-out facilities;

- ☐ the draught requirements on vessels that may be excluded because of insufficient water depth adjacent to the facility;

- ☐ information indicating that treatment of wastes from such pump-out facilities is in conformance with federal law; and

- ☐ information on vessel population and vessel usage of the subject waters.

7.2.2 Prohibition Pursuant to CWA Section 312(f)(4)(A)

A state may apply to the Administrator, Environmental Protection Agency, under section 312(f)(4)(A) of the Act, for the issuance of a regulation completely prohibiting discharge from a vessel of any sewage, whether treated or not, into particular waters of the United States or specified portions thereof, which waters are located within the boundaries of such State. Such application shall specify with particularly the waters, or portions thereof, for which a complete prohibition is desired. The application shall include identification of water recreational areas, drinking water intakes, aquatic sanctuaries, identifiable fish spawning and nursery areas, and areas of intensive boating activities. If, on the basis of the state's application and any other information available to him, the Administrator is unable to make a finding that the waters listed in the application require a complete prohibition of any discharge in the waters or portions thereof covered by the application, he shall state the reasons why he cannot make such a finding, and shall deny the application. If the Administrator makes a finding that the waters listed in the

40

application require a complete prohibition of any discharge in all or any part of the waters or portions thereof covered by the State's application, he shall publish notice of such findings with a notice of proposed rule making, and then shall proceed in accordance with 5 U.S.C. 553. If the Administrator's finding is that applicable water quality standards require a complete prohibition covering a more restricted or more expanded area than that applied for by the state, he shall state the reasons why his finding differs in scope from that requested in the State's application.

For the following waters the discharge from a vessel of any sewage (whether treated or not) is completely prohibited pursuant to CWA section 312(f)(4)(A):

❑ Boundary Waters Canoe Area, formerly designated as the Superior, Little Indian Sioux, and Caribou Roadless Areas, in the Superior National Forest, Minnesota, as described in 16 U.S.C. 577–577d1.

A state may apply to the Administrator of the Environmental Protection Agency under section 312(f)(4)(B) of the Act for the issuance of a regulation establishing a drinking water intake no discharge zone which completely prohibits discharge from a vessel of any sewage, whether treated or untreated, into that zone in particular waters, or portions thereof, within such state. Such application shall:

❑ identify and describe exactly and in detail the location of the drinking water supply intake(s) and the community served by the intake(s), including average and maximum expected amounts of inflow;

❑ specify and describe exactly and in detail, the waters, or portions thereof, for which a complete prohibition is desired, and where appropriate, average, maximum and low flows in million gallons per day (MGD) or the metric equivalent;

❑ include a map, either a USGS topographic quadrant map or a NOAA nautical chart, as applicable, clearly marking by latitude and longitude the waters or portions thereof to be designated a drinking water intake zone; and

❑ include a statement of basis justifying the size of the requested drinking water intake zone, for example, identifying areas of intensive boating activities.

If the Administrator finds that a complete prohibition is appropriate under this paragraph, he or she shall publish notice of such finding with a notice of proposed rulemaking, and then shall proceed in accordance with 5 U.S.C. 553. If the Administrator's finding is that a complete prohibition covering a more restricted or more expanded area than that applied for by the state is appropriate, he or she shall also include a statement of the reasons why the finding differs in scope from that requested in the state's application.

If the Administrator finds that a complete prohibition is inappropriate under this paragraph, he or she shall deny the application and state the reasons for such denial.

7.2.3 Complete Prohibition Pursuant to CWA Section 312(f)(4)(B)

For the following waters the discharge from a vessel of any sewage, whether treated or not, is completely prohibited pursuant to CWA section 312(f)(4)(B):

☐ Two portions of the Hudson River in New York State, the first is bounded by an east–west line through the most northern confluence of the Mohawk River which will be designated by the Troy–Waterford Bridge (126th Street Bridge) on the south and Lock 2 on the north, and the second of which is bounded on the north by the southern end of Houghtaling Island and on the south by a line between the Village of Roseton on the western shore and Low Point on the eastern shore in the vicinity of Chelsea, as described in Items 2 and 3 of 6 NYCRR Part 858.4.

7.3 Analytical Procedures

In determining the composition and quality of effluent discharge from marine sanitation devices, the procedures contained in 40 CFR Part 136, "Guidelines Establishing Test Procedures for the Analysis of Pollutants," or subsequent revisions or amendments thereto, shall be employed.

National Primary Drinking Water Regulations

> *One of the most significant provisions of the SDWA is the establishment of National Primary Drinking Water Regulations at 40 CFR Parts 141 through 143.*

8.1 National Primary Drinking Water Overview

8.1.1 Part 141

The regulations are given life here, with the establishment of maximum contaminant levels (MCLs) for inorganic and organic constituents, Subpart B and maximum contaminant level goals (MCLGs), Subpart F. Much attention is given to the monitoring and analytical requirements for the regulated water quality parameters, Subpart C. Filtration and disinfection are given much the same kind of thorough treatment. Also included are sections covering control of lead and copper, use of non-centralized treatment devices and treatment techniques.

8.1.2 Part 142

With only a few exceptions, 40 CFR Part 142 applies to public water systems in each state. States are given primary enforcement responsibility, given that the state has an EPA-approved program. If a state wishes to revise its program, it may do so if it follows the requirements given in 142.12. All states with enforcement responsibility are required to submit to the EPA Administrator a report containing various components dealing with national primary drinking water regulations. Variances and exemptions to the primary regulations may be granted by either the states or the Administrator. Another section (142.60) discusses best available technologies for a list of contaminants as they pertain to national primary drinking water regulations.

8.1.3 Part 143

While Part 141 of this title is concerned with primary drinking water regulations, 40 CFR Part 143 deals with national secondary drinking water regulations. Secondary regulations control contaminants that primarily affect the aesthetic qualities of drinking water. Levels are given for selected contaminants and it is explained that states may establish higher or lower levels depending on special conditions with that state, given that public health and welfare are not adversely affected. Section 143.4 gives monitoring requirements, stating that monitoring should occur no less frequently than the schedule used for the National Interim Primary Drinking Water Regulations.

8.2 National Primary Drinking Water Regulations (Part 141)

This part establishes primary drinking water regulations pursuant to section 1412 of the Public Health Service Act, as amended by the Safe Drinking Water Act (Pub. L. 93–523); and related regulations applicable to public water systems. This part applies to each public water system, unless the public water system meets all of the following conditions:

- ❑ consists only of distribution and storage facilities (and does not have any collection and treatment facilities);

- ❑ obtains all of its water from, but is not owned or operated by, a public water system to which such regulations apply:

- ❑ does not sell water to any person; and

- ❑ is not a carrier which conveys passengers in interstate commerce.

8.2.1 Variances and Exemptions

Variances or exemptions from certain provisions of these regulations may be granted pursuant to sections 1415 and 1416 of the Act by the entity with primary enforcement responsibility, except that variances or exemptions from the MCL for total coliforms and variances from any of the treatment technique requirements of subpart H of this part may not be granted.

The CFRs indicate that the EPA has stayed the effective date of this section relating to the total coliform MCL of 141.63(a) for systems that demonstrate to the state that the violation of the total coliform MCL is due to a persistent growth of total coliforms in the distribution system rather than fecal or pathogenic contamination, a treatment lapse or deficiency, or a problem in the operation or maintenance of the distribution system.

8.2.2 Siting Requirements

Before a person may enter into a financial commitment for or initiate construction of a new public water system or increase the capacity of an existing public water system, he shall notify the state and, to the extent practicable, avoid locating part or all of the new or expanded facility at a site which:

- ❑ is subject to a significant risk from earthquakes, floods, fires or other disasters which could cause a breakdown of the public water system or a portion thereof; or

- ❑ except for intake structures, is within the floodplain of a 100 year flood or is lower than any recorded high tide where appropriate records exist. The U.S. Environmental Protection Agency will not seek to override land use decisions affecting public water systems siting that are made at the state or local government levels.

8.3 Maximum Contaminant Levels

8.3.1 Maximum Contaminant Levels for Inorganic Chemicals

The maximum contaminant level for arsenic applies only to community water systems. Compliance with the MCL for arsenic is calculated pursuant to 141.23. The maximum contaminant level for arsenic is 0.05 milligrams per liter.

At the discretion of the state, nitrate levels not to exceed 20 mg/l may be allowed in a non-community water system if the supplier of water demonstrates to the satisfaction of the state that:

- ❏ such water will not be available to children under six months of age;

- ❏ there will be continuous posting of the fact that nitrate levels exceed 10 mg/l's and the potential health effects of exposure;

- ❏ local and state public health authorities will be notified annually of nitrate levels that exceed 10 mg/l; and

- ❏ no adverse health effects shall result.

8.3.2 Maximum Contaminant Levels for Organic Chemicals

The following are the maximum contaminant levels for organic chemicals. The maximum contaminant levels for organic chemicals in this section of the CFRs apply to all community water systems. Compliance with the maximum contaminant level in this section of the CFRs is calculated pursuant to 141.24. The maximum contaminant level for total trihalomethanes in this section of the CFRs applies only to community water systems which serve a population of 10,000 or more individuals and which add a disinfectant (oxidant) to the water in any part of the drinking water treatment process. Compliance with the maximum contaminant level for total trihalomethanes is calculated pursuant to 141.30.

8.3.3 Maximum Contaminant Levels for Turbidity

The maximum contaminant levels for turbidity are applicable to both community water systems and non-community water systems using surface water sources in whole or in part. The maximum contaminant levels for turbidity in drinking water, measured at a representative entry point(s) to the distribution system, is one turbidity unit (TU), as determined by a monthly average pursuant to 141.22, except that five or fewer turbidity units may be allowed if the supplier of water can demonstrate to the state that the higher turbidity does not do any of the following:

- ❏ interfere with disinfection;

❏ prevent maintenance of an effective disinfectant agent throughout the distribution system; or

❏ interfere with microbiological determinations.

The five turbidity unit is based on an average for two consecutive days pursuant to 141.22.

8.3.4 Maximum Contaminant Levels for Radium-226, Radium-228, and Gross Alpha Particle Radioactivity

The following are the maximum contaminant levels for radium-226, radium-228, and gross alpha particle radioactivity for community water systems:

❏ Combined radium-226 and radium–228-5 pCi/l.

❏ Gross alpha particle activity (including radium-226 but excluding radon and uranium)-15 pCi/l.

8.3.5 Maximum Contaminant Levels for Beta Particle and Photon Radioactivity from Man-made Radionuclides

The average annual concentration of beta particle and photon radioactivity from man-made radionuclides in community drinking water systems shall not produce an annual dose equivalent to the total body or any internal organ greater than four millirem/year.

Except for the radionuclides listed in Table A of this section of the CFRs, the concentration of man-made radionuclides causing four mrem total body or organ dose equivalents shall be calculated on the basis of a 2 liter per day drinking water intake using the 168-hour data listed in "Maximum Permissible Body Burdens and Maximum Permissible Concentration of Radionuclides in Air or Water for Occupational Exposure," NBS Handbook 69 as amended August 1963, U.S. Department of Commerce. If two or more radionuclides are present, the sum of their annual dose equivalent to the total body or to any organ shall not exceed four millirem/year.

Other Information contained in this part includes:

❏ Monitoring and Analytical Requirements (Subpart C)

❏ Reporting, Public Notification and Recordkeeping (Subpart D)

❏ Special Regulations, Including Monitoring Regulations and Prohibition on Lead Use (Subpart E)

8.4 Maximum Contaminant Level Goals

Maximum contaminant level goals for contaminants, by type of contaminant, are listed below.

8.4.1 Goals for Organic Contaminants

Organic contaminants whose MCLGs are zero include:

- ☐ Benzene
- ☐ Vinyl chloride
- ☐ Carbon tetrachloride
- ☐ 1,2–dichloroethane
- ☐ Trichloroethylene
- ☐ Acrylamide
- ☐ Alachlor
- ☐ Chlordane
- ☐ Dibromochloropropane
- ☐ 1,2–Dichloropropane
- ☐ Epichlorohydrin
- ☐ Ethylene dibromide
- ☐ Heptachlor
- ☐ Heptachlor epoxide
- ☐ Pentachlorophenol
- ☐ Polychlorinated biphenyls (PCBs)
- ☐ Tetrachloroethylene
- ☐ Toxaphene
- ☐ Benzo[a]pyrene
- ☐ Dichloromethane (methylene chloride)
- ☐ Di(2–ethylhexyl)phthalate
- ☐ Hexachlorobenzene
- ☐ 2,3,7,8–TCDD (Dioxin)

8.4.2 Goals for Other Organic Contaminants

MCLGs for Other Organic Contaminants	
Contaminant	MCLG in mg/l
(1) 1,1–Dichloroethylene	0.007
(2) 1,1,1–Trichloroethane	0.20
(3) para–Dichlorobenzene	0.075
(4) Aldicarb	0.001
(5) Aldicarb sulfoxide	0.001
(6) Aldicarb sulfone	0.001
(7) Atrazine	0.003
(8) Carbofuran	0.04
(9) o–Dichlorobenzene	0.6
(10) cis–1,2–Dichloroethylene	0.07
(11) trans–1,2–Dichloroethylene	0.1
(12) 2,4–D	0.07
(13) Ethylbenzene	0.7
(14) Lindane	0.0002
(15) Methoxychlor	0.04
(16) Monochlorobenzene	0.1
(17) Styrene	0.1
(18) Toluene	1
(19) 2,4,5–TP	0.05
(20) Xylenes (total)	10
(21) Dalapon	0.2
(22) Di(2–ethylhexyl)adipate	.4
(23) Dinoseb	.007
(24) Diquat	.02
(25) Endothall	.1
(26) Endrin	.002
(27) Glyphosate	.7
(28) Hexachlorocyclopentadiene	.05
(29) Oxamyl (Vydate)	.2
(30) Picloram	.5
(31) Simazine	.004

MCLGs for Other Organic Contaminants	
Contaminant	MCLG in mg/l
(32) 1,2,4–Trichlorobenzene	.07
(33) 1,1,2–Trichloroethane	.003

8.4.3 Goals for Inorganic Contaminants

MCLGs for Inorganic Contaminants	
Contaminant	MCLG (mg/l)
Antimony	0.006
Asbestos	7 million fibers/liter
Barium	2
Beryllium	.004
Cadmium	0.005
Chromium	0.1
Copper	1.3
Cyanide (as free Cyanide)	.2
Fluoride	4.0
Lead	zero
Mercury	0.002
Nitrate	10 (as Nitrogen).
Nitrite	1 (as Nitrogen).
Total Nitrate+Nitrite	10 (as Nitrogen).
Selenium	0.05
Thallium	.0005

8.4.4 Goals for Microbiological Contaminants

Maximum contaminant level goals for microbiological contaminants	
Contaminant	MCLG
(1) Giardia lamblia	zero
(2) Viruses	zero
(3) Legionella	zero

(4) Total coliforms (including fecal coliforms and Escherichia coli)	zero

8.5 Community and Non-Transient, Non-Community Water Systems

Maximum Contaminant Levels for organic contaminants that apply to community and non-transient, non-community water systems are listed in the following table:

Community and non-transient, non-community water systems		
CAS No.	Contaminant	MCL (mg/l)
(1) 75–01–4	Vinyl chloride	0.002
(2) 71–43–2	Benzene	0.005
(3) 56–23–5	Carbon tetrachloride	0.005
(4) 107–06–2	1,2–Dichloroethane	0.005
(5) 79–01–6	Trichloroethylene	0.005
(6) 106–46–7	para–Dichlorobenzene	0.075
(7) 75–35–4	1,1–Dichloroethylene	0.007
(8) 71–55–6	1,1,1–Trichloroethane	0.2
(9) 156–59–2	cis–1,2–Dichloroethylene	0.07
(10) 78–87–5	1,2–Dichloropropane	0.005
(11) 100–41–4	Ethylbenzene	0.7
(12) 108–90–7	Monochlorobenzene	0.1
(13) 95–50–1	o–Dichlorobenzene	0.6
(14) 100–42–5	Styrene	0.1
(15) 127–18–4	Tetrachloroethylene	0.005
(16) 108–88–3	Toluene	1
(17) 156–60–5	trans–1,2–Dichloroethylene	0.1
(18) 1330–20–7	Xylenes (total)	10
(19) 75–09–2	Dichloromethane	0.005
(20) 120–82–1	1,2,4–Trichloro– benzene	.07
(21) 79–00–5	1,1,2–Trichloro– ethane	.005

8.6 Best Available Technology (BAT) for Organic Contaminants

The Administrator, pursuant to section 1412 of the Act, hereby identifies as shown in the Table below granular activated carbon (GAC), packed tower aeration (PTA), or oxidation (OX) as the best technology treatment technique, or other means available for achieving compliance with the maximum contaminant level for the organic contaminants identified in this section:

BAT for Organic Contaminants Listed in 141.61 (a) and (c)				
CAS No.	Contaminant	GAC	PTA	OX
15972–60–8	Alachlor	X		
116–06–3	Aldicarb	X		
1646–88–4	Aldicarb sulfone	X		
1646–87–3	Aldicarb sulfoxide	X		
1912–24–9	Atrazine	X		
71–43–2	Benzene	X	X	
50–32–8	Benzo[a]pyrene	X		
1563–66–2	Carbofuran	X		
56–23–5	Carbon tetrachloride	X	X	
57–74–9	Chlordane	X		
75–99–0	Dalapon	X		
94–75–7	2,4–D	X		
103–23–1	Di (2–ethylhexyl) adipate	X	X	
117–81–7	Di (2–ethylhexyl) phthalate	X		
96–12–8	Dibromochloropropane (DBCP)	X	X	
95–50–1	o–Dichlorobenzene	X	X	
106–46–7	para–Dichlorobenzene	X	X	
107–06–2	1,2–Dichloroethane	X	X	
75–35–4	1,1–Dichloroethylene	X	X	
156–59–2	cis–1,2–Dichloroethylene	X	X	
156–60–5	trans–1,2–Dichloroethylene	X	X	
75–09–2	Dichloromethane	X		
78–87–5	1,2–Dichloropropane	X	X	
88–85–7	Dinoseb	X		
85–00–7	Diquat	X		
145–73–3	Endothall	X		
72–20–8	Endrin	X		
100–41–4	Ethylbenzene	X	X	
106–93–4	Ethylene Dibromide (EDB)	X	X	
1071–83–6	Gylphosate	X		

BAT for Organic Contaminants Listed in 141.61 (a) and (c)				
CAS No.	Contaminant	GAC	PTA	OX
76–44–8	Heptachlor	X		
1024–57–3	Heptachlor epoxide	X		
118–74–1	Hexachlorobenzene	X		
77–47–3	Hexachlorocyclopentadiene	X	X	
58–89–9	Lindane	X		
72–43–5	Methoxychlor	X		
108–90–7	Monochlorobenzene	X	X	
23135–22–0	Oxamyl (Vydate)	X		
87–86–5	Pentachlorophenol	X		
1918–02–1	Picloram	X		
1336–36–3	Polychlorinated biphenyls (PCB)	X		
122–34–9	Simazine	X		
100–42–5	Styrene	X	X	
1746–01–6	2,3,7,8–TCDD (Dioxin)	X		
127–18–4	Tetrachloroethylene	X	X	
108–88–3	Toluene	X	X	
8001–35–2	Toxaphene	X		
93–72–1	2,4,5–TP (Silvex)	X		
120–82–1	1,2,4–Trichlorobenzene	X	X	
71–55–6	1,1,1–Trichloroethane	X	X	
79–00–5	1,1,2–Trichloroethane	X	X	
79–01–6	Trichloroethylene	X	X	
75–01–4	Vinyl chloride	X		
1330–20–7	Xylene	X	X	

8.7 Synthetic Organic Contaminants

The following maximum contaminant levels for synthetic organic contaminants apply to community water systems and non-transient, non-community water systems:

Synthetic Organic Contaminants		
CAS No.	Contaminant	MCL (mg/l)
(1) 15972–60–8	Alachlor	0.002
(2) 116–06–3	Aldicarb	0.003

Synthetic Organic Contaminants		
CAS No.	Contaminant	MCL (mg/l)
(3) 1646–87–3	Aldicarb sulfoxide	0.004
(4) 1646–87–4	Aldicarb sulfone	0.002
(5) 1912–24–9	Atrazine	0.003
(6) 1563–66–2	Carbofuran	0.04
(7) 57–74–9	Chlordane	0.002
(8) 96–12–8	Dibromochloropropane	0.0002
(9) 94–75–7	2,4–D	0.07
(10) 106–93–4	Ethylene dibromide	0.00005
(11) 76–44–8	Heptachlor	0.0004
(12) 1024–57–3	Heptachlor epoxide	0.0002
(13) 58–89–9	Lindane	0.0002
(14) 72–43–5	Methoxychlor	0.04
(15) 1336–36–3	Polychlorinated biphenyls	0.0005
(16) 87–86–5	Pentachlorophenol	0.001
(17) 8001–35–2	Toxaphene	0.003
(18) 93–72–1	2,4,5–TP	0.05
(19) 50–32–8	Benzo[a]pyrene	0.0002
(20) 75–99–0	Dalapon	0.2
(21) 103–23–1	Di(2–ethylhexyl) adipate	0.4
(22) 117–81–7	Di(2–ethylhexyl) phthalate	0.006
(23) 88–85–7	Dinoseb	0.007
(24) 85–00–7	Diquat	0.02
(25) 145–73–3	Endothall	0.1
(26) 72–20–8	Endrin	0.002
(27) 1071–53–6	Glyphosate	0.7
(28) 118–74–1	Hexacholorbenzene	0.001
(29) 77–47–4	Hexachlorocyclopentadiene	0.05
(30) 23135–22–0	Oxamyl (Vydate)	0.2
(31) 1918–02–1	Picloram	0.5
(32) 122–34–9	Simazine	0.004
(33) 1746–01–6	2,3,7,8–TCDD (Dioxin)	3×10^{-8}

8.8 Maximum Contaminant Levels for Inorganic Contaminants

The maximum contaminant levels for inorganic contaminants specified in this section apply to community water systems and non-transient, non-community water systems. The maximum contaminant level specified in this section of the CFRs only applies to community water systems. The maximum contaminant levels specified in (b)(7), (b)(8), and (b)(9) of this section apply to community water systems; non-transient, non-community water systems; and transient non-community water systems.

MCLs for Inorganic Contaminants	
Contaminant	MCL (mg/l)
Fluoride	4.0
Asbestos	7 million fibers/liter
Barium	2
Cadmium	0.005
Chromium	0.1
Mercury	0.002
Nitrate	10 (as Nitrogen)
Nitrite	1 (as Nitrogen)
Total Nitrate and Nitrite	10 (as Nitrogen)
Selenium	0.05
Antimony	0.006
Beryllium	0.004
Cyanide (as free Cyanide)	0.2
Thallium	0.002

8.9 Best Available Technology (BAT) for Inorganic Compounds Listed in Section 141.62(b)

The Administrator, pursuant to section 1412 of the Act, hereby identifies the following as the best technology, treatment technique, or other means available for achieving compliance with the maximum contaminant levels for inorganic contaminants identified in this section of the CFRs, except fluoride:

BAT for Inorganic Compounds Listed in Section 141.62(b)	
Chemical Name	BAT(s)
Antimony	2,7
Asbestos	2,3,8

BAT for Inorganic Compounds Listed in Section 141.62(b)	
Chemical Name	BAT(s)
Barium	5,6,7,9
Beryllium	1,2,5,6,7
Cadmium	2,5,6,7
Chromium	2,5,62,7
Cyanide	5,7,10
Mercury	21,4,61,71
Nickel	5,6,7
Nitrate	5,7,9
Nitrite	5,7
Selenium	12,3,6,7,9
Thallium	1,5

Key to BATS in Table

Notes: 1BAT only if influent Hg concentrations. 2BAT for Chromium III only. 3BAT for Selenium IV only.

1=Activated Alumina	6=Lime Softening	11=Ultraviolet
2=Coagulation/Filtration	7=Reverse Osmosis	
3=Direct and Diatomite Filtration	8=Corrosion Control	
4=Granular Activated Carbon	9=Electrodialysis	
5=Ion Exchange	10=Chlorine	

8.10 MCLs for Microbiological Contaminants

The MCL is based on the presence or absence of total coliforms in a sample, rather than coliform density. For a system which collects at least 40 samples per month, if no more than 5.0 percent of the samples collected during a month are total coliform positive, the system is in compliance with the MCL for total coliforms. For a system which collects fewer than 40 samples/month, if no more than one sample collected during a month is total coliform positive, the system is in compliance with the MCL for total coliforms.

Any fecal coliform positive repeat sample or E. coli positive repeat sample, or any total coliform positive repeat sample following a fecal coliform positive or E. coli positive routine sample constitutes a violation of the MCL for total coliforms. For purposes of the public notification requirements in 141.32, this is a violation that may pose an acute risk to health.

A public water system must determine compliance with the MCL for total coliforms in paragraphs (a) and (b) of this section for each month in which it is required to monitor for total coliforms.

The Administrator, pursuant to section 1412 of the Act, hereby identifies the following as the best technology, treatment techniques, or other means available for achieving compliance with the maximum contaminant level for total coliforms in paragraphs (a) and (b) of this section:

- ❏ protection of wells from contamination by coliforms by appropriate placement and construction;

- ❏ maintenance of a disinfectant residual throughout the distribution system;

- ❏ proper maintenance of the distribution system including appropriate pipe replacement and repair procedures, main flushing programs, proper operation and maintenance of storage tanks and reservoirs, and continual maintenance of positive water pressure in all Parts of the distribution system;

- ❏ filtration and/or disinfection of surface water, as described in subpart H, or disinfection of ground water using strong oxidants such as chlorine, chlorine dioxide, or ozone; and

- ❏ for systems using ground water, compliance with the requirements of an EPA approved State Wellhead Protection Program developed and implemented under section 1428 of the SDWA.

8.11 Filtration and Disinfection

The requirements of this subpart H constitute national primary drinking water regulations. These regulations establish criteria under which filtration is required as a treatment technique for public water systems supplied by a surface water source and public water systems supplied by a ground water source under the direct influence of surface water.

8.12 Control of Lead and Copper

The requirements of subpart I constitute the national primary drinking water regulations for lead and copper. Unless otherwise indicated, each of the provisions of this subpart applies to community water systems and non-transient, non-community water systems (hereinafter referred to as "water systems" or "systems").

These regulations establish a treatment technique that includes requirements for corrosion control treatment, source water treatment, lead service line replacement, and public education. These requirements are triggered, in some cases, by lead and copper action levels measured in samples collected at consumers' taps.

National Primary Drinking Water Regulations Implementation

This part sets forth, pursuant to sections 1413 through 1416, 1445, and 1450 of the Public Health Service Act, as amended by the Safe Drinking Water Act, Public Law 93–523, regulations for the implementation and enforcement of the national primary drinking water regulations contained in 40 CFR Part 141.

9.1 Overview

Except where otherwise provided, this part applies to each public water system in each state; except that this part shall not apply to a public water system which meets all of the following conditions:

❑ consists only of distribution and storage facilities (and does not have any collection and treatment facilities);

❑ obtains all of its water from, but is not owned or operated by, a public water system to which such regulations apply;

❑ does not sell water to any person; and

❑ is not a carrier which conveys passengers in interstate commerce.

In order to qualify for primary enforcement responsibility, a state's program for enforcement of primary drinking water regulations must apply to all other public water systems in the state, except for:

❑ public water systems on carriers which convey passengers in interstate commerce;

❑ public water systems on indian land with respect to which the state does not have the necessary jurisdiction or its jurisdiction is in question; or

❑ public water systems owned or maintained by a federal agency where the Administrator has waived compliance with national primary drinking water regulations pursuant to section 1447(b) of the Act.

Section 1451 of the SDWA authorizes the Administrator to delegate primary enforcement responsibility for public water systems to indian tribes. An indian tribe must meet the statutory criteria at 42 U.S.C. 300j–11(b)(1) before applying for Public Water System Supervision grants and primary enforcement responsibility is eligible. All primary enforcement responsibility requirements of Parts 141 and 142 apply to indian tribes except where specifically noted.

9.1.1 State and Local Authority

Nothing in this part shall diminish any authority of a state or political subdivision to adopt or enforce any law or regulation respecting drinking water regulations or public water systems, but no such law or regulation shall relieve any person of any requirements otherwise applicable under this part.

9.2 Primary Enforcement Responsibility

A state has primary enforcement responsibility for public water systems in the state during any period for which the Administrator determines, based upon a submission made pursuant to 142.11, and submission under 142.12, that such state, pursuant to appropriate state legal authority: has adopted drinking water regulations which are no less stringent than the national primary drinking water regulations (NPDWRs) in effect under part 141 of this chapter, and is implementing adequate procedures for the enforcement of such state regulations, such procedures to include:

- ☐ maintenance of an inventory of public water systems,

- ☐ a systematic program for conducting sanitary surveys of public water systems in the state, with priority given to sanitary surveys of public water systems not in compliance with state primary drinking water regulations; and

- ☐ the establishment and maintenance of a program for the certification of laboratories conducting analytical measurements of drinking water contaminants pursuant to the requirements of the state primary drinking water regulations including the designation by the state of a laboratory officer, or officers, certified by the Administrator, as the official(s) responsible for the state's certification program.

The requirements of this paragraph may be waived by the Administrator for any state where all analytical measurements required by the state's primary drinking water regulations are conducted at laboratories operated by the state and certified by the agency. Until the agency establishes a national quality assurance program for laboratory certification, the state shall maintain an interim program for approving those laboratories from which the required analytical measurements will be acceptable.

- ☐ assurance of the availability to the state of laboratory facilities certified by the Administrator and capable of performing analytical measurements of all contaminants specified in the state primary drinking water regulations.

- ☐ the establishment and maintenance of an activity to assure that the design and construction of new or substantially modified public water system facilities will be capable of compliance with the state primary drinking water regulations.

States must also demonstrate that they have statutory or regulatory enforcement authority adequate to compel compliance with the state primary drinking water regulations in appropriate cases, such authority to include:

- ❑ authority to apply state primary drinking water regulations to all public water systems in the state covered by the national primary drinking water regulations, except for interstate carrier conveyances and systems on indian land with respect to which the state does not have the necessary jurisdiction or its jurisdiction is in question;

- ❑ authority to sue in courts of competent jurisdiction to enjoin any threatened or continuing violation of the state primary drinking water regulations;

- ❑ right of entry and inspection of public water systems, including the right to take water samples, whether or not the state has evidence that the system is violating an applicable legal requirement;

- ❑ authority to require suppliers of water to keep appropriate records and make appropriate reports to the state;

- ❑ authority to require public water systems to give public notice that is no less stringent than the EPA requirements in 141.32 and 142.16(a);

- ❑ authority to assess civil or criminal penalties for violation of the state's primary drinking water regulations and public notification requirements, including the authority to assess daily penalties or multiple penalties when a violation continues;

- ❑ has established and will maintain record keeping and reporting of its activities under paragraphs (a), (b) and (d) in compliance with 142.14 and 142.15. States with primary enforcement responsibility may adopt procedures different from those set forth in subparts E and F of this part;

- ❑ has adopted and can implement an adequate plan for the provision of safe drinking water under emergency circumstances including, but not limited to, earthquakes, floods, hurricanes, and other natural disasters; and

- ❑ has adopted authority for assessing administrative penalties unless the constitution of the state prohibits the adoption of such authority.

For public water systems serving a population of more than 10,000 individuals, states must have the authority to impose a penalty of at least $1,000 per day per violation. For public water systems serving a population of 10,000 or fewer individuals, states must have penalties that are adequate to ensure compliance with the state regulations as determined by the state.

As long as criteria above are met, states may establish a maximum administrative penalty per violation that may be assessed on a public water system. Indian tribes are not required to exercise criminal enforcement jurisdiction to meet the requirements for primary enforcement responsibility.

9.2.1 Initial Determination of Primary Enforcement Responsibility

A state may apply to the Administrator for a determination that the state has primary enforcement responsibility for public water systems in the state pursuant to section 1413 of the Act. The application shall be as concise as possible and include a side by side comparison of the federal requirements and the corresponding state authorities, including citations to the specific statutes and administrative regulations or ordinances and, wherever appropriate, judicial decisions which demonstrate adequate authority to meet the requirements of 142.10. The following information is to be included with the state application.

The text of the state's primary drinking water regulations, with references to those state regulations that vary from comparable regulations set forth in part 141 of this chapter, and a demonstration that any different state regulation is at least as stringent as the comparable regulation contained in part 141.

A description, accompanied by appropriate documentation, of the state's procedures for the enforcement of the state primary drinking water regulations. The submission shall include:

- ❑ a brief description of the state's program to maintain a current inventory of public water systems;

- ❑ a brief description of the state's program for conducting sanitary surveys, including an explanation of the priorities given to various classes of public water systems;

- ❑ a brief description of the state's laboratory approval or certification program, including the name(s) of the responsible state laboratory officer(s) certified by the Administrator;

- ❑ identification of laboratory facilities, available to the state, certified or approved by the Administrator and capable of performing analytical measurements of all contaminants specified in the state's primary drinking water regulations;

- ❑ a brief description of the state's program activity to assure that the design and construction of new or substantially modified public water system facilities will be capable of compliance with the requirements of the state primary drinking water regulations; and

- ❑ copies of state statutory and regulatory provisions authorizing the adoption and enforcement of state primary drinking water regulations, and a brief description of state procedures for administrative or judicial action with respect to public water systems not in compliance with such regulations.

9.3 Other Requirements

A statement that the state will maintain reports and records as required pursuant to 142.14 and 142.15, is also required. If a state permits variances or exemptions from its primary drinking water regulations, the text of the State's statutory and regulatory provisions concerning variances and exemptions, must be included.

A brief description of the state's plan for the provision of safe drinking water under emergency conditions is also required. To satisfy this requirement for public water supplies from groundwater sources, EPA will accept a contingency plan for providing alternate drinking water supplies that is part of a state's Wellhead Protection Program, where such program has been approved by EPA pursuant to section 1428 of the SDWA.

EPA also requires the following information from the state:

- ❑ a copy of the state statutory and regulatory provisions authorizing the executive branch of the state government to impose an administrative penalty on all public water systems, and a brief description of the state's authority for administrative penalties that will ensure adequate compliance of systems serving a population of 10,000 or fewer individuals, and

- ❑ a statement by the State Attorney General or attorney that certifies that the laws and regulations adopted by the state or tribal ordinances to carry out the program were duly adopted and are enforceable. State statutes and regulations cited by the State Attorney General and tribal ordinances cited by the attorney representing the indian tribe shall be in the form of lawfully adopted state statutes and regulations or tribal ordinances at the time the certification is made and shall be fully effective by the time the program is approved by EPA.

To qualify as "independent legal counsel," the attorney signing the statement required by this section shall have full authority to represent the state primacy agency or indian tribe in court on all matters concerning the state or tribal program independently.

After EPA has received the documents required under this section, EPA may selectively require supplemental statements by the State Attorney General or the attorney representing the indian tribe. Each supplemental statement shall address all issues concerning the adequacy of state authorities to meet the requirements of 142.10 identified by EPA after thorough examination as unresolved by the documents submitted under this section of the CFRs.

The administrator must act on an application within 90 days after receiving such application, and shall promptly inform the state in writing of this action. If he denies the application, his written notification to the state shall include a statement of reasons for the denial.

A final determination by the Administrator that a state has met or has not met the requirements for primary enforcement responsibility shall take effect in accordance with the public notice requirements and related procedures under 142.13. When the Administrator's determination becomes effective pursuant to 142.13, it shall continue in effect unless terminated pursuant to 142.17.

9.4 Revision of State Programs

Either the EPA or the primacy state may initiate actions that require the state to revise its approved state primacy program. To retain primary enforcement responsibility, states must adopt all new and revised national primary drinking water regulations promulgated in part 141 of this chapter and any other requirements specified in this part.

Whenever a state revises its approved primacy program to adopt new or revised federal regulations, the state must submit a request to the Administrator for approval of the program revision, using the procedures described in paragraphs (b), (c), and (d) of this section of the CFRs. The Administrator shall approve or disapprove each state request for approval of a program revision based on the requirements of the Safe Drinking Water Act and of this part. For all state program revisions not covered under 142.12(a)(1), the review procedures outlined in 142.17(a) shall apply.

9.4.1 Timing of State Requests

Complete and final state requests for approval of program revisions to adopt new or revised EPA regulations must be submitted to the Administrator not later than two years after promulgation of the new or revised EPA regulations, unless the state requests an extension and the Administrator has approved the request pursuant to this section. If the state expects to submit a final state request for approval of a program revision to EPA more than two years after promulgation of the new or revised EPA regulations, the state shall request an extension of the deadline before the expiration of the two-year period.

The final date for submission of a complete and final state request for a program revision may be extended by EPA for up to a two-year period upon a written application by the state to the Administrator. In the extension application the state must demonstrate it is requesting the extension because it cannot meet the original deadline for reasons beyond its control despite a good faith effort to do so. The application must include a schedule for the submission of a final request by a certain time and provide sufficient information to demonstrate that the state:

- ❑ currently lacks the legislative or regulatory authority to enforce the new or revised requirements, or

- ❑ currently lacks the program capability adequate to implement the new or revised requirements; or

- ❑ is requesting the extension to group two or more program revisions in a single legislative or regulatory action; and

- ❑ is implementing the EPA requirements to be adopted by the state in its program revision pursuant to this section of the CFRs within the scope of its current authority and capabilities.

To be granted an extension, the state must agree with EPA to meet certain requirements during the extension period, which may include the following types of activities as determined appropriate by the Administrator on a case by case basis:

- ❑ informing public water systems of the new EPA (and upcoming state) requirements and that EPA will be overseeing implementation of the requirements until EPA approves the state program revision;

- ❑ collecting, storing and managing laboratory results, public notices, and other compliance and operation data required by the EPA regulations;

- ❑ assisting EPA in the development of the technical aspects of enforcement actions and conducting informal follow-up on violations (telephone calls, letters, etc.);

❑ providing technical assistance to public water systems;

❑ providing EPA with all information prescribed by 142.15 of this part on state reporting; and

❑ for states whose request for an extension is based on a current lack of program capability adequate to implement the new requirements, taking steps agreed to by EPA and the state during the extension period to remedy the deficiency.

9.4.2 Contents of a State Request for Approval of a Program Revision

The state request for EPA approval of a program revision shall be concise and must include:

❑ the documentation necessary (pursuant to 142.11(a)) to update the approved state primacy program, and identification of those elements of the approved state primacy program that have not changed because of the program revision.

The documentation shall include a side by side comparison of the federal requirements and the corresponding state authorities, including citations to the specific statutes and administrative regulations or ordinances and, wherever appropriate, judicial decisions which demonstrate adequate authority to meet the requirements of 142.10 as they apply to the program revision.

❑ any additional materials listed in 142.16 of this part for a specific EPA regulation, as appropriate; and

❑ a statement by the State Attorney General or the attorney representing the indian tribe that certifies that the laws and regulations adopted by the state or tribal ordinances to carry out the program revision were duly adopted and are enforceable.

State statutes and regulations cited by the State Attorney General and tribal ordinances cited by the attorney for the indian tribe shall be in the form of lawfully adopted state statutes and regulations or tribal ordinances at the time the certification is made and shall be fully effective by the time the request for program revision is approved by EPA. An Attorney General's statement is required as part of the state request for EPA approval of a program revision unless EPA specifically waives this requirement for a specific regulation at the time EPA promulgates the regulation, or by later written notice from the Administrator to the state.

After EPA has received the documents required under this section, EPA may selectively require supplemental statements by the State Attorney General or the attorney representing the indian tribe. Each supplemental statement shall address all issues concerning the adequacy of state authorities to meet the requirements of 142.10 identified by EPA after thorough examination as unresolved by the documents submitted under this section.

Other issues addressed in this section of the CFR's include, but are not limited to:

❑ preliminary state requests

❑ final State requests

❑ EPA's determination on a complete and final request

❑ interim primary enforcement authority

❑ public hearings

9.5 Records Kept by States

Each state which has primary enforcement responsibility shall maintain records of tests, measurements, analyses, decisions, and determinations performed on each public water system to determine compliance with applicable provisions of state primary drinking water regulations.

Records of microbiological analyses shall be retained for not less than 1 year. Actual laboratory reports may be kept or data may be transferred to tabular summaries, provided that the information retained includes the:

❑ analytical method used;

❑ number of samples analyzed each month;

❑ analytical results, set forth in a form which makes possible comparison with the limits specified in 141.63, 141.71, and 141.72 of this chapter.

Records of microbiological analyses of repeat or special samples shall be retained for not less than one year in the form of actual laboratory reports or in an appropriate summary form.

Records of turbidity measurements shall be kept for not less than one year. The information retained must be set forth in a form which makes possible comparison with the limits specified in 141.71 and 141.73 of this chapter. Until June 29, 1993, for any public water system which is providing filtration treatment and until December 30, 1991, for any public water system not providing filtration treatment and not required by the state to provide filtration treatment, records kept must be set forth in a form which makes possible comparison with the limits contained in 141.13.

Records of disinfectant residual measurements and other parameters necessary to document disinfection effectiveness in accordance with 141.72 and 141.74 of this chapter and the reporting requirements of 141.75 of this chapter shall be kept for not less than one year.

9.5.1 Records of Decisions

Records of decisions made on a system by system and case by case basis under provisions of part 141, subpart H, shall be made in writing and kept at the state. Records of decisions made under the following provisions shall be kept for 40 years (or until one year after the decision is reversed or revised) and a copy of the decision must be provided to the system:

❑ Section 141.73(a)(1)–Any decision to allow a public water system using conventional filtration treatment or direct filtration to substitute a turbidity limit greater than 0.5 NTU;

❑ Section 141.73(b)(1)–Any decision to allow a public water system using slow sand filtration to substitute a turbidity limit greater than 1 NTU;

❑ Section 141.74(b)(2)–Any decision to allow an unfiltered public water system to use continuous turbidity monitoring;

❑ Section 141.74(b)(6)(i)–Any decision to allow an unfiltered public water system to sample residual disinfectant concentration at alternate locations if it also has ground water source(s);

❑ Section 141.74(c)(1)–Any decision to allow a public water system using filtration treatment to use continuous turbidity monitoring; or a public water system using slow sand filtration or filtration treatment other than conventional treatment, direct filtration or diatomaceous earth filtration to reduce turbidity sampling to once per day; or for systems serving 500 people or fewer to reduce turbidity sampling to once per day;

❑ Section 141.74(c)(3)(i)–Any decision to allow a filtered public water system to sample disinfectant residual concentration at alternate locations if it also has ground water source(s);

❑ Section 141.75(a)(2)(ix)–Any decision to allow reduced reporting by an unfiltered public water system; and

❑ Section 141.75(b)(2)(iv)–Any decision to allow reduced reporting by a filtered public water system.

Records of decisions made under the following provisions shall be kept for one year after the decision is made:

❑ Section 141.71(b)(1)(i)–Any decision that a violation of monthly CT compliance requirements was caused by circumstances that were unusual and unpredictable.

❑ Section 141.71(b)(1)(iv)–Any decision that a violation of the disinfection effectiveness criteria was not caused by a deficiency in treatment of the source water;

❑ Section 141.71(b)(5)–Any decision that a violation of the total coliform MCL was not caused by a deficiency in treatment of the source water;

❑ Section 141.74(b)(1)–Any decision that total coliform monitoring otherwise required because the turbidity of the source water exceeds 1 NTU is not feasible, except that if such decision allows a system to avoid monitoring without receiving state approval in each instance, records of the decision shall be kept until one year after the decision is rescinded or revised.

Records of decisions made under the following provisions shall be kept for the specified period or 40 years, whichever is less.

❏ Section 141.71(a)(2)(i)–Any decision that an event in which the source water turbidity which exceeded 5 NTU for an unfiltered public water system was unusual and unpredictable shall be kept for 10 years.

❏ Section 141.71(b)(1)(iii)–Any decision by the state that failure to meet the disinfectant residual concentration requirements of 141.72(a)(3)(i) was caused by circumstances that were unusual and unpredictable, shall be kept unless filtration is installed. A copy of the decision must be provided to the system.

❏ Section 141.71(b)(2)–Any decision that a public water system's watershed control program meets the requirements of this section shall be kept until the next decision is available and filed.

❏ Section 141.70(c)–Any decision that an individual is a qualified operator for a public water system using a surface water source or a ground water source under the direct influence of surface water shall be maintained until the qualification is withdrawn. The state may keep this information in the form of a list which is updated periodically. If such qualified operators are classified by category, the decision shall include that classification.

❏ Section 141.71(b)(3)–Any decision that a party other than the state is approved by the state to conduct on-site inspections shall be maintained until withdrawn. The state may keep this information in the form of a list which is updated periodically.

❏ Section 141.71(b)(4)–Any decision that an unfiltered public water system has been identified as the source of a waterborne disease outbreak, and, if applicable, that it has been modified sufficiently to prevent another such occurrence shall be kept until filtration treatment is installed. A copy of the decision must be provided to the system.

❏ Section 141.72–Any decision that certain interim disinfection requirements are necessary for an unfiltered public water system for which the state has determined that filtration is necessary, and a list of those requirements, shall be kept until filtration treatment is installed. A copy of the requirements must be provided to the system.

❏ Section 141.72(a)(2)(ii)–Any decision that automatic shut-off of delivery of water to the distribution system of an unfiltered public water system would cause an unreasonable risk to health or interfere with fire protection shall be kept until rescinded.

❏ Section 141.72(a)(4)(ii)–Any decision by the state, based on site specific considerations, that an unfiltered system has no means for having a sample transported and analyzed for HPC by a certified laboratory under the requisite time and temperature conditions specified by 141.74(a)(3) and that the system is providing adequate disinfection in the distribution system, so that the disinfection requirements contained in 141.72(a)(4)(i) do not apply, and the basis for the decision, shall be kept until the decision is reversed or revised. A copy of the decision must be provided to the system.

❑ Section 141.72(b)(3)(ii)–Any decision by the state, based on site specific conditions, that a filtered system has no means for having a sample transported and analyzed for HPC by a certified laboratory under the requisite time and temperature conditions specified by 141.74(a)(3) and that the system is providing adequate disinfection in the distribution system, so that the disinfection requirements contained in 141.72(b)(3)(i) do not apply, and the basis for the decision, shall be kept until the decision is reversed or revised. A copy of the decision must be provided to the system.

❑ Section 141.73(d)–Any decision that a public water system, having demonstrated to the state that an alternative filtration technology, in combination with disinfection treatment, consistently achieves 99.9 percent removal and/or inactivation of Giardia lamblia cysts and 99.99 percent removal and/or inactivation of viruses, may use such alternative filtration technology, shall be kept until the decision is reversed or revised. A copy of the decision must be provided to the system.

❑ Section 141.74(b), table 3.1–Any decision that a system using either preformed chloramines or chloramines formed by the addition of ammonia prior to the addition of chlorine has demonstrated that 99.99 percent removal and/or inactivation of viruses has been achieved at particular CT values, and a list of those values, shall be kept until the decision is reversed or revised. A copy of the list of required values must be provided to the system.

❑ Section 141.74(b)(3)(v)–Any decision that a system using a disinfectant other than chlorine may use CT99.9 values other than those in tables 2.1 or 3.1 and/or other operational parameters to determine if the minimum total inactivation rates required by 141.72(a)(1) are being met, and what those values or parameters are, shall be kept until the decision is reversed or revised. A copy of the list of required values or parameters must be provided to the system.

❑ Section 142.16(b)(2)(i)(B)–Any decision that a system using a ground water source is under the direct influence of surface water.

Records of any determination that a public water system supplied by a surface water source or a ground water source under the direct influence of surface water is not required to provide filtration treatment shall be kept for 40 years or until withdrawn, whichever is earlier. A copy of the determination must be provided to the system.

Records of each of the following decisions made pursuant to the total coliform provisions of part 141 shall be made in writing and retained by the State. Records of the following decisions must be retained for five years.

❑ Section 141.21(b)(1)–Any decision to waive the 24-hour time limit for collecting repeat samples after a total coliform positive routine sample if the public water system has a logistical problem in collecting the repeat sample that is beyond the system's control, and what alternative time limit the system must meet.

❑ Section 141.21(b)(5)–Any decision to allow a system to waive the requirement for five routine samples the month following a total coliform positive sample. If the waiver decision is made as provided in 141.21(b)(5), the record of the decision must contain all the items listed in that paragraph.

❏ Section 141.21(c)–Any decision to invalidate a total coliform positive sample. If the decision to invalidate a total coliform positive sample as provided in 141.21(c)(1)(iii) is made, the record of the decision must contain all the items listed in that paragraph.

Records of each of the following decisions must be retained in such a manner so that each system's current status may be determined.

❏ Section 141.21(a)(2)–Any decision to reduce the total coliform monitoring frequency for a community water system serving 1,000 persons or fewer that has no history of total coliform contamination in its current configuration and had a sanitary survey conducted within the past five years showing that the system is supplied solely by a protected groundwater source and is free of sanitary defects, to less than once per month, as provided in 141.21(a)(2); and what the reduced monitoring frequency is. A copy of the reduced monitoring frequency must be provided to the system.

❏ Section 141.21(a)(3)(i)–Any decision to reduce the total coliform monitoring frequency for a non-community water system using only ground water and serving 1,000 persons or fewer to less than once per quarter, as provided in 141.21(a)(3)(i), and what the reduced monitoring frequency is. A copy of the reduced monitoring frequency must be provided to the system.

❏ Section 141.21(a)(3)(ii)–Any decision to reduce the total coliform monitoring frequency for a non-community water system using only ground water and serving more than 1,000 persons during any month the system serves 1,000 persons or fewer, as provided in 141.21(a)(3)(ii). A copy of the reduced monitoring frequency must be provided to the system.

❏ Section 141.21(a)(5)–Any decision to waive the 24-hour limit for taking a total coliform sample for a public water system which uses surface water, or ground water under the direct influence of surface water, and which does not practice filtration in accordance with part 141, subpart H, and which measures a source water turbidity level exceeding 1 NTU near the first service connection as provided in 141.21(a)(5).

❏ Section 141.21(d)(1)–Any decision that a non-community water system is using only protected and disinfected ground water and therefore may reduce the frequency of its sanitary survey to less than once every five years, as provided in 141.21(d), and what that frequency is. A copy of the reduced frequency must be provided to the system.

❏ Section 141.21(d)(2)–A list of agents other than the state, if any, approved by the state to conduct sanitary surveys.

❏ Section 141.21(e)(2)–Any decision to allow a public water system to forgo fecal coliform or E. coli testing on a total coliform positive sample if that system assumes that the total coliform positive sample is fecal coliform positive or E. coli positive, as provided in 141.21(e)(2).

Records of analysis for other than microbiological contaminants (including total coliform, fecal coliform, and heterotrophic plate count), residual disinfectant concentration, other parameters necessary to determine disinfection effectiveness (including temperature and pH measurements), and turbidity shall be retained for not less than 12 years and shall include at least the following information:

- ❏ date and place of sampling; and
- ❏ date and results of analyses.

Records required to be kept pursuant to this section must be in a form admissible as evidence in state enforcement proceedings. Each state which has primary enforcement responsibility shall maintain current inventory information for every public water system in the state and shall retain inventory records of public water systems for not less than 12 years. Each state which has primary enforcement responsibility shall retain, for not less than 12 years, files which shall include for each such public water system in the state:

- ❏ reports of sanitary surveys;
- ❏ records of any state approvals;
- ❏ records of any enforcement actions.
- ❏ a record of the most recent vulnerability determination, including the monitoring results and other data supporting the determination, the state's findings based on the supporting data and any additional bases for such determination; except that it shall be kept in perpetuity or until a more current vulnerability determination has been issued.
- ❏ a record of all current monitoring requirements and the most recent monitoring frequency decision pertaining to each contaminant, including the monitoring results and other data supporting the decision, the state's findings based on the supporting data and any additional bases for such decision; except that the record shall be kept in perpetuity or until a more recent monitoring frequency decision has been issued.
- ❏ a record of the most recent asbestos repeat monitoring determination, including the monitoring results and other data supporting the determination, the state's findings based on the supporting data and any additional bases for the determination and the repeat monitoring frequency; except that these records shall be maintained in perpetuity or until a more current repeat monitoring determination has been issued.
- ❏ records of annual certifications received from systems pursuant to part 141, subpart k demonstrating the system's compliance with the treatment techniques for acrylamide and/or epichlorohydrin in 14.111.
- ❏ records of the currently applicable or most recent state determinations, including all supporting information and an explanation of the technical basis for each decision, made for the control of lead and copper;
- ❏ Section 141.82(b)–decisions to require a water system to conduct corrosion control treatment studies;
- ❏ Section 141.82(d)–designations of optimal corrosion control treatment;

- ☐ Section 141.82(f)–designations of optimal water quality parameters;

- ☐ Section 141.82(h)–decisions to modify a public water system's optimal corrosion control treatment or water quality parameters;

- ☐ Section 141.83(b)(2)–determinations of source water treatment;

- ☐ Section 141.83(b)(4)–designations of maximum permissible lead and copper concentrations in source water;

- ☐ Section 141.84(e)–determinations that a system does not control entire lead service lines;

- ☐ Section 141.84(f)–determinations establishing a shorter lead service line replacement schedule than required by 141.84;

- ☐ Records of reports and any other information submitted by PWSs under 141.90;

- ☐ Records of state activities, and the results thereof, to verify compliance with state determinations issued under 141.82(f), 141.82(h), 141.83(b)(2), and 141.83(b)(4) and compliance with lead service line replacement schedules under 141.84; and

- ☐ Records of each system's currently applicable or most recently designated monitoring requirements. If, for the records identified in 142.14(d)(8)(i) through 142.14(d)(8)(viii) above, no change is made to state decision during a 12-year retention period, the state shall maintain the record until a new decision, determination or designation has been issued.

Each state which has primary enforcement responsibility shall retain records pertaining to each variance and exemption granted by it for not less than five years following the expiration of such variance or exemption.

Records required to be kept under this section shall be available to the Regional Administrator upon request. The records required to be kept under this section shall be maintained and made available for public inspection by the state, or, the state at its option may require suppliers of water to make available for public inspection those records maintained in accordance with 141.33.

9.6 Reports by States

Each state which has primary enforcement responsibility shall submit quarterly reports to the Administrator on a schedule and in a format prescribed by the Administrator, consisting of the following information:

- ☐ new violations by public water systems in the state during the previous quarter of state regulations adopted to incorporate the requirements of national primary drinking water regulations;

- ☐ new enforcement actions taken by the state during the previous quarter against public water systems with respect to state regulations adopted to incorporate the requirements of national primary drinking water regulations;

- ☐ notification of any new variance or exemption granted during the previous quarter. The notice shall include a statement of reasons for the granting of the variance or exemption, including documentation of the need for the variance or exemption and the finding that the granting of the variance or exemption will not result in an unreasonable risk to health. The state may use a single notification statement to report two or more similar variances or exemptions.

Each state which has primary enforcement responsibility shall submit annual reports to the Administrator on a schedule and in a format prescribed by the Administrator, consisting of the following information:

- ❏ all additions or corrections to the state's inventory of public water systems;

- ❏ a summary of the status of each variance and exemption currently in effect.

9.6.1 Surface Water Treatment Rule Reports

Surface Water Treatment Rule reports include the following:

- ❏ a list identifying the name, PWS identification number and date of the determination for each public water system supplied by a surface water source or a ground water source under the direct influence of surface water, which the state has determined is not required to provide filtration treatment; and

- ❏ a list identifying the name and PWS identification number of each public water system supplied by a surface water source or ground water source under the direct influence of surface water, which the state has determined, based on an evaluation of site specific considerations, has no means of having a sample transported and analyzed for HPC by a certified laboratory under the requisite time and temperature conditions specified in 141.74(a)(3) and is providing adequate disinfection in the distribution system, regardless of whether the system is in compliance with the criteria of 141.72 (a)(4)(i) or (b)(3)(i) of this chapter, as allowed by 141.72 (a)(4)(ii) and (b)(3)(ii). The list must include the effective date of each determination.

Notification within 60 days of the end of the calendar quarter of any determination that a public water system using a surface water source or a ground water source under the direct influence of surface water is not required to provide filtration treatment. The notification must include a statement describing the system's compliance with each requirement of the state's regulations that implement 141.71 and a summary of comments, if any, received from the public on the determination. A single notification may be used to report two or more such determinations.

9.6.2 Total Coliforms Report

This report requires:

- ❏ A list of public water systems which the state is allowing to monitor less frequently than once per month for community water systems or less frequently than once per quarter for non-community water systems as provided in

141.21(a), including the effective date of the reduced monitoring requirement for each system.

9.6.3 Quarterly Monitoring Reports for Unregulated Contaminants

States shall report to EPA by May 15, August 15, November 15 and February 15 of each year the following information related to each system's compliance with the treatment techniques for lead and copper under 40 CFR Part 141, subpart I during the preceding calendar quarter. Specifically, states shall report the name and PWS identification number of each:

❑ public water system which exceeded the lead and copper action levels and the date upon which the exceedance occurred;

❑ public water system required to complete the corrosion control evaluation specified in 141.82(c) and the date the state received the results of the evaluations from each system;

❑ public water system for which the state has designated optimal corrosion control treatment under 141.82(d), the date of the determination, and each system that completed installation of treatment as certified under 141.90(c)(3);

❑ public water system for which the state has designated optimal water quality parameters under 141.82(f) and the date of the determination;

❑ public water system which the state has required to install source water treatment under 141.83(b)(2), the date of the determination, and each system that completed installation of treatment as certified under 141.90(d)(2);

❑ public water system for which the state has specified maximum permissible source water levels under 141.83(b)(4); and

❑ public water system required to begin replacing lead service lines as specified in 141.84, each public water system for which the state has established a replacement schedule under 141.84(f), and each system reporting compliance with its replacement schedule under 141.90(e)(2).

The reports submitted pursuant to this section shall be made available by the state to the public for inspection at one or more locations within the state.

9.7 States Adoption of Filtration and Disinfection Requirements

Besides the general primacy requirements enumerated elsewhere in this part of the CFRs, including the requirement that state provisions are no less stringent than the federal requirements, an application for approval of a state program revision that adopts 40 CFR Part 141, subpart H Filtration and Disinfection, must contain the information specified in this section, except that states which require without exception all public water systems using a surface water source or a ground water source under the direct influence of surface water to provide filtration need not demonstrate that the state program has provisions that apply to systems which do not provide filtration treatment.

However, such states must provide the text of the state statutes or regulations which specifies that all public water systems using a surface water source or a ground water source under the direct influence of surface water must provide filtration.

9.8 Enforceable Requirements

In addition to adopting criteria no less stringent than those specified in part 141, subpart H of this chapter, the state's application must include enforceable design and operating criteria for each filtration treatment technology allowed or a procedure for establishing design and operating conditions on a system by system basis (e.g., a permit system).

9.9 Other Issues

Additional application information contained in this section of the CFRs includes the following:

- ☐ state practices or procedures
- ☐ total coliform requirements
- ☐ state control of lead and copper
- ☐ review of state programs and procedures for withdrawal of approved primacy programs

9.10 EPA Review of State Monitoring Determinations

A Regional Administrator may annul a state monitoring determination for the types of determinations identified in 141.23(b), 141.23(c), 141.24(f), 141.24(h), and 141.40(n) in accordance with the procedures in this section of the CFRs. When information available to a Regional Administrator, such as the results of an annual review, indicate a state determination fails to apply the standards of the approved state program, he may propose to annul the state monitoring determination by sending the state and the affected PWS a draft Rescission Order. The draft order shall:

- ☐ identify the PWS, the state determination, and the provisions at issue;
- ☐ explain why the state determination is not in compliance with the state program and must be changed; and
- ☐ describe the actions and terms of operation the PWS will be required to implement.

The state and PWS shall have 60 days to comment on the draft Rescission Order and the Regional Administrator may not issue a Rescission Order to impose conditions less stringent than those imposed by the state. The Regional Administrator shall also provide an opportunity for comment upon the draft Rescission Order, by:

- ☐ publishing a notice in a newspaper in general circulation in communities served by the affected system; and
- ☐ providing 30 days for public comment on the draft order.

The state shall demonstrate that the determination is reasonable, based on its approved state program. The Regional Administrator shall decide within 120 days after issuance of the draft Rescission Order to:

- ❑ issue the Rescission Order as drafted;
- ❑ issue a modified Rescission Order; or
- ❑ cancel the Rescission Order.

The Regional Administrator shall set forth the reasons for his decision, including a responsiveness summary addressing significant comments from the state, the PWS and the public. The Regional Administrator shall send a notice of his final decision to the state, the PWS and all parties who commented upon the draft Rescission Order. The Rescission Order shall remain in effect until canceled by the Regional Administrator. The Regional Administrator may cancel a Rescission Order at any time, so long as he notifies those who commented on the draft order.

The Regional Administrator may not delegate the signature authority for a final Rescission Order or the cancellation of an order.

Violation of the actions, or terms of operation, required by a Rescission Order is considered a violation of the Safe Drinking Water Act.

9.10.1 EPA Review of State Implementation of NPDWRs for Lead and Copper

Pursuant to the procedures in this section, the Regional Administrator may review state determinations establishing corrosion control or source water treatment requirements for lead or copper and may issue an order establishing federal treatment requirements for a public water system pursuant to 141.82 (d) and (f) and 141.83(b) (2) and (4) where the Regional Administrator finds that:

- ❑ a state has failed to issue a treatment determination by the applicable deadline;
- ❑ a state has abused its discretion in making corrosion control or source water treatment determinations in a substantial number of cases or in cases affecting a substantial population; or
- ❑ the technical aspects of state's determination would be indefensible in an expected federal enforcement action taken against a system.

If the Regional Administrator determines that review of state determination(s) under this section may be appropriate, he shall request the state to forward to EPA the state determination and all information that was considered by the state in making its determination, including public comments, if any, within 60 days of the Regional Adminstrator's request.

9.10.2 Proposed Review of State Determinations

Where the Regional Administrator finds that review of a state determination under this section of the CFRs is appropriate, he shall issue a proposed review order which shall:

- ❏ identify the public water system(s) affected, the state determination being reviewed and the provisions of state and/or federal law at issue;

- ❏ identify the determination that the state failed to carry out by the applicable deadline, or identify the particular provisions of the state determination which, in the Regional Administrator's judgment, fail to carry out properly applicable treatment requirements, and explain the basis for the Regional Administrator's conclusion;

- ❏ identify the treatment requirements which the Regional Administrator proposes to apply to the affected system(s), and explain the basis for the proposed requirements; and

- ❏ request public comment on the proposed order and the supporting record.

The Regional Administrator shall provide notice of the proposed review order by:

- ❏ mailing the proposed order to the affected public water system(s), the state agency whose order is being reviewed, and any other parties of interest known to the Regional Administrator; and

- ❏ publishing a copy of the proposed order in a newspaper of general circulation in the affected communities.

The Regional Administrator shall make available for public inspection during the comment period the record supporting the proposed order, which shall include all of the information submitted by the state to EPA under this section of the CFRs, all other studies, monitoring data and other information considered by the Agency in developing the proposed order.

9.10.3 Final Review Order

Based upon review of all information obtained regarding the proposed review order, including public comments, the Regional Administrator shall issue a final review order within 120 days after issuance of the proposed order which affirms, modifies, or withdraws the proposed order. The Regional Administrator may extend the time period for issuing the final order for good cause. If the final order modifies or withdraws the proposed order, the final order shall explain the reasons supporting the change.

The record of the final order shall consist of the record supporting the proposed order, all public comments, all other information considered by the Regional Administrator in issuing the final order and a document responding to all significant public comments submitted on the proposed order. If new points are raised or new material supplied during the public comment period, the Regional Administrator may support the responses on those matters by adding new materials to the record. The record shall be complete when the final order is issued.

Notice of the final order shall be provided by mailing the final order to the affected system(s), the state, and all parties who commented on the proposed order. Upon issuance of the final order, its terms constitute requirements of the national primary drinking water regulation for lead and/or copper until the Regional Administrator issues a new order (which may include recision of the previous order) pursuant to the procedures in this section. Such requirements shall supersede any inconsistent treatment requirements established by the state pursuant to the national primary drinking water regulations for lead and copper.

The Regional Administrator may not issue a final order to impose conditions less stringent than those imposed by the State. Nor can the Regional Administrator delegate authority to sign the final order under this section. Other information in this section of the CFRs relate to:

- ❑ state issued variances and exemptions
- ❑ failure by state to assure enforcement
- ❑ requirements for a variance
- ❑ requirements for an exemption
- ❑ variances from the maximum contaminant level for total trihalomethanes
- ❑ requirements for tribal eligibility
- ❑ notices to the states
- ❑ procedures for PWS administrative compliance orders
- ❑ public hearings; opportunity for state conferences
- ❑ issuance, amendment or withdrawal of administrative compliance order
- ❑ administrative assessment of civil penalties for violations of administrative compliance orders

National Secondary Drinking Water Regulations

This part establishes National Secondary Drinking Water Regulations pursuant to section 1412 of the Safe Drinking Water Act, as amended (42 U.S.C. 300g–1). These regulations control contaminants in drinking water that primarily affect the aesthetic qualities relating to the public acceptance of drinking water.

10.1 Overview

At much higher concentrations of these contaminants, health implications may also exist as well as aesthetic degradation. The regulations are not federally enforceable but are intended as guidelines for the states.

These levels represent reasonable goals for drinking water quality. The states may establish higher or lower levels which may be appropriate dependent upon local conditions such as unavailability of alternate source waters or other compelling factors, if public health and welfare are not adversely affected.

10.2 Secondary Maximum Contaminant Levels

The secondary maximum contaminant levels for public water systems are as follows:

Contaminant	Level
Aluminum	0.05 to 0.2 mg/l
Chloride	250 mg/l
Color	15 color units
Copper	1.0 mg/l
Corrosivity	Non–corrosive
Fluoride	2.0 mg/l
Foaming agents	0.5 mg/l
Iron	0.3 mg/l
Manganese	0.05 mg/l
Odor	3 threshold odor number
pH	6.5–8.5

Contaminant	Level
Silver	0.1 mg/l
Sulfate	250 mg/l
Total dissolved solids (TDS)	500 mg/l
Zinc	5 mg/l

10.2.1 Monitoring

It is recommended that the parameters in these regulations should be monitored at intervals no less frequent than the monitoring performed for inorganic chemical contaminants listed in the National Interim Primary Drinking Water Regulations as applicable to community water systems. More frequent monitoring would be appropriate for specific parameters such as pH, color, odor or others under certain circumstances as directed by the state.

Measurement of pH, copper and fluoride to determine compliance under 143.3 may be conducted with one of the methods in 141.23(k)(1). Analyses of aluminum, chloride, foaming agents, iron, manganese, odor, silver, sulfate, total dissolved solids (TDS) and zinc to determine compliance under 143.3 may be conducted with the methods listed in this section of the CFRs. Criteria for analyzing aluminum, copper, iron, manganese, silver and zinc samples with digestion or directly without digestion, and other analytical test procedures are contained in Technical Notes on Drinking Water Methods, EPA–600/R–94–173, October 1994, which is available at NTIS PB95–104766.516. Note: Various reference sources and contact information are included in this section of the CFRs.

10.2.3 Compliance with Secondary Maximum Contaminant Level and Public Notification for Fluoride

Community water systems, as defined in 40 CFR 141.2(e)(i) of this title, that exceed the secondary maximum contaminant level for fluoride as determined by the last single sample taken in accordance with the requirements of 141.23 of this title or any equivalent state law, but do not exceed the maximum contaminant level for flouride as specified by 141.62 of this title or any equivalent state law, shall provide the notice described in paragraph (b) of all billing units annually, all new billing units at the time service begins, and the state public health officer. The notice required contains the following language:

Public Notice

Dear User,

The U.S. Environmental Protection Agency requires that we send you this notice on the level of fluoride in your drinking water. The drinking water in your community has a fluoride concentration of 1 milligram per liter (mg/l).

Federal regulations require that fluoride, which occurs naturally in your water supply, not exceed a concentration of 4.0 mg/l in drinking water. This is an enforceable standard called a Maximum Contaminant Level (MCL), and it has been established to protect the public health. Exposure to drinking water levels above 4.0 mg/l for many years may result in some cases of crippling skeletal fluorosis, which is a serious bone disorder.

Federal law also requires that we notify you when monitoring indicates that the fluoride in your drinking water exceeds 2.0 mg/l. This is intended to alert families about dental problems that might affect children under nine years of age. The fluoride concentration of your water exceeds this federal guideline.

Fluoride in children's drinking water at levels of approximately 1 mg/l reduces the number of dental cavities. However, some children exposed to levels of fluoride greater than about 2.0 mg/l may develop dental fluorosis. Dental fluorosis, in its moderate and severe forms, is a brown staining and/or pitting of the permanent teeth.

Because dental fluorosis occurs only when developing teeth (before they erupt from the gums) are exposed to elevated fluoride levels, households without children are not expected to be affected by this level of fluoride. Families with children under the age of nine are encouraged to seek other sources of drinking water for their children to avoid the possibility of staining and pitting.

Your water supplier can lower the concentration of fluoride in your water so that you will still receive the benefits of cavity prevention while the possibility of stained and pitted teeth is minimized. Removal of fluoride may increase your water costs. Treatment systems are also commercially available for home use. Information on such systems is available at the address given below. Low fluoride bottled drinking water that would meet all standards is also commercially available. For further information, contact _____2 your water system.

1PWS shall insert the compliance result which triggered notification under this part.

2PWS shall insert the name, address, and telephone number of a contact person at the PWS.

National Pollutant Discharge Elimination System

> *This section prescribes criteria and standards for various requirements imposed as conditions for NPDES permit approval. Some criteria expanded upon are those presented for the imposition of technology-based treatment requirements in permits as given under 301(b) and 402(a)(1), those for modifying secondary treatment requirements under 301(h), those for Best Management Practices authorized under 304(e), and those applying to ocean dumping, in Subparts A, G, K, & M, respectively.*

11.1 Overview

This subpart establishes criteria and standards for the imposition of technology based treatment requirements in permits under section 301(b) of the Act, including the application of EPA promulgated effluent limitations and case by case determinations of effluent limitations under section 402(a)(1) of the Act.

11.1.1 Technology-based Treatment Requirements in Permits

Technology-based treatment requirements under section 301(b) of the Act represent the minimum level of control that must be imposed in a permit issued under section 402 of the Act. (See 122.41, 122.42 and 122.44 for a discussion of additional or more stringent effluent limitations and conditions.) Permits shall contain the following technology based treatment requirements in accordance with the statutory deadlines listed in this section of the CFRs.

Technology-based treatment requirements may be imposed through one of the following three methods:

☐ Application of EPA promulgated effluent limitations developed under section 304 of the Act to dischargers by category or subcategory. These effluent limitations are not applicable to the extent that they have been remanded or withdrawn. However, in the case of a court remand, determinations underlying effluent limitations shall be binding in permit issuance proceedings where those determinations are not required to be reexamined by a court remanding the regulations. In addition, dischargers may seek fundamentally different factors variances from these effluent limitations under 122.21 and subpart D of this part.

❏ On a case by case basis under section 402(a)(1) of the Act, to the extent that EPA promulgated effluent limitations are inapplicable.

The permit writer shall apply the appropriate factors listed in 125.3(d) and shall consider:

❏ the appropriate technology for the category or class of point sources of which the applicant is a member, based upon all available information;

❏ any unique factors relating to the applicant; and

❏ through a combination of the methods in this section.

Where promulgated effluent limitations guidelines only apply to certain aspects of the discharger's operation, or to certain pollutants, other aspects or activities are subject to regulation on a case by case basis in order to carry out the provisions of the Act. In setting case by case limitations pursuant to 125.3(c), the permit writer must consider the following factors for BPT requirements:

❏ the total cost of application of technology in relation to the effluent reduction benefits to be achieved from such application;

❏ the age of equipment and facilities involved;

❏ the process employed;

❏ the engineering aspects of the application of various types of control techniques;

❏ process changes; and

❏ non-water quality environmental impact (including energy requirements).

Technology based effluent limitations shall be established under this subpart for solids, sludges, filter backwash, and other pollutants removed during treatment or control of wastewaters in the same manner as for other pollutants. The Director may set a permit limit for a conventional pollutant at a more stringent level under circumstances described in this section.

The Director may not set a more stringent limit under the preceding paragraphs if the method of treatment required to comply with the limit differs from that which would be required if the toxic pollutant(s) or hazardous substance(s) controlled by the limit were limited directly.

11.2 Criteria for Issuance of Permits to Aquaculture Projects

These regulations establish guidelines under sections 318 and 402 of the Act for approval of any discharge of pollutants associated with an aquaculture project. The regulations authorize, on a selective basis, controlled discharges which would otherwise be unlawful under the Act in order to determine the feasibility of using pollutants to grow aquatic organisms which can be harvested and used beneficially. EPA policy is to encourage such projects, while at the same time protecting other beneficial uses of the waters.

Permits issued for discharges into aquaculture projects under this subpart are NPDES permits and are subject to the applicable requirements of parts 122, 123 and 124. Any permit shall include such conditions (including monitoring and reporting requirements) as are necessary to comply with those parts. Technology based effluent limitations need not be applied to discharges into the approved project except with respect to toxic pollutants.

11.3 Criteria and Standards for Determining Alternative Factors

This subpart establishes the criteria and standards to be used in determining whether effluent limitations alternative to those required by promulgated EPA effluent limitations guidelines under sections 301 and 304 of the Act (hereinafter referred to as "national limits") should be imposed on a discharger because factors relating to the discharger's facilities, equipment, processes or other factors related to the discharger are fundamentally different from the factors considered by EPA in development of the national limits. This subpart applies to all national limitations promulgated under sections 301 and 304 of the Act, except for the BPT limits contained in 40 CFR 423.12 (steam electric generating point source category).

In establishing national limits, EPA takes into account all the information it can collect, develop and solicit regarding the factors listed in sections 304(b) and 304(g) of the Act. In some cases, however, data which could affect these national limits as they apply to a particular discharge may not be available or may not be considered during their development. As a result, adjusting the national limits may be necessary on a case by case basis, and make them either more or less stringent as they apply to certain dischargers within an industrial category or subcategory. This will only be done if data specific to that discharger indicates it presents factors fundamentally different from those considered by EPA in developing the limit at issue. Any interested person believing that factors relating to a discharger's facilities, equipment, processes or other facilities related to the discharger is fundamentally different from the factors considered during development of the national limits may request a fundamentally different factors variance under 122.21(l)(1). In addition, such a variance may be proposed by the Director in the draft permit.

11.4 Criteria for Modifying the Secondary Treatment Requirements

This subpart establishes the criteria to be applied by EPA in acting on section 301(h) requests for modifications to the secondary treatment requirements. It also establishes special permit conditions which must be included in any permit incorporating a section 301(h) modification of the secondary treatment requirements ("section 301(h) modified permit").

11.5 Criteria for Determining Alternative Effluent Limitations Under Section 316(a) of the Act

Section 316(a) of the Act provides that:

"With respect to any point source otherwise subject to the provisions of section 301 or section 306 of this Act, whenever the owner or operator of any such source, after opportunity for public hearing, can demonstrate to the satisfaction of the Administrator (or, if appropriate, the State) that any effluent limitation proposed for the control of the thermal component of any discharge from such source will require effluent limitations more stringent than necessary to assure the projection [sic] and propagation of a balanced, indigenous population of shellfish, fish and wildlife in and on the body of water into which the discharge is to be made, the Administrator (or, if appropriate, the State) may impose an effluent limitation under such sections on such plant, with respect to the thermal component of such discharge (taking into account the interaction of such thermal component with other pollutants) that will assure the protection and propagation of a balanced indigenous population of shellfish, fish and wildlife in and on that body of water."

This subpart describes the factors, criteria and standards for the establishment of alternative thermal effluent limitations under section 316(a) of the Act in permits issued under section 402(a) of the Act.

11.6 Criteria and Standards for Best Management Practices Authorized Under Section 304(e) of the Act

This subpart describes how best management practices (BMPs) for ancillary industrial activities under section 304(e) of the Act shall be reflected in permits, including best management practices promulgated in effluent limitations under section 304 and established on a case by case basis in permits under section 402(a)(1) of the Act. Best management practices authorized by section 304(e) are included in permits as requirements for the purposes of section 301, 302, 306, 307, or 403 of the Act, as the case may be.

11.6.1 Applicability of Best Management Practices

Dischargers who use, manufacture, store, handle or discharge any pollutant listed as toxic under section 307(a)(1) of the Act or any pollutant listed as hazardous under section 311 of the Act are subject to the requirements of this Subpart for all activities which may result in significant amounts of those pollutants reaching waters of the United States. These activities are ancillary manufacturing operations including: Materials storage areas; in-plant transfer, process and material handling areas; loading and unloading operations; plant site runoff; and sludge and waste disposal areas.

11.7 Permit Terms and Conditions

Best management practices shall be expressly incorporated into a permit where required by an applicable EPA promulgated effluent limitations guideline under section 304(e); and may also be expressly incorporated into a permit on a case by case basis where determined necessary to carry out the provisions of the Act under section 402(a)(1). In issuing a permit containing BMP requirements, the Director shall consider the following factors:

❏ toxicity of the pollutant(s);

❑ quantity of the pollutant(s) used, produced, or discharged;

❑ history of NPDES permit violations;

❑ history of significant leaks or spills of toxic or hazardous pollutants;

❑ potential for adverse impact on public health (e.g., proximity to a public water supply) or the environment (e.g., proximity to a sport or commerical fishery); and

❑ any other factors determined to be relevant to the control of toxic or hazardous pollutants.

Best management practices may be established in permits under this section alone or in combination with those required under this section of the CFRs. Beyond the requirements of this section, dischargers covered under 125.102 shall develop and implement a best management practices program in accordance with 125.104 which prevents, or minimizes the potential for, the release of toxic or hazardous pollutants from ancillary activities to waters of the United States.

11.8 Best Management Practices Programs

Bmp programs shall be developed in accordance with good engineering practices and with the provisions of this subpart. The BMP program shall:

❑ be documented in narrative form, and shall include any necessary plot plans, drawings or maps;

❑ establish specific objectives for the control of toxic and hazardous pollutants.

Each facility component or system shall be examined for its potential for causing a release of significant amounts of toxic or hazardous pollutants to waters of the United States due to equipment failure, improper operation, natural phenomena such as rain or snowfall, etc.

Where experience indicates a reasonable potential for equipment failure (e.g., a tank overflow or leakage), natural condition (e.g., precipitation), or other circumstances to result in significant amounts of toxic or hazardous pollutants reaching surface waters, the program should include:

❑ a prediction of the direction,

❑ rate of flow, and

❑ total quantity of toxic or hazardous pollutants which could be discharged as a result of each condition or circumstance.

The purpose of the program is to establish specific best management practices to meet the objectives identified under this section of the CFRs, addressing each component or system capable of causing a release of significant amounts of toxic or hazardous pollutants to the waters of the United States.

The BMP program may reflect requirements for Spill Prevention Control and Countermeasure (SPCC) plans under section 311 of the Act and 40 CFR Part 151, and may incorporate any part of such plans into the BMP program by reference; shall assure the proper management of solid and hazardous waste in accordance with regulations promulgated under the Solid Waste Disposal Act, as amended by the Resource Conservation and Recovery Act of 1976 (RCRA) (40 U.S.C. 6901 et seq).

11.9 RCRA Management Practices

Management practices required under RCRA regulations shall be expressly incorporated into the BMP program; and shall address the following points for the ancillary activities in 125.102:

- statement of policy;
- spill control committee;
- material inventory;
- material compatibility;
- employee training:
- reporting and notification procedures;
- visual inspections;
- preventive maintenance;
- housekeeping; and
- security.

Additional technical information on BMPs and the elements of a BMP program is contained in publication entitled "Guidance Manual for Developing Best Management Practices (BMP)." Copies may be obtained by written request to the:

Office of Water Resource Center (mail code: 4100)
Environmental Protection Agency
Washington, D.C. 20460.

NPDES Permit Program

40 CFR Part 122, contains definitions and basic permitting requirements for EPA administered NPDES programs under 318, 402, and 405 of the CWA. The NPDES permit program requires that every industrial or municipal "point source" discharging into public waters obtain an NPDES permit. The NPDES permit performs two distinct functions within the CWA regulatory process: establish a level of performance the discharger must maintain, and require the discharger to self report any failures to maintain those levels of performance.

12.1 Overview

This part contains provisions for the National Pollutant Discharge Elimination System (NPDES) Program under section 318, 402, and 405 of the Clean Water Act (CWA). It covers basic EPA permitting requirements. What a state must do to obtain approval to operate its program instead of a federal program and minimum requirements for administering the approved state program is contained in part 123. Procedures for EPA processing of permit applications and appeals are contained in part 124. Part 124 is also applicable to other EPA permitting programs.

The NPDES program requires permits for the discharge of "pollutants" from any "point source" into "waters of the United States." The following are point sources requiring NPDES permits for discharges:

- ❏ concentrated animal feeding operations (122.23);
- ❏ concentrated aquatic animal production facilities (122.24);
- ❏ discharges into aquaculture projects (122.25);
- ❏ discharges of storm water (122.26); and
- ❏ silvicultural point sources (122.27).

The permit program established under this part also applies to owners or operators of any treatment works treating domestic sewage, whether or not the treatment works is otherwise required to obtain an NPDES permit in accordance with this section of the CFRs, unless all requirements implementing section 405(d) of CWA applicable to the treatment works treating domestic sewage are included in a permit issued under the appropriate provisions of subtitle C of the Solid Waste Disposal Act, Part C of the Safe Drinking Water Act, the Marine Protection, Research, and Sanctuaries Act of 1972, or the Clean Air Act, or under state permit programs approved by the Administrator as adequate to assure compliance with section 405 of the CWA.

12.1.1 State Programs

Certain requirements set forth in part 122 and 124 are made applicable to approved state programs by reference in part 123. These references are set forth in 123.25. If a section or paragraph of part 122 or 124 is applicable to states, through reference in 123.25, that fact is signaled by the following words at the end of the section or paragraph heading: (Applicable to state programs, see 123.25). If these words are absent, the section (or paragraph) applies only to EPA administered permits.

12.1.2 Relation to Other Requirements

Applicants for EPA issued permits must submit their applications on EPA's permit application forms when available. Most of the information requested on these application forms is required by these regulations. The basic information required in the general form (Form 1) and the additional information required for NPDES applications (Forms 2 a through d) are listed in 122.21. Applicants for state issued permits must use state forms which must require at a minimum the information listed in these sections.

12.1.3 Technical Regulations

The NPDES permit program has separate additional regulations. These separate regulations are used by permit issuing authorities to determine what requirements must be placed in permits if they are issued. These separate regulations are located at 40 CFR Parts 125, 129, 133, 136, 40 CFR subchapter N (parts 400 through 460), and 40 CFR Part 503.

12.1.4 Public Participation

This rule establishes the requirements for public participation in EPA and state permit issuance and enforcement and related variance proceedings, and in the approval of state NPDES programs. These requirements carry out the purposes of the public participation requirements of 40 CFR Part 25 (Public Participation), and supersede the requirements of that part as they apply to actions covered under parts 122, 123, and 124. Nothing in part 122, 123, or 124 precludes more stringent state regulation of any activity covered by these regulations, whether or not under an approved state program.

EPA Permit exclusions are listed at 122.3 and 122.4, and state NPDES programs prohibitions can be found at 123.25.

12.2 Effect of a Permit

Except for any toxic effluent standards and prohibitions imposed under section 307 of the CWA and "standards for sewage sludge use or disposal" under 405(d) of the CWA, compliance with a permit during its term constitutes compliance, for purposes of enforcement, with sections 301, 302, 306, 307, 318, 403, and 405 (a)–(b) of CWA. However, a permit may be modified, revoked and reissued, or terminated during its term for cause as set forth in 122.62 and 122.64.

Compliance with a permit condition which implements a particular "standard for sewage sludge use or disposal" shall be an affirmative defense in any enforcement action brought for a violation of that "standard for sewage sludge use or disposal" pursuant to sections 405(e) and 309 of the CWA.

The issuance of a permit does not authorize any injury to persons or property or invasion of other private rights, or any infringement of state or local law or regulations.

12.2.1 Continuation of Expiring Permits

When EPA is the permit–issuing authority, the conditions of an expired permit continue in force under 5 U.S.C. 558(c) until the effective date of a new permit (see 124.15) if:

- ☐ the permittee has submitted a timely application under 122.21 which is a complete (under 122.21(e)) application for a new permit; and

- ☐ the Regional Administrator, through no fault of the permittee does not issue a new permit with an effective date under 124.15 on or before the expiration date of the previous permit (for example, when issuance is impracticable due to time or resource constraints). Permits continued under this section remain fully effective and enforceable.

12.2.3 Enforcement

When the permittee is not in compliance with the conditions of the expiring or expired permit the Regional Administrator may choose to do any or all of the following:

- ☐ initiate enforcement action based upon the permit which has been continued;

- ☐ issue a notice of intent to deny the new permit under 124.6. If the permit is denied, the owner or operator would then be required to cease the activities authorized by the continued permit or be subject to enforcement action for operating without a permit;

- ☐ issue a new permit under part 124 with appropriate conditions; or

- ☐ take other actions authorized by these regulations.

An EPA issued permit does not continue in force beyond its expiration date under federal law if at that time a state is the permitting authority. States authorized to administer the NPDES program may continue either EPA or state issued permits until the effective date of the new permits, if state law allows. Otherwise, the facility or activity is operating without a permit from the time of expiration of the old permit to the effective date of the state issued new permit.

In accordance with 40 CFR Part 2, any information submitted to EPA pursuant to these regulations may be claimed as confidential by the submitter. Any such claim must be asserted at the time of submission in the manner prescribed on the application form or instructions or, in the case of other submissions, by stamping the words "confidential business information" on each page containing such information. If no claim is made at the time of submission, EPA may make the information available to the public without further notice. If a claim is asserted, the information will be treated in accordance with the procedures in 40 CFR Part 2 (Public Information).

12.3 Permit Application and Special NPDES Program Requirements

Any person who discharges or proposes to discharge pollutants or who owns or operates a "sludge-only facility" who does not have an effective permit, except persons covered by general permits under 122.28, excluded under 122.3, or a user of a privately owned treatment works unless the Director requires otherwise under 122.44(m), shall submit a complete application (which shall include a BMP program if necessary under 40 CFR 125.102) to the Director in accordance with this section and part 124. When a facility or activity is owned by one person but is operated by another person, it is the operator's duty to obtain a permit.

12.3.1 Time to apply

Any person proposing a new discharge, shall submit an application at least 180 days before the date on which the discharge is to commence, unless permission for a later date has been granted by the Director. Facilities proposing a new discharge of storm water associated with industrial activity shall submit an application 180 days before that facility commences industrial activity which may result in a discharge of storm water associated with that industrial activity. Facilities described under 122.26(b)(14)(x) shall submit applications at least 90 days before the date on which construction is to commence. Different submittal dates may be required under the terms of applicable general permits. Persons proposing a new discharge are encouraged to submit their applications well in advance of the 90 or 180 day requirements to avoid delay. See this section of the CFRs and 122.26 (c)(1)(i)(G) and (c)(1)(ii). New discharges composed entirely of storm water, other than those dischargers identified by 122.26(a)(1), shall apply for and obtain a permit according to the application requirements in 122.26(g).

12.3.2 Permits under Section 405(f) of CWA

Any existing "treatment works treating domestic sewage" required to have, or requesting site specific pollutant limits as provided in 40 CFR Part 503, must submit the permit application information required by this section of the CFRs within 180 days after publication of a standard applicable to its sewage sludge use or disposal practice(s). After this 180-day period, "treatment works treating domestic sewage" may only apply for site specific pollutant limits for good cause and such requests must be made within 180 days of becoming aware that good cause exists.

Any "treatment works treating domestic sewage" with a currently effective NPDES permit, not addressed in this section, must submit the application information at the time of its next NPDES permit renewal application.

Any other existing "treatment works treating domestic sewage" not addressed in this section must submit the following information to the Director within one year after publication of a standard applicable to its sewage sludge use or disposal practice(s):

- ❑ name, mailing address and location of the "treatment works treating domestic sewage";

- ❑ the operator's name, address, telephone number, ownership status, and status as federal, state, private, public or other entity;

- ❑ a description of the sewage sludge use or disposal practices (including, where applicable, the location of any sites where sewage sludge is transferred for treatment, use, or disposal, as well as the name of the applicator or other contractor who applies the sewage sludge to land, if different from the "treatment works treating domestic sewage," and the name of any distributors if the sewage sludge is sold or given away in a bag or similar enclosure for application to the land, if different from the "treatment works treating domestic sewage");

- ❑ annual amounts of sewage sludge generated, treated, used or disposed (dry weight basis); and

- ❑ the most recent data the "treatment works treating domestic sewage" may have on the quality of the sewage sludge.

12.3.3 Duty to Reapply

Any POTW with a currently effective permit shall submit a new application at least 180 days before the expiration date of the existing permit, unless permission for a later date has been granted by the Director. All other permittees with currently effective permits shall submit a new application 180 days before the existing permit expires. A few exceptions are noted in this section of the CFRs.

12.3.4 Completeness

The Director shall not issue a permit before receiving a complete application for a permit except for NPDES general permits. An application for a permit is complete when the Director receives an application form and any supplemental information which are completed to his or her satisfaction. The completeness of any application for a permit shall be judged independently of the status of any other permit application or permit for the same facility or activity. For EPA administered NPDES programs, an application which is reviewed under 124.3 is complete when the Director receives either a complete application or the information listed in a notice of deficiency.

12.4 Information Requirements

All applicants for NPDES permits shall provide the following information to the Director, using the application form provided by the Director (additional information required of applicants is set forth in this section).

❑ the activities conducted by the applicant which require it to obtain an NPDES permit;

❑ name, mailing address, and location of the facility for which the application is submitted.

❑ up to four SIC codes which best reflect the principal products or services provided by the facility;

❑ the operator's name, address, telephone number, ownership status, and status as federal, state, private, public, or other entity; and

❑ whether the facility is located on indian lands.

12.4.1 Other Permits or Construction Approvals

The owner or operator must also supply a listing of all permits or construction approvals received or applied for under any of the following programs:

❑ Hazardous Waste Management program under RCRA;

❑ UIC program under SDWA;

❑ NPDES program under CWA;

❑ Prevention of Significant Deterioration (PSD) program under the Clean Air Act;

❑ Nonattainment program under the Clean Air Act;

❑ National Emission Standards for Hazardous Pollutants (NESHAPS) preconstruction approval under the Clean Air Act;

❑ ocean dumping permits under the Marine Protection Research and Sanctuaries Act;

❑ dredge or fill permits under section 404 of CWA; and

❑ other relevant environmental permits, including state permits.

12.5 Site Location

A topographic map (or other map if a topographic map is unavailable) extending one mile beyond the property boundaries of the source, depicting the facility and each of its intake and discharge structures; each of its hazardous waste treatment, storage, or disposal facilities; each well where fluids from the facility are injected underground; and those wells, springs, other surface water bodies, and drinking water wells listed in public records or otherwise known to the applicant in the map area, must also be submitted along with a brief description of the nature of the business.

12.6 Existing Manufacturing, Commercial, Mining, and Silvicultural Dischargers

Existing manufacturing, commercial mining, and silvicultural dischargers applying for NPDES permits, except for those facilities subject to the requirements of 122.21(h), shall provide the following information to the Director, using application forms provided by the Director.

Outfall location	The latitude and longitude to the nearest 15 seconds and the name of the receiving water.
Line drawing	A line drawing of the water flow through the facility with a water balance, showing operations contributing wastewater to the effluent and treatment units.
Average flows and treatment	A narrative identification of each type of process, operation, or production area which contributes wastewater to the effluent for each outfall, including process wastewater, cooling water, and stormwater runoff; the average flow which each process contributes; and a description of the treatment the wastewater receives, including the ultimate disposal of any solid or fluid wastes other than by discharge.
Intermittent flows	If any of the discharges described in this section of the CFRs are intermittent or seasonal, a description of the frequency, duration and flow rate of each discharge occurrence (except for stormwater runoff, spillage or leaks).
Maximum production	If an effluent guideline promulgated under section 304 of CWA applies to the applicant and is expressed in terms of production (or other measure of operation), a reasonable measure of the applicant's actual production reported in the units used in the applicable effluent guideline.
Improvements	If the applicant is subject to any present requirements or compliance schedules for construction, upgrading or operation of waste treatment equipment, an identification of the abatement requirement, a description of the abatement project, and a listing of the required and projected final compliance dates.
Effluent characteristics	Information on the discharge of pollutants specified in this section. When "quantitative data" for a pollutant are required, the applicant must collect a sample of effluent and analyze it for the pollutant in accordance with analytical methods approved under 40 CFR Part 136.Grab samples must be used for pH, temperature, cyanide, total phenols, residual chlorine, oil and grease, fecal coliform and fecal streptococcus. For all other pollutants, 24-hour composite samples must be used. For storm water discharges, all samples shall be collected from the discharge resulting from a storm event that is greater than 0.1 inch and at least 72 hours from the previously measurable storm event.

The Director may waive the reporting requirements for individual point sources or for a particular industry category for one or more listed pollutants if the applicant has demonstrated that such a waiver is appropriate because information adequate to support issuance of a permit can be obtained with less stringent requirements.

Each applicant with processes in one or more primary industry category (see appendix A to part 122) contributing to a discharge must report quantitative data for covered pollutants in each outfall containing process wastewater. A number of tables are contained in appendix D of this part:

❏ Table I and II of appendix D of this part - organic toxic pollutants in the fractions;

❏ Table III of appendix D of this part - toxic metals, cyanide, and total phenols;

❏ Table IV of appendix D of this part - certain conventional and nonconventional pollutants; and

❏ Table V of appendix D of this part - certain hazardous substances and asbestos.

Each applicant must indicate whether it knows or has reason to believe that any of the pollutants listed in the tables in appendix D for which quantitative data are not otherwise required under this section, is discharged from each outfall. For every pollutant expected to be discharged in concentrations above regulatory limitations the applicant must report quantitative data.

See this section of the CFRs for listed exemptions.

12.7 Additional information

In addition to the information reported on the application form, applicants shall provide to the Director, at his or her request, such other information as the Director may reasonably require to assess the discharges of the facility and to determine whether to issue an NPDES permit. The additional information may include additional quantitative data and bioassays to assess the relative toxicity of discharges to aquatic life and requirements to determine the cause of the toxicity.

12.8 Non-Process Wastewater Facilities

Except for stormwater discharges, all manufacturing, commercial, mining and silvicultural dischargers applying for NPDES permits which discharge only non-process wastewater not regulated by an effluent limitations guideline or new source performance standard shall provide the following information to the Director, using application forms provided by the Director:

❏ outfall location;

❏ discharge date (for new dischargers); and

❏ type of waste and waste characteristics.

Effluent characteristics, and quantitative data for the following pollutants or parameters, must be reported or estimated in terms of concentration and total mass, except for flow, pH, and temperature:

❏ Biochemical Oxygen Demand (BOD5);

❏ Total Suspended Solids (TSS);

❏ fecal Coliform (if believed present or if sanitary waste is or will be discharged);

❏ total Residual Chlorine (if chlorine is used);

❏ oil and grease;

❏ Chemical Oxygen Demand (COD) (if non-contact cooling water is or will be discharged);

❏ Total Organic Carbon (TOC) (if non-contact cooling water is or will be discharged);

❏ ammonia (as N);

❏ discharge flow;

❏ pH; and

❏ temperature (Winter and Summer).

The Director may waive the testing and reporting requirements for any of the pollutants or flow listed in this section if the applicant submits a request for such a waiver before or with his application which demonstrates that information adequate to support issuance of a permit can be obtained through less stringent requirements. Other data is required for:

❏ flow,

❏ treatment system,

❏ optional information, and

❏ certification.

12.9 Other Information

Other information reporting and application requirements in this section pertain to:

❏ concentrated animal feeding operations

❏ concentrated aquatic animal production facilities

❏ aquaculture projects

❏ storm water discharges

❏ silvicultural activities

❏ new and existing POTWs.

❏ new sources and new discharges.

❏ variance requests by non-POTWs, including expedited variance procedures and time extensions.

12.10 Recordkeeping

Signatories to permit applications and reports must be signed in accordance with the terms set forth in 122.22 for federal permits and/or 123.25 for state permit programs. Any person signing a document under paragraph (a) or (b) of this section shall make the following certification:

> *"I certify under penalty of law that this document and all attachments were prepared under my direction or supervision in accordance with a system designed to assure that qualified personnel properly gather and evaluate the information submitted. Based on my inquiry of the person or persons who manage the system, or those persons directly responsible for gathering the information, the information submitted is, to the best of my knowledge and belief, true, accurate, and complete. I am aware that there are significant penalties for submitting false information, including the possibility of fine and imprisonment for knowing violations."*

12.11 General Permits

The Director may issue a general NPDES permit to cover a category of discharges or sludge use or disposal practices or facilities in accordance with area requirements. For this the general permit must correspond to existing geographic or political boundaries, such as:

- ❑ designated planning areas under sections 208 and 303 of CWA;
- ❑ sewer districts or sewer authorities;
- ❑ city, county, or state political boundaries;
- ❑ state highway systems;
- ❑ Standard metropolitan statistical areas as defined by the Office of Management and Budget;
- ❑ urbanized areas as designated by the Bureau of the Census according to criteria in 30 FR 15202; or
- ❑ any other appropriate division or combination of boundaries.

12.11.1 Sources

The general permit regulates the area for either storm water point sources; a category of point sources, or a category of "treatment works treating domestic sewage," if the sources or "treatment works treating domestic sewage" all:

- ❑ involve the same or substantially similar types of operations;
- ❑ discharge the same types of wastes or engage in the same types of sludge use or disposal practices;

❑ require the same effluent limitations, operating conditions, or standards for sewage sludge use or disposal;

❑ require the same or similar monitoring; and

❑ in the opinion of the Director, are more appropriately controlled under a general permit than under individual permits.

General permits may be issued, modified, revoked and reissued, or terminated in accordance with applicable requirements of part 124 or corresponding state regulations. Special procedures for issuance are found at 123.44 for states and 124.58 for EPA. These general permits cover authorization to discharge, or authorization to engage in sludge use and disposal practices, and specify deadlines for submitting notices of intent to be covered and the date(s).

Discharges other than discharges from publicly owned treatment works, combined sewer overflows, primary industrial facilities, and storm water discharges associated with industrial activity, may, at the discretion of the Director, be authorized to discharge under a general permit without submitting a notice of intent where the Director finds that a notice of intent requirement would be inappropriate. In making such a finding, the Director considers the:

❑ type of discharge;

❑ expected nature of the discharge;

❑ potential for toxic and conventional pollutants in the discharges;

❑ expected volume of the discharges;

❑ other means of identifying discharges covered by the permit; and

❑ estimated number of discharges to be covered by the permit.

12.12 Individual NPDES Permit

The Director may require any discharger authorized by a general permit to apply for and obtain an individual NPDES permit. Any interested person may petition the Director to take action under this paragraph. Cases where an individual NPDES permit may be required include the following:

❑ the discharger or "treatment works treating domestic sewage" is not in compliance with the conditions of the general NPDES permit;

❑ a change has occurred in the availability of demonstrated technology or practices for the control or abatement of pollutants applicable to the point source or treatment works treating domestic sewage;

❑ effluent limitation guidelines are promulgated for point sources covered by the general NPDES permit;

❑ a Water Quality Management plan containing requirements applicable to such point sources is approved;

❏ circumstances have changed since the time of the request to be covered so that the discharger is no longer appropriately controlled under the general permit, or either a temporary or permanent reduction or elimination of the authorized discharge is necessary;

❏ standards for sewage sludge use or disposal have been promulgated for the sludge use and disposal practice covered by the general NPDES permit; or

❏ the discharge(s) is a significant contributor of pollutants.

In making this determination, the Director may consider the following factors:

❏ location of the discharge with respect to waters of the United States;

❏ size of the discharge;

❏ quantity and nature of the pollutants discharged to waters of the United States; and

❏ other relevant factors.

For EPA issued general permits only, the Regional Administrator may require any owner or operator authorized by a general permit to apply for an individual NPDES permit, only if the owner or operator has been notified in writing that a permit application is required. This notice shall include a brief statement of the reasons for this decision, an application form, a statement setting a time for the owner or operator to file the application, and a statement that on the effective date of the individual NPDES permit the general permit as it applies to the individual permittee shall automatically terminate. The Director may grant additional time upon request of the applicant.

Any owner or operator authorized by a general permit may request to be excluded from the coverage of the general permit by applying for an individual permit. When an individual NPDES permit is issued to an owner or operator otherwise subject to a general NPDES permit, the applicability of the general permit to the individual NPDES permittee is automatically terminated on the effective date of the individual permit. Other requirements outlined in this section pertain to offshore oil and gas facilities.

12.13 New Sources and New Dischargers

Except as otherwise provided in an applicable new source performance standard, a source is a "new source" if it meets the definition of "new source" in 122.2, and it is constructed at a site at which no other source is located; or it totally replaces the process or production equipment that causes the discharge of pollutants at an existing source; or its processes are substantially independent of an existing source at the same site.

In determining whether these processes are substantially independent, the Director shall consider such factors as the extent to which the new facility is integrated with the existing plant; and the extent to which the new facility is engaged in the same general type of activity as the existing source.

12.13.1 Requirement for an Environmental Impact Statement (EIS)

The issuance of a NPDES permit to new source by EPA may be a major federal action significantly affecting the quality of the human environment within the meaning of the National Environmental Policy Act of 1969 (NEPA), 33 U.S.C. 4321 et seq. and is subject to the environmental review provisions of NEPA as set out in 40 CFR Part 6, subpart F. EPA will determine whether an Environmental Impact Statement (EIS) is required under 122.21(k) (special provisions for applications from new sources) and 40 CFR Part 6, subpart F.

The Regional Administrator, to the extent allowed by law, shall issue, condition (other than imposing effluent limitations), or deny the new source NPDES permit following a complete evaluation of any significant beneficial and adverse impacts of the proposed action and a review of the recommendations contained in the EIS or finding of no significant impact.

The issuance of a NPDES permit to new source by a NPDES- approved state is not a federal action and therefore does not require EPA to conduct an environmental review. After the effective date of new source performance standards, operating the source in violation of those standards applicable to the source is unlawful for any owner or operator of any new source.

12.14 Conditions Applicable to All Permits

The following conditions apply to all NPDES permits. Additional conditions applicable to NPDES permits are in 122.42. All conditions applicable to NPDES permits shall be incorporated into the permits either expressly or by reference. If incorporated by reference, a specific citation to these regulations (or the corresponding approved state regulations) must be given in the permit.

12.14.1 Duty to comply

The permittee must comply with all conditions of this permit. Any permit noncompliance constitutes a violation of the Clean Water Act and is grounds for enforcement action, permit termination, revocation and reissuance, modification, or denial of a permit renewal application. The permittee shall comply with:

- ❏ effluent standards or prohibitions established under section 307(a) of the Clean Water Act for toxic pollutants and with standards for sewage sludge use or disposal established under section 405(d) of the CWA within the time provided in the regulations that establish these standards; and

- ❏ the Clean Water Act sections 301, 302, 306, 307, 308, 318 or 405, or any permit condition or limitation implementing any such sections in a permit issued under section 402, or any requirement imposed in an approved pretreatment program.

12.14.2 Administrative Penalties

Noncompliance is subject to criminal penalties of $2,500 to $25,000 per day of violation, or imprisonment of not more than 1 year, or both. In the case of a second or subsequent conviction for a negligent violation, a person shall be subject to criminal penalties of not more than $50,000 per day of violation, or by imprisonment of not more than 2 years, or both. Any person who knowingly violates such sections, or such conditions or limitations is subject to criminal penalties of $5,000 to $50,000 per day of violation, or imprisonment for not more than 3 years, or both. In the case of a second or subsequent conviction for a knowing violation, a person shall be subject to criminal penalties of not more than $100,000 per day of violation, or imprisonment of not more than 6 years, or both.

Any person who knowingly violates section 301, 302, 303, 306, 307, 308, 318 or 405 of the Act, or any permit condition or limitation implementing any of such sections in a permit issued under section 402 of the Act, and who knows at that time that he thereby places another person in imminent danger of death or serious bodily injury, shall, upon conviction, be subject to a fine of not more than $250,000 or imprisonment of not more than 15 years, or both.

In the case of a second or subsequent conviction for a knowing endangerment violation, a person shall be subject to a fine of not more than $500,000 or by imprisonment of not more than 30 years, or both. An organization, as defined in section 309(c)(3)(B)(iii) of the CWA, shall, upon conviction of violating the imminent danger provision, be subject to a fine of not more than $1,000,000 and can be fined up to $2,000,000 for second or subsequent convictions.

Other requirements outlined in this section of the CFRs include, but are not limited to:

- ❏ duty to reapply
- ❏ need to halt or reduce activity not a defense
- ❏ duty to mitigate
- ❏ proper operation and maintenance
- ❏ permit actions
- ❏ property rights
- ❏ duty to provide information
- ❏ inspection and entry
- ❏ signatory requirements
- ❏ reporting requirements
- ❏ anticipated noncompliance

12.15 Monitoring Records and Reports

Records of monitoring information shall include the:

❏ date, exact place, and time of sampling or measurements;

❏ individual(s) who performed the sampling or measurements;

❏ date(s) analyses were performed;

❏ individual(s) who performed the analyses;

❏ analytical techniques or methods used; and

❏ results of such analyses.

Monitoring results must be conducted according to test procedures approved under 40 CFR Part 136 or, in the case of sludge use or disposal, approved under 40 CFR Part 136 unless otherwise specified in 40 CFR Part 503, unless other test procedures have been specified in the permit.

Monitoring results shall be reported at the intervals specified in the permit and must be reported on a Discharge Monitoring Report (DMR) or forms provided or specified by the Director for reporting results of monitoring of sludge use or disposal practices.

If the permittee monitors any pollutant more frequently than required by the permit using test procedures approved under 40 CFR Part 136 or, in the case of sludge use or disposal, approved under 40 CFR Part 136 unless otherwise specified in 40 CFR Part 503, or as specified in the permit, the results of this monitoring shall be included in the calculation and reporting of the data submitted in the DMR or sludge reporting form specified by the Director.

12.16 Compliance Schedules and Twenty-Four Hour Reporting

Reports of compliance or noncompliance with, or any progress reports on, interim and final requirements contained in any compliance schedule of this permit shall be submitted no later than 14 days following each schedule date.

The permittee shall report any noncompliance which may endanger health or the environment. Any information shall be provided orally within 24 hours from the time the permittee becomes aware of the circumstances. A written submission shall also be provided within five days of the time the permittee becomes aware of the circumstances. The written submission shall contain a description of the noncompliance and its cause; the period of noncompliance, including exact dates and times, and if the noncompliance has not been corrected, the anticipated time it is expected to continue; and steps taken or planned to reduce, eliminate, and prevent reoccurrence of the noncompliance.

The following shall be included as information which must be reported within 24 hours under this section:

❏ any unanticipated bypass which exceeds any effluent limitation in the permit. (See 122.41(g);

❏ any upset which exceeds any effluent limitation in the permit; and

❑ volations of a maximum daily discharge limitation for any of the pollutants listed in the permit to be reported within 24 hours. (See 122.44(g)).

The Director may waive the written report on a case by case basis for reports under this section of the I)(6)(ii)CFRs of this section if the oral report has been received within 24 hours. Additional conditions applicable to specified categories of NPDES permits applicable to EPA are listed in section 122.42, for those applicable to state NPDES programs, see 123.25.

12.17 Establishing Limitations, Standards, and Other Permit Conditions

Limitations must control all pollutants or pollutant parameters (either conventional, nonconventional, or toxic pollutants) which the Director determines are or may be discharged at a level which will cause, have the reasonable potential to cause, or contribute to an excursion above any state water quality standard, including state narrative criteria for water quality.

Where a state has not established a water quality criterion for a specific chemical pollutant that is present in an effluent at a concentration that causes, has the reasonable potential to cause, or contributes to an excursion above a narrative criterion within an applicable state water quality standard, the permitting authority must establish effluent limits using one or more of the following options:

❑ Establish effluent limits using a calculated numeric water quality criterion for the pollutant which the permitting authority demonstrates will attain and maintain applicable narrative water quality criteria and will fully protect the designated use. Such a criterion may be derived using a proposed state criterion, or an explicit state policy or regulation interpreting its narrative water quality criterion, supplemented with other relevant information which may include EPA's Water Quality Standards Handbook, October 1983, risk assessment data, exposure data, information about the pollutant from the Food and Drug Administration, and current EPA criteria documents; or

❑ Establish effluent limits on a case by case basis, using EPA's water quality criteria, published under section 304(a) of the CWA, supplemented where necessary by other relevant information; or

❑ Establish effluent limitations on an indicator parameter for the pollutant of concern, (see this section of the CFRs for specific details).

When developing water quality based effluent limits under this paragraph the permitting authority shall ensure that:

❑ The level of water quality to be achieved by limits on point sources established under this paragraph is derived from, and complies with all applicable water quality standards; and

❑ Effluent limits developed to protect a narrative water quality criterion, a numeric water quality criterion, or both, are consistent with the assumptions and requirements of any available wasteload allocation for the discharge prepared by the state and approved by EPA pursuant to 40 CFR 130.7. The methods used for calculating NPDES permit conditions are listed in the table below.

Calculating NPDES permit conditions (122.45) (for State NPDES programs, see 123.25)	
Outfalls and discharge points	All permit effluent limitations, standards and prohibitions shall be established for each outfall or discharge point of the permitted facility, except as otherwise provided under 122.44(k) (BMPs where limitations are infeasible) and this section of the CFRs (limitations on internal waste streams).
Production based limitations	In the case of POTWs, permit effluent limitations, standards, or prohibitions shall be calculated based on design flow.
Metals	All permit effluent limitations, standards, or prohibitions for a metal shall be expressed in terms of "total recoverable metal" as defined in 40 CFR Part 136 unless: an applicable effluent limitation has been promulgated that specifies the limitation for the metal in the dissolved or valent or total form; or all approved analytical methods for the metal inherently measure only its dissolved form (e.g., hexavalent chromium).
Continuous discharges	For continuous discharges all permit effluent limitations, standards, and prohibitions, including those necessary to achieve water quality standards, should be stated as: maximum daily and average monthly discharge limitations for all dischargers other than publicly owned treatment works; and average weekly and average monthly discharge limitations for POTWs.
Non-continuous discharges	Discharges which are not continuous, as defined in 122.2, shall be particularly described and limited, considering the following factors, as appropriate: frequency; total mass; maximum rate of discharge of pollutants during the discharge; and prohibition or limitation of specified pollutants by mass, concentration, or other appropriate measure.
Mass limitations	All pollutants limited in permits shall have limitations, standards or prohibitions expressed in terms of mass except: for pH, temperature, radiation, or other pollutants which cannot appropriately be expressed by mass; when applicable standards and limitations are expressed in terms of other units of measurement.
Pollutants in intake water	Upon request of the discharger, technology based effluent limitations or standards shall be adjusted to reflect credit for pollutants in the discharger's intake water if: the applicable effluent limitations and standards contained in 40 CFR subchapter N specifically provide that they shall be applied on a net basis; or the discharger demonstrates that the control system it proposes or uses would meet the limitations and standards.
Internal waste streams	When permit effluent limitations or standards imposed at the point of discharge are impractical or infeasible, effluent limitations or standards for discharges of pollutants may be imposed on internal waste streams before mixing with other waste streams or cooling water streams, if so, the monitoring required by 122.44(i) shall also be applied to the internal waste streams.
Disposal of pollutants	Permit limitations and standards shall be calculated as provided in 122.50 for disposal in wells, POTWs or land application.

12.17.1 Duration of Permits

NPDES permits shall be effective for a fixed term not to exceed five years. Except as provided in 122.6, the term of a permit shall not be extended by modification beyond the maximum duration specified in this section. The Director may issue any permit for a duration that is less than the full allowable term under this section.

12.17.2 Schedules of Compliance

Any schedules of compliance under this section shall require compliance as soon as possible, but not later than the applicable statutory deadline under the CWA. The first NPDES permit issued to a new source or a new discharger shall contain a schedule of compliance only when necessary to allow a reasonable opportunity to attain compliance with requirements issued or revised after commencement of construction but less than three years before commencement of the relevant discharge. For recommencing dischargers, a schedule of compliance shall be available only when necessary to allow a reasonable opportunity to attain compliance with requirements issued or revised less than three years before recommencement of discharge.

An NPDES permit applicant or permittee may cease conducting regulated activities (by terminating of direct discharge for NPDES sources) rather than continuing to operate and meet permit requirements as follows:

If the permittee decides to cease conducting regulated activities at a given time within the term of a permit which has already been issued:

- ☐ the permit may be modified to contain a new or additional schedule leading to timely cessation of activities; or

- ☐ the permittee shall cease conducting permitted activities before noncompliance with any interim or final compliance schedule requirement already specified in the permit.

If the decision to cease conducting regulated activities is made before issuance of a permit whose term will include the termination date, the permit shall contain a schedule leading to termination which will ensure timely compliance with applicable requirements no later than the statutory deadline. If the permittee is undecided whether to cease conducting regulated activities, the Director may issue or modify a permit to contain alternative schedules:

- ☐ one schedule shall lead to timely compliance with applicable requirements, no later than the statutory deadline;

- ☐ the second schedule shall lead to cessation of regulated activities by a date which will ensure timely compliance with applicable requirements no later than the statutory deadline.

12.17.3 Requirements for Recording and Reporting

All NPDES permits shall specify:

☐ requirements concerning the proper use, maintenance, and installation, when appropriate, of monitoring equipment or methods (including biological monitoring methods when appropriate);

☐ required monitoring including type, intervals, and frequency sufficient to yield data which represent the monitored activity including, when appropriate, continuous monitoring;

☐ applicable reporting requirements based upon the impact of the regulated activity and as specified in 122.44. Reporting shall be no less frequent than specified in the above regulation.

12.18 Considerations under Federal law

The following table contains a list of federal laws under these rules. When any of these laws are applicable, its procedures must be followed. When the applicable law requires consideration or adoption of particular permit conditions or requires the denial of a permit, those requirements also must be followed.

Federal laws that may apply to the issuance of NPDES permits	
Wild and Scenic Rivers Act, 16 U.S.C. 1273 et seq.	section 7 of the Act prohibits the Regional Administrator from assisting by license or otherwise the construction of any water resources projects that would have a direct, adverse effect on the values for which a national wild and scenic river was established.
National Historic Preservation Act of 1966, 16 U.S.C. 470 et seq.	section 106 of the Act and implementing regulations (36 CFR Part 800) require the Regional Administrator, before issuing a license, to adopt measures when feasible to mitigate potential adverse effects of the licensed activity and properties listed or eligible for listing in the National Register of Historic Places. The Act's requirements are to be implemented in cooperation with State Historic Preservation Officers and upon notice to, and when appropriate, in consultation with the Advisory Council on Historic Preservation.
Endangered Species Act, 16 U.S.C. 1531 et seq.	section 7 of the Act and implementing regulations (50 CFR Part 402) require the Regional Administrator to ensure, in consultation with the Secretary of the Interior or Commerce, that any action authorized by EPA is not likely to jeopardize the continued existence of any endangered or threatened species or adversely affect its critical habitat.
Coastal Zone Management Act, 16 U.S.C. 1451 et seq.	section 307(c) of the Act and implementing regulations (15 CFR Part 930) prohibit EPA from issuing a permit for an activity affecting land or water use in the coastal zone until the applicant certifies that the proposed activity complies with the State Coastal Zone Management program, and the state or its designated agency concurs with the certification (or the Secretary of Commerce overrides the state's nonconcurrence).

Federal laws that may apply to the issuance of NPDES permits	
Fish and Wildlife Coordination Act, 16 U.S.C. 661 et seq.	requires that the Regional Administrator, before issuing a permit proposing or authorizing the impoundment (with certain exemptions), diversion, or other control or modification of any body of water, consult with the appropriate state agency exercising jurisdiction over wildlife resources to conserve those resources.
National Environmental Policy Act, 42 U.S.C. 4321 et seq.	may require preparation of an Environmental Impact Statement and consideration of EIS related permit conditions (other than effluent limitations) as provided in 122.29(c).

12.19 Other Information

Other Sections in this part include:

- ❏ disposal of pollutants into wells, into publicly owned treatment works or by land application
- ❏ transfer of permits
- ❏ modification or revocation and reissuance of permits
- ❏ minor modifications of permits
- ❏ termination of permits

For NPDES permit requirements applicable to state programs, see 123.25. Any permit issued after June 30, 1981 to dischargers in the following categories shall include effluent limitations and a compliance schedule to meet the requirements of section 301(b)(2)(A), (C), (D), (E) and (F) of CWA, whether or not applicable effluent limitations guidelines have been promulgated. See 122.44 and 122.46.

12.20 Appendices to Part 122

The table below lists industries by NPDES Primary Industry Categories:

Appendix A - NPDES Primary Industry Categories	
Adhesives and sealants	Nonferrous metals manufacturing
Aluminum forming	Ore mining
Auto and other laundries	Organic chemicals manufacturing
Battery manufacturing	Paint and ink formulation
Coal mining	Pesticides
Coil coating	Petroleum refining
Copper forming	Pharmaceutical preparations
Electrical and electronic components	Photographic equipment and supplies
Electroplating	Plastics processing

Appendix A - NPDES Primary Industry Categories	
Explosives manufacturing	Plastic and synthetic materials manufacturing
Foundries	Porcelain enameling
Gum and wood chemicals	Printing and publishing
Inorganic chemicals manufacturing	Pulp and paper mills
Iron and steel manufacturing	Rubber processing
Leather tanning and finishing	Soap and detergent manufacturing
Mechanical products manufacturing	Steam electric power plants
Mills, Textile	Timber products processing

In addition to the table above (Appendix A to Part 122), the following appendices are included in part 122:

Appendix	Contents
B	Criteria for Determining a Concentrated Animal Feeding Operation (122.23)
C	Criteria for Determining a Concentrated Aquatic Animal Production Facility (122.24)
D	NPDES Permit Application Testing Requirements (122.21)
E	Rainfall Zones of the United States
F	Incorporated Places With Populations Greater Than 250,000
G	Places With Populations Greater Than 100,000 and Less Than 250,000
H	Counties with Unincorporated Urbanized Areas With a Population of 250,000 or More
I	Counties With Unincorporated Urbanized Areas Greater Than 100,000, But Less Than 250,000

Ocean Dumping

This section of the CFRs presents EPA specifications for the exact contents of special, interim, emergency, general and research permits as required under section 102 of the MPRSA. Revision procedures for such permits are also presented.

13.1 Overview

Criteria for the Evaluation of Permit Applications for Ocean Dumping of Materials. Along with 40 CFR Part 228, this regulation comprises the criteria established pursuant to section 102 of the Act. The decision to issue or deny a permit and to impose special conditions on any permit will be based on an evaluation of the permit application according to the criteria set forth here. Subpart B provides the real guts of this part by examining environmental impact. First, the criterion for evaluating environmental impact is given, followed by prohibited materials, constituents prohibited as other than trace contaminants, limits established for specific wastes, limitations in the disposal rates of toxic wastes, limitations on quantities of waste materials, hazards to fishing, navigation, shorelines or beaches, containerized wastes, insoluble wastes, and dredged materials.

Criteria for the Management of Disposal Sites for Ocean Dumping. Working closely with Part 227, this part relates to decisions to issue or deny a permit based on the requirements for effective disposal site management to prevent unreasonable degradation of the marine environment. Procedures and criteria are given for the selection of sites by the EPA Administrator. Most of what remains in this regulation are listings of both interim and final designated dumping sites (§ 28.14 & 228.15). These listings need to be referred to when any project requires the transport of material for the purpose of ocean dumping.

13.1.1 Permits for Discharges of Dredged or Fill Material into Waters of the United States, Army Corps of Engineers

33 CFR Part 322, contains definitions and special policies, practices and procedures to be followed by the Corps in connection with review of permit applications for the discharge of dredged or fill materials under 404 of CWA. Permits issued under 404 are required for the discharge of dredged or fill materials not exempted by 323.4 of this part or permitted by 33 CFR Part 330. Please refer to 323.4 for a detailed listing of exemptions.

13.1.2 Permits for Ocean Dumping of Dredged Material, Army Corps of Engineers

33 CFR Part 324-325, applies to activities of federal agencies in relation to special policies that the Corps must follow for the review of permits for the transport and dumping of dredged materials into ocean waters. Focused attention should be given to § 324.3(b). Here, it states, "federal agencies are not required to obtain and provide certification of compliance with effluent limitations and water quality standards from state or interstate water pollution control agencies in connection with activities involving the transport of dredged material for dumping into ocean waters beyond the territorial sea."

13.1.3 Processing of Department of the Army Permits, Army Corps of Engineers

33 CFR Part 325, contains general processing procedures for all Department of the Army permits. Attention is given to transportation of dredged materials in § 325.1(d)(4). Federal agencies that initiate or authorize proposed actions that include transportation of dredged materials must ensure that the appropriate permits are obtained. In states with approved programs, permit application is done through the appropriate state agency.

13.2 Ocean Discharge Criteria

This subpart establishes guidelines for issuance of National Pollutant Discharge Elimination System (NPDES) permits for the discharge of pollutants from a point source into the territorial seas, the contiguous zone, and the oceans.

The director shall determine whether a discharge will cause unreasonable degradation of the marine environment based on consideration of the:

- ❏ quantities, composition and potential for bioaccumulation or persistence of the pollutants to be discharged;

- ❏ potential transport of such pollutants by biological, physical or chemical processes;

- ❏ composition and vulnerability of the biological communities which may be exposed to such pollutants, including the presence of unique species or communities of species, the presence of species identified as endangered or threatened pursuant to the Endangered Species Act, or the presence of those species critical to the structure or function of the ecosystem, such as those important for the food chain;

- ❏ importance of the receiving water area to the surrounding biological community, including the presence of spawning sites, nursery/forage areas, migratory pathways, or areas necessary for other functions or critical stages in the life cycle of an organism.

- ❏ existence of special aquatic sites including, but not limited to marine sanctuaries and refuges, parks, national and historic monuments, national seashores, wilderness areas and coral reefs;

- ❑ potential impacts on human health through direct and indirect pathways;

- ❑ existing or potential recreational and commercial fishing, including finfishing and shellfishing;

- ❑ applicable requirements of an approved Coastal Zone Management plan;

- ❑ other factors relating to the effects of the discharge as may be appropriate; and

- ❑ marine water quality criteria developed pursuant to section 304(a)(1).

Discharges in compliance with section 301(g), 301(h), or 316(a) variance requirements or state water quality standards shall be presumed not to cause unreasonable degradation of the marine environment, for any specific pollutants or conditions specified in the variance or the standard.

13.3 Permit Requirements

If the director on the basis of available information including that supplied by the applicant pursuant to 125.124 determines prior to permit issuance that the discharge will not cause unreasonable degradation of the marine environment after application of any necessary conditions specified in 125.123(d), he may issue an NPDES permit containing such conditions.

If the director, on the basis of available information including that supplied by the applicant pursuant to 125.124 determines prior to permit issuance that the discharge will cause unreasonable degradation of the marine environment after application of all possible permit conditions specified in 125.123(d), he may not issue an NPDES permit which authorizes the discharge of pollutants.

If the director has insufficient information to determine prior to permit issuance that there will be no unreasonable degradation of the marine environment pursuant to 125.122, there shall be no discharge of pollutants into the marine environment unless the director on the basis of available information, including that supplied by the applicant pursuant to 125.124 determines that:

- ❑ such discharge will not cause irreparable harm to the marine environment during the period in which monitoring is undertaken, and

- ❑ there are no reasonable alternatives to the on-site disposal of these materials, and

- ❑ the discharge will be in compliance with all permit conditions established pursuant to this section of the CFRs.

All permits which authorize the discharge of pollutants pursuant to this section shall:

- ❑ require that a discharge of pollutants will: i) following dilution as measured at the boundary of the mixing zone, not exceed the limiting permissible concentration for the liquid and suspended particulate phases of the waste material as described in 227.27(a) (2) and (3), 227.27(b), and 227.27(c) of the Ocean Dumping Criteria; and ii) not exceed the limiting permissible concentration for the solid phase of the waste material or cause an accumulation of toxic materials in the human food chain as described in 227.27 (b) and (d) of the Ocean Dumping Criteria;

❑ specify a monitoring program, which is sufficient to assess the impact of the discharge on water, sediment, and biological quality including, where appropriate, analysis of the bioaccumulative and/or persistent impact on aquatic life of the discharge;

❑ contain any other conditions, such as performance of liquid or suspended particulate phase bioaccumulation tests, seasonal restrictions on discharge, process modifications, dispersion of pollutants, or schedule of compliance for existing discharges, which are determined to be necessary because of local environmental conditions, and

❑ contain the following clause: In addition to any other grounds specified herein, this permit shall be modified or revoked at any time if, on the basis of any new data, the director determines that continued discharges may cause unreasonable degradation of the marine environment.

13.3.1 Information Required to Be Submitted by Applicant

The applicant is responsible for providing information which the director may request to make the determination required by this subpart. The director may require the following information as well as any other pertinent information:

❑ an analysis of the chemical constituents of any discharge;

❑ appropriate bioassays necessary to determine the limiting permissible concentrations for the discharge;

❑ an analysis of initial dilution;

❑ available process modifications which will reduce the quantities of pollutants which will be discharged;

❑ analysis of the location where pollutants are sought to be discharged, including the biological community and the physical description of the discharge facility; and

❑ an evaluation of available alternatives to the discharge of the pollutants including an evaluation of the possibility of land-based disposal or disposal in an approved ocean dumping site.

Section 404 Disposal Site Guidelines for Dredged or Fill Material

> *The purpose of Section 404(b)(1) Guidelines is to restore and maintain the chemical, physical, and biological integrity of waters of the United States through the control of discharges of dredged or fill material.*

14.1 Overview

Fundamental to these Guidelines is the precept that dredged or fill material should not be discharged into the aquatic ecosystem, unless it can be demonstrated that such a discharge will not have an unacceptable adverse impact either individually or in combination with known and/or probable impacts of other activities affecting the ecosystems of concern.

From a national perspective, the degradation or destruction of special aquatic sites, such as filling operations in wetlands, is considered among the most severe environmental impacts covered by these Guidelines. The principle should be that degradation or destruction of special sites may represent an irreversible loss of valuable aquatic resources.

14.2 Guidelines for Discharges of Dredged or Fill Material

These Guidelines have been developed by the Administrator of the Environmental Protection Agency in conjunction with the Secretary of the Army acting through the Chief of Engineers under section 404(b)(1) of the Clean Water Act (33 U.S.C. 1344). The Guidelines are applicable to the specification of disposal sites for discharges of dredged or fill material into waters of the United States. Sites may be specified through:

- ❏ the regulatory program of the U.S. Army Corps of Engineers under sections 404(a) and (e) of the Act (see 33 CFR Parts 320, 323 and 325);

- ❏ the civil works program of the U.S. Army Corps of Engineers (see 33 CFR 209.145 and section 150 of Pub. L. 94–587, Water Resources Development Act of 1976);

- ❏ permit programs of states approved by the Administrator of the Environmental Protection Agency in accordance with section 404(g) and (h) of the Act (see 40 CFR Parts 122, 123 and 124);

- ❏ statewide dredged or fill material regulatory programs with best management practices approved under section 208(b)(4)(B) and (C) of the Act (see 40 CFR 35.1560);

❑ federal construction projects which meet criteria specified in section 404(r) of the Act.

These Guidelines will be applied in the review of proposed discharges of dredged or fill material into navigable waters which lie inside the baseline from which the territorial sea is measured, and the discharge of fill material into the territorial sea, pursuant to the procedures referred to in paragraphs (a)(1) and (2) of this section of the CFRs. The discharge of dredged material into the territorial sea is governed by the Marine Protection, Research, and Sanctuaries Act of 1972, Pub. L. 92–532, and regulations and criteria issued pursuant thereto (40 CFR Parts 220 through 228).

Guidance on interpreting and implementing these Guidelines may be prepared jointly by EPA and the Corps at the national or regional level from time to time. No modifications to the basic application, meaning, or intent of these Guidelines will be made without rulemaking by the Administrator under the Administrative Procedure Act (5 U.S.C. 551 et seq.).

14.2.1 Section 404 Guidelines Organization

The Guidelines are divided into eight subparts:

❑ Subpart A presents those provisions of general applicability, such as purposes and definitions.

❑ Subpart B establishes the four conditions which must be satisfied in order to make a finding that a proposed discharge of dredged or fill material complies with the Guidelines. Section 230.11 of subpart B, sets forth factual determinations which are to be considered in determining whether or not a proposed discharge satisfies the subpart B conditions of compliance.

❑ Subpart C describes the physical and chemical components of a site and provides guidance about how proposed discharges of dredged or fill material may affect these components.

❑ Subparts D through F detail the special characteristics of particular aquatic ecosystems in terms of their values, and the possible loss of these values due to discharges of dredged or fill material.

❑ Subpart G prescribes a number of physical, chemical, and biological evaluations and testing procedures to be used in reaching the required factual determinations.

❑ Subpart H details the means to prevent or minimize adverse effects.

❑ Subpart I concerns advanced identification of disposal areas.

14.2.2 General Procedures

In evaluating whether a particular discharge site may be specified, the permitting authority should use these Guidelines in the following sequence:

☐ in order to obtain an overview of the principal regulatory provisions of the Guidelines, review the restrictions on discharge in 230.10(a) through (d), the measures to minimize adverse impact of subpart H, and the required factual determinations of 230.11; and

☐ determine if a general permit (230.7) is applicable, if so, the applicant needs merely to comply with its terms, and no further action by the permitting authority is necessary.

Special conditions for evaluation of proposed general permits are contained in 230.7. If the discharge is not covered by a general permit:

☐ examine practicable alternatives to the proposed discharge, that is, not discharging into the waters of the U.S. or discharging into an alternative aquatic site with potentially less damaging consequences (230.10(a));

☐ delineate the candidate disposal site consistent with the criteria and evaluations of 230.11(f);

☐ evaluate the various physical and chemical components which characterize the nonliving environment of the candidate site, the substrate and the water including its dynamic characteristics (subpart C);

☐ identify and evaluate any special or critical characteristics of the candidate disposal site, and surrounding areas which might be affected by use of such site, related to their living communities or human uses (subparts D, E, and F);

☐ review factual determinations in 230.11 to determine whether the information in the project file is sufficient to provide the documentation required by 230.11 or to perform the pretesting evaluation described in 230.60, or other information is necessary;

☐ evaluate the material to be discharged to determine the possibility of chemical contamination or physical incompatibility of the material to be discharged (230.60);

☐ if there is a reasonable probability of chemical contamination, conduct the appropriate tests according to the section on Evaluation and Testing (230.61);

☐ identify appropriate and practicable changes to the project plan to minimize the environmental impact of the discharge, based upon the specialized methods of minimization of impacts in subpart H;

☐ make and document factual determinations in 230.11; and

☐ make and document findings of compliance (230.12) by comparing factual determinations with the requirements for discharge of 230.10.

This outline of the steps to follow in using the Guidelines is simplified for purposes of illustration. The actual process followed may be iterative, with the results of one step leading to a reexamination of previous steps. The permitting authority must address all of the relevant provisions of the Guidelines in reaching a Finding of Compliance in an individual case.

14.3 Adaptability

The manner in which these Guidelines are used depends on the physical, biological, and chemical nature of the proposed extraction site, the material to be discharged, and the candidate disposal site, including any other important components of the ecosystem being evaluated. Documentation to demonstrate knowledge about the extraction site, materials to be extracted, and the candidate disposal site is an essential component of guideline application. These Guidelines allow evaluation and documentation for a variety of activities, ranging from those with large, complex impacts on the aquatic environment to those for which the impact is likely to be innocuous.

It is unlikely that the Guidelines will apply in their entirety to any one activity, no matter how complex. It is anticipated that substantial numbers of permit applications will be for minor, routine activities that have little, if any, potential for significant degradation of the aquatic environment. It generally is not intended or expected that extensive testing, evaluation or analysis will be needed to make findings of compliance in such routine cases. Where the conditions for general permits are met, and where numerous applications for similar activities are likely, the use of general permits will eliminate repetitive evaluation and documentation for individual discharges.

The Guidelines user, including the agency or agencies responsible for implementing the Guidelines, must recognize the different levels of effort that should be associated with varying degrees of impact and require or prepare commensurate documentation. The documentation should reflect the significance and complexity of the discharge activity.

An essential part of the evaluation process involves discovering the relevance of any portion(s) of the Guidelines and conducting further evaluation only as needed. However, where portions of the Guidelines review procedure are "short form" evaluations, there still must be sufficient information (including consideration of both individual and cumulative impacts) to support the decision of whether to specify the site for disposal of dredged or fill material and to support the decision to curtail or abbreviate the evaluation process. The presumption against the discharge in 230.1 applies to this decision making.

In the case of activities covered by general permits or section 208(b)(4)(B) and (C) Best Management Practices, the analysis and documentation required by the Guidelines will be performed at the time of general permit issuance or Best Management Practices promulgation and will not be repeated. These Guidelines do not require reporting or formal written communication at the time individual activities are initiated under a general permit or section 208(b)(4)(B) and (C) Best Management Practices. However, a particular general permit may require appropriate reporting.

14.4 General Permits

Conditions for the issuance of general permits. A general permit for a category of activities involving the discharge of dredged or fill material complies with the Guidelines if it meets the applicable restrictions on the discharge in 230.10 and if the permitting authority determines that the:

❏ activities in such category are similar in nature and similar in their impact upon water quality and the aquatic environment;

❏ activities in such category will have only minimal adverse effects when performed separately; and

❏ activities in such category will have only minimal cumulative adverse effects on water quality and the aquatic environment.

14.4.1 Evaluation process

To reach the determinations required in this section of the CFRs, the permitting authority shall set forth in writing an evaluation of the potential individual and cumulative impacts of the category of activities to be regulated under the general permit. While some information necessary for this evaluation can be obtained from potential permittees and others through the proposal of general permits for public review, the evaluation must be completed before any general permit is issued, and the results must be published with the final permit.

This evaluation shall be based upon consideration of the prohibitions and factors listed in 230.10(b-c), and shall include documented information supporting each factual determination in 230.11 of the Guidelines.

The evaluation shall include a precise description of the activities to be permitted under the General permit, explaining why they are sufficiently similar in nature and in environmental impact to warrant regulation under a single general permit based on subparts C through F of the Guidelines. Allowable differences between activities which will be regulated under the same general permit shall be specified. Activities otherwise similar in nature may differ in environmental impact due to their location in or near ecologically sensitive areas, areas with unique chemical or physical characteristics, areas containing concentrations of toxic substances, or areas regulated for specific human uses or by specific land or water management plans (e.g., areas regulated under an approved Coastal Zone Management Plan).

If there are specific geographic areas within the purview of a proposed general permit (called a draft general permit under a State 404 program), which are more appropriately regulated by individual permit due to the considerations cited in this paragraph, they shall be clearly delineated in the evaluation and excluded from the permit. In addition, the permitting authority may require an individual permit for any proposed activity under a general permit where the nature or location of the activity makes an individual permit more appropriate.

To predict cumulative effects, the evaluation shall include the number of individual discharge activities likely to be regulated under a general permit until its expiration, including repetitions of individual discharge activities at a single location.

14.5 Compliance With the Guidelines

14.5.1 Restrictions on Discharge

Other laws may apply to particular discharges and because the Corps of Engineers or State 404 agencies may have additional procedural and substantive requirements, a discharge complying with the requirement of these Guidelines will not automatically receive a permit. Although all requirements in 230.10 must be met, the compliance evaluation procedures will vary to reflect the seriousness of the potential for adverse impacts on the aquatic ecosystems posed by specific dredged or fill material discharge activities.

Except as provided under section 404(b)(2), no discharge of dredged or fill material shall be permitted if there is a practicable alternative to the proposed discharge which would have less adverse impact on the aquatic ecosystem, so long as the alternative does not have other significant adverse environmental consequences. For the purpose of this requirement, practicable alternatives include, but are not limited to:

- ☐ activities which do not involve a discharge of dredged or fill material into the waters of the United States or ocean waters; and

- ☐ discharges of dredged or fill material at other locations in waters of the United States or ocean waters.

An alternative is practicable if it is available and capable of being done after taking into consideration cost, existing technology, and logistics in light of overall project purposes. If it is otherwise a practicable alternative, an area not presently owned by the applicant which could reasonably be obtained, utilized, expanded or managed in order to fulfill the basic purpose of the proposed activity may be considered.

Where the activity associated with a discharge which is proposed for a special aquatic site (as defined in subpart E) does not require access or proximity to or siting within the special aquatic site in question to fulfill its basic purpose (i.e., is not "water dependent"), practicable alternatives that do not involve special aquatic sites are presumed to be available, unless clearly demonstrated otherwise. In addition, where a discharge is proposed for a special aquatic site, all practicable alternatives to the proposed discharge which do not involve a discharge into a special aquatic site are presumed to have less adverse impact on the aquatic ecosystem, unless clearly demonstrated otherwise.

For actions subject to NEPA, where the Corps of Engineers is the permitting agency, the analysis of alternatives required for NEPA environmental documents, including supplemental Corps NEPA documents, will usually provide the information for the evaluation of alternatives under these Guidelines. On occasion, these NEPA documents may address a broader range of alternatives than required to be considered under this paragraph or may not have considered the alternatives in sufficient detail to respond to the requirements of these Guidelines. In the latter case, supplementing these NEPA documents with this additional information may be necessary.

To the extent that practicable alternatives have been identified and evaluated under a Coastal Zone Management program, a section 208 program, or other planning process, such evaluation shall be considered by the permitting authority as part of the consideration of alternatives under the Guidelines. Where such evaluation is less comprehensive than that contemplated under this subsection, it must be supplemented accordingly.

No discharge of dredged or fill material shall be permitted if it:

- ☐ causes or contributes, after consideration of disposal site dilution and dispersion, to violations of any applicable state water quality standard;

- ☐ violates any applicable toxic effluent standard or prohibition under section 307 of the Act;

- ☐ jeopardizes the continued existence of species listed as endangered or threatened under the Endangered Species Act of 1973, as amended, or results in likelihood of the destruction or adverse modification of a habitat which is determined by the Secretary of Interior or Commerce, as appropriate, to be a critical habitat under the Endangered Species Act of 1973, as amended. If an exemption has been granted by the Endangered Species Committee, the terms of such exemption shall apply instead of this subparagraph; or

- ☐ volates any requirement imposed by the Secretary of Commerce to protect any marine sanctuary designated under title III of the Marine Protection, Research, and Sanctuaries Act of 1972.

Except as provided under section 404(b)(2), no discharge of dredged or fill material shall be permitted which will cause or contribute to significant degradation of the waters of the United States. Findings of significant degradation related to the proposed discharge shall be based upon appropriate factual determinations, evaluations, and tests required by subparts B and G, after consideration of subparts C through F, with special emphasis on the persistence and permanence of the effects outlined in those subparts. Under these Guidelines, effects contributing to significant degradation considered individually or collectively, include:

- ☐ significantly adverse effects of the discharge of pollutants on human health or welfare, including but not limited to effects on municipal water supplies, plankton, fish, shellfish, wildlife, and special aquatic sites.

- ☐ significantly adverse effects of the discharge of pollutants on life stages of aquatic life and other wildlife dependent on aquatic ecosystems, including the transfer, concentration, and spread of pollutants or their byproducts outside of the disposal site through biological, physical, and chemical processes;

- ☐ significantly adverse effects of the discharge of pollutants on aquatic ecosystem diversity, productivity, and stability. Such effects may include, but are not limited to, losses of fish and wildlife habitat or loss of the capacity of a wetland to assimilate nutrients, purify water, or reduce wave energy; or

- ☐ significantly adverse effects of discharge of pollutants on recreational, aesthetic, and economic values.

Except as provided under section 404(b)(2), no discharge of dredged or fill material shall be permitted unless appropriate and practicable steps have been taken which will minimize potential adverse impacts of the discharge on the aquatic ecosystem. Subpart H identifies such possible steps.

14.5.2 Factual Determinations

The permitting authority shall determine in writing the potential short-term or long-term effects of a proposed discharge of dredged or fill material on the physical, chemical, and biological components of the aquatic environment in light of subparts C through F. Such factual determinations shall be used in 230.12 in making findings of compliance or noncompliance with the restrictions on discharge in 230.10. The evaluation and testing procedures described in 230.60 and 230.61 of subpart G shall be used as necessary to make, and shall be described in, such determination. The determinations of effects of each proposed discharge shall include the following:

14.5.2.1 Physical Substrate Determinations

Determine the nature and degree of effect that the proposed discharge will have, individually and cumulatively, on the characteristics of the substrate at the proposed disposal site. Consideration shall be given to the similarity in particle size, shape, and degree of compaction of the material proposed for discharge and the material constituting the substrate at the disposal site, and any potential changes in substrate elevation and bottom contours, including changes outside the disposal site which may occur as a result of erosion, slumpage, or other movement of the discharged material. The duration and physical extent of substrate changes shall also be considered. The possible loss of environmental values (230.20) and actions to minimize impact (subpart H) shall also be considered in making these determinations. Potential changes in substrate elevation and bottom contours shall be predicted on the basis of the proposed method, volume, location, and rate of discharge, as well as on the individual and combined effects of current patterns, water circulation, wind and wave action, and other physical factors that may affect the movement of the discharged material.

14.5.2.2 Water Circulation, Fluctuation, and Salinity Determinations

Determine the nature and degree of effect that the proposed discharge will have individually and cumulatively on water, current patterns, circulation including downstream flows, and normal water fluctuation. Consideration shall be given to water chemistry, salinity, clarity, color, odor, taste, dissolved gas levels, temperature, nutrients, and eutrophication plus other appropriate characteristics. Consideration shall also be given to the potential diversion or obstruction of flow, alterations of bottom contours, or other significant changes in the hydrologic regime. Additional consideration of the possible loss of environmental values (230.23 through 230.25) and actions to minimize impacts (subpart H), shall be used in making these determinations. Potential significant effects on the current patterns, water circulation, normal water fluctuation and salinity shall be evaluated on the basis of the proposed method, volume, location, and rate of discharge.

14.5.2.3 Suspended Particulate/Turbidity Determinations

Determine the nature and degree of effect that the proposed discharge will have, individually and cumulatively, in terms of potential changes in the kinds and concentrations of suspended particulate/turbidity in the vicinity of the disposal site. Consideration shall be given to the grain size of the material proposed for discharge, the shape and size of the plume of suspended particulates, the duration of the discharge and resulting plume and whether or not the potential changes will cause violations of applicable water quality standards. Consideration should also be given to the possible loss of environmental values (230.21) and to actions for minimizing impacts (subpart H). Consideration shall include the proposed method, volume, location, and rate of discharge, as well as the individual and combined effects of current patterns, water circulation and fluctuations, wind and wave action, and other physical factors on the movement of suspended particulates.

14.5.2.4 Contaminant Determinations

Determine the degree to which the material proposed for discharge will introduce, relocate, or increase contaminants. This determination shall consider the material to be discharged, the aquatic environment at the proposed disposal site, and the availability of contaminants.

14.5.2.5 Aquatic Ecosystem and Organism Determinations

Determine the nature and degree of effect that the proposed discharge will have, both individually and cumulatively, on the structure and function of the aquatic ecosystem and organisms. Consideration shall be given to the effect at the proposed disposal site of potential changes in substrate characteristics and elevation, water or substrate chemistry, nutrients, currents, circulation, fluctuation, and salinity, on the recolonization and existence of indigenous aquatic organisms or communities. Possible loss of environmental values (230.31), and actions to minimize impacts (subpart H) shall be examined. Tests as described in 230.61 (Evaluation and Testing), may be required to provide information on the effect of the discharge material on communities or populations of organisms expected to be exposed to it.

14.5.2.6 Proposed Disposal Site Determinations

Each disposal site shall be specified through the application of these Guidelines. The mixing zone shall be confined to the smallest practicable zone within each specified disposal site that is consistent with the type of dispersion determined to be appropriate by the application of these Guidelines. In a few special cases under unique environmental conditions, where there is adequate justification to show that widespread dispersion by natural means will result in no significantly adverse environmental effects, the discharged material may be intended to be spread naturally in a very thin layer over a large area of the substrate rather than be contained within the disposal site.

The permitting authority and the Regional Administrator shall consider the following factors in determining the acceptability of a proposed mixing zone:

- ❏ depth of water at the disposal site;

- ❏ current velocity, direction, and variability at the disposal site;

- ❏ degree of turbulence;

- ❏ stratification attributable to causes such as obstructions, salinity or density profiles at the disposal site;

- ❏ discharge vessel speed and direction, if appropriate;

- ❏ rate of discharge;

- ❏ ambient concentration of constituents of interest;

- ❏ dredged material characteristics, particularly concentrations of constituents, amount of material, type of material (sand, silt, clay, etc.) and settling velocities;

- ❏ number of discharge actions per unit of time;

- ❏ other factors of the disposal site that affect the rates and patterns of mixing.

14.6 Aquatic Ecosystems

Cumulative impacts are the changes in an aquatic ecosystem that are attributable to the collective effect of a number of individual discharges of dredged or fill material. Although the impact of a particular discharge may constitute a minor change in itself, the cumulative effect of many such piecemeal changes can result in a major impairment of the water resources and interfere with the productivity and water quality of existing aquatic ecosystems.

Cumulative effects attributable to the discharge of dredged or fill material in waters of the United States should be predicted to the extent reasonable and practical. The permitting authority shall collect information and solicit information from other sources about the cumulative impacts on the aquatic ecosystem. This information shall be documented and considered during the decision–making process concerning the evaluation of individual permit applications, the issuance of a general permit, and monitoring and enforcement of existing permits.

14.6.1 Determination of Secondary Effects on the Aquatic Ecosystem

Secondary effects are effects on an aquatic ecosystem associated with a discharge of dredged or fill materials, but do not result from the actual placement of the dredged or fill material. Information about secondary effects on aquatic ecosystems shall be considered prior to the time final section 404 action is taken by permitting authorities.

Some examples of secondary effects on an aquatic ecosystem are fluctuating water levels in an impoundment and downstream associated with the operation of a dam, septic tank leaching and surface runoff from residential or commercial developments on fill, and leachate and runoff from a sanitary landfill located in waters of the U.S. activities to be conducted on fast land created by the discharge of dredged or fill material in waters of the United States may have secondary impacts within those waters which should be considered in evaluating the impact of creating those fast lands.

14.6.2 Findings of Compliance or Noncompliance

On the basis of these Guidelines (subparts C through G) the proposed disposal sites for the discharge of dredged or fill material must be specified:

- ❑ as complying with the requirements of these Guidelines; or
- ❑ as complying with the requirements of these Guidelines with the inclusion of appropriate and practicable discharge conditions (see subpart H) to minimize pollution or adverse effects to the affected aquatic ecosystems; or
- ❑ as failing to comply with the requirements of these Guidelines.

This failure to comply is determined where:

- ❑ there is a practicable alternative to the proposed discharge that would have less adverse effect on the aquatic ecosystem, so long as such alternative does not have other significant adverse environmental consequences; or
- ❑ the proposed discharge will result in significant degradation of the aquatic ecosystem under 230.10(b) or (c); or
- ❑ the proposed discharge does not include all appropriate and practicable measures to minimize potential harm to the aquatic ecosystem; or
- ❑ there does not exist sufficient information to make a reasonable judgment about whether the proposed discharge will comply with these Guidelines.

Findings under this section shall be set forth in writing by the permitting authority for each proposed discharge and made available to the permit applicant. These findings shall include the factual determinations required by 230.11, and a brief explanation of any adaptation of these Guidelines to the activity under consideration. In the case of a general permit, such findings shall be prepared at the time of issuance of that permit rather than for each subsequent discharge under the authority of that permit.

14.7 Potential Impacts on Physical and Chemical Characteristics of the Aquatic Ecosystem

The effects described in this subpart should be considered in making the factual determinations and the findings of compliance or noncompliance in subpart B.

14.7.1 Substrate

The substrate of the aquatic ecosystem underlies open waters of the United States and constitutes the surface of wetlands. It consists of organic and inorganic solid materials and includes water and other liquids or gases that fill the spaces between solid particles.

❏ Possible loss of environmental characteristics and values

The discharge of dredged or fill material can result in varying degrees of change in the complex physical, chemical, and biological characteristics of the substrate. Discharges which alter substrate elevation or contours can result in changes in water circulation, depth, current pattern, water fluctuation and water temperature. Discharges may adversely affect bottom dwelling organisms at the site by smothering immobile forms or forcing mobile forms to migrate. Benthic forms present prior to a discharge are unlikely to recolonize on the discharged material if it is very dissimilar from that of the discharge site. Erosion, slumping, or lateral displacement of surrounding bottom of such deposits can adversely affect areas of the substrate outside the perimeters of the disposal site by changing or destroying habitat. The bulk and composition of the discharged material and the location, method, and timing of discharges may all influence the degree of impact on the substrate.

14.7.2 Suspended Particulates/Turbidity

Suspended particulates in the aquatic ecosystem consist of fine grained mineral particles, usually smaller than silt, and organic particles. Suspended particulates may enter water bodies as a result of land runoff, flooding, vegetative and planktonic breakdowns, resuspension of bottom sediments, and man's activities including dredging and filling. Particulates may remain suspended in the water column for variable periods of time as a result of such factors as agitation of the water mass, particulate specific gravity, particle shape, and physical and chemical properties of particle surfaces.

❏ Possible loss of environmental characteristics and values

The discharge of dredged or fill material can result in greatly elevated levels of suspended particulates in the water column for varying lengths of time. These new levels may reduce light penetration and lower the rate of photosynthesis and the primary productivity of an aquatic area if they last long enough. Sight dependent species may suffer reduced feeding ability leading to limited growth and lowered resistance to disease if high levels of suspended particulates persist. The biological and the chemical content of the suspended material may react with the dissolved oxygen in the water, which can result in oxygen depletion. Toxic metals and organics, pathogens, and viruses absorbed or adsorbed to fine grained particulates in the material may become biologically available to organisms either in the water column or on the substrate. Significant increases in suspended particulate levels create turbid plumes which are highly visible and aesthetically displeasing. The extent and persistence of these adverse impacts caused by discharges depend upon the relative increase in suspended particulates above the amount occurring naturally, the duration of the higher levels, the current patterns, water level, and fluctuations present when such discharges occur, the volume, rate, and duration of the discharge, particulate deposition, and the seasonal timing of the discharge.

14.7.3 Water

Water is the part of the aquatic ecosystem in which organic and inorganic constituents are dissolved and suspended. It constitutes part of the liquid phase and is contained by the substrate. Water forms part of a dynamic aquatic life supporting system. Water clarity, nutrients and chemical content, physical and biological content, dissolved gas levels, pH, and temperature contribute to its life sustaining capabilities.

 ❑ Possible loss of environmental characteristics and values

The discharge of dredged or fill material can change the chemistry and the physical characteristics of the receiving water at a disposal site through the introduction of chemical constituents in suspended or dissolved form. Changes in the clarity, color, odor, and taste of water and the addition of contaminants can reduce or eliminate the suitability of water bodies for populations of aquatic organisms, and for human consumption, recreation, and aesthetics. The introduction of nutrients or organic material to the water column as a result of the discharge can lead to a high biochemical oxygen demand (BOD), which in turn can lead to reduced dissolved oxygen, thereby potentially affecting the survival of many aquatic organisms. Increases in nutrients can favor one group of organisms such as algae to the detriment of other more desirable types such as submerged aquatic vegetation, potentially causing adverse health effects, objectionable tastes and odors, and other problems.

14.7.4 Current Patterns and Water Circulation

Current patterns and water circulation are the physical movements of water in the aquatic ecosystem. Currents and circulation respond to natural forces as modified by basin shape and cover, physical and chemical characteristics of water strata and masses, and energy dissipating factors.

 ❑ Possible loss of environmental characteristics and values

The discharge of dredged or fill material can modify current patterns and water circulation by obstructing flow, changing the direction or velocity of water flow, changing the direction or velocity of water flow and circulation, or otherwise changing the dimensions of a water body. As a result, adverse changes can occur in: Location, structure, and dynamics of aquatic communities; shoreline and substrate erosion and depositon rates; the deposition of suspended particulates; the rate and extent of mixing of dissolved and suspended components of the water body; and water stratification.

14.7.5 Normal Water Fluctuations

Normal water fluctuations in a natural aquatic system consist of daily, seasonal, and annual tidal and flood fluctuations in water level. Biological and physical components of such a system are either attuned to or characterized by these periodic water fluctuations.

❏ Possible loss of environmental characteristics and values

The discharge of dredged or fill material can alter the normal water level fluctuation pattern of an area, resulting in prolonged periods of inundation, exaggerated extremes of high and low water, or a static, nonfluctuating water level. Such water level modifications may change salinity patterns, alter erosion or sedimentation rates, aggravate water temperature extremes, and upset the nutrient and dissolved oxygen balance of the aquatic ecosystem. In addition, these modifications can alter or destroy communities and populations of aquatic animals and vegetation, induce populations of nuisance organisms, modify habitat, reduce food supplies, restrict movement of aquatic fauna, destroy spawning areas, and change adjacent, upstream, and downstream areas.

14.7.6 Salinity Gradients

Salinity gradients form where salt water from the ocean meets and mixes with fresh water from land.

❏ Possible loss of environmental characteristics and values

Obstructions which divert or restrict flow of either fresh or salt water may change existing salinity gradients. For example, partial blocking of the entrance to an estuary or river mouth that significantly restricts the movement of the salt water into and out of that area can effectively lower the volume of salt water available for mixing within that estuary. The downstream migration of the salinity gradient can occur, displacing the maximum sedimentation zone and requiring salinity dependent aquatic biota to adjust to the new conditions, move to new locations if possible, or perish. In the freshwater zone, discharge operations in the upstream regions can have equally adverse impacts. A significant reduction in the volume of fresh water moving into an estuary below that which is considered normal can affect the location and type of mixing thereby changing the characteristic salinity patterns. The resulting changed circulation pattern can cause the upstream migration of the salinity gradient displacing the maximum sedimentation zone. This migration may affect those organisms that are adapted to freshwater environments. It may also affect municipal water supplies.

Note: Possible actions to minimize adverse impacts regarding site characteristics can be found in subpart H.

14.8 Potential Impacts on Biological Characteristics of the Aquatic Ecosystem

The impacts described in this subpart should be considered in making the factual determinations and the findings of compliance or noncompliance in subpart B.

❏ Possible loss of threatened and endangered species

An endangered species is a plant or animal in danger of extinction throughout all or a significant portion of its range. A threatened species is one in danger of becoming an endangered species in the foreseeable future throughout all or a significant portion of its range. Listings of threatened and endangered species as well as critical habitats are maintained by some individual states and by the U.S. Fish and Wildlife Service of the Department of the Interior (codified annually at 50 CFR 17.11). The Department of Commerce has authority over some threatened and endangered marine mammals, fishes and reptiles.

The major potential impacts on threatened or endangered species from the discharge of dredged or fill material include:

❑ covering or otherwise directly killing species; and

❑ the impairment or destruction of habitat to which these species are limited.

Elements of the aquatic habitat which are particularly crucial to the continued survival of some threatened or endangered species include adequate good quality water, spawning and maturation areas, nesting areas, protective cover, adequate and reliable food supply, and resting areas for migratory species.

Each of these elements can be adversely affected by changes in either the normal water conditions for clarity, chemical content, nutrient balance, dissolved oxygen, pH, temperature, salinity, current patterns, circulation and fluctuation, or the physical removal of habitat, and facilitating incompatible activities.

Where consultation with the Secretary of the Interior occurs under section 7 of the Endangered Species Act, the conclusions of the Secretary concerning the impact(s) of the discharge on threatened and endangered species and their habitat shall be considered final.

❑ Possible loss of Fish, crustaceans, mollusks, and other aquatic organisms in the food web

Aquatic organisms in the food web include, but are not limited to, finfish, crustaceans, mollusks, insects, annelids, planktonic organisms, and the plants and animals on which they feed and depend upon for their needs. All forms and life stages of an organism, throughout its geographic range, are included in this category.

The discharge of dredged or fill material can variously affect populations of fish, crustaceans, mollusks and other food web organisms through the release of contaminants which adversely affect adults, juveniles, larvae, or eggs, or result in the establishment or proliferation of an undesirable competitive species of plant or animal at the expense of the desired resident species. Suspended particulates settling on attached or buried eggs can smother the eggs by limiting or sealing off their exposure to oxygenated water. Discharge of dredged and fill material may result in the debilitation or death of sedentary organisms by smothering, exposure to chemical contaminants in dissolved or suspended form, exposure to high levels of suspended particulates, reduction in food supply, or alteration of the substrate upon which they are dependent. Mollusks are particularly sensitive to the discharge of material during periods of reproduction and growth and development due primarily to their limited mobility. They can be rendered unfit for human consumption by tainting, by production and accumulation of toxins, or by ingestion and retention of pathogenic organisms, viruses, heavy metals or persistent synthetic organic chemicals.

The discharge of dredged or fill material can redirect, delay, or stop the reproductive and feeding movements of some species of fish and crustacea, thus preventing their aggregation in accustomed places such as spawning or nursery grounds and potentially leading to reduced populations. Reduction of detrital feeding species or other representatives of lower trophic levels can impair the flow of energy from primary consumers to higher trophic levels. The reduction or potential elimination of food chain organism populations decreases the overall productivity and nutrient export capability of the ecosystem.

❑ Possible loss of other wildlife

Wildlife associated with aquatic ecosystems are resident and transient mammals, birds, reptiles, and amphibians.

The discharge of dredged or fill material can result in the loss or change of breeding and nesting areas, escape cover, travel corridors, and preferred food sources for resident and transient wildlife species associated with the aquatic ecosystem. These adverse impacts upon wildlife habitats may result from changes in water levels, water flow and circulation, salinity, chemical content, and substrate characteristics and elevation. Increased water turbidity can adversely affect wildlife species which rely upon sight to feed, and disrupt the respiration and feeding of certain aquatic wildlife and food chain organisms. The availability of contaminants from the discharge of dredged or fill material may lead to the bioaccumulation of such contaminants in wildlife. Changes in such physical and chemical factors of the environment may favor the introduction of undesirable plant and animal species at the expense of resident species and communities. In some aquatic environments lowering plant and animal species diversity may disrupt the normal functions of the ecosystem and lead to reductions in overall biological productivity.

Note: Possible actions to minimize adverse impacts regarding characteristics of biological components of the aquatic ecosystem can be found in subpart H.

14.9 Potential Impacts on Special Aquatic Sites

❑ Possible loss of sanctuaries and refuges

Sanctuaries and refuges consist of areas designated under state and federal laws or local ordinances to be managed principally for the preservation and use of fish and wildlife resources. Sanctuaries and refuges may be affected by discharges of dredged or fill material which will:

❑ disrupt the breeding, spawning, migratory movements or other critical life requirements of resident or transient fish and wildlife resources;

❑ create unplanned, easy and incompatible human access to remote aquatic areas;

❑ create the need for frequent maintenance activity;

❑ result in the establishment of undesirable competitive species of plants and animals;

❑ change the balance of water and land areas needed to provide cover, food, and other fish and wildlife habitat requirements in a way that modifies sanctuary or refuge management practices; and/or

❑ result in any of the other adverse impacts discussed in subparts C and D as they relate to a particular sanctuary or refuge.

14.9.1 Wetlands

Wetlands consist of areas inundated or saturated by surface or ground water at a frequency and duration sufficient to support, and that under normal circumstances do support, a prevalence of vegetation typically adapted for life in saturated soil conditions.

Where wetlands are adjacent to open water, they generally constitute the transition to upland. The margin between wetland and open water can best be established by specialists familiar with the local environment, particularly where emergent vegetation merges with submerged vegetation over a broad area in such places as the lateral margins of open water, headwaters, rainwater catch basins, and groundwater seeps. The landward margin of wetlands also can best be identified by specialists familiar with the local environment when vegetation from the two regions merges over a broad area.

Wetland vegetation consists of plants that require saturated soils to survive (obligate wetland plants) as well as plants, including certain trees, that gain a competitive advantage over others because they can tolerate prolonged wet soil conditions and their competitors cannot. In addition to plant populations and communities, wetlands are delimited by hydrological and physical characteristics of the environment. These characteristics should be considered when information about them is needed to supplement information available about vegetation, or where wetland vegetation has been removed or is dormant.

❑ Possible loss of wetlands

The discharge of dredged or fill material in wetlands is likely to damage or destroy habitat and adversely affect the biological productivity of wetlands ecosystems by smothering, by dewatering, by permanently flooding, or by altering substrate elevation or periodicity of water movement. The addition of dredged or fill material may destroy wetland vegetation or result in advancement of succession to dry land species. It may reduce or eliminate nutrient exchange by a reduction of the system's productivity, or by altering current patterns and velocities. Disruption or elimination of the wetland system can degrade water quality by obstructing circulation patterns that flush large expanses of wetland systems, by interfering with the filtration function of wetlands, or by changing the aquifer recharge capability of a wetland. Discharges can also change the wetland habitat value for fish and wildlife as discussed in subpart D. When disruptions in flow and circulation patterns occur, apparently minor loss of wetland acreage may result in major losses through secondary impacts. Discharging fill material in wetlands as part of municipal, industrial or recreational development may modify the capacity of wetlands to retain and store floodwaters and to serve as a buffer zone shielding upland areas from wave actions, storm damage and erosion.

❑ Possible loss of mud flats

Mud flats are broad flat areas along the sea coast and in coastal rivers to the head of tidal influence and in inland lakes, ponds, and riverine systems. When mud flats are inundated, wind and wave action may resuspend bottom sediments. Coastal mud flats are exposed at extremely low tides and inundated at high tides with the water table at or near the surface of the substrate. The substrate of mud flats contains organic material and particles smaller than sand. They are either unvegetated or vegetated only by algal mats.

The discharge of dredged or fill material can cause changes in water circulation patterns which may permanently flood or dewater the mud flat or disrupt periodic inundation, resulting in an increase in the rate of erosion or accretion. Such changes can deplete or eliminate mud flat biota, foraging areas, and nursery areas. Changes in inundation patterns can affect the chemical and biological exchange and decomposition process occurring on the mud flat and change the deposition of suspended material affecting the productivity of the area. Changes may reduce the mud flat's capacity to dissipate storm surge runoff.

❑ Possible loss of vegetated shallows

Vegetated shallows are permanently inundated areas that under normal circumstances support communities of rooted aquatic vegetation, such as turtle grass and eelgrass in estuarine or marine systems as well as a number of freshwater species in rivers and lakes.

The discharge of dredged or fill material can smother vegetation and benthic organisms. It may also create unsuitable conditions for their continued vigor by:

❑ changing water circulation patterns;

❑ releasing nutrients that increase undesirable algal populations;

❑ releasing chemicals that adversely affect plants and animals;

❑ increasing turbidity levels, thereby reducing light penetration and hence photosynthesis; and

❑ changing the capacity of a vegetated shallow to stabilize bottom materials and decrease channel shoaling.

The discharge of dredged or fill material may reduce the value of vegetated shallows as nesting, spawning, nursery, cover, and forage areas, as well as their value in protecting shorelines from erosion and wave actions. It may also encourage the growth of nuisance vegetation.

❑ Possible loss of coral reefs

Coral reefs consist of the skeletal deposit, usually of calcareous or silicaceous materials, produced by the vital activities of anthozoan polyps or other invertebrate organisms present in growing portions of the reef.

The discharge of dredged or fill material can adversely affect colonies of reef building organisms by burying them, by releasing contaminants such as hydrocarbons into the water column, by reducing light penetration through the water, and by increasing the level of suspended particulates. Coral organisms are extremely sensitive to even slight reductions in light penetration or increases in suspended particulates. These adverse effects will cause a loss of productive colonies which in turn provide habitat for many species of highly specialized aquatic organisms.

❏ Possible loss of riffle and pool complexes

Steep gradient sections of streams are sometimes characterized by riffle and pool complexes. Such stream sections are recognizable by their hydraulic characteristics. The rapid movement of water over a coarse substrate in riffles results in a rough flow, a turbulent surface, and high dissolved oxygen levels in the water. Pools are deeper areas associated with riffles. Pools are characterized by a slower stream velocity, a steaming flow, a smooth surface, and a finer substrate. Riffle and pool complexes are particularly valuable-habitat for fish and wildlife.

Discharge of dredged or fill material can eliminate riffle and pool areas by displacement, hydrologic modification, or sedimentation. Activities which affect riffle and pool areas and especially riffle/pool ratios, may reduce the aeration and filtration capabilities at the discharge site and downstream, may reduce stream habitat diversity, and may retard repopulation of the disposal site and downstream waters through sedimentation and the creation of unsuitable habitats. The discharge of dredged or fill material which alters stream hydrology may cause scouring or sedimentation of riffles and pools. Sedimentation induced through hydrological modification or as a direct result of the deposition of unconsolidated dredged or fill material may clog riffle and pool areas, destroy habitats, and create anaerobic conditions. Eliminating pools and meanders by the discharge of dredged or fill material can reduce water holding capacity of streams and cause rapid runoff from a watershed. Rapid runoff can deliver large quantities of flood water in a short time to downstream areas resulting in the destruction of natural habitat, high property loss, and the need for further hydraulic modification.

Note: Possible actions to minimize adverse impacts on site or material characteristics can be found in subpart H.

14.10 Potential Effects on Human Use Characteristics

❏ Possible loss of municipal and private water supplies

Municipal and private water supplies consist of surface water or ground water which is directed to the intake of a municipal or private water supply system.

Discharges can affect the quality of water supplies with respect to color, taste, odor, chemical content and suspended particulate concentration, in a way that reduces the fitness of the water for consumption. Water can be rendered unpalatable or unhealthy by the addition of suspended particulates, viruses and pathogenic organisms, and dissolved materials. The expense of removing such substances before the water is delivered for consumption can be high. Discharges may also affect the quantity of water available for municipal and private water supplies. In addition, certain commonly used water treatment chemicals have the potential for combining with some suspended or dissolved substances from dredged or fill material to form other products that can have a toxic effect on consumers.

❑ Possible loss of recreational and commercial fisheries

Recreational and commercial fisheries consist of harvestable fish, crustaceans, shellfish, and other aquatic organisms used by man.

The discharge of dredged or fill materials can affect the suitability of recreational and commercial fishing grounds as habitat for populations of consumable aquatic organisms. Discharges can result in the chemical contamination of recreational or commercial fisheries. They may also interfere with the reproductive success of recreational and commercially important aquatic species through disruption of migration and spawning areas. The introduction of pollutants at critical times in their life cycle may directly reduce populations of commercially important aquatic organisms or indirectly reduce them by reducing organisms upon which they depend for food. Any of these impacts can be of short duration or prolonged, depending upon the physical and chemical impacts of the discharge and the biological availability of contaminants to aquatic organisms.

❑ Possible loss of water related recreation

Water related recreation encompasses activities undertaken for amusement and relaxation. Activities encompass two broad categories of use: consumptive, e.g., harvesting resources by hunting and fishing; and non-consumptive, e.g., canoeing and sightseeing.

One of the more important direct impacts of dredged or fill disposal is to impair or destroy the resources which support recreation activities. The disposal of dredged or fill material may adversely modify or destroy water use for recreation by changing turbidity, suspended particulates, temperature, dissolved oxygen, dissolved materials, toxic materials, pathogenic organisms, quality of habitat, and the aesthetic qualities of sight, taste, odor, and color.

❑ Possible loss of aesthetic values

Aesthetics associated with the aquatic ecosystem consist of the perception of beauty by one or a combination of the senses of sight, hearing, touch, and smell. Aesthetics of aquatic ecosystems apply to the quality of life enjoyed by the general public and property owners.

The discharge of dredged or fill material can mar the beauty of natural aquatic ecosystems by degrading water quality, creating distracting disposal sites, inducing inappropriate development, encouraging unplanned and incompatible human access, and by destroying vital elements that contribute to the compositional harmony or unity, visual distinctiveness, or diversity of an area. The discharge of dredged or fill material can adversely affect the particular features, traits, or characteristics of an aquatic area which make it valuable to property owners. Activities which degrade water quality, disrupt natural substrate and vegetational characteristics, deny access to or visibility of the resource, or result in changes in odor, air quality, or noise levels may reduce the value of an aquatic area to private property owners.

☐ Possible loss of parks, national and historical monuments, national seashores, wilderness areas, research sites, and similar preserves

These preserves consist of areas designated under federal and state laws or local ordinances to be managed for their aesthetic, educational, historical, recreational, or scientific value.

The discharge of dredged or fill material into such areas may modify the aesthetic, educational, historical, recreational and/or scientific qualities thereby reducing or eliminating the uses for which such sites are set aside and managed.

Note: Possible actions to minimize adverse impacts regarding site or material characteristics can be found in subpart H.

14.11 General Evaluation of Dredged or Fill Material

The purpose of these evaluation procedures and the chemical and biological testing sequence outlined in 230.61 is to provide information to reach the determinations required by 230.11. Where the results of prior evaluations, chemical and biological tests, scientific research, and experience can provide information helpful in making a determination, these should be used. Such prior results may make new testing unnecessary. The information used shall be documented. Where the same information applies to more than one determination, it may be documented once and referenced in later determinations.

If the evaluation under this section indicates the dredged or fill material is not a carrier of contaminants, then the required determinations pertaining to the presence and effects of contaminants can be made without testing. Dredged or fill material is most likely to be free from chemical, biological, or other pollutants when it is composed primarily of sand, gravel, or other naturally occurring inert material. Dredged material so composed is generally found in areas of high current or wave energy such as streams with large bed loads or coastal areas with shifting bars and channels. However, when such material is discolored or contains other indications that contaminants may be present, further inquiry should be made.

The extraction site shall be examined in order to assess whether it is sufficiently removed from sources of pollution to provide reasonable assurance that the proposed discharge material is not a carrier of contaminants. Factors to be considered include, but are not limited to:

☐ potential routes of contaminants or contaminated sediments to the extraction site, based on hydrographic or other maps, aerial photography, or other materials that show watercourses, surface relief, proximity to tidal movement, private and public roads, location of buildings, municipal and industrial areas, and agricultural or forest lands;

❏ pertinent results from tests previously carried out on the material at the extraction site, or carried out on similar material for other permitted projects in the vicinity. Materials shall be considered similar if the sources of contamination, the physical configuration of the sites and the sediment composition of the materials are comparable, in light of water circulation and stratification, sediment accumulation and general sediment characteristics;

❏ any potential for significant introduction of persistent pesticides from land runoff or percolation;

❏ any records of spills or disposal of petroleum products or substances designated as hazardous under section 311 of the Clean Water Act (See 40 CFR Part 116);

❏ information in federal, state and local records indicating significant introduction of pollutants from industries, municipalities, or other sources, including types and amounts of waste materials discharged along the potential routes of contaminants to the extraction site; and

❏ any possibility of the presence of substantial natural deposits of minerals or other substances which could be released to the aquatic environment in harmful quantities by man induced discharge activities.

To reach the determinations in 230.11 involving potential effects of the discharge on the characteristics of the disposal site, the narrative guidance in subparts C through F shall be used along with the general evaluation procedure in 230.60 and, if necessary, the chemical and biological testing sequence in 230.61. Where the discharge site is adjacent to the extraction site and subject to the same sources of contaminants, and materials at the two sites are substantially similar, the fact that the material to be discharged may be a carrier of contaminants is not likely to result in degradation of the disposal site. In such circumstances, when dissolved material and suspended particulates can be controlled to prevent carrying pollutants to less contaminated areas, testing will not be required.

Even if the 230.60(b) evaluation (previous tests, the presence of polluting industries and information about their discharge or runoff into waters of the U.S., bioinventories, etc.) leads to the conclusion that there is a high probability that the material proposed for discharge is a carrier of contaminants, testing may not be necessary if constraints are available to reduce contamination to acceptable levels within the disposal site and to prevent contaminants from being transported beyond the boundaries of the disposal site, if such constraints are acceptable to the permitting authority and the Regional Administrator, and if the potential discharger is willing and able to implement such constraints. However, even if tests are not performed, the permitting authority must still determine the probable impact of the operation on the receiving aquatic ecosystem. Any decision not to test must be explained in the determinations made under 230.11.

14.12 Chemical, Biological, and Physical Evaluation and Testing

No single test or approach can be applied in all cases to evaluate the effects of proposed discharges of dredged or fill materials. This section provides some guidance in determining which test and/or evaluation procedures are appropriate in a given case. Interim guidance to applicants concerning the applicability of specific approaches or procedures will be furnished by the permitting authority.

The principal concerns of discharge of dredged or fill materials that contain contaminants are the potential effects on the water column and on communities of aquatic organisms.

14.12.1 Evaluation of chemical-biological interactive effects

Dredged or fill material may be excluded from the evaluation procedures specified in paragraphs (b) (2) and (3) of this section if it is determined, on the basis of the evaluation in 230.60, that the likelihood of contamination by contaminants is acceptably low, unless the permitting authority, after evaluating and considering any comments received from the Regional Administrator, determines that these procedures are necessary. The Regional Administrator may require, on a case by case basis, testing approaches and procedures by stating what additional information is needed through further analyses and how the results of the analyses will be of value in evaluating potential environmental effects.

If the general evaluation indicates the presence of a sufficiently large number of chemicals to render impractical the identification of all contaminants by chemical testing, information may be obtained from bioassays in lieu of chemical tests.

14.12.2 Water Column Effects

Sediments normally contain constituents that exist in various chemical forms and in various concentrations in several locations within the sediment. An elutriate test may be used to predict the effect on water quality due to release of contaminants from the sediment to the water column. However, in the case of fill material originating on land which may be a carrier of contaminants, a water leachate test is appropriate.

Major constituents to be analyzed in the elutriate are those deemed critical by the permitting authority, after evaluating and considering any comments received from the Regional Administrator, and considering results of the evaluation in 230.60. Elutriate concentrations should be compared to concentrations of the same constituents in water from the disposal site. Results should be evaluated considering the volume and rate of the intended discharge, the type of discharge, the hydrodynamic regime at the disposal site, and other information relevant to the impact on water quality. The permitting authority should consider the mixing zone in evaluating water column effects. The permitting authority may specify bioassays when such procedures will be of value.

14.12.3 Effects on Benthos

The permitting authority may use an appropriate benthic bioassay (including bioaccumulation tests) when such procedures will be of value in assessing ecological effects and in establishing discharge conditions.

14.12.4 Procedure for Comparison of Sites

When an inventory of the total concentration of contaminants would be of value in comparing sediment at the dredging site with sediment at the disposal site, the permitting authority may require a sediment chemical analysis. Markedly different concentrations of contaminants between the excavation and disposal sites may aid in making an environmental assessment of the proposed disposal operation. Such differences should be interpreted in terms of the potential for harm as supported by any pertinent scientific literature.

When an analysis of biological community structure will be of value to assess the potential for adverse environmental impact at the proposed disposal site, a comparison of the biological characteristics between the excavation and disposal sites may be required by the permitting authority. Biological indicator species may be useful in evaluating the existing degree of stress at both sites. Sensitive species representing community components colonizing various substrate types within the sites should be identified as possible bioassay organisms if tests for toxicity are required. Community structure studies should be performed only when they will be of value in determining discharge conditions. This is particularly applicable to large quantities of dredged material known to contain adverse quantities of toxic materials. Community studies should include benthic organisms such as microbiota and harvestable shellfish and finfish. Abundance, diversity, and distribution should be documented and correlated with substrate type and other appropriate physical and chemical environmental characteristics.

The effect of a discharge of dredged or fill material on physical substrate characteristics at the disposal site, as well as on the water circulation, fluctuation, salinity, and suspended particulates content there, is important in making factual determinations in 230.11. Where information on such effects is not otherwise available to make these factual determinations, the permitting authority shall require appropriate physical tests and evaluations as are justified and deemed necessary. Such tests may include sieve tests, settleability tests, compaction tests, mixing zone and suspended particulate plume determinations, and site assessments of water flow, circulation, and salinity characteristics.

14.13 Actions To Minimize Adverse Effects

There are many actions which can be undertaken in response to 203.10(d) to minimize the adverse effects of discharges of dredged or fill material. Some of these, grouped by type of activity, are listed in this subpart.

14.13.1 Actions Concerning the Location of the Discharge

The effects of the discharge can be minimized by the choice of the disposal site. Some of the ways to accomplish this are by:

❑ locating and confining the discharge to minimize smothering of organisms;

❑ designing the discharge to avoid a disruption of periodic water inundation patterns;

❑ selecting a disposal site that has been used previously for dredged material discharge;

❑ selecting a disposal site at which the substrate is composed of material similar to that being discharged, such as discharging sand on sand or mud on mud;

❑ selecting the disposal site, the discharge point, and the method of discharge to minimize the extent of any plume; and

❑ designing the discharge of dredged or fill material to minimize or prevent the creation of standing bodies of water in areas of normally fluctuating water levels, and minimize or prevent the drainage of areas subject to such fluctuations.

14.13.2 Actions Concerning Material to Be Discharged

The effects of a discharge can be minimized by treatment of, or limitations on the material itself, such as:

❑ disposal of dredged material so that physicochemical conditions are maintained and the potency and availability of pollutants are reduced.

❑ imiting the solid, liquid, and gaseous components of material to be discharged at a particular site;

❑ adding treatment substances to the discharge material;

❑ utilizing chemical flocculants to enhance the deposition of suspended particulates in diked disposal areas.

The effects of the dredged or fill material after discharge may be controlled by selecting discharge methods and disposal sites where the potential for erosion, slumping or leaching of materials into the surrounding aquatic ecosystem will be reduced. These sites or methods include, but are not limited to:

❑ using containment levees, sediment basins, and cover crops to reduce erosion;

❑ using lined containment areas to reduce leaching where leaching of chemical constituents from the discharged material is expected to be a problem;

❑ capping in place contaminated material with clean material or selectively discharging the most contaminated material first to be capped with the remaining material;

❑ maintaining and containing discharged material properly to prevent point and nonpoint sources of pollution;

❑ timing the discharge to minimize impact, for instance during periods of unusual high water flows, wind, wave, and tidal actions.

14.13.3 Actions Affecting the Method of Dispersion

The effects of a discharge can be minimized by the manner in which it is dispersed, such as:

❏ where environmentally desirable, distributing the dredged material widely in a thin layer at the disposal site to maintain natural substrate contours and elevation;

❏ orienting a dredged or fill material mound to minimize undesirable obstruction to the water current or circulation pattern, and utilizing natural bottom contours to minimize the size of the mound;

❏ using silt screens or other appropriate methods to confine suspended particulate/turbidity to a small area where settling or removal can occur;

❏ making use of currents and circulation patterns to mix, disperse and dilute the discharge;

❏ minimizing water column turbidity by using a submerged diffuser system. A similar effect can be accomplished by submerging pipeline discharges or otherwise releasing materials near the bottom;

❏ selecting sites or managing discharges to confine and minimize the release of suspended particulates to give decreased turbidity levels and to maintain light penetration for organisms;

❏ setting limitations on how much material to be discharged per unit of time or volume of receiving water.

14.13.4 Actions Related to Technology

Discharge technology should be adapted to the needs of each site. In determining whether the discharge operation sufficiently minimizes adverse environmental impacts, the applicant should consider:

❏ using appropriate equipment or machinery, including protective devices, and the use of such equipment or machinery in activities related to the discharge of dredged or fill material;

❏ employing appropriate maintenance and operation on equipment or machinery, including adequate training, staffing, and working procedures;

❏ using machinery and techniques that are especially designed to reduce damage to wetlands. This may include machines equipped with devices that scatter rather than mound excavated materials, machines with specially designed wheels or tracks, and the use of mats under heavy machines to reduce wetland surface compaction and rutting;

❏ designing access roads and channel spanning structures using culverts, open channels, and diversions that will pass both low and high water flows, accommodate fluctuating water levels, and maintain circulation and faunal movement; and

❑ employing appropriate machinery and methods of transport of the material for discharge.

14.13.5 Actions Affecting Plant and Animal Populations

Minimization of adverse effects on populations of plants and animals can be achieved by:

❑ avoiding changes in water current and circulation patterns which would interfere with the movement of animals;

❑ selecting sites or managing discharges to prevent or avoid creating habitat conducive to the development of undesirable predators or species which have a competitive edge ecologically over indigenous plants or animals;

❑ avoiding sites having unique habitat or other value, including habitat of threatened or endangered species;

❑ using planning and construction practices to institute habitat development and restoration to produce a new or modified environmental state of higher ecological value by displacement of some or all of the existing environmental characteristics. Habitat development and restoration techniques can be used to minimize adverse impacts and to compensate for a destroyed habitat. Use techniques that have been demonstrated to be effective in circumstances similar to those under consideration wherever possible. Where proposed development and restoration techniques have not yet advanced to the pilot demonstration stage, initiate their use on a small scale to allow corrective action if unanticipated adverse impacts occur;

❑ timing discharge to avoid spawning or migration seasons and other biologically critical time periods; and

❑ avoiding the destruction of remnant natural sites within areas already affected by development.

14.13.6 Actions Affecting Human Use

Minimization of adverse effects on human use potential may be achieved by:

❑ selecting discharge sites and following discharge procedures to prevent or minimize any potential damage to the aesthetically pleasing features of the aquatic site (e.g., viewscapes), particularly with respect to water quality;

❑ selecting disposal sites which are not valuable as natural aquatic areas;

❑ timing the discharge to avoid the seasons or periods when human recreational activity associated with the aquatic site is most important;

❑ following discharge procedures which avoid or minimize the disturbance of aesthetic features of an aquatic site or ecosystem;

❑ selecting sites that will not be detrimental or increase incompatible human activity, or require the need for frequent dredge or fill maintenance activity in remote fish and wildlife areas; and

❑ locating the disposal site outside the vicinity of a public water supply intake.

14.13.7 Other Actions

❑ in the case of fills, controlling runoff and other discharges from activities to be conducted on the fill;

❑ in the case of dams, designing water releases to accommodate the needs of fish and wildlife;

❑ in dredging projects funded by federal agencies other than the Corps of Engineers, maintain desired water quality of the return discharge through agreement with the federal funding authority on scientifically defensible pollutant concentration levels in addition to any applicable water quality standards; and

❑ when a significant ecological change in the aquatic environment is proposed by the discharge of dredged or fill material, the permitting authority should consider the ecosystem that will be lost as well as the environmental benefits of the new system.

14.14 Advanced Identification of Disposal Areas

Consistent with these Guidelines, EPA and the permitting authority, on their own initiative or at the request of any other party and after consultation with any affected state that is not the permitting authority, may identify sites which will be considered as:

❑ possible future disposal sites, including existing disposal sites and non-sensitive areas; or

❑ areas generally unsuitable for disposal site specification.

The identification of any area as a possible future disposal site should not be deemed to constitute a permit for the discharge of dredged or fill material within such area or a specification of a disposal site.

The identification of areas that generally will not be available for disposal site specification should not be deemed as prohibiting applications for permits to discharge dredged or fill material in such areas. Either type of identification constitutes information to facilitate individual or general permit application and processing.

To provide the basis for advanced identification of disposal areas, and areas unsuitable for disposal, EPA and the permitting authority shall consider the likelihood that use of the area in question for dredged or fill material disposal will comply with these Guidelines.

To facilitate this analysis, EPA and the permitting authority should review available water resources management data including data available from the public, other federal and state agencies, and information from approved Coastal Zone Management programs and River Basin Plans.

The permitting authority should always maintain a public record of the identified areas and a written statement of the basis for identification.

Sole Source Aquifers

The purpose of this subpart is to provide criteria for identifying critical aquifer protection areas, pursuant to section 1427 of the Safe Drinking Water Act (SDWA).

15.1 Overview

Pursuant to the SDWA, this regulation was written to provide criteria for identifying critical aquifer protection areas. Section 149.3 refers to a Critical Aquifer Protection Area as one which was designated as a sole or principal source aquifer for which an area wide groundwater quality protection plan was approved.

15.1.1 Critical Aquifer Protection Areas

A Critical Aquifer Protection Area is either all or part of an area which was designated as a sole or principal source aquifer prior to June 19, 1986, and for which an areawide groundwater quality protection plan was approved, under section 208 of the Clean Water Act, prior to that date; or all or part of a major recharge area of a sole or principal source aquifer, for which:

- ☐ the sole or principal source aquifer is particularly vulnerable to contamination due to the hydrogeologic characteristics of the unsaturated or saturated zone within the suggested critical aquifer protection area;

- ☐ contamination of the sole or principal source aquifer is reasonably likely to occur, unless a program to reduce or prevent such contamination is implemented; and

- ☐ lacking any program to reduce or prevent contamination, reasonably foreseeable contamination would result in significant cost, taking into account the cost of replacing the drinking water supply from the sole or principal source aquifer, and other economic costs and environmental and social costs resulting from such contamination.

Spill Prevention Control and Countermeasure Plans

This section repeats the mandate of 311(b)(3) of the CWA. It generally prohibits the discharge of oil into navigable waters in such quantities as may be harmful. This requires that owners or operators of non-transportation-related onshore and offshore facilities engaged in any type of oil and gas operation prepare a Spill Prevention Control and Countermeasure Plan, and provide guidelines for preparation of the plan.

16.1 Overview

Spill Prevention Control and Countermeasure Plans may be required of an applicant for USGS approval of any oil and gas activities. This part establishes procedures, methods and equipment and other requirements for equipment to prevent the discharge of oil from non-transportation-related onshore and offshore facilities into or upon the navigable waters of the United States or adjoining shorelines.

Except as provided in this section of the CFRs, this part applies to owners or operators of non-transportation-related onshore and offshore facilities engaged in drilling, producing, gathering, storing, processing, refining, transferring, distributing or consuming oil and oil products, and which, due to their location, could reasonably be expected to discharge oil in harmful quantities, as defined in part 110 of this chapter, into or upon the navigable waters of the United States or adjoining shorelines.

As provided in section 313 (86 Stat. 875) departments, agencies, and instrumentalities of the federal government are subject to these regulations to the same extent as any person, except for the provisions of 112.6. This part does not apply to facilities, equipment or operations which are not subject to the jurisdiction of the Environmental Protection Agency, as follows:

❑ Onshore and offshore facilities, which, due to their location, could not reasonably be expected to discharge oil into or upon the navigable waters of the United States or adjoining shorelines. This determination shall be based solely upon a consideration of the geographical, locational aspects of the facility (such as proximity to navigable waters or adjoining shorelines, land contour, drainage, etc.) and shall exclude consideration of manmade features such as dikes, equipment or other structures which may serve to restrain, hinder, contain, or otherwise prevent a discharge of oil from reaching navigable waters of the United States or adjoining shorelines; and

❏ Equipment or operations of vessels or transportation–related onshore and offshore facilities which are subject to authority and control of the Department of Transportation, as defined in the Memorandum of Understanding between the Secretary of Transportation and the Administrator of the Environmental Protection Agency, dated November 24, 1971, 36 FR 24000.

It also does not apply to facilities which, although otherwise subject to the jurisdiction of the Environmental Protection Agency, meet both of the following requirements:

❏ the underground buried storage capacity of the facility is 42,000 gallons or less of oil, and

❏ the storage capacity, which is not buried, of the facility is 1,320 gallons or less of oil, provided no single container has a capacity greater than 660 gallons.

This part provides for the preparation and implementation of Spill Prevention Control and Countermeasure Plans prepared in accordance with 112.7, designed to complement existing laws, regulations, rules, standards, policies and procedures pertaining to safety standards, fire prevention and pollution prevention rules, so as to form a comprehensive balanced federal/state spill prevention program to minimize the potential for oil discharges. Compliance with this part does not in any way relieve the owner or operator of an onshore or an offshore facility from compliance with other federal, state or local laws.

16.2 Requirements for Preparation and Implementation of Spill Prevention Control and Countermeasure Plans

Owners or operators of onshore and offshore facilities in operation on or before the effective date of this part that have discharged or, due to their location, could reasonably be expected to discharge oil in harmful quantities, as defined in 40 CFR Part 110, into or upon the navigable waters of the United States or adjoining shorelines, shall prepare a Spill Prevention Control and Countermeasure Plan (hereinafter "SPCC Plan"), in writing and in accordance with 112.7. Except as provided for in this section of the CFRs, such SPCC Plan shall be prepared within six months after the effective date of this part and shall be fully implemented as soon as possible, but not later than one year after the effective date of this part.

Owners or operators of onshore and offshore facilities that become operational after the effective date of this part, and that has discharged or could reasonably be expected to discharge oil in harmful quantities, as defined in 40 CFR Part 110, into or upon the navigable waters of the United States or adjoining shorelines, shall prepare an SPCC Plan in accordance with 112.7. Except as provided for in this section of the CFRs, such SPCC Plan shall be prepared within six months after the date such facility begins operations and shall be fully implemented as soon as possible, but not later than one year after such facility begins operations.

Owners or operators of onshore and offshore mobile or portable facilities, such as onshore drilling or workover rigs, barge mounted offshore drilling or workover rigs, and portable fueling facilities shall prepare and implement an SPCC Plan as required by this section. The owners or operators of such facility need not prepare a new SPCC Plan each time the facility is moved to a new site. The SPCC Plan may be a general plan, prepared in accordance with 112.7, using good engineering practice. When the mobile or portable facility is moved, it must be located and installed using the spill prevention practices outlined in the SPCC Plan for the facility. No mobile or portable facility subject to this regulation shall operate unless the SPCC Plan has been implemented. The SPCC Plan shall only apply while the facility is in a fixed (non-transportation) operating mode.

No SPCC Plan shall be effective to satisfy the requirements of this part unless it has been reviewed by a Registered Professional Engineer and certified to by such Professional Engineer. By means of this certification the engineer, having examined the facility and being familiar with the provisions of this part, shall attest that the SPCC Plan has been prepared in accordance with good engineering practices. Such certification shall in no way relieve the owner or operator of an onshore or offshore facility of his duty to prepare and fully implement such Plan in accordance with 112.7, as required this section.

Owners or operators of a facility for which an SPCC Plan is required pursuant to paragraph (a), (b) or (c) of this section shall maintain a complete copy of the Plan at such facility if the facility is normally attended at least 8 hours per day, or at the nearest field office if the facility is not so attended, and shall make such Plan available to the Regional Administrator for on-site review during normal working hours.

16.2.1 Extensions of Time

The Regional Administrator may authorize an extension of time for the preparation and full implementation of an SPCC Plan beyond the time permitted for the preparation and implementation of an SPCC Plan pursuant to paragraph (a), (b) or (c) of this section where he finds that the owner or operator of a facility subject to paragraphs (a), (b) or (c) of this section cannot fully comply with the requirements of this part as a result of either nonavailability of qualified personnel, or delays in construction or equipment delivery beyond the control and without the fault of such owner or operator or their respective agents or employees.

Any owner or operator seeking an extension of time pursuant to this section of the CFRs may submit a letter of request to the Regional Administrator. Such letter shall include:

- ☐ a complete copy of the SPCC Plan, if completed;
- ☐ a full explanation of the cause for any such delay and the specific aspects of the SPCC Plan affected by the delay;
- ☐ a full discussion of actions being taken or contemplated to minimize or mitigate such delay; and
- ☐ a proposed time schedule for the implementation of any corrective actions being taken or contemplated, including interim dates for completion of tests or studies, installation and operation of any necessary equipment or other preventive measures.

In addition, such owner or operator may present additional oral or written statements in support of his letter of request.

The submission of a letter of request for extension of time pursuant to this section shall in no way relieve the owner or operator from his obligation to comply with the requirements of 112.3 (a), (b) or (c). Where an extension of time is authorized by the Regional Administrator for particular equipment or other specific aspects of the SPCC Plan, such extension shall in no way affect the owner's or operator's obligation to comply with the requirements of 112.3 (a), (b) or (c) with respect to other equipment or other specific aspects of the SPCC Plan for which an extension of time has not been expressly authorized.

16.2.2 Amendment of SPCC Plans by Regional Administrator

Notwithstanding compliance with 112.3, whenever a facility subject to 112.3 (a), (b) or (c) has discharged more than 1,000 U.S. gallons of oil into or upon the navigable waters of the United States or adjoining shorelines in a single spill event, or discharged oil in harmful quantities, as defined in 40 CFR Part 110, into or upon the navigable waters of the United States or adjoining shorelines in two spill events, reportable under section 311(b)(5) of the FWPCA, occurring within any twelve month period, the owner or operator of such facility shall submit to the Regional Administrator, within 60 days from the time such facility becomes subject to this section, the following:

- ❑ name of the facility;
- ❑ name(s) of the owner or operator of the facility;
- ❑ location of the facility;
- ❑ date and year of initial facility operation;
- ❑ maximum storage or handling capacity of the facility and normal daily throughput;
- ❑ description of the facility, including maps, flow diagrams, and topographical maps;
- ❑ a complete copy of the SPCC Plan with any amendments;
- ❑ the cause(s) of such spill, including a failure analysis of system or subsystem in which the failure occurred;
- ❑ the corrective actions and/or countermeasures taken, including an adequate description of equipment repairs and/or replacements;
- ❑ additional preventive measures taken or contemplated to minimize the possibility of recurrence; and
- ❑ such other information as the Regional Administrator may reasonably require pertinent to the Plan or spill event.

Section 112.4 shall not apply until the expiration of the time permitted for the preparation and implementation of an SPCC Plan pursuant to 112.3 (a), (b), (c) and (f). A complete copy of all information provided to the Regional Administrator pursuant to this section of the CFRs shall be sent at the same time to the state agency in charge of water pollution control activities in and for the state in which the facility is located. Upon receipt of such information such state agency may conduct a review and make recommendations to the Regional Administrator as to further procedures, methods, equipment and other requirements for equipment necessary to prevent and to contain discharges of oil from such facility.

After review of the SPCC Plan for a facility subject to this section of the CFRs, together with all other information submitted by the owner or operator of such facility, and by the state agency under this section of the CFRs, the Regional Administrator may require the owner or operator of such facility to amend the SPCC Plan if he finds that the Plan does not meet the requirements of this part or that the amendment of the Plan is necessary to prevent and to contain discharges of oil from such facility.

When the Regional Administrator proposes to require an amendment to the SPCC Plan, he shall notify the facility operator by certified mail addressed to, or by personal delivery to, the facility owner or operator, that he proposes to require an amendment to the Plan, and shall specify the terms of such amendment. If the facility owner or operator is a corporation, a copy of such notice shall also be mailed to the registered agent, if any, of such corporation in the state where such facility is located. Within 30 days from receipt of such notice, the facility owner or operator may submit written information, views, and arguments on the amendment. After considering all relevant material presented, the Regional Administrator shall notify the facility owner or operator of any amendment required or shall rescind the notice.

The amendment required by the Regional Administrator shall become part of the Plan 30 days after such notice, unless the Regional Administrator, for good cause, shall specify another effective date. The owner or operator of the facility shall implement the amendment of the Plan as soon as possible, but not later than six months after the amendment becomes part of the Plan, unless the Regional Administrator specifies another date.

An owner or operator may appeal a decision made by the Regional Administrator requiring an amendment to an SPCC Plan. The appeal shall be made to the Administrator of the United States Environmental Protection Agency and must be made in writing within 30 days of receipt of the notice from the Regional Administrator requiring the amendment. A complete copy of the appeal must be sent to the Regional Administrator at the time the appeal is made. The appeal shall contain a clear and concise statement of the issues and points of fact in the case. It may also contain additional information from the owner or operator, or from any other person. The Administrator or his designee may request additional information from the owner or operator, or from any other person. The Administrator or his designee shall render a decision within 60 days of receiving the appeal and shall notify the owner or operator of his decision.

16.2.3 Amendment of Spill Prevention Control and Countermeasure Plans

Owners or operators of facilities subject to 112.3 (a), (b) or (c) shall amend the SPCC Plan for such facility in accordance with 112.7 whenever there is a change in facility design, construction, operation or maintenance which materially affects the facility's potential for the discharge of oil into or upon the navigable waters of the United States or adjoining shore lines. Such amendments shall be fully implemented as soon as possible, but not later than six months after such change occurs.

Notwithstanding compliance with this section of the CFRs, owners and operators of facilities subject to 112.3 (a), (b) or (c) shall complete a review and evaluation of the SPCC Plan at least once every three years from the date such facility becomes subject to this part. As a result of this review and evaluation, the owner or operator shall amend the SPCC Plan within six months of the review to include more effective prevention and control technology if (1) such technology will significantly reduce the likelihood of a spill event from the facility, and (2) if such technology has been field proven at the time of the review.

No amendment to an SPCC Plan shall be effective to satisfy the requirements of this section unless it has been certified by a professional engineer in accordance with 112.3(d).

16.3 Guidelines for the Spill Prevention Control and Countermeasure Plan

The SPCC Plan shall be a carefully thoughtout plan, prepared in accordance with good engineering practices, and which has the full approval of management at a level with authority to commit the necessary resources. If the plan calls for additional facilities or procedures, methods, or equipment not yet fully operational, these items should be discussed in separate paragraphs, and the details of installation and operational start-up should be explained separately. The complete SPCC Plan shall follow the sequence outlined below, and include a discussion of the facility's conformance with the appropriate guidelines listed:

- ❑ a facility which has experienced one or more spill events within twelve months prior to the effective date of this part should include a written description of each such spill, corrective action taken and plans for preventing recurrence.

- ❑ where experience indicates a reasonable potential for equipment failure (such as tank overflow, rupture, or leakage), the plan should include a prediction of the direction, rate of flow, and total quantity of oil which could be discharged from the facility as a result of each major type of failure.

- ❑ appropriate containment and/or diversionary structures or equipment to prevent discharged oil from reaching a navigable water course should be provided. One of the following preventive systems or its equivalent should be used as a minimum—

Onshore facilities:

- dikes, berms or retaining walls sufficiently impervious to contain spilled oil;

- curbing;

- culverting, gutters or other drainage systems;

- weirs, booms or other barriers;

- spill diversion ponds;

- retention ponds; and

- sorbent materials.

Offshore facilities:

- curbing, drip pans;

- sumps and collection systems.

When it is determined that the installation of structures or equipment listed in 112.7(c) to prevent discharged oil from reaching the navigable waters is not practicable from any onshore or offshore facility, the owner or operator should clearly demonstrate such impracticability and provide the following:

❑ a strong oil spill contingency plan following the provision of 40 CFR Part 109.

❑ a written commitment of manpower, equipment and materials required to expeditiously control and remove any harmful quantity of oil discharged.

In addition to the minimal prevention standards listed under 112.7(c), sections of the Plan should include a complete discussion of conformance with the following applicable guidelines, other effective spill prevention and containment procedures (or, if more stringent, with state rules, regulations and guidelines)—

16.3.1 Facility Drainage (onshore)

Drainage from diked storage areas should be restrained by valves or other positive means to prevent a spill or other excessive leakage of oil into the drainage system or inplant effluent treatment system, except where plan systems are designed to handle such leakage. Diked areas may be emptied by pumps or ejectors; however, these should be manually activated and the condition of the accumulation should be examined before starting to be sure no oil will be discharged into the water.

Flapper type drain valves should not be used to drain diked areas. Valves used for the drainage of diked areas should, as far as practical, be of manual, open and closed design. When plant drainage drains directly into water courses and not into wastewater treatment plants, retained storm water should be inspected as provided in paragraphs (e)(2)(iii) (B), (C) and (D) of this section before drainage.

Plant drainage systems from undiked areas should, if possible, flow into ponds, lagoons or catchment basins, designed to retain oil or return it to the facility. Catchment basins should not be located in areas subject to periodic flooding. If plant drainage is not engineered as above, the final discharge of all in-plant ditches should be equipped with a diversion system that could, in the event of an uncontrolled spill, return the oil to the plant.

Where drainage waters are treated in more than one treatment unit, natural hydraulic flow should be used. If pump transfer is needed, two "lift" pumps should be provided, and at least one of the pumps should be permanently installed when such treatment is continuous. In any event, whatever techniques are used facility drainage systems should be adequately engineered to prevent oil from reaching navigable waters in the event of equipment failure or human error at the facility.

16.3.2 Bulk Storage Tanks (onshore)

No tank should be used for the storage of oil unless its material and construction are compatible with the material stored and conditions of storage such as pressure and temperature, etc.

All bulk storage tank installations should be constructed so that a secondary means of containment is provided for the entire contents of the largest single tank plus sufficient freeboard to allow for precipitation. Diked areas should be sufficiently impervious to contain spilled oil. Dikes, containment curbs, and pits are commonly employed for this purpose, but they may not always be appropriate. An alternative system could consist of a complete drainage trench enclosure arranged so that a spill could terminate and be safely confined in an in-plant catchment basin or holding pond.

Drainage of rainwater from the diked area into a storm drain or an effluent discharge that empties into an open water course, lake, or pond, and bypassing the in-plant treatment system may be acceptable if:

- ☐ the bypass valve is normally sealed closed;

- ☐ inspection of the runoff rain water ensures compliance with applicable water quality standards and will not cause a harmful discharge as defined in 40 CFR Part 110;

- ☐ the bypass valve is opened, and resealed following drainage under responsible supervision; and

- ☐ adequate records are kept of such events.

16.3.3 Metallic Storage Tanks

Buried metallic storage tanks represent a potential for undetected spills. A new buried installation should be protected from corrosion by coatings, cathodic protection or other effective methods compatible with local soil conditions. Such buried tanks should at least be subjected to regular pressure testing.

Partially buried metallic tanks for the storage of oil should be avoided, unless the buried section of the shell is adequately coated, since partial burial in damp earth can cause rapid corrosion of metallic surfaces, especially at the earth/air interface. Aboveground tanks should be subject to periodic integrity testing, taking into account tank design (floating roofs, etc.) and using such techniques as hydrostatic testing, visual inspection or a system of nondestructive shell thickness testing. Comparison records should be kept where appropriate, and tank supports and foundations should be included in these inspections. In addition, the outside of the tank should frequently be observed by operating personnel for signs of deterioration, leaks which might cause a spill, or accumulation of oil inside diked areas.

To control leakage through defective internal heating coils, the following factors should be considered and applied, as appropriate:

- ❏ The steam return or exhaust lines from internal heating coils which discharge into an open water course should be monitored for contamination, or passed through a settling tank, skimmer, or other separation or retention system.

- ❏ The feasibility of installing an external heating system should also be considered.

New and old tank installations should, as far as practical, be fail safe engineered or updated into a fail safe engineered installation to avoid spills. Consideration should be given to providing one or more of the following devices:

- ❏ high liquid level alarms with an audible or visual signal at a constantly manned operation or surveillance station; in smaller plants an audible air vent may suffice;

- ❏ considering size and complexity of the facility, high liquid level pump cutoff devices set to stop flow at a predetermined tank content level;

- ❏ direct audible or code signal communication between the tank gauger and the pumping station;

- ❏ a fast response system for determining the liquid level of each bulk storage tank such as digital computers, telepulse, or direct vision gauges or their equivalent;

- ❏ liquid level sensing devices should be regularly tested to insure proper operation;

- ❏ plant effluents which are discharged into navigable waters should have disposal facilities observed frequently enough to detect possible system upsets that could cause an oil spill event;

- ❏ visible oil leaks which result in a loss of oil from tank seams, gaskets, rivets and bolts sufficiently large to cause the accumulation of oil in diked areas should be promptly corrected; and

- ❏ mobile or portable oil storage tanks (onshore) should be positioned or located so as to prevent spilled oil from reaching navigable waters. A secondary means of containment, such as dikes or catchment basins, should be furnished for the largest single compartment or tank. These facilities should be located where they will not be subject to periodic flooding or washout.

16.4 Facility Transfer Operations, Pumping, and In-Plant Process (Onshore)

Buried piping installations should have a protective wrapping and coating and should be cathodically protected if soil conditions warrant. If a section of buried line is exposed for any reason, it should be carefully examined for deterioration. If corrosion damage is found, additional examination and corrective action should be taken as indicated by the magnitude of the damage. An alternative would be the more frequent use of exposed pipe corridors or galleries.

- ❑ When a pipeline is not in service, or in standby service for an extended time the terminal connection at the transfer point should be capped or blank-flanged, and marked as to origin.

- ❑ Pipe supports should be properly designed to minimize abrasion and corrosion and allow for expansion and contraction.

- ❑ All aboveground valves and pipelines should be subjected to regular examinations by operating personnel at which time the general condition of items, such as flange joints, expansion joints, valve glands and bodies, catch pans, pipeline supports, locking of valves, and metal surfaces should be assessed. In addition, periodic pressure testing may be warranted for piping in areas where facility drainage is such that a failure might lead to a spill event.

- ❑ Vehicular traffic granted entry into the facility should be warned verbally or by appropriate signs to be sure that the vehicle, because of its size, will not endanger above ground piping.

16.5 Facility Tank Car and Tank Truck Loading/Unloading Rack (Onshore)

Tank car and tank truck loading/unloading procedures should meet the minimum requirements and regulation established by the Department of Transportation.

Where rack area drainage does not flow into a catchment basin or treatment facility designed to handle spills, a quick drainage system should be used for tank truck loading and unloading areas. The containment system should be designed to hold at least maximum capacity of any single compartment of a tank car or tank truck loaded or unloaded in the plant.

An interlocked warning light or physical barrier system, or warning signs, should be provided in loading/unloading areas to prevent vehicular departure before complete disconnect of flexible or fixed transfer lines.

Prior to filling and departure of any tank car or tank truck, the lowermost drain and all outlets of such vehicles should be closely examined for leakage, and if necessary, tightened, adjusted, or replaced to prevent liquid leakage while in transit.

16.6 Oil Production Facilities (Onshore) Drainage

At tank batteries and central treating stations where an accidental discharge of oil would have a reasonable possibility of reaching navigable waters, the dikes or equivalent required under 112.7(c)(1) should have drains closed and sealed at all times unless rainwater is being drained. Prior to drainage, the diked area should be inspected as provided in paragraphs (e)(2)(iii) (B), (C), and (D) of this section of the CFRs.

❑ Accumulated oil on the rainwater should be picked up and returned to storage or disposed of in accordance with approved methods.

❑ Field drainage ditches, road ditches, and oil traps, sumps or skimmers, if such exist, should be inspected at regularly scheduled intervals for accumulation of oil that may have escaped from small leaks. Any such accumulations should be removed.

No tank should be used for the storage of oil unless its material and construction are compatible with the material stored and the conditions of storage.

❑ All tank battery and central treating plant installations should be provided with a secondary means of containment for the entire contents of the largest single tank if feasible, or alternate systems such as those outlined in 112.7(c)(1). Drainage from undiked areas should be safely confined in a catchment basin or holding pond.

❑ All tanks containing oil should be visually examined by a competent person for condition and need for maintenance on a scheduled periodic basis. Such examination should include the foundation and supports of tanks that are above the surface of the ground.

New and old tank battery installations should, as far as practical, be fail-safe engineered or updated into a fail-safe engineered installation to prevent spills. Consideration should be given to one or more of the following:

❑ adequate tank capacity to assure that a tank will not overfill should a pumper/gauger be delayed in making his regular rounds;

❑ overflow equalizing lines between tanks so that a full tank can overflow to an adjacent tank;

❑ adequate vacuum protection to prevent tank collapse during a pipeline run; and

❑ high level sensors to generate and transmit an alarm signal to the computer where facilities are a part of a computer production control system.

16.7 Facility Transfer Operations, Oil Production Facility (Onshore)

All above ground valves and pipelines should be examined periodically on a scheduled basis for general condition of items such as flange joints, valve glands and bodies, drip pans, pipeline supports, pumping well polish rod stuffing boxes, bleeder and gauge valves.

❏ Salt water (oil field brine) disposal facilities should be examined often, particularly following a sudden change in atmospheric temperature to detect possible system upsets that could cause an oil discharge.

❏ Production facilities should have a program of flowline maintenance to prevent spills from this source. The program should include periodic examinations, corrosion protection, flowline replacement, and adequate records, as appropriate, for the individual facility.

16.8 Oil Drilling and Workover Facilities (Onshore)

Mobile drilling or workover equipment should be positioned or located so as to prevent spilled oil from reaching navigable waters. Depending on the location, catchment basins or diversion structures may be necessary to intercept and contain spills of fuel, crude oil, or oily drilling fluids.

❏ Before drilling below any casing string or during workover operations, a blowout prevention (BOP) assembly and well control system should be installed that is capable of controlling any well head pressure expected to be encountered while that BOP assembly is on the well. Casing and BOP installations should be in accordance with state regulatory agency requirements.

"An oil drilling, production or workover facility (offshore)" may include all drilling or workover equipment, wells, flowlines, gathering lines, platforms, and auxiliary nontransportation-related equipment and facilities in a single geographical oil or gas field operated by a single operator.

Oil drainage collection equipment should be used to prevent and control small oil spillage around pumps, glands, valves, flanges, expansion joints, hoses, drain lines, separators, treaters, tanks, and allied equipment. Drains on the facility should be controlled and directed toward a central collection sump or equivalent collection system sufficient to prevent discharges of oil into the navigable waters of the United States. Where drains and sumps are not practicable oil contained in collection equipment should be removed as often as necessary to prevent overflow.

❏ For facilities employing a sump system, sump and drains should be adequately sized and a spare pump or equivalent method should be available to remove liquid from the sump and assure that oil does not escape. A regular scheduled preventive maintenance inspection and testing program should be employed to assure reliable operation of the liquid removal system and pump start-up device. Redundant automatic sump pumps and control devices may be required on some installations.

❏ In areas where separators and treaters are equipped with dump valves whose predominant mode of failure is in the closed position and pollution risk is high, the facility should be specially equipped to prevent the escape of oil. This could be accomplished by extending the flare line to a diked area if the separator is near shore, equipping it with a high liquid level sensor that will automatically shut-in wells producing to the separator, parallel redundant dump valves, or other feasible alternatives to prevent oil discharges.

❑ Atmospheric storage or surge tanks should be equipped with high liquid level sensing devices or other acceptable alternatives to prevent oil discharges.

❑ Pressure tanks should be equipped with high and low pressure sensing devices to activate an alarm and/or control the flow or other acceptable alternatives to prevent oil discharges.

❑ Tanks should be equipped with suitable corrosion protection.

❑ A written procedure for inspecting and testing pollution prevention equipment and systems should be prepared and maintained at the facility. Such procedures should be included as part of the SPCC Plan.

❑ Testing and inspection of the pollution prevention equipment and systems at the facility should be conducted by the owner or operator on a scheduled periodic basis commensurate with the complexity, conditions and circumstances of the facility or other appropriate regulations.

❑ Surface and subsurface well shut-in valves and devices in use at the facility should be sufficiently described to determine method of activation or control, e.g., pressure differential, change in fluid or flow conditions, combination of pressure and flow, manual or remote control mechanisms. Detailed records for each well, while not necessarily part of the plan should be kept by the owner or operator.

❑ Before drilling below any casing string, and during workover operations a blowout preventer (BOP) assembly and well control system should be installed that is capable of controlling any wellhead pressure expected to be encountered while that BOP assembly is on the well. Casing and BOP installations should be in accordance with state regulatory agency requirements.

❑ Extraordinary well control measures should be provided should emergency conditions, including fire, loss of control and other abnormal conditions, occur. The degree of control system redundancy should vary with hazard exposure and probable consequences of failure. It is recommended that surface shut-in systems have redundant or "fail close" valving. Subsurface safety valves may not be needed in producing wells that will not flow but should be installed as required by applicable state regulations.

❑ So that there will be no misunderstanding of joint and separate duties and obligations to perform work in a safe and pollution free manner, written instructions should be prepared by the owner or operator for contractors and subcontractors to follow whenever contract activities include servicing a well or systems appurtenant to a well or pressure vessel. Such instructions and procedures should be maintained at the offshore production facility. Under certain circumstances and conditions such contractor activities may require the presence at the facility of an authorized representative of the owner or operator who would intervene when necessary to prevent a spill event.

❑ All manifolds (headers) should be equipped with check valves on individual flowlines.

❑ If the shut-in well pressure is greater than the working pressure of the flowline and manifold valves up to and including the header valves associated with that individual flowline, the flowline should be equipped with a high pressure sensing device and shut-in valve at the wellhead unless provided with a pressure relief system to prevent over pressuring.

❑ All pipelines appurtenant to the facility should be protected from corrosion. Methods used, such as protective coatings or cathodic protection, should be discussed.

❑ Sub-marine pipelines appurtenant to the facility should be adequately protected against environmental stresses and other activities such as fishing operations.

❑ Sub-marine pipelines appurtenant to the facility should be in good operating condition at all times and inspected on a scheduled periodic basis for failures. Such inspections should be documented and maintained at the facility.

16.8.1 Inspections and Records

Inspections required by this part should be in accordance with written procedures developed for the facility by the owner or operator. These written procedures and a record of the inspections, signed by the appropriate supervisor or inspector, should be made part of the SPCC Plan and maintained for a period of three years.

16.8.2 Security (excluding oil production facilities)

All plants handling, processing, and storing oil should be fully fenced, and entrance gates should be locked and/or guarded when the plant is not in production or is unattended. Other issues include:

❑ The master flow and drain valves and any other valves that will permit direct outward flow of the tank's content to the surface should be securely locked in the closed position when in nonoperating or nonstandby status.

❑ The starter control on all oil pumps should be locked in the "off" position or located at a site accessible only to authorized personnel when the pumps are in a nonoperating or nonstandby status.

❑ The loading/unloading connections of oil pipelines should be securely capped or blank flanged when not in service or standby service for an extended time. This security practice should also apply to pipelines that are emptied of liquid content either by draining or by inert gas pressure.

Facility lighting should be commensurate with the type and location of the facility. Consideration should be given to:

❑ Discovery of spills occurring during hours of darkness, both by operating personnel, if present, and by nonoperating personnel (the general public, local police, etc.) and prevention of spills occurring through acts of vandalism.

16.9 Personnel, Training and Spill Prevention Procedures

Owners or operators are responsible for properly instructing their personnel in the operation and maintenance of equipment to prevent the discharges of oil and applicable pollution control laws, rules and regulations.

❑ Each applicable facility should have a designated person who is accountable for oil spill prevention and who reports to line management.

❑ Owners or operators should schedule and conduct spill prevention briefings for their operating personnel at intervals frequent enough to assure adequate understanding of the SPCC Plan for that facility. Such briefings should highlight and describe known spill events or failures, malfunctioning components, and recently developed precautionary measures.

16.10 Facility Response Plans

The owner or operator of any non-transportation related onshore facility that, because of its location, could reasonably be expected to cause substantial harm to the environment by discharging oil into or on the navigable waters or adjoining shorelines shall prepare and submit a facility response plan to the Regional Administrator.

The owner or operator of a facility in operation on or after August 30, 1994 that satisfies the criteria in this section or that is notified by the Regional Administrator pursuant to this section shall prepare and submit a facility response plan that satisfies the requirements of this section to the Regional Administrator.

For a newly constructed facility that commences operation after August 30, 1994, the owner or operator is required to prepare and submit a response plan based on the criteria in this section, the owner or operator shall submit the response plan, along with a completed version of the response plan cover sheet contained in Appendix F to this part, to the Regional Administrator prior to the start of operations (adjustments to the response plan to reflect changes that occur at the facility during the start-up phase of operations must be submitted to the Regional Administrator after an operational trial period of 60 days).

For a facility required to prepare and submit a response plan after August 30, 1994, as a result of a planned change in design, construction, operation, or maintenance that renders the facility subject to the criteria in this section of the CFRs, the owner or operator shall submit the response plan, along with a completed version of the response plan cover sheet contained in Appendix F to this part, to the Regional Administrator before the portion of the facility undergoing change commences operations (adjustments to the response plan to reflect changes that occur at the facility during the start-up phase of operations must be submitted to the Regional Administrator after an operational trial period of 60 days).

For a facility required to prepare and submit a response plan after August 30, 1994, as a result of an unplanned event or change in facility characteristics that renders the facility subject to the criteria in this section of the CFRs, the owner or operator shall submit the response plan, along with a completed version of the response plan cover sheet contained in Appendix F to this part, to the Regional Administrator within six months of the unplanned event or change.

16.10.1 Review of Plans

The Regional Administrator shall review plans submitted by such facilities to determine whether the facility could, because of its location, reasonably be expected to cause significant and substantial harm to the environment by discharging oil into or on the navigable waters or adjoining shorelines.

The Regional Administrator shall determine whether a facility could, because of its location, reasonably be expected to cause significant and substantial harm to the environment by discharging oil into or on the navigable waters or adjoining shorelines, based on the factors in paragraph (f)(3) of this section. If such a determination is made, the Regional Administrator shall notify the owner or operator of the facility in writing and:

- ☐ promptly review the facility response plan;
- ☐ require amendments to any response plan that does not meet the requirements of this section;
- ☐ approve any response plan that meets the requirements of this section; and
- ☐ review each response plan periodically thereafter on a schedule established by the Regional Administrator provided that the period between plan reviews does not exceed five years.

The owner or operator of a facility for which a response plan is required under this part shall revise and resubmit revised portions of the response plan within 60 days of each facility change that materially may affect the response to a worst case discharge, including:

- ☐ a change in the facility's configuration that materially alters the information included in the response plan;
- ☐ a change in the type of oil handled, stored, or transferred that materially alters the required response resources;
- ☐ a material change in capabilities of the oil spill removal organization(s) that provide equipment and personnel to respond to discharges of oil described in this section of the CFRs;
- ☐ a material change in the facility's spill prevention and response equipment or emergency response procedures; and
- ☐ any other changes that materially affect the implementation of the response plan.

Except as provided in this section, amendments to personnel and telephone number lists included in the response plan and a change in the oil spill removal organization(s) that does not result in a material change in support capabilities do not require approval by the Regional Administrator. Facility owners or operators shall provide a copy of such changes to the Regional Administrator as the revisions occur.

The owner or operator of a facility that submits changes to a response plan as provided in this section shall provide the EPA issued facility identification number (where one has been assigned) with the changes.

The Regional Administrator shall review, for approval, changes to a response plan submitted pursuant to this section of the CFRs for a facility determined pursuant to this section to have the potential to cause significant and substantial harm to the environment. If the owner or operator of a facility determines that the facility could not, because of its location, reasonably be expected to cause substantial harm to the environment by discharging oil into or on the navigable waters or adjoining shorelines, the owner or operator shall complete and maintain at the facility the certification form contained in Appendix C to this part and, in the event an alternative formula that is comparable to one contained in Appendix C to this part is used to evaluate the criterion in this section, the owner or operator shall attach documentation to the certification form that demonstrates the reliability and analytical soundness of the comparable formula and shall notify the Regional Administrator, in writing, that an alternative formula was used.

A facility could, because of its location, reasonably be expected to cause substantial harm to the environment by discharging oil into or on the navigable waters or adjoining shorelines pursuant to this section of the CFRs, if it meets any of the following criteria applied in accordance with the flowchart contained in Attachment C–I to Appendix C to this part:

☐ The facility transfers oil over water to or from vessels and has a total oil storage capacity greater than or equal to 42,000 gallons; or

☐ The facility's total oil storage capacity is greater than or equal to 1 million gallons, and one of the following is true:

- The facility does not have secondary containment for each aboveground storage area sufficiently large to contain the capacity of the largest aboveground oil storage tank within each storage area plus sufficient freeboard to allow for precipitation;

- The facility is located at a distance (as calculated using the appropriate formula in Appendix C to this part or a comparable formula) such that a discharge from the facility could cause injury to fish and wildlife and sensitive environments. For further description of fish and wildlife and sensitive environments, see Appendices I, II, and III of the "Guidance for Facility and Vessel Response Plans: Fish and Wildlife and Sensitive Environments" (see Appendix E to this part, section 10, for availability) and the applicable Area Contingency Plan prepared pursuant to section 311(j)(4) of the Clean Water Act;

- The facility is located at a distance (as calculated using the appropriate formula in Appendix C to this part or a comparable formula) such that a discharge from the facility would shut down a public drinking water intake; or

- The facility has had a reportable oil spill in an amount greater than or equal to 10,000 gallons within the last five years.

To determine whether a facility could, because of its location, reasonably be expected to cause substantial harm to the environment by discharging oil into or on the navigable waters or adjoining shorelines pursuant to this section of the CFRs, the Regional Administrator shall consider the following:

❏ type of transfer operation;

❏ oil storage capacity;

❏ lack of secondary containment;

❏ proximity to fish and wildlife and sensitive environments and other areas determined by the Regional Administrator to possess ecological value;

❏ proximity to drinking water intakes;

❏ spill history; and

❏ other site sepecific characteristics and environmental factors that the Regional Administrator determines to be relevant to protecting the environment from harm by discharges of oil into or on navigable waters or adjoining shorelines.

Any person, including a member of the public or any representative from a federal, state, or local agency who believes that a facility subject to this section could, because of its location, reasonably be expected to cause substantial harm to the environment by discharging oil into or on the navigable waters or adjoining shorelines may petition the Regional Administrator to determine whether the facility meets the criteria in this section. Such petitions shall include a discussion of how the factors in this section apply to the facility in question. The RA shall consider such petitions and respond in an appropriate amount of time.

To determine whether a facility could, because of its location, reasonably be expected to cause significant and substantial harm to the environment by discharging oil into or on the navigable waters or adjoining shorelines, the Regional Administrator may consider the factors in this section of the f)(2)CFRs of this section as well as the following:

❏ frequency of past spills;

❏ proximity to navigable waters;

❏ age of oil storage tanks; and

❏ other facility specific and region specific information, including local impacts on public health.

16.10.2 Response Plan Consistency

All facility response plans shall be consistent with the requirements of the National Oil and Hazardous Substance Pollution Contingency Plan (40 CFR Part 300) and applicable Area Contingency Plans prepared pursuant to section 311(j)(4) of the Clean Water Act. The facility response plan should be coordinated with the local emergency response plan developed by the local emergency planning committee under section 303 of Title III of the Superfund Amendments and Reauthorization Act of 1986 (42 U.S.C. 11001 et seq.). Upon request, the owner or operator should provide a copy of the facility response plan to the local emergency planning committee or state emergency response commission.

The owner or operator shall review relevant portions of the National Oil and Hazardous Substances Pollution Contingency Plan and applicable Area Contingency Plan annually and, if necessary, revise the facility response plan to ensure consistency with these plans. The owner or operator shall review and update the facility response plan periodically to reflect changes at the facility.

16.10.3 Model Facility Specific Response Plan

A response plan shall follow the format of the model facility specific response plan included in Appendix F to this part, unless an equivalent response plan has been prepared to meet state or other federal requirements. A response plan that does not follow the specified format in Appendix F to this part shall have an emergency response action plan as specified in paragraphs (h)(1) of this section and be supplemented with a cross reference section to identify the location of the elements listed in paragraphs (h)(2) through (h)(10) of this section of the CFRs. To meet the requirements of this part, a response plan shall address the following elements, as further described in Appendix F to this part—

16.11 Emergency Response Action Plan

The response plan shall include an emergency response action plan in the format specified in this section that is maintained in the front of the response plan, or as a separate document accompanying the response plan, and that includes the following information:

- ❏ the identity and telephone number of a qualified individual having full authority, including contracting authority, to implement removal actions;

- ❏ the identity of individuals or organizations to be contacted in the event of a discharge so that immediate communications between the qualified individual identified in this section of the CFRs and the appropriate federal officials and the persons providing response personnel and equipment can be ensured;

- ❏ a description of information to pass to response personnel in the event of a reportable spill;

- ❏ a description of the facility's response equipment and its location;

❑ a description of response personnel capabilities, including the duties of persons at the facility during a response action and their response times and qualifications;

❑ plans for evacuation of the facility and a reference to community evacuation plans, as appropriate;

❑ a description of immediate measures to secure the source of the discharge, and to provide adequate containment and drainage of spilled oil; and

❑ a diagram of the facility.

The response plan shall identify and discuss the location and type of facility, the identity and tenure of the present owner and operator, and the identity of the qualified individual identified in this section.

16.11.1 Information about Emergency Responses

The response plan shall include:

❑ the identity of private personnel and equipment necessary to remove to the maximum extent practicable a worst case discharge and other discharges of oil described in this section of the CFRs, and to mitigate or prevent a substantial threat of a worst case discharge (To identify response resources to meet the facility response plan requirements of this section, owners or operators shall follow Appendix E to this part or, where not appropriate, shall clearly demonstrate in the response plan why use of Appendix E of this part is not appropriate at the facility and make comparable arrangements for response resources);

❑ evidence of contracts or other approved means for ensuring the availability of such personnel and equipment;

❑ the identity and the telephone number of individuals or organizations to be contacted in the event of a discharge so that immediate communications between the qualified individual identified in this section of the CFRs and the appropriate federal official and the persons providing response personnel and equipment can be ensured;

❑ a description of information to pass to response personnel in the event of a reportable spill;

❑ a description of response personnel capabilities, including the duties of persons at the facility during a response action and their response times and qualifications;

❑ a description of the facility's response equipment, the location of the equipment, and equipment testing;

❑ plans for evacuation of the facility and a reference to community evacuation plans, as appropriate;

❑ a diagram of evacuation routes; and

❏ a description of the duties of the qualified individual.

A description of the duties of the qualified individual identified in this section, includes responsibilities to:

❏ activate internal alarms and hazard communication systems to notify all facility personnel;

❏ notify all response personnel, as needed;

❏ identify the character, exact source, amount, and extent of the release, as well as the other items needed for notification;

❏ notify and provide necessary information to the appropriate federal, state, and local authorities with designated response roles, including the National Response Center, state Emergency Response Commission, and Local Emergency Planning Committee;

❏ assess the interaction of the spilled substance with water and/or other substances stored at the facility and notify response personnel at the scene of that assessment;

❏ assess the possible hazards to human health and the environment due to the release. This assessment must consider both the direct and indirect effects of the release (i.e., the effects of any toxic, irritating, or asphyxiating gases that may be generated, or the effects of any hazardous surface water runoffs from water or chemical agents used to control fire and heat induced explosion);

❏ assess and implement prompt removal actions to contain and remove the substance released;

❏ coordinate rescue and response actions as previously arranged with all response personnel;

❏ use authority to immediately access company funding to initiate cleanup activities; and

❏ direct cleanup activities until properly relieved of this responsibility.

16.12 Hazard Evaluation

The response plan shall discuss the facility's known or reasonably identifiable history of discharges reportable under 40 CFR Part 110 for the entire life of the facility and shall identify areas within the facility where discharges could occur and what the potential effects of the discharges would be on the affected environment. To assess the range of areas potentially affected, owners or operators shall, where appropriate, consider the distance calculated in this section of the CFRs to determine whether a facility could, because of its location, reasonably be expected to cause substantial harm to the environment by discharging oil into or on the navigable waters or adjoining shorelines.

16.12.1 Response Planning Levels

The response plan shall include discussion of specific planning scenarios for:

❑ a worst case discharge, as calculated using the appropriate worksheet in Appendix D to this part. In cases where the Regional Administrator determines that the worst case discharge volume calculated by the facility is not appropriate, the Regional Administrator may specify the worst case discharge amount to be used for response planning at the facility. For complexes, the worst case planning quantity shall be the larger of the amounts calculated for each component of the facility;

❑ a discharge of 2,100 gallons or less, provided that this amount is less than the worst case discharge amount. For complexes, this planning quantity shall be the larger of the amounts calculated for each component of the facility; and

❑ a discharge greater than 2,100 gallons and less than or equal to 36,000 gallons or 10 percent of the capacity of the largest tank at the facility, whichever is less, provided that this amount is less than the worst case discharge amount. For complexes, this planning quantity shall be the larger of the amounts calculated for each component of the facility.

The response plan shall also describe the procedures and equipment used to detect discharges.

16.13 Plan Implementation

The response plan shall describe:

❑ response actions to be carried out by facility personnel or contracted personnel under the response plan to ensure the safety of the facility and to mitigate or prevent discharges described in this section of the CFRs or the substantial threat of such discharges;

❑ a description of the equipment to be used for each scenario;

❑ plans to dispose of contaminated cleanup materials; and

❑ measures to provide adequate containment and drainage of spilled oil.

16.13.1 Self-Inspection, Drills/Exercises, and Response Training

The response plan shall include:

❑ a checklist and record of inspections for tanks, secondary containment, and response equipment;

❑ a description of the drill/exercise program to be carried out under the response plan as described in 112.21;

❑ a description of the training program to be carried out under the response plan as described in 112.21; and

❑ logs of discharge prevention meetings, training sessions, and drills/exercises. Logs that may be maintained as an annex to the response plan include, site plan and drainage plan diagrams, descriptions of facility security systems, and a response plan cover sheet provided in Section 2.0 of Appendix F to this part.

16.13.2 Disagreement with the Administrator's Finding

In the event the owner or operator of a facility does not agree with the Regional Administrator's determination that the facility could, because of its location, reasonably be expected to cause substantial harm or significant and substantial harm to the environment by discharging oil into or on the navigable waters or adjoining shorelines, or that amendments to the facility response plan are necessary prior to approval, such as changes to the worst case discharge planning volume, the owner or operator may submit a request for reconsideration to the Regional Administrator and provide additional information and data in writing to support the request. The request and accompanying information must be submitted to the Regional Administrator within 60 days of receipt of notice of the Regional Administrator's original decision. The Regional Administrator shall consider the request and render a decision as rapidly as practicable.

In the event the owner or operator of a facility believes a change in the facility's classification status is warranted because of an unplanned event or change in the facility's characteristics (i.e., substantial harm or significant and substantial harm), the owner or operator may submit a request for reconsideration to the Regional Administrator and provide additional information and data in writing to support the request. The Regional Administrator shall consider the request and render a decision as rapidly as practicable.

After a request for reconsideration has been denied by the Regional Administrator, an owner or operator may appeal a determination made by the Regional Administrator. The appeal shall be made to the EPA Administrator and shall be made in writing within 60 days of receipt of the decision from the Regional Administrator that the request for reconsideration was denied. A complete copy of the appeal must be sent to the Regional Administrator at the time the appeal is made. The appeal shall contain a clear and concise statement of the issues and points of fact in the case. It also may contain additional information from the owner or operator, or from any other person. The EPA Administrator may request additional information from the owner or operator, or from any other person. The EPA Administrator shall render a decision as rapidly as practicable and shall notify the owner or operator of the decision.

16.13.3 Facility Response Training and Drills/Exercises

The owner or operator of any facility required to prepare a facility response plan under 112.20 shall develop and implement a facility response training program and a drill/exercise program that satisfy the requirements of this section of the CFRs. The owner or operator shall describe the programs in the response plan as provided in 112.20(h)(8).

The facility owner or operator shall develop a facility response training program to train those personnel involved in oil spill response activities. It is recommended that the training program be based on the USCG's Training Elements for Oil Spill Response, as applicable to facility operations. An alternative program can also be acceptable subject to approval by the Regional Administrator.

❑ The owner or operator shall be responsible for the proper instruction of facility personnel in the procedures to respond to discharges of oil and in applicable oil spill response laws, rules, and regulations.

❑ Training shall be functional in nature according to job tasks for both supervisory and non-supervisory operational personnel.

❑ Trainers shall develop specific lesson plans on subject areas relevant to facility personnel involved in oil spill response and cleanup.

The facility owner or operator shall develop a program of facility response drills/exercises, including evaluation procedures. A program that follows the National Preparedness for Response Exercise Program (PREP) (see Appendix E to this part, section 10, for availability) will be deemed satisfactory for purposes of this section of the CFRs. An alternative program can also be acceptable subject to approval by the Regional Administrator.

16.14 Required Response Resources for Facility Response Plans

The purpose of Appendix E to Part 112 is to describe the procedures to identify response resources to meet the requirements of 112.20. To identify response resources to meet the facility response plan requirements of 40 CFR 112.20(h), owners or operators shall follow this appendix or, where not appropriate, shall clearly demonstrate in the response plan why use of this appendix is not appropriate at the facility and make comparable arrangements for response resources.

16.14.1 Equipment Operability and Readiness

All equipment identified in a response plan must be designed to operate in the conditions expected in the facility's geographic area (i.e., operating environment). These conditions vary widely based on location and season. Therefore, it is difficult to identify a single stockpile of response equipment that will function effectively in each geographic location (i.e., operating area).

Facilities handling, storing, or transporting oil in more than one operating environment as indicated in Table 1 of this appendix must identify equipment capable of successfully functioning in each operating environment. When identifying equipment for the response plan (based on the use of this appendix), a facility owner or operator must consider the inherent limitations of the operability of equipment components and response systems. The criteria in Table 1 of this appendix shall be used to evaluate the operability in a given environment. These criteria reflect the general conditions in certain operating environments. Table 1 of this appendix lists criteria for oil recovery devices and boom. All other equipment necessary to sustain or support response operations in an operating environment must be designed to function in the same conditions.

16.14.2 Determining Response Resources Required for Small Discharges

A facility owner or operator shall identify sufficient response resources available, by contract or other approved means as described in 112.2, to respond to a small discharge. A small discharge is defined as any discharge volume less than or equal to 2,100 gallons, but not to exceed the calculated worst case discharge. The equipment must be designed to function in the operating environment at the point of expected use. Complexes that are regulated by EPA and the USCG must also consider planning quantities for the transportation related transfer portion of the facility. The USCG planning level that corresponds to EPA's "small discharge" is termed "the average most probable discharge." The USCG revisions to 33 CFR Part 154 define "the average most probable discharge" as a discharge of 50 barrels (2,100 gallons). Owners or operators of complexes must compare oil spill volumes for a small discharge and an average most probable discharge and plan for whichever quantity is greater.

16.14.3 Determining Response Resources Required for Medium Discharges

A facility owner or operator shall identify sufficient response resources available, by contract or other approved means as described in 112.2, to respond to a medium discharge of oil for that facility. This will require response resources capable of containing and collecting up to 36,000 gallons of oil or 10 percent of the worst case discharge, whichever is less. All equipment identified must be designed to operate in the applicable operating environment specified in Table 1 of this appendix. Complexes that are regulated by EPA and the USCG must also consider planning quantities for the transportation related transfer portion of the facility. The USCG planning level that corresponds to EPA's "medium discharge" is termed "the maximum most probable discharge." The USCG revisions to 33 CFR Part 154 define "the maximum most probable discharge" as a discharge of 1,200 barrels (50,400 gallons) or 10 percent of the worst case discharge, whichever is less. Owners or operators of complexes must compare spill volumes for a medium discharge and a maximum most probable discharge and plan for whichever quantity is greater.

In addition to oil recovery capacity, the plan shall, as appropriate, identify sufficient quantity of containment boom available, by contract or other approved means as described in 112.2, to arrive within the required response times for oil collection and containment and for protection of fish and wildlife and sensitive environments. For further description of fish and wildlife and sensitive environments, see Appendices I, II, and III to DOC/NOAA's "Guidance for Facility and Vessel Response Plans: Fish and Wildlife and Sensitive Environments" (see Appendix E to this part, section 10, for availability) and the applicable ACP. While the regulation does not set required quantities of boom for oil collection and containment, the response plan shall identify and ensure, by contract or other approved means as described in 112.2, the availability of the quantity of boom identified in the plan for this purpose.

16.14.4 Determining Response Resources Required for the Worst Case Discharge to the Maximum Extent Practicable

A facility owner or operator shall identify and ensure the availability of, by contract or other approved means as described in 112.2, sufficient response resources to respond to the worst case discharge of oil to the maximum extent practicable. Section 7 of this appendix describes the method to determine the necessary response resources. A worksheet is provided as Attachment E–1 at the end of this appendix to simplify the procedures involved in calculating the planning volume for response resources for the worst case discharge. Complexes that are regulated by EPA and the USCG must also consider planning for the worst case discharge at the transportation related portion of the facility. The USCG requires that transportation related facility owners or operators use a different calculation for the worst case discharge in the revisions to 33 CFR Part 154. Owners or operators of complex facilities that are regulated by EPA and the USCG must compare both calculations of worst case discharge derived by EPA and the USCG and plan for whichever volume is greater.

Oil spill response resources identified in the response plan and available, by contract or other approved means as described in 112.2, to meet the applicable worst case discharge planning volume must be located such that they are capable of arriving at the scene of a discharge within the times specified for the applicable response tier listed below:

Area	Tier 1	Tier 2	Tier 3
Higher volume port areas	6 hrs	30 hrs	54 hrs
Great Lakes	12 hrs	36 hrs	60 hrs
All other river and canal, inland, and nearshore areas	12 hrs	36 hrs	60 hrs

16.15 Three Levels of Response Tiers

The three levels of response tiers apply to the amount of time in which facility owners or operators must plan for response resources to arrive at the scene of a spill to respond to the worst case discharge planning volume. For example, at a worst case discharge in an inland area, the first tier of response resources would arrive at the scene of the discharge within 12 hours; the second tier of response resources would arrive within 36 hours; and the third tier of response resources would arrive within 60 hours. A facility owner or operator shall identify the storage locations of all response resources used for each tier. The owner or operator of a facility whose calculated planning volume exceeds the applicable contracting caps shall, as appropriate, identify sources of additional equipment equal to twice the cap listed in Tier 3 or the amount necessary to reach the calculated planning volume, whichever is lower. The resources identified above the cap shall be capable of arriving on-scene not later than the Tier 3 response times.

When listing USCG classified oil spill removal organization(s) that have sufficient removal capacity to recover the volume above the response capacity cap for the specific facility, as specified in Table 5 of this appendix, listing specific quantities of equipment is not necessary.

When selecting response resources necessary to meet the response plan requirements, the facility owner or operator shall, as appropriate, ensure that a portion of those resources is capable of being used in close to shore response activities in shallow water. For any EPA regulated facility that is required to plan for response in shallow water, at least 20 percent of the on-water response equipment identified for the applicable operating area shall, as appropriate, be capable of operating in water of 6 feet or less depth.

In addition to oil spill recovery devices, a facility owner or operator shall identify sufficient quantities of boom that are available, to arrive on-scene within the specified response times for oil containment and collection. The specific quantity of boom required for collection and containment will depend on the facility specific information and response strategies employed. A facility owner or operator shall, as appropriate, also identify sufficient quantities of oil containment boom to protect fish and wildlife and sensitive environments. For further description of fish and wildlife and sensitive environments, see Appendices I, II, and III to DOC/NOAA's "Guidance for Facility and Vessel Response Plans: Fish and Wildlife and Sensitive Environments" (see Appendix F, section 10, of this part of the CFRs for availability).

16.16 Other Information

Other information contained in this section of the CFRs includes:

- ❑ Determining Effective Daily Recovery Capacity for Oil Recovery Devices
- ❑ Calculating Planning Volumes for a Worst Case Discharge
- ❑ Determining the Availability of Alternative Response Methods
- ❑ Additional Equipment Necessary to Sustain Response Operations
- ❑ References and Availability of Information
- ❑ Response Resource Operating Criteria (Table 1)
- ❑ Removal Capacity Planning (Table 2)
- ❑ Emulsification Factors for Petroleum Oil Groups (Table 3)
- ❑ On-Water Oil Recovery Resource Mobilization Factors (Table 4)
- ❑ Response Capability Caps by Operating Area (Table 5)

16.16.1 Part 112 Appendices

The following tables lists the other appendices contained in this part:

Part 112 Appendices	Subject
Appendix A	Memorandum of Understanding Between the Secretary of Transportation and the Administrator of the Environmental Protection Agency
Appendix B	Memorandum of Understanding Among the Secretary of the Interior, Secretary of Transportation, and Administrator of the Environmental Protection Agency
Appendix C	Substantial Harm Criteria
Appendix D	Determination of a Worst Case Discharge Planning Volume
Appendix E	Determination and Evaluation of Required Response Resources for Facility Response Plans

State and Federal 404 Programs

40 CFR Part 232 contains definitions applicable to the section 404 program for discharges of dredged or fill material. These definitions apply to both the federally operated program and state administered programs after program approval. This part also describes those activities which are exempted from regulation.

17.1 Overview

Regulations prescribing the substantive environmental criteria for issuance of section 404 permits appear at 40 CFR Part 230. Regulations establishing procedures to be followed by the EPA in denying or restricting a disposal site appear at 40 CFR Part 231. Regulations containing the procedures and policies used by the Corps in administering the 404 program appear at 33 CFR Parts 320–330. Regulations specifying the procedures EPA will follow, and the criteria EPA will apply in approving, monitoring, and withdrawing approval of section 404 state programs appear at 40 CFR Part 233.

17.2 Activities Not Requiring Permits

Except as specified in this section, any discharge of dredged or fill material that may result from any of the activities described in this section of the CFRs is not prohibited by or otherwise subject to regulation under this part.

❑ If any discharge of dredged or fill material resulting from the activities listed in this section of the CFRs contains any toxic pollutant listed under section 307 of the Act, such discharge shall be subject to any applicable toxic effluent standard or prohibition, and shall require a section 404 permit.

❑ Any discharge of dredged or fill material into waters of the United States incidental to any of the activities identified in this section of the CFRs must have a permit if it is part of an activity whose purpose is to convert an area of the waters of the United States into a use to which it was not previously subject, where the flow or circulation of waters of the United States may be impaired or the reach of such waters reduced. Where the proposed discharge will result in significant discernable alterations to flow or circulation, the presumption is that flow or circulation may be impaired by such alteration.

For example, a permit will be required for the conversion of a cypress swamp to some other use or the conversion of a wetland from silvicultural to agricultural use when there is a discharge of dredged or fill material into waters of the United States in conjunction with construction of dikes, drainage ditches or other works or structures used to effect such conversion. A conversion of section 404 wetland to a non-wetland is a change in

173

use of an area of waters of the United States. A discharge which elevates the bottom of waters of the United States without converting it to dry land does not thereby reduce the reach of, but may alter the flow or circulation of, waters of the United States.

The following activities are exempt from section 404 permit requirements, except as specified in this section:

❑ Normal farming, silviculture and ranching activities such as plowing, seeding, cultivating, minor drainage, and harvesting for the production of food, fiber, and forest products, or upland soil and water conservation practices, as defined in this section of the CFRs.

To fall under this exemption, the activities specified in this section of the CFRs must be part of an established (i.e., ongoing) farming, silviculture, or ranching operation, and must be in accordance with definitions in this section of the CFRs. Activities on areas lying fallow as part of a conventional rotational cycle are part of an established operation.

❑ Activities which bring an area into farming, silviculture or ranching use is not part of an established operation. An operation ceases to be established when the area in which it was conducted has been converted to another use or has lain idle so long that modifications to the hydrological regime are necessary to resume operation. If an activity takes place outside the waters of the United States, or if it does not involve a discharge, it does not need a section 404 permit whether or not it was part of an established farming, silviculture or ranching operation.

❑ Maintenance, including emergency reconstruction of recently damaged parts, of currently serviceable structures such as dikes, dams, levees, groins, riprap, breakwaters, causeways, bridge abutments or approaches, and transportation structures. Maintenance does not include any modification that changes the character, scope, or size of the original fill design. Emergency reconstruction must occur within a reasonable period of time after damage occurs in order to qualify for this exemption.

❑ Construction or maintenance of farm or stock ponds or irrigation ditches or the maintenance (but not construction) of drainage ditches. Discharge associated with siphons, pumps, headgates, wingwalls, wiers, diversion structures, and such other facilities as are appurtenant and functionally related to irrigation ditches are included in this exemption.

❑ Construction of temporary sedimentation basins on a construction site which does not include placement of fill material into waters of the United States. The term "construction site" refers to any site involving the erection of buildings, roads, and other discrete structures and the installation of support facilities necessary for construction and utilization of such structures. The term also includes any other land areas which involve land disturbing excavation activities, including quarrying or other mining activities, where an increase in the runoff of sediment is controlled through the use of temporary sedimentation basins.

❏ Any activity with respect to which a state has an approved program under section 208(b)(4) of the Act which meets the requirements of section 208(b)(4)(B) and (C).

Construction or maintenance of farm roads, forest roads, or temporary roads for moving mining equipment, where such roads are constructed and maintained in accordance with best management practices (BMPs) to assure that flow and circulation patterns and chemical and biological characteristics of waters of the United States are not impaired, that the reach of the waters of the United States is not reduced, and that any adverse effect on the aquatic environment will be otherwise minimized are also exempted. The BMPs which must be applied to satisfy this provision include the following baseline provisions:

❏ Permanent roads (for farming or forestry activities), temporary access roads (for mining, forestry, or farm purposes) and skid trails (for logging) in waters of the United States shall be held to the minimum feasible number, width, and total length consistent with the purpose of specific farming, silvicultural or mining operations, and local topographic and climatic conditions;

❏ All roads, temporary or permanent, shall be located sufficiently far from streams or other water bodies (except for portions of such roads which must cross water bodies) to minimize discharges of dredged or fill material into waters of the United States;

❏ The road fill shall be bridged, culverted, or otherwise designed to prevent the restriction of expected flood flows;

❏ The fill shall be properly stabilized and maintained to prevent erosion during and following construction;

❏ Discharges of dredged or fill material into waters of the United States to construct a road fill shall be made in a way that minimizes the encroachment of trucks, tractors, bulldozers, or other heavy equipment within the waters of the United States (including adjacent wetlands) that lie outside the lateral boundaries of the fill itself;

❏ In designing, constructing, and maintaining roads, vegetative disturbance in the waters of the United States shall be kept to a minimum;

❏ The design, construction and maintenance of the road crossing shall not disrupt the migration or other movement of those species of aquatic life inhabiting the water body;

❏ Borrow material shall be taken from upland sources whenever feasible;

❏ The discharge shall not take, or jeopardize the continued existence of, a threatened or endangered species as defined under the Endangered Species Act, or adversely modify or destroy the critical habitat of such species;

❏ Discharges into breeding and nesting areas for migratory waterfowl, spawning areas, and wetlands shall be avoided if practical alternatives exist;

❏ The discharge shall not be located in the proximity of a public water supply intake;

❑ The discharge shall not occur in areas of concentrated shellfish production;

❑ The discharge shall not occur in a component of the National Wild and Scenic River System;

❑ The discharge of material shall consist of suitable material free from toxic pollutants in toxic amounts; and

❑ All temporary fills shall be removed in their entirety and the area restored to its original elevation.

17.3 State 404 Program Regulations 40 CFR Part 233

State assumption of the section 404 program is limited to certain waters, as provided in section 404(g)(1). The federal program operated by the Corps of Engineers continues to apply to the remaining waters in the state even after program approval. However, this does not restrict states from regulating discharges of dredged or fill material into those waters over which the Secretary retains section 404 jurisdiction.

This part specifies the procedures EPA will follow, and the criteria EPA will apply, in approving, reviewing, and withdrawing approval of state programs under section 404 of the Act. Except as provided in 232.3, a state program must regulate all discharges of dredged or fill material into waters regulated by the state under section 404(g)–(1). Partial state programs are not approvable under section 404.

A state's decision not to assume existing Corps' general permits does not constitute a partial program. The discharges previously authorized by general permit will be regulated by state individual permits. However, in many cases, states other than indian tribes will lack authority to regulate activities on indian lands. This lack of authority does not impair that state's ability to obtain full program approval in accordance with this part, i.e., inability of a state which is not an indian tribe to regulate activities on indian lands does not constitute a partial program. The Secretary of the Army acting through the Corps of Engineers will continue to administer the program on indian lands if a state which is not an indian tribe does not seek and have authority to regulate activities on indian lands.

Any approved state program shall, at all times, be conducted in accordance with the requirements of the Act and of this part. While states may impose more stringent requirements, they may not impose any less stringent requirements for any purpose.

17.3.1 Elements of a Program Submission

Any state that seeks to administer a 404 program under this part shall submit to the Regional Administrator at least three copies of the following:

❑ a letter from the Governor of the state requesting program approval;

❑ a complete program description, as set forth in 233.11;

❑ an Attorney General's statement, as set forth in 233.12;

☐ a Memorandum of Agreement with the Regional Administrator, as set forth in 233.13;

☐ a Memorandum of Agreement with the Secretary, as set forth in 233.14; and

☐ copies of all applicable state statutes and regulations, including those governing applicable state administrative procedures.

17.4 State 404 Program Description

The program description as required under 233.10 shall include:

☐ a description of the scope and structure of the state's program. The description should include extent of state's jurisdiction, scope of activities regulated, anticipated coordination, scope of permit exemptions if any, and permit review criteria;

☐ a description of the state's permitting, administrative, judicial review, and other applicable procedures;

☐ a description of the basic organization and structure of the state agency (agencies) which will have responsibility for administering the program. If more than one state agency is responsible for the administration of the program, the description shall address the responsibilities of each agency and how the agencies intend to coordinate administration and evaluation of the program;

☐ a description of the funding and manpower which will be available for program administration;

☐ an estimate of the anticipated workload, e.g., number of discharges.

☐ copies of permit application forms, permit forms, and reporting forms;

☐ a description of the state's compliance evaluation and enforcement programs, including a description of how the state will coordinate its enforcement strategy with that of the Corps and EPA;

☐ a description of the waters of the United States within a state over which the state assumes jurisdiction under the approved program; a description of the waters of the United States within a state over which the Secretary retains jurisdiction subsequent to program approval; and a comparison of the state and federal definitions of wetlands.

☐ a description of the specific best management practices proposed to be used to satisfy the exemption provisions of section 404(f)(1)(E) of the Act for construction or maintenance of farm roads, forest roads, or temporary roads for moving mining equipment.

Any state that seeks to administer a program under this part must also submit a statement from the State Attorney General (or the attorney for those state or interstate agencies which have independence legal counsel), that the laws and regulations of the state, or an interstate compact, provide adequate authority to carry out the program and meet the applicable requirements of this part. This statement shall cite specific statutes and administrative regulations which are lawfully adopted at the time the statement is signed and which shall be fully effective by the time the program is approved, and, where appropriate, judicial decisions which demonstrate adequate authority. The attorney signing the statement required by this section must have authority to represent the state agency in court on all matters pertaining to the state program.

If a state seeks approval of a program covering activities on indian lands, the statement shall contain an analysis of the state's authority over such activities. The State Attorney General's statement shall contain a legal analysis of the effect of state law regarding the prohibition on taking private property without just compensation on the successful implementation of the State's program.

In those states where more than one agency has responsibility for administering the state program, the statement must include certification that each agency has full authority to administer the program within its category of jurisdiction and that the state, as a whole, has full authority to administer a complete state section 404 program.

17.4.1 Memorandum of Agreement with Regional Administrator

Any state that seeks to administer a program under this part shall submit a Memorandum of Agreement executed by the Director and the Regional Administrator. The Memorandum of Agreement shall become effective upon approval of the state program. When more than one agency within a state has responsibility for administering the state program, Directors of each of the responsible state agencies shall be parties to the Memorandum of Agreement.

The Memorandum of Agreement shall set out the state and federal responsibilities for program administration and enforcement. These shall include, but not be limited to:

- ❑ provisions specifying classes and categories of permit applications for which EPA will waive federal review (as specified in 233.51);

- ❑ provisions specifying the frequency and content of reports, documents and other information which the state may be required to submit to EPA in addition to the annual report, as well as a provision establishing the submission date for the annual report;

- ❑ provisions addressing EPA and state roles and coordination with respect to compliance monitoring and enforcement activities; and

- ❑ provisions addressing modification of the Memorandum of Agreement.

Before a state program is approved under this part, the Director shall enter into a Memorandum of Agreement with the Secretary. When more than one agency within a state has responsibility for administering the state program, Directors of each of the responsible agencies shall be parties of the Memorandum of Agreement.

17.4.2 Procedures for Approving State Programs

After determining that a state program submission is complete, the Regional Administrator shall publish notice of the state's application in the Federal Register and in enough of the largest newspapers in the state to attract statewide attention. The Regional Administrator shall also mail notice to persons known to be interested in such matters. Existing state, EPA, Corps, FWS, and NMFS mailing lists shall be used as a basis for this mailing. However, failure to mail all such notices shall not be grounds for invalidating approval (or disapproval) of an otherwise acceptable (or unacceptable) program. This notice shall:

- ☐ provide for a comment period of not less than 45 days during which interested members of the public may express their views on the state program;

- ☐ provide for a public hearing within the state to be held not less than 30 days after notice of hearing is published in the Federal Register;

- ☐ indicate where and when the state's submission may be reviewed by the public;

- ☐ indicate whom an interested member of the public with questions should contact; and

- ☐ briefly outline the fundamental aspects of the state's proposed program and the process for EPA review and decision.

Within 90 days of EPA's receipt of a complete program submission, the Corps, FWS, and NMFS shall submit to EPA any comments on the state's program.

The Regional Administrator shall respond individually to comments received from the Corps, FWS, and NMFS. If the Regional Administrator approves the State's section 404 program, he shall notify the state and the Secretary of the decision and publish notice in the Federal Register. Transfer of the program to the state shall not be considered effective until such notice appears in the Federal Register. The Secretary shall suspend the issuance by the Corps of section 404 permits in state regulated waters on such effective date.

If the Regional Administrator disapproves the state's program based on the state not meeting the requirements of the Act and this part, the Regional Administrator shall notify the state of the reasons for the disapproval and of any revisions or modifications to the State's program which are necessary to obtain approval. If the state resubmits a program submission remedying the identified problem areas, the approval procedure and statutory review period shall begin upon receipt of the revised submission.

The state shall keep the Regional Administrator fully informed of any proposed or actual changes to the state's statutory or regulatory authority or any other modifications which are significant to administration of the program. Any approved program which requires revision because of a modification to this part or to any other applicable federal statute or regulation shall be revised within one year of the date of promulgation of such regulation, except that if a state must amend or enact a statute in order to make the required revision, the revision shall take place within two years.

17.5 General Permits

Under section 404(h)(5) of the Act, states may, after program approval, administer and enforce general permits previously issued by the Secretary in state regulated waters.

The Director may issue a general permit for categories of similar activities if he determines that the regulated activities will cause only minimal adverse environmental effects when performed separately and will have only minimal cumulative adverse effects on the environment. Any general permit issued shall be in compliance with the section 404(b)(1) Guidelines. In addition to the conditions specified in 233.23, each general permit shall contain:

- ❏ a specific description of the type(s) of activities which are authorized, including limitations for any single operation. The description shall be detailed enough to ensure that the requirements of this section of the CFRs are met; and

- ❏ a precise description of the geographic area to which the general permit applies, including limitations on the type(s) of water where operations may be conducted sufficient to ensure that the requirements of this section of the CFRs are met;

The Director may, without revoking the general permit, require any person authorized under a general permit to apply for an individual permit. This discretionary authority will be based on concerns for the aquatic environment including compliance with this section and the 404(b)(1) Guidelines (40 CFR Part 230.) This provision in no way affects the legality of activities undertaken pursuant to the general permit prior to notification by the Director of such requirement.

Once the Director notifies the discharger of his decision to exercise discretionary authority to require an individual permit, the discharger's activity is no longer authorized by the general permit.

17.6 Emergency Permits

Notwithstanding any other provision of this part, the Director may issue a temporary emergency permit for a discharge of dredged or fill material if unacceptable harm to life or severe loss of physical property is likely to occur before a permit could be issued or modified under procedures normally required. Emergency permits shall incorporate, to the extent possible and not inconsistent with the emergency situation, all applicable requirements of 233.23.

- ❏ Any emergency permit shall be limited to the duration of time (typically no more than 90 days) required to complete the authorized emergency action.

- ❏ The emergency permit shall have a condition requiring appropriate restoration of the site.

The emergency permit may be terminated at any time without process (233.36) if the Director determines that termination is necessary to protect human health or the environment. The emergency permit may be oral or written. If oral, it must be followed within five days by a written emergency permit. A copy of the written permit shall be sent to the Regional Administrator.

Notice of the emergency permit shall be published and public comments solicited in accordance with 233.32 as soon as possible but no later than 10 days after the issuance date.

17.7 Permit Conditions

For each permit the Director shall establish conditions which assure compliance with all applicable statutory and regulatory requirements, including the 404(b)(1) Guidelines, applicable section 303 water quality standards, and applicable section 307 effluent standards and prohibitions.

Section 404 permits shall be effective for a fixed term not to exceed five years. Each 404 permit shall include conditions meeting or implementing the following requirements:

❏ A specific identification and complete description of the authorized activity including name and address of permittee, location and purpose of discharge, type and quantity of material to be discharged. (This subsection is not applicable to general permits).

❏ Only the activities specifically described in the permit are authorized.

❏ The permittee shall comply with all conditions of the permit even if that requires halting or reducing the permitted activity to maintain compliance. Any permit violation constitutes a violation of the Act as well as of state statute and/or regulation.

❏ The permittee shall take all reasonable steps to minimize or prevent any discharge in violation of this permit.

❏ The permittee shall inform the Director of any expected or known actual noncompliance.

❏ The permittee shall provide such information to the Director, as the Director requests, to determine compliance status, or whether cause exists for permit modification, revocation or termination.

❏ Monitoring, reporting and recordkeeping requirements as needed to safeguard the aquatic environment. (Such requirements will be determined on a case by case basis, but at a minimum shall include monitoring and reporting of any expected leachates, reporting of noncompliance, planned changes or transfer of the permit.)

17.7.1 Inspection and Entry

The permittee shall allow the Director, or his authorized representative, upon presentation of proper identification, at reasonable times to:

❏ enter upon the permittee's premises where a regulated activity is located or where records must be kept under the conditions of the permit,

❏ have access to and copy any records that must be kept under the conditions of the permit,

❏ inspect operations regulated or required under the permit, and

❏ sample or monitor, for the purposes of assuring permit compliance or as otherwise authorized by the Act, any substances or parameters at any location.

Conditions assuring that the discharge will be conducted in a manner which minimizes adverse impacts upon the physical, chemical and biological integrity of the waters of the United States, such as requirements for restoration or mitigation.

17.8 Application for a Permit

Except when an activity is authorized by a general permit issued pursuant to 233.21 or is exempt from the requirements to obtain a permit under 232.3, any person who proposes to discharge dredged or fill material into state regulated waters shall complete, sign and submit a permit application to the Director. Persons proposing to discharge dredged or fill material under the authorization of a general permit must comply with any reporting requirements of the general permit. A complete application shall include:

❏ Name, address, telephone number of the applicant and name(s) and address(es) of adjoining property owners.

❏ A complete description of the proposed activity including necessary drawings, sketches or plans sufficient for public notice (the applicant is not generally expected to submit detailed engineering plans and specifications); the location, purpose and intended use of the proposed activity; scheduling of the activity; the location and dimensions of adjacent structures; and a list of authorizations required by other federal, interstate, state or local agencies for the work, including all approvals received or denials already made.

❏ The application must include a description of the type, composition, source and quantity of the material to be discharged, the method of discharge, and the site and plans for disposal of the dredged or fill material.

❏ A certification that all information contained in the application is true and accurate and acknowledging awareness of penalties for submitting false information.

❏ All activities which the applicant plans to undertake which are reasonably related to the same project should be included in the same permit application.

In addition to the information indicated in 233.30(b), the applicant will be required to furnish such additional information as the Director deems appropriate to assist in the evaluation of the application. Such additional information may include environmental data and information on alternate methods and sites as may be necessary for the preparation of the required environmental documentation.

The level of detail shall be reasonably commensurate with the type and size of discharge, proximity to critical areas, likelihood of long–lived toxic chemical substances, and potential level of environmental degradation.

EPA encourages states to provide permit applicants guidance regarding the level of detail of information and documentation required under this subsection. This guidance can be provided either through the application form or on an individual basis. EPA also encourages the state to maintain a program to inform potential applicants for permits of the requirements of the state program and of the steps required to obtain permits for activities in state regulated waters.

17.9 Other Issues

Other issues described in this section include, but are not limited to:

- ☐ coordination requirements
- ☐ public notice
- ☐ public hearing
- ☐ making a decision on the permit application
- ☐ issuance and effective date of permit
- ☐ modification, suspension or revocation of permits
- ☐ signatures on permit applications and reports
- ☐ continuation of expiring permits
- ☐ requirements for compliance evaluation programs
- ☐ requirements for enforcement authority
- ☐ federal oversight
- ☐ review of and objection to state permits

17.10 Program Reporting

The starting date for the annual period to be covered by reports shall be established in the Memorandum of Agreement with the Regional Administrator (233.13.)

The Director shall submit to the Regional Administrator within 90 days after completion of the annual period, a draft annual report evaluating the state's administration of its program identifying problems the state has encountered in the administration of its program and recommendations for resolving these problems. Items that shall be addressed in the annual report include:

- ☐ an assessment of the cumulative impacts of the state's permit program on the integrity of the state regulated waters;
- ☐ identification of areas of particular concern and/or interest within the state;
- ☐ the number and nature of individual and general permits issued, modified, and denied;

- ❏ number of violations identified and number and nature of enforcement actions taken;

- ❏ number of suspected unauthorized activities reported and nature of action taken;

- ❏ an estimate of extent of activities regulated by general permits; and

- ❏ the number of permit applications received but not yet processed.

The state shall make the draft annual report available for public inspection. Within 60 days of receipt of the draft annual report, the Regional Administrator will complete review of the draft report and transmit comments, questions, and/or requests for additional evaluation and/or information to the Director. Within 30 days of receipt of the Regional Administrator's comments, the Director will finalize the annual report, incorporating and/or responding to the Regional Administrator's comments, and transmit the final report to the Regional Administrator.

Upon acceptance of the annual report, the Regional Administrator shall publish notice of availability of the final annual report.

17.11 Withdrawal of Program Approval

A state with a program approved under this part may voluntarily transfer program responsibilities required by federal law to the Secretary by taking the following actions, or in such other manner as may be agreed upon with the Administrator.

The state shall give the Administrator and the Secretary 180 days notice of the proposed transfer. The state shall also submit a plan for the orderly transfer of all relevant program information not in the possession of the Secretary (such as permits, permit files, reports, permit applications) which are necessary for the Secretary to administer the program.

Within 60 days of receiving the notice and transfer plan, the Administrator and the Secretary shall evaluate the state's transfer plan and shall identify for the state any additional information needed by the federal government for program administration.

At least 30 days before the transfer is to occur the Administrator shall publish notice of transfer in the Federal Register and in a sufficient number of the largest newspapers in the state to provide statewide coverage, and shall mail notice to all permit holders, permit applicants, other regulated persons and other interested persons on appropriate EPA, Corps and state mailing lists.

The Administrator may withdraw program approval when a state program no longer complies with the requirements of this part, and the state fails to take corrective action. Such circumstances include the following:

- ❏ when the state's legal authority no longer meets the requirements of this part, including:

(i) failure of the state to promulgate or enact new authorities when necessary; or

(ii) action by a state legislature or court striking down or limiting state authorities.

❏ when the operation of the state program fails to comply with the requirements of this part, including:

> (i) failure to exercise control over activities required to be regulated under this part,

including   failure to issue permits;

> (ii) issuance of permits which do not conform to the requirements of this part; or

> (iii) failure to comply with the public participation requirements of this part.

❏ when the state's enforcement program fails to comply with the requirements of this part, including:

> (i) failure to act on violations of permits or other program requirements;

> (ii) failure to seek adequate enforcement penalties or to collect administrative fines when imposed, or to implement alternative enforcement methods approved by the

Administrator; or

> (iii) failure to inspect and monitor activities subject to regulation.

❏ when the state program fails to comply with the terms of the Memorandum of Agreement required under 233.13.

The Administrator may order the commencement of withdrawal proceedings on the Administrator's initiative or in response to a petition from an interested person alleging failure of the state to comply with the requirements of this part as set forth in subsection (b) of this section of the CFRs. The Administrator shall respond in writing to any petition to commence withdrawal proceedings. He may conduct an informal review of the allegations in the petition to determine whether cause exists to commence proceedings under this paragraph. The Administrator's order commencing proceedings under this paragraph shall fix a time and place for the commencement of the hearing, shall specify the allegations against the state which are to be considered at the hearing, and shall be published in the Federal Register. Within 30 days after publication of the Administrator's order in the Federal Register, the state shall admit or deny these allegations in a written answer. The party seeking withdrawal of the State's program shall have the burden of coming forward with the evidence in a hearing under this paragraph.

17.12 Procedures

The following provisions of 40 CFR Part 22 [Consolidated Rules of Practice] are applicable to proceedings under this section of the CFRs:

❏ Section 22.02–(use of number/gender);

❏ Section 22.04–(authorities of presiding officer);

❏ Section 22.06–(filing/service of rulings and orders);

❏ Section 22.09–(examination of filed documents);

❏ Section 22.19 (a), (b) and (c)–(prehearing conference);

❏ Section 22.22–(evidence);

❏ Section 22.23–(objections/offers of proof);

❑ Section 22.25–(filing the transcript; and

❑ Section 22.26–(findings/conclusions).

❑ Computation and extension of time

❑ Extensions of time

❑ Ex parte discussion of proceeding

❑ Intervention

❑ Disposition

❑ Amicus curiae

Subpart H of this part contains information on Approved State Programs.

State Permit Program (SPDES) Requirements

---

40 CFR Part 123 describes the general requirements and additional requirements for states and the EPA to obtain and give approval, revision, and withdrawal of state NPDES programs. State program information shall be made available to EPA upon request.

18.1 Overview

This part specifies the procedures EPA will follow in approving, revising, and withdrawing state programs and the requirements state programs must meet to be approved by the Administrator under sections 318, 402, and 405 (National Pollutant Discharge Elimination System–NPDES) of CWA. These regulations are promulgated under the authority of sections 304(i), 101(e), 405, and 518(e) of the CWA, and implement the requirements of those sections.

The Administrator shall approve state programs which conform to the applicable requirements of this part. A state NPDES program will not be approved by the Administrator under section 402 of CWA unless it has authority to control the discharges specified in sections 318 and 405(a) of CWA. Permit programs under sections 318 and 405(a) will not be approved independent of a section 402 program. (Permit programs under section 405(f) of CWA (sludge management programs) may be approved under 40 CFR Part 501 independently of a section 402 permit program.)

Upon approval of a state program, the Administrator shall suspend the issuance of federal permits for those activities subject to the approved state program. After program approval EPA shall retain jurisdiction over any permits (including general permits) which it has issued unless arrangements have been made with the state in the Memorandum of Agreement for the state to assume responsibility for these permits. Retention of jurisdiction shall include the processing of any permit appeals, modification requests, or variance requests; the conduct of inspections, and the receipt and review of self-monitoring reports. If any permit appeal, modification request or variance request is not finally resolved when the federally issued permit expires, EPA may, with the consent of the state, retain jurisdiction until the matter is resolved.

The procedures outlined in this section for suspension of permitting authority and transfer of existing permits will also apply when EPA approves an indian tribe's application to operate a state program and a state was the authorized permitting authority under 123.23(b) for activities within the scope of the newly approved program. The authorized state will retain jurisdiction over its existing permits as described in this section of the CFRs absent a different arrangement stated in the Memorandum of Agreement executed between EPA and the Tribe.

Upon submission of a complete program, EPA will conduct a public hearing, if interest is shown, and determine whether to approve or disapprove the program taking into consideration the requirements of this part, the CWA and any comments received.

Any state program approved by the Administrator shall at all times be conducted in accordance with the requirements of this part.

Except as may be authorized pursuant to this section or excluded by 122.3, the state program must prohibit all point source discharges of pollutants, all discharges into aquaculture projects, and all disposal of sewage sludge which results in any pollutant from such sludge entering into any waters of the United States within the State's jurisdiction except as authorized by a permit in effect under the state program or under section 402 of CWA. NPDES authority may be shared by two or more state agencies but each agency must have statewide jurisdiction over a class of activities or discharges. When more than one agency is responsible for issuing permits, each agency must make a submission meeting the requirements of 123.21 before EPA will begin formal review.

A state may seek approval of a partial or phased program in accordance with section 402(n) of the CWA.

In many cases, states (other than indian tribes) will lack authority to regulate activities on indian lands. This lack of authority does not impair that State's ability to obtain full program approval in accordance with this part, i.e., inability of a state to regulate activities on indian lands does not constitute a partial program. EPA will administer the program on indian lands if a state (or indian tribe) does not seek or have authority to regulate activities on indian lands.

States are advised to contact the United States Department of the Interior, Bureau of Indian Affairs, concerning authority over indian lands. Nothing in this part precludes a state from:

❑ adopting or enforcing requirements which are more stringent or more extensive than those required under this part;

❑ operating a program with a greater scope of coverage than that required under this part. If an approved state program has greater scope of coverage than required by federal law the additional coverage is not part of the federally approved program.

Issuance of state permits under this part may be coordinated with issuance of RCRA, UIC, NPDES, and 404 permits whether they are controlled by the state, EPA, or the Corps of Engineers. See 124.4.

18.2 State Program Submissions

Any state that seeks to administer a program under this part shall submit to the Administrator at least three copies of a program submission. The submission shall contain the following:

❑ a letter from the Governor of the state (or in the case of an indian tribe in accordance with 123.33(b), the tribal authority exercising powers substantially similar to those of a State Governor) requesting program approval;

❑ a complete program description, as required by 123.22, describing how the state intends to carry out its responsibilities under this part;

❑ an Attorney General's statement as required by 123.23;

❑ a Memorandum of Agreement with the Regional Administrator as required by 123.24; and

❑ copies of all applicable state statutes and regulations, including those governing state administrative procedures.

Within 30 days of receipt by EPA of a state program submission, EPA will notify the state whether its submission is complete. If EPA finds that a state's submission is complete, the statutory review period (i.e., the period of time allotted for formal EPA review of a proposed state program under CWA) shall be deemed to have begun on the date of receipt of the state's submission. If EPA finds that a state's submission is incomplete, the statutory review period shall not begin until all the necessary information is received by EPA.

In the case of an indian tribe eligible under 123.33(b), EPA shall take into consideration the contents of the Tribe's request submitted under 123.32, in determining if the program submission required by 123.21(a) is complete.

If the state's submission is materially changed during the statutory review period, the statutory review period shall begin again upon receipt of the revised submission. The state and EPA may extend the statutory review period by agreement.

18.3 Program Description

Any state that seeks to administer a program under this part shall submit a description of the program it proposes to administer in lieu of the federal program under state law or under an interstate compact. The program description shall include:

❑ a description in narrative form of the scope, structure, coverage and processes of the state program; and

❑ a description (including organization charts) of the organization and structure of the state agency or agencies which will have responsibility for administering the program, including the information listed below.

If more than one agency is responsible for administration of a program, each agency must have statewide jurisdiction over a class of activities. The responsibilities of each agency must be delineated, their procedures for coordination set forth, and an agency may be designated as a "lead agency" to facilitate communications between EPA and the state agencies having program responsibility. If the state proposes to administer a program of greater scope of coverage than is required by federal law, the information provided under this paragraph shall indicate the resources dedicated to administering the federally required portion of the program.

- ❑ a description of the state agency staff who will carry out the state program, including the number, occupations, and general duties of the employees. The state need not submit complete job descriptions for every employee carrying out the state program;

- ❑ an itemization of the estimated costs of establishing and administering the program for the first two years after approval, including cost of the personnel listed in this section of the CFRs, cost of administrative support, and cost of technical support;

- ❑ an itemization of the sources and amounts of funding, including an estimate of federal grant money, available to the State Director for the first two years after approval to meet the costs listed in this section of the CFRs, identifying any restrictions or limitations upon this funding;

- ❑ a description of applicable state procedures, including permitting procedures and any state administrative or judicial review procedures;

- ❑ copies of the permit form(s), application form(s), and reporting form(s) the state intends to employ in its program. Forms used by states need not be identical to the forms used by EPA but should require the same basic information, except that state NPDES programs are required to use standard Discharge Monitoring Reports (DMR). The state need not provide copies of uniform national forms it intends to use but should note its intention to use such forms;

- ❑ a complete description of the state's compliance tracking and enforcement program.

A state seeking approval of a sludge management program under section 405(f) of the CWA as part of its NPDES program, in addition to the above requirements of this section, shall include the inventory as required in 40 CFR 501.12(f).

In the case of indian tribes eligible under 123.33(b), if a state has been authorized by EPA to issue permits on the federal Indian reservation in accordance with 123.23(b), a description of how responsibility for pending permit applications, existing permits, and supporting files will be transferred from the state to the eligible indian tribe. To the maximum extent practicable, this should include a Memorandum of Agreement negotiated between the state and the indian tribe addressing the arrangements for such transfer.

18.4 Attorney General's Statement

Any state that seeks to administer a program under this part shall submit a statement from the State Attorney General (or the attorney for those state or interstate agencies which have independent legal counsel) that the laws of the state, or an interstate compact, provide adequate authority to carry out the program described under 123.22 and to meet the requirements of this part. This statement shall include citations to the specific statutes, administrative regulations, and, where appropriate, judicial decisions which demonstrate adequate authority. State statutes and regulations cited by the State Attorney General or independent legal counsel shall be in the form of lawfully adopted state statutes and regulations at the time the statement is signed and shall be fully effective by the time the program is approved. To qualify as "independent legal counsel" the attorney signing the statement required by this section must have full authority to independently represent the state agency in court on all matters pertaining to the state program.

Note: EPA will supply states with an Attorney General's statement format on request.

If a state (which is not an indian tribe) seeks authority over activities on Indian lands, the statement shall contain an appropriate analysis of the state's authority. The Attorney General's statement shall certify that the state has adequate legal authority to issue and enforce general permits if the state seeks to implement the general permit program under 122.28.

18.5 Memorandum of Agreement with the Regional Administrator

Any state that seeks to administer a program under this part shall submit a Memorandum of Agreement. The Memorandum of Agreement shall be executed by the State Director and the Regional Administrator and shall become effective when approved by the Administrator. In addition to meeting the requirements of this section of the CFRs, the Memorandum of Agreement may include other terms, conditions, or agreements consistent with this part and relevant to the administration and enforcement of the state's regulatory program. The Administrator shall not approve any Memorandum of Agreement which contains provisions which restrict EPA's statutory oversight responsibility.

The Memorandum of Agreement shall include the following:

❑ Provisions for the prompt transfer from EPA to the state of pending permit applications and any other information relevant to program operation not already in the possession of the State Director (e.g., support files for permit issuance, compliance reports, etc.). If existing permits are transferred from EPA to the state for administration, the Memorandum of Agreement shall contain provisions specifying a procedure for transferring the administration of these permits. If a state lacks the authority to directly administer permits issued by the federal government, a procedure may be established to transfer responsibility for these permits.

❑ Where a state has been authorized by EPA to issue permits in accordance with 123.23(b) on the federal Indian reservation of the indian tribe seeking program approval, provisions describing how the transfer of pending permit applications, permits, and any other information relevant to the program operation not already in the possession of the indian tribe (support files for permit issuance, compliance reports, etc.) will be accomplished.

❑ Provisions specifying classes and categories of permit applications, draft permits, and proposed permits that the state will send to the Regional Administrator for review, comment and, where applicable, objection.

❑ Provisions specifying the frequency and content of reports, documents and other information which the state is required to submit to EPA. The state shall allow EPA to routinely review state records, reports, and files relevant to the administration and enforcement of the approved program. state reports may be combined with grant reports where appropriate. These procedures shall implement the requirements of 123.43.

❑ Provisions on the state's compliance monitoring and enforcement program, including:

  • provisions for coordination of compliance monitoring activities by the state and by EPA. These may specify the basis on which the Regional Administrator will select facilities or activities within the state for EPA inspection. The Regional Administrator will normally notify the state at least seven days before any such inspection; and

  • Procedures to assure coordination of enforcement activities.

When appropriate, provisions for joint processing of permits by the state and EPA for facilities or activities which require permits from both EPA and the state under different programs. (See 124.4.)

To promote efficiency and to avoid duplication and inconsistency, states are encouraged to enter into joint processing agreements with EPA for permit issuance. Likewise, states are encouraged (but not required) to consider steps to coordinate or consolidate their own permit programs and activities.

The Memorandum of Agreement shall also specify the extent to which EPA will waive its right to review, object to, or comment upon state issued permits under section 402(d)(3), (e) or (f) of CWA. While the Regional Administrator and the state may agree to waive EPA review of certain "classes or categories" of permits, no waiver of review may be granted for the following classes or categories:

❑ discharges into the territorial sea;

❑ discharges which may affect the waters of a state other than the one in which the discharge originates;

❑ discharges proposed to be regulated by general permits (see 122.28);

❑ discharges from publicly owned treatment works with a daily average discharge exceeding one million gallons per day;

❑ discharges of uncontaminated cooling water with a daily average discharge exceeding 500 million gallons per day;

❑ discharges from any major discharger or from any discharger within any of the 21 industrial categories listed in appendix A to part 122; and

❑ discharges from other sources with a daily average discharge exceeding 0.5 (one-half) million gallons per day, except that EPA review of permits for discharges of non-process wastewater may be waived regardless of flow.

Whenever a waiver is granted under this section of the CFRs, the Memorandum of Agreement shall contain:

❑ a statement that the Regional Administrator retains the right to terminate the waiver as to future permit actions, in whole or in part, at any time by sending the State Director written notice of termination; and

❑ a statement that the state shall supply EPA with copies of final permits.

18.6 Requirements for Permitting

All state programs under this part must have legal authority to implement each of the following provisions and must be administered in conformance with each, except that a state which chooses not to administer a sludge management program pursuant to section 405(f) of the CWA as part of its NPDES program is not required to have legal authority to implement the portions of the following provisions which were promulgated after the enactment of the Water Quality Act of 1987 (Pub. L. 100–4) and which govern sewage sludge use and disposal. In all cases, states are not precluded from omitting or modifying any provisions to impose more stringent requirements:

❑ (1)122.4–(prohibitions):

❑ (2)122.5(a) and (b)–(effect of permit);

❑ (3)122.7(b) and (c)–(confidential information);

❑ (4)122.21 (a)–(b), (c)(2), (e)–(k), and (m)–(p)–(application for a permit);

❑ (5)122.22–(signatories);

❑ (6)122.23–(concentrated animal feeding operations);

❑ (7)122.24–(concentrated aquatic animal production facilities);

❑ (8)122.25–(aquaculture projects);

❑ (9)122.26–(storm water discharges);

❑ (10)122.27–(silviculture);

❑ (11)122.28–(general permits), provided that states which do not seek to implement the general permit program under 122.28 need not do so.

❑ (12) Section 122.41–(applicable permit conditions)(Indian Tribes can satisfy enforcement authority requirements under 123.34).

- ❏ (13)122.42–(conditions applicable to specified categories of permits);
- ❏ (14)122.43–(establishing permit conditions);
- ❏ (15)122.44–(establishing NPDES permit conditions);
- ❏ (16)122.45–(calculating permit conditions);
- ❏ (17)122.46–(duration);
- ❏ (18)122.47(a)–(schedules of compliance);
- ❏ (19)122.48–(monitoring requirements);
- ❏ (20)122.50–(disposal into wells);
- ❏ (21)122.61–(permit transfer);
- ❏ (22)122.62–(permit modification);
- ❏ (23)122.64–(permit termination);
- ❏ (24)124.3(a)–(application for a permit);
- ❏ (25)124.5 (a), (c), (d), and (f)–(modification of permits);
- ❏ (26)124.6 (a), (c), (d), and (e)–(draft permit);
- ❏ (27)124.8–(fact sheets);
- ❏ (28)124.10 (a)(1)(ii), (a)(1)(iii), (a)(1)(v), (b), (c), (d), and (e)–(public notice);
- ❏ (29)124.11–(public comments and requests for hearings);
- ❏ (30)124.12(a)–(public hearings); and
- ❏ (31)124.17 (a) and (c)–(response to comments);
- ❏ (32)124.56–(fact sheets);
- ❏ (33)124.57(a)–(public notice);
- ❏ (34)124.59–(comments from government agencies);
- ❏ (35)124.62–(decision on variances);
- ❏ (36)Subparts A, B, C, D, H, I, J, K and L of part 125;
- ❏ (37)40 CFR Parts 129, 133, subchapter N and 40 CFR Part 503; and
- ❏ (38) For a Great Lakes State or Tribe (as defined in 40 CFR 132.2), 40 CFR Part 132 (NPDES permitting implementation procedures only).

States need not implement provisions identical to the above listed provisions. Implemented provisions must, however, establish requirements at least as stringent as the corresponding listed provisions. While states may impose more stringent requirements, they may not make one requirement more lenient as a tradeoff for making another requirement more stringent.

18.7 State NPDES programs

State NPDES programs shall have an approved continuing planning process under 40 CFR 35.1500 and shall assure that the approved planning process is at all times consistent with CWA.

State NPDES programs shall ensure that any board or body which approves all or portions of permits shall not include as a member any person who receives, or has during the previous two years received, a significant portion of income directly or indirectly from permit holders or applicants for a permit.

18.7.1 Requirements for Compliance Evaluation Programs

State programs shall have procedures for receipt, evaluation, retention and investigation for possible enforcement of all notices and reports required of permittees and other regulated persons (and for investigation for possible enforcement of failure to submit these notices and reports).

State programs shall have inspection and surveillance procedures to determine, independent of information supplied by regulated persons, compliance or noncompliance with applicable program requirements. The state shall maintain:

- ❏ a program which is capable of making comprehensive surveys of all facilities and activities subject to the State Director's authority to identify persons subject to regulation who have failed to comply with permit application or other program requirements. Any compilation, index or inventory of such facilities and activities shall be made available to the Regional Administrator upon request;

- ❏ a program for periodic inspections of the facilities and activities subject to regulation. These inspections shall be conducted in a manner designed to: determine compliance or noncompliance with issued permit conditions and other program requirements; verify the accuracy of information submitted by permittees and other regulated persons in reporting forms and other forms supplying monitoring data; and verify the adequacy of sampling, monitoring, and other methods used by permittees and other regulated persons to develop that information;

- ❏ a program for investigating information obtained regarding violations of applicable program and permit requirements; and

- ❏ procedures for receiving and ensuring proper consideration of information submitted by the public about violations. Public effort in reporting violations shall be encouraged, and the State Director shall make available information on reporting procedures.

18.7.2 Inspections

Investigatory inspections shall be conducted, samples shall be taken and other information shall be gathered in a manner (e.g., using proper "chain of custody" procedures) that will produce evidence admissible in an enforcement proceeding or in court. State NPDES compliance evaluation programs shall also have procedures and ability for:

❑ maintaining a comprehensive inventory of all sources covered by NPDES permits and a schedule of reports required to be submitted by permittees to the state agency;

❑ initial screening (i.e., pre-enforcement evaluation) of all permit or grant related compliance information to identify violations and to establish priorities for further substantive technical evaluation;

❑ when warranted, conducting a substantive technical evaluation following the initial screening of all permit or grant related compliance information to determine the appropriate agency response;

❑ maintaining a management information system which supports the compliance evaluation activities of this part; and

❑ inspecting the facilities of all major dischargers and all Class I sludge management facilities (as defined in 40 CFR 501.2) where applicable at least annually.

18.7.3 Enforcement Authority

Any state agency administering a program shall have available the following remedies for violations of state program requirements:

❑ to restrain immediately and effectively any person by order or by suit in state court from engaging in any unauthorized activity which is endangering or causing damage to public health or the environment;

❑ procedures for assessment by the state of the cost of investigations, inspections, or monitoring surveys which lead to the establishment of violations;

❑ to sue in courts of competent jurisdiction to enjoin any threatened or continuing violation of any program requirement, including permit conditions, without the necessity of a prior revocation of the permit; and

❑ to assess or sue to recover in court civil penalties and to seek criminal remedies, including fines.

Civil penalties shall be recoverable for the violation of any NPDES permit condition; any NPDES filing requirement; any duty to allow or carry out inspection, entry or monitoring activities; or, any regulation or orders issued by the State Director. These penalties shall be assessable in at least the amount of $5,000 a day for each violation.

Criminal fines shall be recoverable against any person who willfully or negligently violates any applicable standards or limitations; any NPDES permit condition; or any NPDES filing requirement. These fines shall be assessable in at least the amount of $10,000 a day for each violation.

The burden of proof and degree of knowledge or intent required under state law for establishing violations under this section, shall be no greater than the burden of proof or degree of knowledge or intent EPA must provide when it brings an action under the appropriate Act.

A civil penalty assessed, sought, or agreed upon by the State Director under this section of the CFRs shall be appropriate to the violation.

In addition to the requirements above, the state may have other enforcement remedies.

18.7.4 Public Participation

Any state administering a program shall provide for public participation in the state enforcement process by providing either:

❑ authority which allows intervention as of right in any civil or administrative action to obtain remedies specified in this section by any citizen having an interest which is or may be adversely affected; or

❑ assurance that the state agency or enforcement authority will:

- investigate and provide written responses to all citizen complaints submitted pursuant to the procedures specified in 123.26(b)(4);

- not oppose intervention by any citizen when permissive intervention may be authorized by statute, rule, or regulation; and

- publish notice of and provide at least 30 days for public comment on any proposed settlement of a state enforcement action.

18.7.5 Control of Disposal of Pollutants into Wells

State law must provide authority to issue permits to control the disposal of pollutants into wells. Such authority shall enable the state to protect the public health and welfare and to prevent the pollution of ground and surface waters by prohibiting well discharges or by issuing permits for such discharges with appropriate permit terms and conditions. A program approved under section 1422 of SDWA satisfies the requirements of this section of the CFRs.

State permit programs shall provide that no permit shall be issued when the Regional Administrator has objected in writing under 123.44. Other issues addressed in this section of the CFRs includes, but is not limited to:

❑ judicial review of approval or denial of permits

❑ transfer of information and permit review

- ❑ sharing of information
- ❑ receipt and use of federal information
- ❑ transmission of information to EPA
- ❑ EPA review of and objections to state permits

18.8 Noncompliance and Program Reporting by the Director

The Director shall prepare quarterly, semiannual, and annual reports as detailed below. When the state is the permit issuing authority, the State Director shall submit all reports required under this section to the Regional Administrator, and the EPA Region in turn shall submit the state reports to EPA Headquarters. When EPA is the permit–issuing authority, the Regional Administrator shall submit all reports required under this section to EPA Headquarters.

All permittees under current enforcement orders (i.e., administrative and judicial orders and consent decrees) for previous instances of noncompliance must be listed in the QNCR until the orders have been satisfied in full and the permittee is in compliance with permit conditions. If the permittee is in compliance with the enforcement order, but has not achieved full compliance with permit conditions, the compliance status shall be reported as "resolved pending," but the permittee will continue to be listed on the QNCR.

18.8.1 Category I Noncompliance

The following instances of noncompliance by major dischargers are Category I noncompliance:

- ❑ violations of conditions in enforcement orders except compliance schedules and reports;
- ❑ violations of compliance schedule milestones for starting construction, completing construction, and attaining final compliance by 90 days or more from the date of the milestone specified in an enforcement order or a permit.
- ❑ violations of permit effluent limits that exceed the Appendix A "Criteria for Noncompliance Reporting in the NPDES Program;" and
- ❑ failure to provide a compliance schedule report for final compliance or a monitoring report. This applies when the permittee has failed to submit a final compliance schedule progress report, pretreatment report, or a Discharge Monitoring Report within 30 days from the due date specified in an enforcement order or a permit.

18.8.2 Category II Noncompliance

Category II noncompliance includes violations of permit conditions which the Agency believes to be of substantial concern and may not meet the Category I criteria. The following are instances of noncompliance which must be reported as Category II noncompliance unless the same violation meets the criteria for Category I noncompliance:

- ❏ violation of a permit limit;

- ❏ an unauthorized bypass;

- ❏ an unpermitted discharge; or

- ❏ a pass-through of pollutants which causes or has the potential to cause a water quality problem (e.g., fish kills, oil sheens) or health problems (e.g., beach closings, fishing bans, or other restrictions of beneficial uses).

- ❏ failure of an approved POTW to implement its approved pretreatment program adequately including failure to enforce industrial pretreatment requirements on industrial users as required in the approved program.

- ❏ violations of any compliance schedule milestones (except those milestones listed in this section of the CFRs) by 90 days or more from the date specified in an enforcement order or a permit.

- ❏ failure of the permittee to provide reports (other than those reports listed in this section of the CFRs) within 30 days from the due date specified in an enforcement order or a permit.

- ❏ instances when the required reports provided by the permittee are so deficient or incomplete as to cause misunderstanding by the Director and thus impede the review of the status of compliance.

- ❏ violations of narrative requirements (e.g., requirements to develop Spill Prevention Control and Countermeasure Plans and requirements to implement Best Management Practices), which are of substantial concern to the regulatory agency.

- ❏ any other violation or group of permit violations which the Director or Regional Administrator considers to be of substantial concern.

18.8.3 Semiannual Statistical Summary Reports

Summary information shall be provided twice a year on the number of major permittees with two or more violations of the same monthly average permit limitation in a six-month period, including those otherwise reported under this section of the CFRs. This report shall be submitted at the same time, according to the federal fiscal year calendar, as the first and third quarter QNCRs.

18.8.4 Annual Reports for NPDES

Annual noncompliance statistical reports shall be submitted by the Director on non-major NPDES permittees indicating the total number reviewed, the number of noncomplying non-major permittees, the number of enforcement actions, and number of permit modifications extending compliance deadlines. The statistical information shall be organized to follow the types of noncompliance listed in this section.

A separate list of non-major discharges which are one or more years behind in construction phases of the compliance schedule shall also be submitted in alphabetical order by name and permit number.

18.8.5 Schedule for Reports

On the last working day of May, August, November, and February, the State Director shall submit to the Regional Administrator information concerning noncompliance with NPDES permit requirements by major dischargers in the state in accordance with the following schedule. The Regional Administrator shall prepare and submit information for EPA issued permits to EPA Headquarters in accordance with the same schedule.

The period for annual reports shall be for the calendar year ending December 31, with reports completed and available to the public no more than 60 days later.

Appendix A to 123.45, Criteria for Noncompliance Reporting in the NPDES Program describes the criteria for reporting violations of NPDES permit effluent limits in the quarterly noncompliance report (QNCR). Any violation of an NPDES permit is a violation of the Clean Water Act (CWA) for which the permittee is liable. An agency's decision about what enforcement action, if any, should be taken in such cases, will be based on an analysis of facts and legal requirements.

Cases in which violations of permit effluent limits must be reported depend upon the magnitude and/or frequency of the violation. Effluent violations should be evaluated on a parameter-by-parameter and outfall-by-outfall basis. The criteria for reporting effluent violations are listed in this section of the CFRs.

18.9 Individual Control Strategies

For the purposes of this section the term individual control strategy, as set forth in section 304(l) of the CWA, means a final NPDES permit with supporting documentation showing that effluent limits are consistent with an approved wasteload allocation, or other documentation which shows that applicable water quality standards will be met not later than three years after the individual control strategy is established. If a point source is subject to section 304(l)(1)(C) of the CWA and is also subject to an on-site response action under sections 104 or 106 of the Comprehensive Environmental Response, Compensation, and Liability Act of 1980 (CERCLA), (42 U.S.C. 9601 et seq.), an individual control strategy may be the decision document (which incorporates the applicable or relevant and appropriate requirements under the CWA) prepared under sections 104 or 106 of CERCLA to address the release or threatened release of hazardous substances to the environment.

A petition submitted pursuant to section 304(l)(3) of the CWA must be submitted to the appropriate Regional Administrator. Petitions must identify a waterbody in sufficient detail so that EPA is able to determine the location and boundaries of the waterbody. The petition must also identify the list or lists for which the waterbody qualifies, and the petition must explain why the waterbody satisfies the criteria for listing under CWA section 304(l) and 40 CFR 130.10(d)(6).

State UIC Program Requirements

> *The State UIC Program contains the procedures EPA will follow in approving, revising, and withdrawing state programs under section 1422 (underground injection control–UIC) of SDWA, and includes the elements which must be part of submissions to EPA for program approval and the substantive provisions which must be present in state programs for them to be approved.*

19.1 Overview

State submissions for program approval must be made in accordance with the procedures set out in subpart C. This includes developing and submitting to EPA a program description (145.23), an Attorney General's Statement (145.24), and a Memorandum of Agreement with the Regional Administrator (145.25).

The substantive provisions which must be included in state programs to obtain approval include requirements for permitting, compliance evaluation, enforcement, public participation, and sharing of information. The requirements are found in subpart B. Many of the requirements for state programs are made applicable to states by cross-referencing other EPA regulations. In particular, many of the provisions of Parts 144 and 124 are made applicable to states by the references contained in 145.11.

Upon submission of a complete program, EPA will conduct a public hearing, if interest is shown, and determine whether to approve or disapprove the program taking into consideration the requirements of this part, the Safe Drinking Water Act and any comments received.

Upon approval of a state program, the Administrator shall suspend the issuance of federal permits for those activities subject to the approved state program.

Any state program approved by the Administrator shall at all times be conducted in accordance with the requirements of this part. Nothing in this part precludes a state from:

- ☐ adopting or enforcing requirements which are more stringent or more extensive than those required under this part; and

- ☐ operating a program with a greater scope of coverage than that required under this part. Where an approved state program has a greater scope of coverage than required by federal law the additional coverage is not part of the federally approved program.

Section 1451 of the SDWA authorizes the Administrator to delegate primary enforcement responsibility for the Underground Injection Control Program to eligible indian tribes. An indian tribe must establish its eligibility to be treated as a state before it is eligible to apply for Underground Injection Control grants and primary enforcement responsibility. All requirements of Parts 124, 144, 145, and 146 that apply to states with UIC primary enforcement responsibility also apply to indian tribes except where specifically noted.

19.2 Requirements for Permitting

All state programs under this part must have legal authority to implement each of the following provisions and must be administered in conformance with each; except that states are not precluded from omitting or modifying any provisions to impose more stringent requirements.

- ❏ Section 144.5(b)–(confidential information);
- ❏ Section 144.6–(classification of injection wells);
- ❏ Section 144.7–(identification of underground sources of drinking water and exempted aquifers);
- ❏ Section 144.8–(noncompliance reporting);
- ❏ Section 144.11–(prohibition of unauthorized injection);
- ❏ Section 144.12–(Prohibition of movement of fluids into underground sources of drinking water);
- ❏ Section 144.13–(elimination of Class IV wells);
- ❏ Section 144.14–(requirements for wells managing hazardous waste);
- ❏ Sections 144.21–144.26–(authorization by rule);
- ❏ Section 144.31–(application for a permit);
- ❏ Section 144.32–(signatories);
- ❏ Section 144.33–(area permits);
- ❏ Section 144.34–(emergency permits);
- ❏ Section 144.35–(effect of permit);
- ❏ Section 144.36–(duration);
- ❏ Section 144.38–(permit transfer);
- ❏ Section 144.39–(permit modification);
- ❏ Section 144.40–(permit termination);
- ❏ Section 144.51–(applicable permit conditions);
- ❏ Section 144.52–(establishing permit conditions);
- ❏ Section 144.53(a)–(schedule of compliance);

- ☐ Section 144.54–(monitoring requirements);

- ☐ Section 144.55–(corrective action);

- ☐ Section 124.3(a)–(application for a permit);

- ☐ Section 124.5 (a), (c), (d), and (f)–(modification of permits);

- ☐ Section 124.6 (a), (c), (d), and (e)–(draft permit);

- ☐ Section 124.8–(fact sheets);

- ☐ Section 124.10 (a)(1)(ii), (a)(1)(iii), (a)(1)(v), (b), (c), (d), and (e)–(public notice);

- ☐ Section 124.11–(public comments and requests for hearings);

- ☐ Section 124.12(a)–(public hearings); and

- ☐ Section 124.17 (a) and (c)–(response to comments).

States need not implement provisions identical to the provisions listed in the above sections. Implemented provisions must, however, establish requirements at least as stringent as the corresponding listed provisions. While states may impose more stringent requirements, they may not make one requirement more lenient as a tradeoff for making another requirement more stringent; for example, by requiring that public hearings be held prior to issuing any permit while reducing the amount of advance notice of such a hearing.

State programs may, if they have adequate legal authority, implement any of the provisions of Parts 144 and 124. See, for example 144.37(d) (continuation of permits) and 124.4 (consolidation of permit processing).

19.3 Requirements for Compliance Evaluation Programs

State programs shall have procedures for receipt, evaluation, retention and investigation for possible enforcement of all notices and reports required of permittees and other regulated persons (and for investigation for possible enforcement of failure to submit these notices and reports).

State programs shall have inspection and surveillance procedures to determine, independent of information supplied by regulated persons, compliance or noncompliance with applicable program requirements. The state shall maintain:

- ☐ a program which is capable of making comprehensive surveys of all facilities and activities subject to the State Director's authority to identify persons subject to regulation who have failed to comply with permit application or other program requirements. Any compilation, index, or inventory of such facilities and activities shall be made available to the Regional Administrator upon request;

- ☐ a program for periodic inspections of the facilities and activities subject to regulation. These inspections shall be conducted in a manner designed to:

  - determine compliance or noncompliance with issued permit conditions and other program requirements;

- verify the accuracy of information submitted by permittees and other regulated persons in reporting forms and other forms supplying monitoring data; and

- verify the adequacy of sampling, monitoring, and other methods used by permittees and other regulated persons to develop that information;

❑ a program for investigating information obtained regarding violations of applicable program and permit requirements; and

❑ procedures for receiving and ensuring proper consideration of information submitted by the public about violations. Public effort in reporting violations shall be encouraged and the State Director shall make available information on reporting procedures.

The State Director and state officers engaged in compliance evaluation shall have authority to enter any site or premises subject to regulation or in which records relevant to program operation are kept in order to copy any records, inspect, monitor or otherwise investigate compliance with permit conditions and other program requirements. States whose law requires a search warrant before entry conform with this requirement.

Investigatory inspections shall be conducted, samples shall be taken and other information shall be gathered in a manner [e.g., using proper "chain of custody" procedures] that will produce evidence admissible in an enforcement proceeding or in court.

19.3.1 Requirements for Enforcement Authority

Any state agency administering a program shall have available the following remedies for violations of state program requirements:

❑ to restrain immediately and effectively any person by order or by suit in state court from engaging in any unauthorized activity which is endangering or causing damage to public health or environment;

❑ to sue in courts of competent jurisdiction to enjoin any threatened or continuing violation of any program requirement, including permit conditions, without the necessity of a prior revocation of the permit;

❑ to assess or sue to recover in court civil penalties and to seek criminal remedies, including fines, as follows:

For all wells except Class II wells, civil penalties shall be recoverable for any program violation in at least the amount of $2,500 per day. For Class II wells, civil penalties shall be recoverable for any program violation in at least the amount of $1,000 per day. Criminal fines shall be recoverable in at least the amount of $5,000 per day against any person who willfully violates any program requirement, or for Class II wells, pipeline (production) severance shall be imposable against any person who willfully violates any program requirement.

Note: In many states the State Director will be represented in state courts by the State Attorney General or other appropriate legal officer. Although the State Director need not appear in court actions he or she should have power to request that any of the above actions be brought.

The maximum civil penalty or criminal fine (as provided in this section of the CFRs) shall be assessable for each instance of violation and, if the violation is continuous, shall be assessable up to the maximum amount for each day of violation.

The burden of proof and degree of knowledge or intent required under state law for establishing violations under this section of the CFRs, shall be no greater than the burden of proof or degree of knowledge or intent EPA must provide when it brings an action under the Safe Drinking Water Act.

A civil penalty assessed, sought, or agreed upon by the State Director under this section of the CFRs shall be appropriate to the violation. To the extent that state judgments or settlements provide penalties in amounts which EPA believes to be substantially inadequate in comparison to the amounts which EPA would require under similar facts, EPA, when authorized by the applicable statute, may commence separate actions for penalties.

In addition to the requirements of this paragraph, the state may have other enforcement remedies. The following enforcement options, while not mandatory, are highly recommended:

❑ procedures for assessment by the state of the costs of investigations, inspections, or monitoring surveys which lead to the establishment of violations;

❑ procedures which enable the state to assess or to sue any persons responsible for unauthorized activities for any expenses incurred by the state in removing, correcting, or terminating any adverse effects upon human health and the environment resulting from the unauthorized activity, or both; and

❑ procedures for the administrative assessment of penalties by the Director.

Any state administering a program shall provide for public participation in the state enforcement process by providing either:

❑ authority which allows intervention as of right in any civil or administrative action to obtain remedies specified in paragraph (a) (1), (2) or (3) of this section by any citizen having an interest which is or may be adversely affected; or

❑ assurance that the state agency or enforcement authority will:

- investigate and provide written responses to all citizen complaints submitted pursuant to the procedures specified in 145.12(b)(4);

- not oppose intervention by any citizen when permissive intervention may be authorized by statute, rule, or regulation; and

- publish notice of and provide at least 30 days for public comment on any proposed settlement of a state enforcement action.

To the extent that an indian tribe does not assert or is precluded from asserting criminal enforcement authority the Administrator will assume primary enforcement responsibility for criminal violations. The Memorandum of Agreement in 145.25 shall reflect a system where the tribal agency will refer such violations to the Administrator in an appropriate and timely manner.

19.3.2 Sharing of Information

Any information obtained or used in the administration of a state program shall be available to EPA upon request without restriction. If the information has been submitted to the state under a claim of confidentiality, the state must submit that claim to EPA when providing information under this section. Any information obtained from a state and subject to a claim of confidentiality will be treated in accordance with the regulations in 40 CFR Part 2. If EPA obtains from a state information that is not claimed to be confidential, EPA may make that information available to the public without further notice.

EPA shall furnish to states with approved programs the information in its files not submitted under a claim of confidentiality which the state needs to implement its approved program. EPA shall furnish to states with approved programs information submitted to EPA under a claim of confidentiality, which the state needs to implement its approved program, subject to the conditions in 40 CFR Part 2.

19.4 General Requirements for State Program Approvals

States shall submit to the Administrator a proposed state UIC program complying with 145.22 of this part within 270 days of the date of promulgation of the UIC regulations on June 24, 1980. The administrator may, for good cause, extend the date for submission of a proposed state UIC program for up to an additional 270 days.

States shall submit to the Administrator six months after the date of promulgation of the UIC regulations a report describing the state's progress in developing a UIC program. If the Administrator extends the time for submission of a UIC program an additional 270 days, pursuant to 145.21(a), the state shall submit a second report six months after the first report is due. The Administrator may prescribe the manner and form of the report. The requirements of 145.21 (a) and (b) shall not apply to indian tribes.

EPA will establish a UIC program in any state which does not comply with this section of the CFRs. EPA will continue to operate a UIC program in such a state until the state receives approval of a UIC program in accordance with the requirements of this part.

Note: States which are authorized to administer the NPDES permit program under section 402 of CWA are encouraged to rely on existing statutory authority, to the extent possible, in developing a state UIC program. Section 402(b)(1)(D) of CWA requires that NPDES states have the authority "to issue permits which control the disposal of pollutants into wells." In many instances, therefore, NPDES states will have existing statutory authority to regulate well disposal which satisfies the requirements of the UIC program. Note, however, that CWA excludes certain types of well injections from the definition of "pollutant." If the state's statutory authority contains a similar exclusion it may need to be modified to qualify for UIC program approval.

If a state can demonstrate to EPA's satisfaction that there are no underground injections within the state for one or more classes of injection wells (other than Class IV wells) subject to SDWA and that such injections cannot legally occur in the state until the state has developed an approved program for those classes of injections, the state need not submit a program to regulate those injections and a partial program may be approved. The demonstration of legal prohibition shall be made by either explicitly banning new injections of the class not covered by the state program or providing a certification from the State Attorney General that such new injections cannot legally occur until the state has developed an approved program for that class. The state shall submit a program to regulate both those classes of injections for which a demonstration is not made and class IV wells.

When a state UIC program is fully approved by EPA to regulate all classes of injections, the state assumes primary enforcement authority under section 1422(b)(3) of SDWA. EPA retains primary enforcement responsibility whenever the state program is disapproved in whole or in part. States which have partially approved programs have authority to enforce any violation of the approved portion of their program. EPA retains authority to enforce violations of state underground injection control programs, except that, when a state has a fully approved program, EPA will not take enforcement actions without providing prior notice to the state and otherwise complying with section 1423 of SDWA.

A state can assume primary enforcement responsibility for the UIC program, notwithstanding 145.21(3), when the state program is unable to regulate activities on Indian lands within the state. EPA will administer the program on Indian lands if the state does not seek this authority.

19.4.1 Elements of a Program Submission

Any state that seeks to administer a program under this part shall submit to the Administrator at least three copies of a program submission. The submission shall contain the following:

- ❑ a letter from the Governor of the state requesting program approval;

- ❑ a complete program description, as required by 145.23, describing how the state intends to carry out its responsibilities under this part;

- ❑ an Attorney General's statement as required by 145.24;

- ❑ a Memorandum of Agreement with the Regional Administrator as required by 145.25;

- ❑ copies of all applicable state statutes and regulations, including those governing state administrative procedures; and

- ❑ the showing required by 145.31(b) of the state's public participation activities prior to program submission.

Within 30 days of receipt by EPA of a state program submission, EPA will notify the state whether its submission is complete. If EPA finds that a state's submission is complete, the statutory review period (i.e., the period of time allotted for formal EPA review of a proposed state program under the Safe Drinking Water Act) shall be deemed to have begun on the date of receipt of the state's submission. If EPA finds that a State's submission is incomplete, the statutory review period shall not begin until all the necessary information is received by EPA.

If the state's submission is materially changed during the statutory review period, the statutory review period shall begin again upon receipt of the revised submission.

The state and EPA may extend the statutory review period by agreement.

19.4.2 Program Description

Any state that seeks to administer a program under this part shall submit a description of the program it proposes to administer in lieu of the federal program under state law or under an interstate compact. The program description shall include:

- ❑ a description in narrative form of the scope, structure, coverage and processes of the state program;

- ❑ a description (including organization charts) of the organization and structure of the state agency or agencies which will have responsibility for administering the program, including the information listed below. If more than one agency is responsible for administration of a program, each agency must have statewide jurisdiction over a class of activities. The responsibilities of each agency must be delineated, their procedures for coordination set forth, and an agency may be designated as a "lead agency" to facilitate communications between EPA and the state agencies having program responsibility. When the state proposes to administer a program of greater scope of coverage than is required by federal law, the information provided under this paragraph shall indicate the resources dedicated to administering the federally required portion of the program;

- ❑ a description of the state agency staff who will carry out the state program, including the number, occupations, and general duties of the employees. The state need not submit complete job descriptions for every employee carrying out the state program;

- ❑ an itemization of the estimated costs of establishing and administering the program for the first two years after approval, including cost of the personnel listed in this section of the CFRs, cost of administrative support, and cost of technical support;

- ❑ an itemization of the sources and amounts of funding, including an estimate of federal grant money, available to the State Director for the first two years after approval to meet the costs listed in this section of the CFRs, identifying any restrictions or limitations upon this funding;

- ❑ a description of applicable state procedures, including permitting procedures and any state administrative or judicial review procedures; and

- ❑ copies of the permit form(s), application form(s), reporting form(s), and manifest format the state intends to employ in its program. Forms used by states need not be identical to the forms used by EPA but should require the same basic information. The state need not provide copies of uniform national forms it intends to use but should note its intention to use such forms.

Note: States are encouraged to use uniform national forms established by the Administrator. If uniform national forms are used, they may be modified to include the State Agency's name, address, logo, and other similar information, as appropriate, in place of EPA's.

❏ A complete description of the state's compliance tracking and enforcement program.

A state UIC program description shall also include:

❏ a schedule for issuing permits within five years after program approval to all injection wells within the state which are required to have permits under this part and part 144;

❏ the priorities (according to criteria set forth in 40 CFR 146.09) for issuing permits, including the number of permits in each class of injection well which will be issued each year during the first five years of program operation;

❏ a description of how the Director will implement the mechanical integrity testing requirements of 40 CFR 146.08, including the frequency of testing that will be required and the number of tests that will be reviewed by the Director each year;

❏ a description of the procedure whereby the Director will notify owners and operators of injection wells of the requirement that they apply for and obtain a permit. The notification required by this paragraph shall require applications to be filed as soon as possible, but not later than four years after program approval for all injection wells requiring a permit;

❏ a description of any rule under which the Director proposes to authorize injections, including the text of the rule;

❏ for any existing enhanced recovery and hydrocarbon storage wells which the Director proposes to authorize by rule, a description of the procedure for reviewing the wells for compliance with applicable monitoring, reporting, construction, and financial responsibility requirements of 144.51 and 144.52, and 40 CFR Part 146;

❏ a description of and schedule for the state's program to establish and maintain a current inventory of injection wells which must be permitted under state law;

❏ where the Director had designated underground sources of drinking water in accordance with 144.7(a), a description and identification of all such designated sources in the state;

❏ a description of aquifers, or parts thereof, which the Director has identified under 144.7(b) as exempted aquifers, and a summary of supporting data;

❏ A description of and schedule for the state's program to ban Class IV wells prohibited under 144.13; and

❑ A description of and schedule for the state's program to establish an inventory of Class V wells and to assess the need for a program to regulate Class V wells.

Any state that seeks to administer a program under this part shall submit a statement from the State Attorney General (or the attorney for those state or interstate agencies which have independent legal counsel) that the laws of the state, or an interstate compact, provide adequate authority to carry out the program described under 145.23 and to meet the requirements of this part.

19.5 Approval Process

Prior to submitting an application to the Administrator for approval of a state UIC program, the state shall issue public notice of its intent to adopt a UIC program and to seek program approval from EPA. This public notice shall:

❑ be circulated in a manner calculated to attract the attention of interested persons. Circulation of the public notice shall include publication in enough of the largest newspapers in the state to attract statewide attention and mailing to persons on appropriate state mailing lists and to any other persons whom the agency has reason to believe are interested;

❑ indicate when and where the state's proposed program submission may be reviewed by the public;

❑ indicate the cost of obtaining a copy of the submission;

❑ provide for a comment period of not less than 30 days during which interested persons may comment on the proposed UIC program;

❑ schedule a public hearing on the state program for no less than 30 days after notice of the hearing is published;

❑ briefly outline the fundamental aspects of the state UIC program; and

❑ identify a person that an interested member of the public may contact for further information.

After complying with the requirements above any state may submit a proposed UIC program under section 1422 of SDWA and 145.22 of this part to EPA for approval. Such a submission shall include a showing of compliance with this section of the CFRs; copies of all written comments received by the state; a transcript, recording or summary of any public hearing which was held by the state; and a responsiveness summary which identifies the public participation activities conducted, describes the matters presented to the public, summarizes significant comments received, and responds to these comments. A copy of the responsiveness summary shall be sent to those who testified at the hearing, and others upon request.

After determining that a state's submission for UIC program approval is complete the Administrator shall issue public notice of the submission in the Federal Register and in accordance with this section of the CFRs. Such notice shall:

☐ indicate that a public hearing will be held by EPA no earlier than 30 days after notice of the hearing. The notice may require persons wishing to present testimony to file a request with the Regional Administrator, who may cancel the public hearing if sufficient public interest in a hearing is not expressed;

☐ afford the public 30 days after the notice to comment on the state's submission; and

☐ note the availability of the state submission for inspection and copying by the public.

Within 90 days of the receipt of a complete submission (as provided in 145.22) or material amendment thereto, the Administrator shall by rule either fully approve, disapprove, or approve in part the state's UIC program taking into account any comments submitted. The Administrator shall give notice of this rule in the Federal Register and in accordance with this section of the CFRs. If the Administrator determines not to approve the state program or to approve it only in part, the notice shall include a concise statement of the reasons for this determination. A responsiveness summary shall be prepared by the Regional Office which identifies the public participation activities conducted, describes the matters presented to the public, summarizes significant comments received, and explains the Agency's response to these comments. The responsiveness summary shall be sent to those who testified at the public hearing, and to others upon request.

19.6 Procedures for Revision of State Programs

Either EPA or the approved state may initiate program revision. Program revision may be necessary when the controlling federal or state statutory or regulatory authority is modified or supplemented. The state shall keep EPA fully informed of any proposed modifications to its basic statutory or regulatory authority, its forms, procedures, or priorities.

Revision of a state program shall be accomplished as follows:

☐ The state shall submit a modified program description, Attorney General's statement, Memorandum of Agreement, or such other documents as EPA determines to be necessary under the circumstances.

☐ Whenever EPA determines that the proposed program revision is substantial, EPA shall issue public notice and provide an opportunity to comment for a period of at least 30 days. The public notice shall be mailed to interested persons and shall be published in the Federal Register and in enough of the largest newspapers in the state to provide statewide coverage. The public notice shall summarize the proposed revisions and provide for the opportunity to request a public hearing. Such a hearing will be held is there if significant public interest based on requests received.

☐ The Administrator shall approve or disapprove program revisions based on the requirements of this part and of the Safe Drinking Water Act.

☐ A program revision shall become effective upon the approval of the Administrator. Notice of approval of any substantial revision shall be published in the Federal Register. Notice of approval of non-substantial program revisions may be given by a letter from the Administrator to the State Governor or his designee.

States with approved programs shall notify EPA whenever they propose to transfer all or part of any program from the approved state agency to any other state agency, and shall identify any new division of responsibilities among the agencies involved. The new agency is not authorized to administer the program until approval by the Administrator under this section of the CFRs. Organizational charts required under 145.23(b) shall be revised and resubmitted.

Whenever the Administrator has reason to believe that circumstances have changed with respect to a state program, he may request, and the state shall provide, a supplemental Attorney General's statement, program description, or such other documents or information as are necessary.

The state shall submit the information required under this section of the CFRs within 270 days of any amendment to this part or 40 CFR Part 144, 146, or 124 which revises or adds any requirement respecting an approved UIC program.

19.7 Criteria for Withdrawal of State Programs

The Administrator may withdraw program approval when a state program no longer complies with the requirements of this part, and the state fails to take corrective action. Such circumstances include the following—

When the state's legal authority no longer meets their requirements of this part, including:

❑ failure of the state to promulgate or enact new authorities when necessary; or

❑ action by a state legislature or court striking down or limiting state authorities.

When the operation of the state program fails to comply with the requirements of this part, including:

❑ failure to exercise control over activities required to be regulated under this part, including failure to issue permits;

❑ repeated issuance of permits which do not conform to the requirements of this part; or

❑ failure to comply with the public participation requirements of this part.

When the state's enforcement program fails to comply with the requirements of this part, including:

❑ failure to act on violations of permits or other program requirements;

❑ failure to seek adequate enforcement penalties or to collect administrative fines when imposed; or

❏ failure to inspect and monitor activities subject to regulation.

When the state program fails to comply with the terms of the Memorandum of Agreement required under 145.24.

19.8 Requirements for Tribal Eligibility

The Administrator is authorized to treat an indian tribe as eligible to apply for primary enforcement responsibility for the Underground Injection Control Program if it meets the criteria outlined in Subpart E.

State Underground Injection Control Programs

> *The applicable UIC program for a state is either a state administered program approved by EPA, or a federally administered program promulgated by EPA. In some cases, the UIC program may consist of a state administered program applicable to some classes of wells and a federally administered program applicable to other classes of wells.*

20.1 Overview

40 CFR Part 147, sets forth the applicable Underground Injection Control (UIC) programs for each of the states, territories, and possessions identified pursuant to the Safe Drinking Water Act (SDWA) as needing a UIC program.

Approval of a state program is based upon a determination by the Administrator that the program meets the requirements of section 1422 or section 1425 of the Safe Drinking Water Act and the applicable provisions of parts 124, 144, and 146 of this chapter. A federally administered program is promulgated in those instances where the state has failed to submit a program for approval or where the submitted program does not meet the minimum statutory and regulatory requirements.

In the case of state programs approved by EPA pursuant to section 1422 of the SDWA, 'each state subpart describes the major elements of such programs, including state statutes and regulations, statement of legal authority, memorandum of agreement, and program description. State statutes and regulations that contain standards, requirements, and procedures applicable to owners or operators have been incorporated by reference pursuant to regulations of the Office of the Federal Register. Material incorporated by reference is available for inspection in the appropriate EPA Regional Office, in EPA Headquarters, and at the Office of the Federal Register Information Center, Room 8301, 800 North Capitol Street, NW, suite 621700, Washington, DC. Other state statutes and regulations containing standards and procedures that constitute elements of the state program but do not apply directly to owners or operators have been listed but have not been incorporated by reference.

In the case of state programs promulgated under section 1422 that are to be administered by EPA, the state subpart makes applicable the provisions of parts 124, 144, and 146, and provides additional requirements pertinent to the specific state program.

Regulatory provisions incorporated by reference (in the case of approved state programs) or promulgated by EPA (in the case of EPA administered programs), and all permit conditions or permit denials issued pursuant to such regulations, are enforceable by the Administrator pursuant to section 1423 of the SDWA.

20.2 Severability of Provisions

The provisions in this part and the various applications thereof are distinct and severable. If any provision of this part or the application thereof to any person or circumstances is held invalid, such invalidity shall not affect other provisions or application of such provision to other persons or circumstances which can be given effect without the invalid provision or application.

- ❏ Subpart B–Alabama
- ❏ Subpart C–Alaska
- ❏ Subpart D–Arizona
- ❏ Subpart E–Arkansas
- ❏ Subpart F–California
- ❏ Subpart G–Colorado
- ❏ Subpart H–Connecticut
- ❏ Subpart I–Delaware
- ❏ Subpart J–District of Columbia
- ❏ Subpart K–Florida
- ❏ Subpart L–Georgia
- ❏ Subpart M–Hawaii
- ❏ Subpart N–Idaho
- ❏ Subpart O–Illinois
- ❏ Subpart P–Indiana
- ❏ Subpart Q–Iowa
- ❏ Subpart R–Kansas
- ❏ Subpart S–Kentucky
- ❏ Subpart T–Louisiana
- ❏ Subpart U–Maine
- ❏ Subpart V–Maryland
- ❏ Subpart W–Massachusetts
- ❏ Subpart X–Michigan
- ❏ Subpart Y–Minnesota
- ❏ Subpart Z–Mississippi

- ❏ Subpart AA–Missouri
- ❏ Subpart BB–Montana
- ❏ Subpart CC–Nebraska
- ❏ Subpart DD–Nevada
- ❏ Subpart EE–New Hampshire
- ❏ Subpart FF–New Jersey
- ❏ Subpart GG–New Mexico
- ❏ Subpart HH–New York
- ❏ Subpart II–North Carolina
- ❏ Subpart JJ–North Dakota
- ❏ Subpart KK–Ohio
- ❏ Subpart LL–Oklahoma
- ❏ Subpart MM–Oregon
- ❏ Subpart NN–Pennsylvania
- ❏ Subpart OO–Rhode Island
- ❏ Subpart PP–South Carolina
- ❏ Subpart QQ–South Dakota
- ❏ Subpart RR–Tennessee
- ❏ Subpart SS–Texas
- ❏ Subpart TT–Utah
- ❏ Subpart UU–Vermont
- ❏ Subpart VV–Virginia
- ❏ Subpart WW–Washington
- ❏ Subpart XX–West Virginia
- ❏ Subpart YY–Wisconsin
- ❏ Subpart ZZ–Wyoming
- ❏ Subpart AAA–Guam
- ❏ Subpart BBB–Puerto Rico
- ❏ Subpart CCC–Virgin Islands
- ❏ Subpart DDD–American Samoa
- ❏ Subpart EEE–Commonwealth of the Northern Mariana Islands
- ❏ Subpart FFF–Trust Territory of the Pacific Islands

❑ Subpart GGG–Osage Mineral Reserve–Class II Wells

❑ Subpart HHH–Lands of the Navajo, Ute Mountain Ute, and All Other New Mexico Tribes

Other information in this section of the CFRs includes:

• Appendix A to Subpart HHH–Exempted Aquifers in New Mexico.

• Subpart III–Lands of Certain Oklahoma Indian Tribes

Toxic Pollutant Effluent Standards

This section designates toxic pollutant effluent standards and applies to owners or operators of specified facilities discharging into navigable waters. Section 129.4 listed the pollutants to be regulated. Each owner/operator is given 60 days to notify the Regional Administrator of any listed pollutant discharged. Much of the regulation gives specific information on each of the toxic pollutants.

21.1 Overview

The provisions of this subpart apply to owners or operators of specified facilities discharging into navigable waters. The effluent standards or prohibitions for toxic pollutants established in this subpart are applicable to the sources and pollutants set forth herein, and may be incorporated in any NPDES permit, modification or renewal thereof, in accordance with the provisions of this subpart.

The provisions of 40 CFR Parts 124 and 125 shall apply to any NPDES permit proceedings for any point source discharge containing any toxic pollutant for which a standard or prohibition is established under this part.

21.1.1 Toxic Pollutants

The following are the pollutants subject to regulation under the provisions of this subpart:

- Aldrin/Dieldrin–Aldrin means the compound aldrin as identified by the chemical name, 1,2,3,4,10,10–hexachloro–1,4,4a,5,8,8a–hexahydro–1,4 –endo–5,8–exo–dimethanonaphthalene; "Dieldrin" means the compound the dieldrin as identified by the chemical name 1,2,3,4,10,10–hexachloro–6,7–epoxy–1,4,4a,5,6,7,8,8a–octahydro–1,4–endo–5,8–exo–dimethanonap hthalene.

- DDT–DDT means the compounds DDT, DDD, and DDE as identified by the chemical names:(DDT)–1,1,1–trichloro–2,2–bis(p–chlorophenyl) ethane and some o,p'–isomers; (DDD) or (TDE)–1,1–dichloro–2,2–bis(p–chlorophenyl) ethane and some o,p'–isomers; (DDE)–1,1–dichloro–2,2–bis(p–chlorophenyl) ethylene.

- Endrin–Endrin means the compound endrin as identified by the chemical name 1,2,3,4,10,10–hexachloro–6,7–epoxy–1,4,4a,5,6,7,8,8a–octahydro–1,4–endo–5,8–endodimethanonap hthalene.

- Toxaphene–Toxaphene means a material consisting of technical grade chlorinated camphene having the approximate formula of C10 H10 Cl8 and normally containing 67–69 percent chlorine by weight.

- Benzidine–Benzidine means the compound benzidine and its salts as identified by the chemical name 4,4'–diaminobiphenyl.

- Polychlorinated Biphenyls (PCBs) polychlorinated biphenyls (PCBs) means a mixture of compounds composed of the biphenyl molecule which has been chlorinated to varying degrees.

21.1.2 Compliance

Within 60 days from the date of promulgation of any toxic pollutant effluent standard or prohibition each owner or operator with a discharge subject to that standard or prohibition must notify the Regional Administrator (or State Director, if appropriate) of such discharge. Such notification shall include such information and follow such procedures as the Regional Administrator (or State Director, if appropriate) may require.

Any owner or operator who does not have a discharge subject to any toxic pollutant effluent standard at the time of such promulgation, but who thereafter commences or intends to commence any activity which would result in such a discharge shall first notify the Regional Administrator (or State Director, if appropriate) in the manner herein provided at least 60 days prior to any such discharge.

Upon receipt of any application for issuance or reissuance of a permit or for a modification of an existing permit for a discharge subject to a toxic pollutant effluent standard or prohibition the permitting authority shall proceed thereon in accordance with 40 CFR Part 124 or 125, whichever is applicable.

Every permit which contains limitations based upon a toxic pollutant effluent standard or prohibition under this part is subject to revision following the completion of any proceeding revising such toxic pollutant effluent standard or prohibition regardless of the duration specified on the permit.

For purposes of this section, all toxic pollutants for which standards are set under this part are deemed to be injurious to human health within the meaning of section 402(k) of the Act unless otherwise specified in the standard established for any particular pollutant.

Upon the compliance date for any section 307(a) toxic pollutant effluent standard or prohibition, each owner or operator of a discharge subject to such standard or prohibition shall comply with such monitoring, sampling, recording, and reporting conditions as the Regional Administrator (or State Director, if appropriate) may require for that discharge. Notice of such conditions shall be provided in writing to the owner or operator.

In addition to any conditions required pursuant to this section of the CFRs and to the extent not required in conditions contained in NPDES permits, within 60 days following the close of each calendar year each owner or operator of a discharge subject to any toxic standard or prohibition shall report to the Regional Administrator (or State Director, if appropriate) concerning the compliance of such discharges. Such report shall include, as a minimum, information concerning:

❑ relevant identification of the discharger such as name, location of facility, discharge points, receiving waters, and the industrial process or operation emitting the toxic pollutant;

❑ relevant conditions (pursuant to this section of the CFRs or to an NPDES permit) as to flow, section 307(a) toxic pollutant concentrations, and section 307(a) toxic pollutant mass emission rate;

❑ compliance by the discharger with such conditions.

When samples collected for analysis are composited, such samples shall be composited in proportion to the flow at time of collection and preserved in compliance with requirements of the Regional Administrator (or State Director, if appropriate), but shall include at least five samples, collected at approximately equal intervals throughout the working day.

Nothing in these regulations shall preclude a Regional Administrator from requiring in any permit a more stringent effluent limitation or standard pursuant to section 301(b)(1)(C) of the Act and implemented in 40 CFR 125.11 and other related provisions of 40 CFR Part 125. Nothing in these regulations shall preclude the Director of a State Water Pollution Control Agency or interstate agency operating a National Pollutant Discharge Elimination System Program which has been approved by the Administrator pursuant to section 402 of the Act from requiring in any permit a more stringent effluent limitation or standard pursuant to section 301(b)(1)(C) of the Act and implemented in 40 CFR 124.42 and other related provisions of 40 CFR Part 124.

Any owner or operator of a facility which discharges a toxic pollutant to the navigable waters and to a publicly owned treatment system shall limit the summation of the mass emissions from both discharges to the less restrictive standard, either the direct discharge standard or the pretreatment standard; but in no case will this paragraph allow a discharge to the navigable waters greater than the toxic pollutant effluent standard established for a direct discharge to the navigable waters.

In any permit hearing or other administrative proceeding relating to the implementation or enforcement of these standards, or any modification thereof, or in any judicial proceeding other than a petition for review of these standards pursuant to section 509(b)(1)(C) of the Act, the parties thereto may not contest the validity of any national standards established in this part, or the ambient water criterion established herein for any toxic pollutant.

21.2 Adjustment of Effluent Standards for Toxic Pollutants in the Intake Water

Upon the request of the owner or operator of a facility discharging a pollutant subject to a toxic pollutant effluent standard or prohibition, the Regional Administrator (or State Director, if appropriate) shall give credit, and shall adjust the effluent standard(s) in such permit to reflect credit for the toxic pollutant(s) in the owner's or operator's water supply if:

❏ the source of the owner's or operator's water supply is the same body of water into which the discharge is made; and if

❏ it is demonstrated to the Regional Administrator (or State Director, if appropriate) that the toxic pollutant(s) present in the owner's or operator's intake water will not be removed by any wastewater treatment systems whose design capacity and operation were such as to reduce toxic pollutants to the levels required by the applicable toxic pollutant effluent standards in the absence of the toxic pollutant in the intake water.

Effluent limitations established pursuant to this section shall be calculated on the basis of the amount of section 307(a) toxic pollutant(s) present in the water after any water supply treatment steps have been performed by or for the owner or operator.

Any permit which includes toxic pollutant effluent limitations established pursuant to this section shall also contain conditions requiring the permittee to conduct additional monitoring in the manner and locations determined by the Regional Administrator (or State Director, if appropriate) for those toxic pollutants for which the toxic pollutant effluent standards have been adjusted.

21.3 Requirement and Procedure for Establishing a More Stringent Effluent Limitation

In exceptional cases where the Regional Administrator (or State Director, if appropriate) determines that the ambient water criterion established in these standards is not being met or will not be met in the receiving water as a result of one or more discharges at levels allowed by these standards, and where he further determines that this is resulting in or may cause or contribute to significant adverse effects on aquatic or other organisms usually or potentially present, or on human health, he may issue to an owner or operator a permit or a permit modification containing a toxic pollutant effluent limitation at a more stringent level than that required by the standard set forth in these regulations.

Any such action shall be taken pursuant to the procedural provisions of 40 CFR Parts 124 and 125, as appropriate. In any proceeding in connection with such action the burden of proof and of going forward with evidence with regard to such more stringent effluent limitation shall be upon the Regional Administrator (or State Director, if appropriate) as the proponent of such more stringent effluent limitation.

Evidence in such proceeding shall include, at a minimum, an analysis using data and other information to demonstrate receiving water concentrations of the specified toxic pollutant, projections of the anticipated effects of the proposed modification on such receiving water concentrations, and the hydrologic and hydrographic characteristics of the receiving waters including the occurrence of dispersion of the effluent. Detailed specifications for presenting relevant information by any interested party may be prescribed in guidance documents published from time to time, whose availability will be announced in the Federal Register.

Any effluent limitation in an NPDES permit which a state proposes to issue which is more stringent than the toxic pollutant effluent standards promulgated by the Administrator is subject to review by the Administrator under section 402(d) of the Act. The Administrator may approve or disapprove such limitation(s) or specify another limitation(s) upon review of any record of any proceedings held in connection with the permit issuance or modification and any other evidence available to him. If he takes no action within ninety days of his receipt of the notification of the action of the permit issuing authority and any record thereof, the action of the state permit issuing authority shall be deemed to be approved.

21.4 Compliance Date

The effluent standards or prohibitions set forth herein shall be complied with not later than one year after promulgation unless an earlier date is established by the Administrator for an industrial subcategory in the promulgation of the standards or prohibitions.

Toxic pollutant effluent standards or prohibitions set forth herein shall become enforceable under sections 307(d) and 309 of the Act on the date established in this section of the CFRs regardless of proceedings in connection with the issuance of any NPDES permit or application therefor, or modification or renewal thereof.

21.4.1 Standards

Effluent standards outlined in this section of the CFRS pertain to:

- ❑ Aldrin/Dieldrin;
- ❑ DDT, DDD and DDE;
- ❑ Endrin;
- ❑ Toxaphene;
- ❑ Benzidine;
- ❑ Benzidine based dye applicators; and
- ❑ Polychlorinated biphenyls (PCBs).

21.5 Test Procedure Guidelines for Pollutant Analysis

The procedures prescribed herein shall, except as noted in 136.5, be used to perform the measurements indicated whenever the waste constituent specified is required to be measured for:

- ❑ An application submitted to the Administrator, or to a state having an approved NPDES program for a permit under section 402 of the Clean Water Act of 1977, as amended (CWA), and/or to reports required to be submitted under NPDES permits or other requests for quantitative or qualitative effluent data under parts 122 to 125 of title 40, and,

❏ Reports required to be submitted by discharges under the NPDES established by parts 124 and 125 of this chapter, and,

❏ Certifications issued by states pursuant to section 401 of the CWA, as amended.

21.5.1 Identification of Test Procedures

Parameters or pollutants, for which methods are approved, are listed together with test procedure descriptions and references in tables IA, IB, IC, ID, and IE. The references and the sources from which they are available are given in this section of the CFRs. These test procedures are incorporated as they exist on the day of approval and a notice of any change in these test procedures will be published in the Federal Register. Under certain circumstances (136.3 (b) or (c) or 40 CFR 401.13) other test procedures may be used. Typically, discharge parameter values for which reports are required must be determined by one of the standard analytical test procedures incorporated by reference and described in the following table references:

Table IA   List of Approved Biological Methods

Table IB   List of Approved Inorganic Test Procedures

Table IC   List of Approved Test Procedures for Non-Pesticide Organic Compounds

Table ID   List of Approved Test Procedures for Pesticides

Table IE   List of Approved Radiologic Test Procedures

Underground Injection Control Programs

> *This regulation stems from Part C of the SDWA which allows for the establishment of an Underground Injection Control (UIC) program in each state. General program requirements address prohibition of unauthorized injection, prohibition of movement of fluid into underground sources of drinking water, prohibition of Class IV wells and requirements for wells injecting hazardous waste.*

22.1 Overview

A UIC program is necessary in any state listed by EPA under section 1422 of the SDWA. Because all states have been listed, the SDWA required all states to submit an UIC program within 270 days after the effective date of 40 CFR Part 146, which was the final element of the UIC minimum requirements to be originally promulgated, unless the Administrator grants an extension, which can be for a period not to exceed an additional 270 days. If a state fails to submit an approvable program, EPA will establish a program for that state. Once a program is established, SDWA provides that all underground injections in listed states are unlawful and subject to penalties unless authorized by a permit or a rule. This part sets forth the requirements governing all UIC programs, authorizations by permit or rule and prohibits certain types of injection. The technical regulations governing these authorizations appear in 40 CFR Part 146.519

22.1.1 Structure of the UIC Program Part 144

This part sets forth the permitting and other program requirements that must be met by UIC Programs, whether run by a state or by EPA. It is divided into the following subparts:

❏ Subpart A describes general elements of the program, including definitions and classifications.

❏ Subpart B sets forth the general program requirements, including the performance standards applicable to all injection activities, basic elements that all UIC programs must contain, and provisions for waiving permit of rule requirements under certain circumstances.

❏ Subpart C sets forth requirements for wells authorized by rule.

❏ Subpart D sets forth permitting procedures.

❏ Subpart E sets forth specific conditions, or types of conditions, that must at a minimum be included in all permits.

❑   Subpart F sets forth the financial responsibility requirements for owners and operators of all existing and new Class I hazardous waste injection wells.

22.1.2 Part 145

While part 144 sets forth minimum requirements for all UIC Programs, these requirements are specifically identified as elements of a state application for primacy to administer an UIC Program in part 145. Part 145 also sets forth the necessary elements of a state submission and the procedural requirements for approval of state programs.

22.1.3 Part 124

The public participation requirements that must be met by UIC Programs, whether administered by the state or by EPA, are set forth in part 124. EPA must comply with all part 124 requirements; state administered programs must comply with part 124 as required by part 145. These requirements carry out the purposes of the public participation requirement of 40 CFR Part 25 (Public Participation), and supersede the requirements of that part as they apply to the UIC Program.

22.1.4 Part 146

This part sets forth the technical criteria and standards that must be met in permits and authorizations by rule as required by part 144.

22.2 Scope of the Permit or Rule Requirement

The UIC Permit Program regulates underground injections by five classes of wells (see definition of "well injection," 144.3). The five classes of wells are set forth in 144.6. All owners or operators of these injection wells must be authorized either by permit or rule by the Director. In carrying out the mandate of the SDWA, this subpart provides that no injection shall be authorized by permit or rule if it results in the movement of fluid containing any contaminant into Underground Sources of Drinking Water (USDWs–see 144.3 for definition), if the presence of that contaminant may cause a violation of any primary drinking water regulation under 40 CFR Part 142 or may adversely affect the health of persons (144.12). Existing Class IV wells which inject hazardous waste directly into an underground source of drinking water are to be eliminated over a period of six months and new such Class IV wells are to be prohibited (144.13). Class V wells will be inventoried and assessed and regulatory action will be established at a later date.

In the meantime, if remedial action appears necessary, an individual permit may be required (144.25) or the Director must require remedial action or closure by order (144.12(c)). During UIC program development, the Director may identify aquifers and portions of aquifers which are actual or potential sources of drinking water. This will provide an aid to the Director in carrying out his or her duty to protect all USDWs. An aquifer is a USDW if it fits the definition, even if it has not been "identified." The Director may also designate "exempted aquifers" using criteria in 146.04. Such aquifers are those which would otherwise qualify as "underground sources of drinking water" to be protected, but which have no real potential to be used as drinking water sources.

Therefore, they are not USDWs. No aquifer is an "exempted aquifer" until it has been affirmatively designated under the procedures in 144.7. Aquifers which do not fit the definition of "underground sources of drinking water" are not "exempted aquifers." They are simply not subject to the special protection afforded USDWs.

22.2.1 Specific Inclusions

The following wells are included among those types by injection activities which are covered by the UIC regulations. (This list is not intended to be exclusive but is for clarification only.)

- ❑ any injection well located on a drilling platform inside the state's territorial waters;
- ❑ any dug hole or well that is deeper than its largest surface dimension, where the principal function of the hole is emplacement of fluids;
- ❑ any septic tank or cesspool used by generators of hazardous waste, or by owners or operators of hazardous waste management facilities, to dispose of fluids containing hazardous waste; and
- ❑ any septic tank, cesspool, or other well used by a multiple dwelling, community, or regional system for the injection of wastes.

22.2.2 Specific Exclusions

The following are not covered by these regulations:

- ❑ injection wells located on a drilling platform or other site that is beyond the state's territorial waters;
- ❑ individual or single family residential waste disposal systems such as domestic cesspools or septic systems;
- ❑ non-residential cesspools, septic systems or similar waste disposal systems if such systems (A) are used solely for the disposal of sanitary waste, and (B) have the capacity to serve fewer than 20 persons a day;
- ❑ injection wells used for injection of hydrocarbons which are of pipeline quality and are gases at standard temperature and pressure for the purpose of storage; and
- ❑ any dug hole which is not used for emplacement of fluids underground.

The prohibition applicable to Class IV wells under 144.13 does not apply to injections of hazardous wastes into aquifers or portions thereof which have been exempted pursuant to 146.04.

22.3 Interim Status Under RCRA for Class I Hazardous Waste Injection Wells

The minimum national standards which define acceptable injection of hazardous waste during the period of interim status under RCRA are set out in the applicable provisions of this part, Parts 146 and 147, and 265.430 of this chapter. The issuance of a UIC permit does not automatically terminate RCRA interim status. A Class I well's interim status does, however, automatically terminate upon issuance to that well of a RCRA permit, or upon the well's receiving a RCRA permit-by-rule under 270.60(b) of this chapter. Thus, until a Class I well injecting hazardous waste receives a RCRA permit or RCRA permit-by-rule, the well's interim status requirements are the applicable requirements imposed pursuant to this part and Parts 146, 147, and 265 of this chapter, including any requirements imposed in the UIC permit.

22.4 Considerations Under Other Federal Laws

The following is a list of federal laws that may apply to the issuance of permits under these rules. When any of these laws are applicable, its procedures must be followed. When the applicable law requires consideration or adoption of particular permit conditions or requires the denial of a permit, those requirements also must be followed.

- ❑ The Wild and Scenic Rivers Act, 16 U.S.C. 1273 et seq. Section 7 of the Act prohibits the Regional Administrator from assisting by license or otherwise the construction of any water resources projects that would have a direct, adverse effect on the values for which a national wild and scenic river was established.

- ❑ The National Historic Preservation Act of 1966, 16 U.S.C. 470 et seq. Section 106 of the Act and implementing regulations (36 CFR Part 800) require the Regional Administrator, before issuing a license, to adopt measures when feasible to mitigate potential adverse effects of the licensed activity and properties listed or eligible for listing in the National Register of Historic Places. The Act's requirements are to be implemented in cooperation with State Historic Preservation Officers and upon notice to, and when appropriate, in consultation with the Advisory Council on Historic Preservation.

- ❑ The Endangered Species Act, 16 U.S.C. 1531 et seq. Section 7 of the Act and implementing regulations (50 CFR Part 402) require the Regional Administrator to ensure, in consultation with the Secretary of the Interior or Commerce, that any action authorized by EPA is not likely to jeopardize the continued existence of any endangered or threatened species or adversely affect its critical habitat.

- ❑ The Coastal Zone Management Act, 16 U.S.C. 1451 et seq. Section 307(c) of the Act and implementing regulations (15 CFR Part 930) prohibit EPA from issuing a permit for an activity affecting land or water use in the coastal zone until the applicant certifies that the proposed activity complies with the State Coastal Zone Management program, and the state or its designated agency concurs with the certification (or the Secretary of Commerce overrides the states nonconcurrence).

- ❑ The Fish and Wildlife Coordination Act, 16 U.S.C. 661 et seq., requires the Regional Administrator, before issuing a permit proposing or authorizing the impoundment (with certain exemptions), diversion, or other control or modification of any body of water, consult with the appropriate state agency exercising jurisdiction over wildlife resources to conserve these resources.

22.4.1 Authority Under the Safe drinking Water Act (SDWA)

❑ Section 1421 of SDWA requires the Administrator to promulgate regulations establishing minimum requirements for effective UIC programs.

❑ Section 1422 of SDWA requires the Administrator to list in the Federal Register "each state for which in his judgment a state underground injection control program may be necessary to assure that underground injection will not endanger drinking water sources" and to establish by regulation a program for EPA administration of UIC programs in the absence of an approved state program in a listed state.

❑ Section 1423 of SDWA provides procedures for EPA enforcement of UIC requirements.

❑ Section 1431 authorizes the Administrator to take action to protect the health of persons when a contaminant which is present in or may enter a public water system or underground source of drinking water may present an imminent and substantial endangerment to the health of persons.

❑ Section 1445 of SDWA authorizes the promulgation of regulations for such recordkeeping, reporting, and monitoring requirements "as the Administrator may reasonably require to assist him in establishing regulations under this title," and a "right of entry and inspection to determine compliance with this title, including for this purpose, inspection, at reasonable time, or records, files, papers, processes, controls, and facilities."

❑ Section 1450 of SDWA authorizes the Administrator "to prescribe such regulations as are necessary or appropriate to carry out his functions" under SDWA.

22.5 Confidentiality of Information

In accordance with 40 CFR Part 2, any information submitted to EPA pursuant to these regulations may be claimed as confidential by the submitter. Any such claim must be asserted at the time of submission in the manner prescribed on the application form or instructions or, in the case of other submissions, by stamping the words "confidential business information" on each page containing such information. If no claim is made at the time of submission, EPA may make the information available to the public without further notice. If a claim is asserted, the information will be treated in accordance with the procedures in 40 CFR Part 2 (Public Information). Claims of confidentiality for the following information will be denied:

❑ the name and address of any permit applicant or permittee;

❑   information which deals with the existence, absence, or level of contaminants in drinking water.

22.6 Classification of Wells

Injection wells are classified as follows:

❑   Class I

Wells used by generators of hazardous waste or owners or operators of hazardous waste management facilities to inject hazardous waste beneath the lowermost formation containing, within one-quarter mile of the well bore, an underground source of drinking water.

Other industrial and municipal disposal wells which inject fluids beneath the lowermost formation containing, within one quarter mile of the well bore, an underground source of drinking water.

❑   Class II

Wells which inject fluids which are brought to the surface in connection with natural gas storage operations, or conventional oil or natural gas production and may be commingled with waste waters from gas plants which are an integral part of production operations, unless those waters are classified as a hazardous waste at the time of injection.

For enhanced recovery of oil or natural gas; and for storage of hydrocarbons which are liquid at standard temperature and pressure.

❑   Class III

Wells which inject for extraction of minerals including:

- mining of sulfur by the Frasch process;

- in situ production of uranium or other metals; this category includes only in situ production from ore bodies which have not been conventionally mined. Solution mining of conventional mines such as stopes leaching is included in Class V.

- solution mining of salts or potash.

❑   Class IV

Wells used by generators of hazardous waste or of radioactive waste, by owners or operators of hazardous waste management facilities, or by owners or operators of radioactive waste disposal sites to dispose of hazardous waste or radioactive waste into a formation which within one-quarter mile of the well contains an underground source of drinking water.

Wells used by generators of hazardous waste or of radioactive waste, by owners or operators of hazardous waste management facilities, or by owners or operators of radioactive waste disposal sites to dispose of hazardous waste or radioactive waste above a formation which, within one-quarter mile of the well, contains an underground source of drinking water.

Wells used by generators of hazardous waste or owners or operators of hazardous waste management facilities to dispose of hazardous waste, which cannot be classified under paragraph (a)(1) or (d) (1) and (2) of this section (e.g., wells used to dispose of hazardous waste into or above a formation which contains an aquifer which has been exempted pursuant to 146.04).

❑ Class V

Injection wells not included in Classes I, II, III, or IV.

22.6.1 Identification of Underground Sources of Drinking Water and Exempted Aquifers

The Director may identify (by narrative description, illustrations, maps, or other means) and shall protect, except where exempted under this section of the CFRs, as an underground source of drinking water, all aquifers or parts of aquifers which meet the definition of an "underground source of drinking water" in 144.3. Even if an aquifer has not been specifically identified by the Director, it is an underground source of drinking water if it meets the definition in 144.3.

The Director may identify (by narrative description, illustrations, maps, or other means) and describe in geographic and/or geometric terms (such as vertical and lateral limits and gradient) which are clear and definite, all aquifers or parts thereof which the Director proposes to designate as exempted aquifers using the criteria in 40 CFR 146.04.

No designation of an exempted aquifer submitted as part of a UIC Program shall be final until approved by the Administrator as part of a UIC program. Subsequent to program approval or promulgation, the Director may, after notice and opportunity for a public hearing, identify additional exempted aquifers. For approved state programs exemption of aquifers identified (i) under 146.04(b) shall be treated as a program revision under 145.32; (ii) under 146.04(c) shall become final if the State Director submits the exemption in writing to the Administrator and the Administrator has not disapproved the designation within 45 days. Any disapproval by the Administrator shall state the reasons and shall constitute final Agency action for purposes of judicial review.

For Class III wells, the Director shall require an applicant for a permit which necessitates an aquifer exemption under 146.04(b)(1) to furnish the data necessary to demonstrate that the aquifer is expected to be mineral or hydrocarbon producing. Information contained in the mining plan for the proposed project, such as a map and general description of the mining zone, general information on the mineralogy and geochemistry of the mining zone, analysis of the amenability of the mining zone to the proposed mining method, and a timetable of planned development of the mining zone shall be considered by the Director in addition to the information required by 144.31(g).

For Class II wells, a demonstration of commercial producibility shall be made as follows:

❑   For a Class II well to be used for enhanced oil recovery processes in a field or project containing aquifers from which hydrocarbons were previously produced, commercial producibility shall be presumed by the Director upon a demonstration by the applicant of historical production having occurred in the project area or field.

❑   For Class II wells not located in a field or project containing aquifers from which hydrocarbons were previously produced, information such as logs, core data, formation description, formation depth, formation thickness and formation parameters such as permeability and porosity shall be considered by the Director, to the extent such information is available.

22.6.2 Noncompliance and Program Reporting by the Director

The Director shall prepare quarterly and annual reports as detailed below. When the state is the permit issuing authority, the State Director shall submit any reports required under this section to the Regional Administrator. When EPA is the permit issuing authority, the Regional Administrator shall submit any report required under this section to EPA Headquarters.

The Director shall submit quarterly narrative reports for major facilities that use the following format:

❑   provide an alphabetized list of permittees. When two or more permittees have the same name, the lowest permit number shall be entered first.

For each entry on the list, include the following information in the following order:

❑   name, location, and permit number of the noncomplying permittees;

❑   a brief description and date of each instance of noncompliance for that permittee. Instances of noncompliance may include one or more the kinds set forth in this section of the CFRs. When a permittee has noncompliance of more than one kind, combine the information into a single entry for each such permittee;

❑   the date(s) and a brief description of the action(s) taken by the Director to ensure compliance;

❑   status of the instance(s) of noncompliance with the date of the review of the status or the date of resolution; and

❑   any details which tend to explain or mitigate the instance(s) of noncompliance.

22.6.3 Instances of Noncompliance

Any instances of noncompliance within the following categories shall be reported in successive reports until the noncompliance is reported as resolved. Once noncompliance is reported as resolved it need not appear in subsequent reports.

Failure to complete construction elements - When the permittee has failed to complete, by the date specified in the permit, an element of a compliance schedule involving either planning for construction or a construction step (for example, begin construction, attain operation level); and the permittee has not returned to compliance by accomplishing the required elements of the schedule within 30 days from the date a compliance schedule report is due under the permit.

Modifications to schedules of compliance - When a schedule of compliance in the permit has been modified under 144.39 or 144.41 because of the permittee's noncompliance.

Failure to complete or provide compliance schedule or monitoring reports - When the permittee has failed to complete or provide a report required in a permit compliance schedule (for example, progress report or notice of noncompliance or compliance) or a monitoring report; and the permittee has not submitted the complete report within 30 days from the date it is due under the permit for compliance schedules, or from the date specified in the permit for monitoring reports.

Deficient reports - When the required reports provided by the permittee are so deficient as to cause misunderstanding by the Director and thus impede the review of the status of compliance.

Noncompliance with other permit requirements. Noncompliance shall be reported in the following circumstances:

- ❑ whenever the permittee has violated a permit requirement (other than reported under paragraph (a)(2) (i) or (ii) of this section), and has not returned to compliance within 45 days from the date reporting of noncompliance was due under the permit; or

- ❑ when the Director determines that a pattern of noncompliance exists for a major facility permittee over the most recent four consecutive reporting periods. This pattern includes any violation of the same requirement in two consecutive reporting periods, and any violation of one or more requirements in each of four consecutive reporting periods; or

- ❑ when the Director determines significant permit noncompliance or other significant event has occurred, such as a migration of fluids into a USDW.

Other statistical information shall be reported quarterly on all other instances of noncompliance by major facilities with permit requirements not otherwise reported under this section of the CFRs.

22.7 Annual reports

Annual noncompliance report. Statistical reports shall be submitted by the Director on non-major UIC permittees indicating the total number reviewed, the number of noncomplying non-major permittees, the number of enforcement actions, and number of permit modifications extending compliance deadlines. The statistical information shall be organized to follow the types of noncompliance listed in this section of the CFRs.

In addition to the annual noncompliance report, the State Director shall submit each year a program report to the Administrator (in a manner and form prescribed by the Administrator) consisting of:

❑ a detailed description of the state's implementation of its program;

❑ suggested changes, if any to the program description (see 145.23(f)) which are necessary to reflect more accurately the state's progress in issuing permits; and

❑ an updated inventory of active underground injection operations in the state.

In addition to complying with the requirements of this section of the CFRs, the Director shall provide the Administrator, on February 28th and August 31st of each of the first two years of program operation, the information required in 40 CFR 146.15, 146.25, and 146.35.

22.7.1 Reporting Schedule

Quarterly reports must be submitted on, or before, the last working day of May, August, November, and February. The period for annual reports shall be for the calendar year ending December 31, with reports completed and available to the public no more than 60 days later.

22.8 General Program Requirements

Any underground injection, except into a well authorized by rule or except as authorized by permit issued under the UIC program, is prohibited. The construction of any well required to have a permit is prohibited until the permit has been issued.

22.8.1 Prohibition of Movement of Fluid into Underground Sources of Drinking Water

No owner or operator shall construct, operate, maintain, convert, plug, abandon, or conduct any other injection activity in a manner that allows the movement of fluid containing any contaminant into underground sources of drinking water, if the presence of that contaminant may cause a violation of any primary drinking water regulation under 40 CFR Part 142 or may otherwise adversely affect the health of persons. The applicant for a permit shall have the burden of showing that the requirements of this paragraph are met.

For Class I, II and III wells, if any water quality monitoring of an underground source of drinking water indicates the movement of any contaminant into the underground source of drinking water, except as authorized under part 146, the Director shall prescribe such additional requirements for construction, corrective action, operation, monitoring, or reporting (including closure of the injection well) as are necessary to prevent such movement. In the case of wells authorized by permit, these additional requirements shall be imposed by modifying the permit in accordance with 144.39, or the permit may be terminated under 144.40 if cause exists, or appropriate enforcement action may be taken if the permit has been violated. In the case of wells authorized by rule, see 144.21 through 144.24. For EPA administered programs, such enforcement action shall be taken in accordance with appropriate sections of the SDWA.

For Class V wells, if at any time the Director learns that a Class V well may cause a violation of primary drinking water regulations under 40 CFR Part 142, he or she shall:

- ☐ require the injector to obtain an individual permit;

- ☐ order the injector to take such actions (including, where required, closure of the injection well) as may be necessary to prevent the violation. For EPA administered programs, such orders shall be issued in accordance with the appropriate provisions of the SDWA; or

- ☐ take enforcement action.

Whenever the Director learns that a Class V well may be otherwise adversely affecting the health of persons, he or she may prescribe such actions as may be necessary to prevent the adverse effect, including any action authorized under this section of the CFRs.

Notwithstanding any other provision of this section, the Director may take emergency action upon receipt of information that a contaminant which is present in or likely to enter a public water system or underground source of drinking water may present an imminent and substantial endangerment to the health of persons. If the Director is an EPA official, he must first determine that the appropriate state and local authorities have not taken appropriate action to protect the health of such persons, before taking emergency action.

22.8.2 Prohibition of Class IV Wells

The following are prohibited, except as provided in this section of the CFRs:

- ☐ the construction of any Class IV well;

- ☐ the operation or maintenance of any Class IV well not in operation prior to July 18, 1980;

- ☐ the operation or maintenance of any Class IV well that was in operation prior to July 18, 1980, after six months following the effective date of a UIC program approved or promulgated for the state; and

- ☐ any increase in the amount of hazardous waste or change in the type of hazardous waste injected into a Class IV well.

The owner or operator of a Class IV well shall comply with the requirements of 144.14, and with the requirements of 144.23 regarding closure of Class IV wells. Wells used to inject contaminated ground water that has been treated and is being reinjected into the same formation from which it was drawn are not prohibited by this section if such injection is approved by EPA pursuant to provisions for cleanup of releases under the Comprehensive Environmental Response, Compensation, and Liability Act of 1980 (CERCLA), 42 U.S.C. 9601–9657, or pursuant to requirements and provisions under the Resource Conservation and Recovery Act (RCRA), 42 U.S.C. 6901 through 6987.

The following wells are not prohibited by this action:

❑ wells used to inject hazardous waste into aquifers or portions thereof that have been exempted pursuant to 146.4, if the exempted aquifer into which waste is injected underlies the lowermost formation containing a USDW. Such wells are Class I wells as specified in 144.6(a)(1), and the owner or operator must comply with the requirements applicable to Class I wells.

❑ wells used to inject hazardous waste where no USDW exists within one quarter mile of the well bore in any underground formation, provided that the Director determines that such injection is into a formation sufficiently isolated to ensure that injected fluids do not migrate from the injection zone. Such wells are Class I wells as specified in 144.6(a)(1), and the owner or operator must comply with the requirements applicable to Class I wells.

22.9 Requirements for Wells Injecting Hazardous Waste

The regulations in this section apply to all generators of hazardous waste, and to the owners or operators of all hazardous waste management facilities, using any class of well to inject hazardous wastes accompanied by a manifest. (See also 144.13.)

The owner or operator of any well used to inject hazardous waste required to be accompanied by a manifest or delivery document shall apply for authorization to inject as specified in 144.31 within six months after the approval or promulgation of the state UIC program.

In addition to complying with the applicable requirements of this part and 40 CFR Part 146, the owner or operator of each facility meeting the requirements of this section of the CFRs, shall comply with the following:

❑ Notification. The owner or operator shall comply with the notification requirements of section 3010 of Public Law 94–580.

❑ Identification number. The owner or operator shall comply with the requirements of 40 CFR 264.11.

❑ Manifest system. The owner or operator shall comply with the applicable recordkeeping and reporting requirements for manifested wastes in 40 CFR 264.71.

❑ Manifest discrepancies. The owner or operator shall comply with 40 CFR 264.72.

- ☐ Operating record. The owner or operator shall comply with 40 CFR 264.73(a), (b)(1), and (b)(2).

- ☐ Annual report. The owner or operator shall comply with 40 CFR 264.75.

- ☐ Unmanifested waste report. The owner or operator shall comply with 40 CFR 264.75.

- ☐ Personnel training. The owner or operator shall comply with the applicable personnel training requirements of 40 CFR 264.16.

- ☐ Certification of closure. When abandonment is completed, the owner or operator must submit to the Director certification by the owner or operator and certification by an independent registered professional engineer that the facility has been closed in accordance with the specifications in 144.52(a)(6).

22.9.1 Waiver of Requirement by Director

When injection does not occur into, through or above an underground source of drinking water, the Director may authorize a well or project with less stringent requirements for area of review, construction, mechanical integrity, operation, monitoring, and reporting than required in 40 CFR Part 146 or 144.52 to the extent that the reduction in requirements will not result in an increased risk of movement of fluids into an underground source of drinking water.

When injection occurs through or above an underground source of drinking water, but the radius of endangering influence when computed under 146.06(a) is smaller or equal to the radius of the well, the Director may authorize a well or project with less stringent requirements for operation, monitoring, and reporting than required in 40 CFR Part 146 or 144.52 to the extent that the reduction in requirements will not result in an increased risk of movement of fluids into an underground source of drinking water.

When reducing requirements under paragraph (a) or (b) of this section, the Director shall prepare a fact sheet under 124.8 explaining the reasons for the action.

22.9.2 Records

The Director or the Administrator may require, by written notice on a selective well-by-well basis, an owner or operator of an injection well to establish and maintain records, make reports, conduct monitoring, and provide other information as is deemed necessary to determine whether the owner or operator has acted or is acting in compliance with Part C of the SDWA or its implementing regulations.

22.10 Authorization of Underground Injection by Rule

22.10.1 Existing Class I, II and III Wells

An existing Class I, II (except enhanced recovery and hydrocarbon storage) and III injection well is authorized by rule if the owner or operator injects into the existing well within one year after the date at which a UIC program authorized under the SDWA becomes effective for the first time or inventories the well pursuant to the requirements of 144.26. An owner or operator of a well which is authorized by rule pursuant to this section shall rework, operate, maintain, convert, plug, abandon or inject into the well in compliance with applicable regulations.

Well authorization under this section expires upon the effective date of a permit issued pursuant to 144.25, 144.31, 144.33 or 144.34; after plugging and abandonment in accordance with an approved plugging and abandonment plan pursuant to 144.28(c) and 146.10, and upon submission of a plugging and abandonment report pursuant to 144.28(k); or upon conversion in compliance with 144.28(j).

An owner or operator of a well authorized by rule pursuant to this section is prohibited from injecting into the well:

- ☐ upon the effective date of an applicable permit denial;
- ☐ upon failure to submit a permit application in a timely manner pursuant to 144.25 or 144.31;
- ☐ upon failure to submit inventory information in a timely manner pursuant to 144.26;
- ☐ upon failure to comply with a request for information in a timely manner pursuant to 144.27;
- ☐ upon failure to provide alternative financial assurance pursuant to 144.28(d)(7);
- ☐ forty-eight hours after receipt of a determination by the Director pursuant to 144.28(f)(3) that the well lacks mechanical integrity, unless the Director requires immediate cessation; or
- ☐ upon receipt of notification from the Director pursuant to 144.28(l) that the transferee has not demonstrated financial responsibility pursuant to 144.28(d).

Prohibition for Class I and III wells is as follows:

- ☐ in states with approved programs, five years after the effective date of the UIC program unless a timely and complete permit application is pending the Director's decision; or
- ☐ in states with programs administered by EPA, one year after the effective date of the UIC program unless a timely and complete permit application is pending the Director's decision; or for Class II wells (except enhanced recovery and hydrocarbon storage), five years after the effective date of the UIC program unless a timely and complete permit application is pending the Director's decision.

22.10.2 Class II and III Wells in Existing Fields or Projects

Notwithstanding the prohibition in 144.11, this section authorizes Class II and Class III wells or projects in existing fields or projects to continue normal operations until permitted, including construction, operation, and plugging and abandonment of wells as part of the operation, provided the owner or operator maintains compliance with all applicable requirements.

The owner or operator of a well authorized under this section shall comply with the applicable requirements of 144.28 and part 147 of this chapter no later than one year after authorization.

22.10.3 Existing Class II Enhanced Recovery and Hydrocarbon Storage Wells

An existing Class II enhanced recovery or hydrocarbon storage injection well is authorized by rule for the life of the well or project, if the owner or operator injects into the existing well within one year after the date which a UIC program authorized under the SDWA becomes effective for the first time or inventories the well pursuant to the requirements of 144.26. An owner or operator of a well which is authorized by rule pursuant to this section shall rework, operate, maintain, convert, plug, abandon or inject into the well in compliance with applicable regulations.

Well authorization under this section expires upon the effective date of a permit issued pursuant to 144.25, 144.31, 144.33 or 144.34; after plugging and abandonment in accordance with an approved plugging and abandonment plan pursuant to 144.28(c) and 146.10 of this chapter, and upon submission of a plugging and abandonment report pursuant to 144.28(k); or upon conversion in compliance with 144.28(j).

An owner or operator of a well authorized by rule pursuant to this section is prohibited from injecting into the well:

- ❏ upon the effective date of an applicable permit denial;
- ❏ upon failure to submit a permit application in a timely manner pursuant to 144.25 or 144.31;
- ❏ upon failure to submit inventory information in a timely manner pursuant to 144.26;
- ❏ upon failure to comply with a request for information in a timely manner pursuant to 144.27;
- ❏ upon failure to provide alternative financial assurance pursuant to 144.28(d)(7);
- ❏ forty-eight hours after receipt of a determination by the Director pursuant to 144.28(f)(3) that the well lacks mechanical integrity, unless the Director requires immediate cessation; or
- ❏ upon receipt of notification from the Director pursuant to 144.28(l) that the transferee has not demonstrated financial responsibility pursuant to 144.28(d).

The owner or operator of a well authorized under this section shall comply with the applicable requirements of 144.28 and part 147 of this chapter. Such owner or operator shall comply with the casing and cementing requirements no later than three years and other requirements no later than one year after authorization.

239

22.11 Class IV Wells

Injection into existing Class IV wells is authorized for up to six months after approval or promulgation of the UIC Program. Such wells are subject to the requirements of 144.13 and 144.14(c).

For EPA administered programs only, prior to abandoning any Class IV well, the owner or operator shall plug or otherwise close the well in a manner acceptable to the Regional Administrator. The owner or operator of a Class IV well must notify the Regional Administrator of intent to abandon the well at least thirty days prior to abandonment.

22.12 Class V Wells

A Class V injection well is authorized by rule until further requirements under future regulations become applicable. Well authorization under this section expires upon the effective date of a permit issued pursuant to 144.25, 144.31, 144.33 or 144.34, or upon proper closure of the well.

An owner or operator of a well which is authorized by rule pursuant to this section is prohibited from injecting into the well:

- [ ] upon the effective date of an applicable permit denial;
- [ ] upon failure to submit a permit application in a timely manner pursuant to 144.25 or 144.31;
- [ ] upon failure to submit inventory information in a timely manner pursuant to 144.26; or
- [ ] upon failure to comply with a request for information in a timely manner pursuant to 144.27.

22.13 Requiring a Permit

The Director may require the owner or operator of any Class I, II, III or V injection well which is authorized by rule under this subpart to apply for and obtain an individual or area UIC 532permit. Cases where individual or area UIC permits may be required include:

- [ ] the injection well is not in compliance with any requirement of the rule;
- [ ] the injection well is not or no longer is within the category of wells and types of well operations authorized in the rule;
- [ ] the protection of USDWs requires that the injection operation be regulated by requirements, such as for corrective action, monitoring and reporting, or operation, which are not contained in the rule.

When the injection well is a Class I, II (except existing enhanced recovery and hydrocarbon storage) or III well, in accordance with a schedule established by the Director pursuant to 144.31(c).

For EPA administered programs, the Regional Administrator may require an owner or operator of any well which is authorized by rule under this subpart to apply for an individual or area UIC permit under this paragraph only if the owner or operator has been notified in writing that a permit application is required. The owner or operator of a well which is authorized by rule under this subpart is prohibited from injecting into the well upon the effective date of permit denial, or upon failure by the owner or operator to submit an application in a timely manner as specified in the notice. The notice shall include: a brief statement of the reasons for requiring a permit; an application form; a statement setting a time for the owner or operator to file the application; and a statement of the consequences of denial or issuance of the permit, or failure to submit an application, as described in this paragraph.

An owner or operator of a well authorized by rule may request to be excluded from the coverage of this subpart by applying for an individual or area UIC permit. The owner or operator shall submit an application under 144.31 with reasons supporting the request, to the Director. The Director may grant any such requests.

22.14 Inventory Requirements

The owner or operator of an injection well which is authorized by rule under this subpart shall submit inventory information to the Director. Such an owner or operator is prohibited from injecting into the well upon failure to submit inventory information for the well within the time specified in paragraph (d) or (e) of this section of the CFRs.

As part of the inventory, the Director shall require and the owner/operator shall provide at least the following information:

- ❏ facility name and location;
- ❏ name and address of legal contact;
- ❏ ownership of facility;
- ❏ nature and type of injection wells; and
- ❏ operating status of injection wells.

Note: This information is requested on national form "Inventory of Injection Wells," OMB No. 158–R0170.

This section applies to Class II enhanced recovery wells; Class IV wells; and the following Class V wells:

- ❏ sand or other backfill wells [146.5(e)(8)];
- ❏ radioactive waste disposal wells [146.5(e)(11)];
- ❏ geothermal energy recovery wells [146.5(e)(12)];
- ❏ brine return flow wells [146.5(e)(14)];
- ❏ wells used in experimental technologies [146.5(e)(15)];

❑ municipal and industrial disposal wells other than Class I; and

❑ any other Class V wells at the discretion of the Regional Administrator.

The owner or operator of a well shall provide a listing of all wells owned or operated setting forth the following information for each well. (A single description of wells at a single facility with substantially the same characteristics is acceptable).

❑ for Class II only, the field name(s);

❑ location of each well or project given by township, range, section, and quarter-section, or by latitude and longitude to the nearest second, according to the conventional practice in the state;

❑ date of completion of each well;

❑ identification and depth of the formation(s) into which each well is injecting;

❑ total depth of each well;

❑ casing and cementing record, tubing size, and depth of packer;

❑ nature of the injected fluids;

❑ average and maximum injection pressure at the wellhead;

❑ average and maximum injection rate; and

❑ date of the last mechanical integrity test, if any.

Upon approval of the UIC Program in a state, the Director shall notify owners or operators of injection wells of their duty to submit inventory information. The method of notification selected by the Director must assure that the owners or operators will be made aware of the inventory requirement.

22.15 Deadlines

Except as provided in this section of the CFRs, the owner or operator of an injection well shall submit inventory information no later than one year after the date of approval or effective date of the UIC program for the State. The Director need not require inventory information from any facility with interim status under RCRA.

For EPA administered programs the information need not be submitted if a complete permit application is submitted within one year of the effective data of the UIC program. The owner or operator of Class IV well shall submit inventory information no later than 60 days after the effective date of the program.

22.15.1 Deadlines for Class V Wells (EPA administered programs)

The owner or operator of a Class V well in which injection took place within one year after the date at which a UIC program authorized under the SDWA first became effective, and who failed to submit inventory for the well within the time specified in this section of the CFRs may resume injection 90 days after submittal of the inventory information to the Director unless the owner or operator receives notice that injection may not resume or may resume sooner.

The owner or operator of a Class V well in which injection started after the first anniversary date at which a UIC program authorized under the SDWA became effective, shall submit inventory information no later than one year after May 2, 1994.

The owner or operator of a Class V well in which injection will start after May 2, 1994, shall submit inventory information prior to starting injection.

The owner or operator of a Class V injection well prohibited from injecting for failure to submit inventory information for the well within the time specified in paragraphs (e) (2) and (3) of this section, may resume injection 90 days after submittal of the inventory information to the Director unless the owner or operator receives notice from the Director that injection may not resume or may resume sooner.

22.15.2 Requiring Other Information

For EPA administered programs only, in addition to the inventory requirements of 144.26, the Regional Administrator may require the owner or operator of any well authorized by rule under this subpart to submit information as deemed necessary by the Regional Administrator to determine whether a well may be endangering an underground source of drinking water in violation of 144.12 of this part.

Such information requirements may include, but are not limited to:

- ❑ performance of groundwater monitoring and the periodic submission of reports of such monitoring;

- ❑ an analysis of injected fluids, including periodic submission of such analyses; and

- ❑ a description of the geologic strata through and into which injection is taking place.

Any request for information under this section shall be made in writing, and include a brief statement of the reasons for requiring the information. An owner or operator shall submit the information within the time period(s) provided in the notice.

An owner or operator of an injection well authorized by rule under this subpart is prohibited from injecting into the well upon failure of the owner or operator to comply with a request for information within the time period(s) specified by the Director pursuant to this section of the CFRs. An owner or operator of a well prohibited from injection under this section shall not resume injection except under a permit issued pursuant to 144.25, 144.31, 144.33 or 144.34.

22.16 Requirements for Class I, II, and III Wells Authorized by Rule

The following requirements apply to the owner or operator of a Class I, II or III well authorized by rule under this subpart, as provided by 144.21(e) and 144.22(d).

The owner or operator shall comply with all applicable requirements of this subpart and subpart B of this part. Any noncompliance with these requirements constitutes a violation of the Safe Drinking Water Act and is grounds for enforcement action, except that the owner or operator need not comply with these requirements to the extent and for the duration such noncompliance is authorized by an emergency permit under 144.34.

22.16.1 Twenty-Four Hour Reporting

The owner or operator shall report any noncompliance which may endanger health or the environment, including:

- ❑ any monitoring or other information which indicates that any contaminant may cause an endangerment to a USDW; or

- ❑ any noncompliance or malfunction of the injection system which may cause fluid migration into or between USDWs.

Any information shall be provided orally within 24 hours from the time the owner or operator becomes aware of the circumstances. A written submission shall also be provided within five days of the time the owner or operator becomes aware of the circumstances. The written submission shall contain a description of the noncompliance and its cause, the period of noncompliance, including exact dates and times, and if the noncompliance has not been corrected, the anticipated time it is expected to continue; and steps taken or planned to reduce, eliminate, and prevent recurrence of the noncompliance.

22.16.2 Plugging and Abandonment Plan

The owner or operator shall prepare, maintain, and comply with a plan for plugging and abandonment of the well or project that meets the requirements of 146.10 of this chapter and is acceptable to the Director. For purposes of this paragraph, temporary intermittent cessation of injection operations is not abandonment.

For EPA administered programs:

- ❑ The owner or operator shall submit the plan, on a form provided by the Regional Administrator, no later than one year after the effective date of the UIC program in the state.

- ❑ The owner or operator shall submit any proposed significant revision to the method of plugging reflected in the plan no later than the notice of plugging required by 144.28(j)(2) (i.e., 45 days prior to plugging unless shorter notice is approved).

The plan shall include the following information:

- ☐ the nature and quantity and material to be used in plugging;
- ☐ the location and extent (by depth) of the plugs;
- ☐ any proposed test or measurement to be made;
- ☐ the amount, size, and location (by depth) of casing to be left in the well;
- ☐ the method and location where casing is to be parted; and
- ☐ the estimated cost of plugging the well.

After a cessation of operations of two years the owner or operator shall plug and abandon the well in accordance with the plan unless he:

- ☐ provides notice to the Regional Administrator;
- ☐ describe actions or procedures, satisfactory to the Regional Administrator, that the owner or operator will take to ensure that the well will not endanger USDWs during the period of temporary abandonment. These actions and procedures shall include compliance with the technical requirements applicable to active injection wells unless waived by the Regional Administrator.

The owner or operator of any well that has been temporarily abandoned [ceased operations for more than two years and has met the requirements of paragraphs (c)(2) (A) and (B) of this section] shall notify the Regional Administrator prior to resuming operation of the well.

22.17 Financial Responsibility

The owner, operator and/or, for EPA administered programs, the transferor of a Class I, II or III well, is required to demonstrate and maintain financial responsibility and resources to close, plug and abandon the underground injection operation in a manner prescribed by the Director until:

- ☐ the well has been plugged and abandoned in accordance with an approved plugging and abandonment plan pursuant to 144.28(c) and 146.10 and submission of a plugging and abandonment report has been made pursuant to 144.28(k);
- ☐ the well has been converted in compliance with the requirements of 144.28(j); or
- ☐ for EPA administered programs, the transferor has received notice from the Director that the transferee has demonstrated financial responsibility for the well. The owner or operator shall show evidence of such financial responsibility to the Director by the submission of a surety bond, or other adequate assurance, such as a financial statement.

For EPA administered programs, the owner or operator shall submit such evidence no later than one year after the effective date of the UIC program in the state. Where the ownership or operational control of the well is transferred more than one year after the effective date of the UIC program, the transferee shall submit such evidence no later than the date specified in the notice required pursuant to 144.28(l)(2).

For EPA administered programs the Regional Administrator may require the owner or operator to submit a revised demonstration of financial responsibility if the Regional Administrator has reason to believe that the original demonstration is no longer adequate to cover the cost of closing, plugging and abandoning the well.

For EPA administered programs the owner or operator of a well injecting hazardous waste must comply with the financial responsibility requirements of subpart F of this part.

For EPA administered programs, an owner or operator must notify the Regional Administrator by certified mail of the commencement of any voluntary or involuntary proceeding under Title 11 (Bankruptcy) of the United States Code which names the owner or operator as debtor, within 10 business days after the commencement of the proceeding. Any party acting as guarantor for the owner or operator for the purpose of financial responsibility must so notify the Regional Administrator, if the guarantor is named as debtor in any such proceeding.

In the event of commencement of a proceeding specified in this section of the CFRs, an owner or operator who has furnished a financial statement for the purpose of demonstrating financial responsibility under this section shall be deemed to be in violation of this paragraph until an alternative financial assurance demonstration acceptable to the Regional Administrator is provided either by the owner or operator or by its trustee in bankruptcy, receiver, or other authorized party. All parties shall be prohibited from injecting into the well until such alternate financial assurance is provided.

22.18 Casing and Cementing Requirements

For enhanced recovery and hydrocarbon storage wells the owner or operator shall case and cement the well to prevent movement of fluids into or between underground sources of drinking water. In determining and specifying casing and cementing requirements, the following factors shall be considered:

- ❑ depth to the injection zone;

- ❑ depth to the bottom of all USDWs; and

- ❑ estimated maximum and average injection pressures.

In addition, in determining and specifying casing and cementing requirements the Director may consider information on:

- ❑ nature of formation fluids;

- ❑ lithology of injection and confining zones;

- ❑ external pressure, internal pressure, and axial loading;

- ❑ hole size;

- ❑ size and grade of all casing strings; and

❑ class of cement.

The requirements in paragraphs (e) (1) and (2) of this section may not apply if regulatory controls for casing and cementing existed at the time of drilling of the well and the well is in compliance with those controls; and well injection will not result in the movement of fluids into an underground source of drinking water so as to create a significant risk to the health of persons.

When a state did not have regulatory controls for casing and cementing prior to the time of the submission of the state program to the Administrator, the Director need not apply the casing and cementing requirements in this section of the CFRs if he submits as a part of his application for primacy, an appropriate plan for casing and cementing of existing, newly converted, and newly drilled wells in existing fields, and the Administrator approves the plan.

22.18.1 Operating Requirements

Injection between the outermost casing protecting underground sources of drinking water and the well bore is prohibited. The owner or operator of a Class I, II or III injection well authorized by rule shall establish and maintain mechanical integrity as defined in 146.8 of this chapter until the well is properly plugged in accordance with an approved plugging and abandonment plan pursuant to 144.28(c) and 146.10, and a plugging and abandonment report pursuant to 144.28(k) is submitted, or until the well is converted in compliance with 144.28(j). For EPA administered programs, the Regional Administrator may require by written notice that the owner or operator comply with a schedule describing when mechanical integrity demonstrations shall be made.

When the Director determines that a Class I (non-hazardous), II or III injection well lacks mechanical integrity pursuant to 146.8 of this chapter, the Director shall give written notice of his determination to the owner or operator. Unless the Director requires immediate cessation, the owner or operator shall cease injection into the well within 48 hours of receipt of the Director's determination. The Director may allow plugging of the well in accordance with the requirements of 146.10 of this chapter, or require the owner or operator to perform such additional construction, operation, monitoring, reporting and corrective action as is necessary to prevent the movement of fluid into or between USDWs caused by the lack of mechanical integrity. The owner or operator may resume injection upon receipt of written notification from the Director that the owner or operator has demonstrated mechanical integrity pursuant to 146.8 of this chapter.

The Director may allow the owner or operator of a well which lacks mechanical integrity pursuant to 146.8(a)(1) of this chapter to continue or resume injection if the owner or operator has made a satisfactory demonstration that there is no movement of fluid into or between USDWs.

For Class I wells, unless an alternative to a packer has been approved under 146.12(c) of this chapter, the owner or operator shall fill the annulus between the tubing and the long string of casings with a fluid approved by the Director and maintain a pressure, also approved by the Director, on the annulus. For EPA administered programs, the owner or operator of a Class I well completed with tubing and packer shall fill the annulus between tubing and casing with a noncorrosive fluid and maintain a positive pressure on the annulus. For other Class I wells, the owner or operator shall insure that the alternative completion method will reliably provide a comparable level of protection to underground sources of drinking water.

22.18.2 Injection Pressure

For Class I and III wells:

- ❏ except during stimulation, the owner or operator shall not exceed an injection pressure at the wellhead which shall be calculated so as to assure that the pressure during injection does not initiate new fractures or propagate existing fractures in the injection zone; and

- ❏ the owner or operator shall not inject at a pressure which will initiate fractures in the confining zone or cause the movement of injection or formation fluids into an underground source of drinking water.

For Class II wells:

- ❏ the owner or operator shall not exceed a maximum injection pressure at the wellhead which shall be calculated so as to assure that the pressure during injection does not initiate new fractures of propagate existing fractures in the confining zone adjacent to the USDWs; and

- ❏ the owner or operator shall not inject at a pressure which will cause the movement of injection or formation fluids into an underground source of drinking water.

22.19 Monitoring Requirements

For EPA administered programs, monitoring of the nature of the injected fluids shall comply with applicable analytical methods cited and described in table I of 40 CFR 136.3 or in appendix III of 40 CFR Part 261 or by other methods that have been approved by the Regional Administrator. The owner or operator of a Class I well shall:

- ❏ analyze the nature of the injected fluids with sufficient frequency to yield data representative of their characteristics;

- ❏ install and use continuous recording devices to monitor injection pressure, flow rate and volume, and the pressure on the annulus between the tubing and the long string of casing;

- ❏ install and use monitoring wells within the area of review if required by the Director, to monitor any migration of fluids into and pressure in the underground sources of drinking water. The type, number and location of the wells, the parameters to be measured, and the frequency of monitoring must be approved by the Director.

For Class II wells the owner or operator shall monitor the nature of the injected fluids with sufficient frequency to yield data representative of their characteristics. For EPA administered programs, this frequency shall be at least once within the first year of the authorization and thereafter when changes are made to the fluid.

The owner or operator shall observe the injection pressure, flow rate, and cumulative volume at least with the following frequencies:

❑ weekly for produced fluid disposal operations;

❑ monthly for enhanced recovery operations;

❑ daily during the injection of liquid hydrocarbons and injection for withdrawal of stored hydrocarbons; and

❑ daily during the injection phase of cyclic steam operations.

The owner or operator shall record one observation of injection pressure, flow rate and cumulative volume at reasonable intervals no greater than thirty days.

For enhanced recovery and hydrocarbon storage wells:

❑ the owner or operator shall demonstrate mechanical integrity pursuant to 146.8 of this chapter at least once every five years during the life of the injection well;

❑ for EPA administered programs, the Regional Administrator by written notice may require the owner or operator to comply with a schedule describing when such demonstrations shall be made; and

❑ for EPA administered programs, the owner or operator of any well required to be tested for mechanical integrity shall notify the Regional Administrator at least 30 days prior to any required mechanical integrity test.

The Regional Administrator may allow a shorter notification period if it would be sufficient to enable EPA to witness the mechanical integrity testing if it chose. Notification may be in the form of a yearly or quarterly schedule of planned mechanical integrity tests, or it may be on an individual basis.

The owner or operator of a hydrocarbon storage or enhanced recovery wells may monitor them by manifold monitoring on a field or project basis rather than on an individual well basis if such facilities consist of more than one injection well, operate with a common manifold, and provided the owner or operator demonstrates to the Director that manifold monitoring is comparable to individual well monitoring.

For Class III wells the owner or operator shall provide to the Director a qualitative analysis and ranges in concentrations of all constituents of injected fluids at least once within the first year of authorization and thereafter whenever the injection fluid is modified to the extent that the initial data are incorrect or incomplete. The owner or operator may request federal confidentiality as specified in 40 CFR Part 2.

If the information is proprietary the owner or operator may in lieu of the ranges in concentrations choose to submit maximum concentrations which shall not be exceeded. In such a case the owner or operator shall retain records of the undisclosed concentrations and provide them upon request to the Regional Administrator as part of any enforcement investigation; and

- ❏ monitor injection pressure and either flow rate or volume semimonthly, or meter and record daily injected and produced fluid volumes as appropriate; and

- ❏ monitor the fluid level in the injection zone semimonthly, where appropriate.

All Class III wells may be monitored on a field or project basis rather than an individual well basis by manifold monitoring. Manifold monitoring may be used in cases of facilities consisting of more than one injection well, operating with a common manifold. Separate monitoring systems for each well are not required provided the owner or operator demonstrates to the Director that manifold monitoring is comparable to individual well monitoring.

22.20 Reporting Requirements

The owner or operator shall submit reports to the Director as follows for Class I wells; quarterly reporting on:

- ❏ the physical, chemical, and other relevant characteristics of the injection fluids;

- ❏ monthly average, maximum, and minimum values for injection pressure, flow rate and volume, and annular pressure;

- ❏ the results from groundwater monitoring wells prescribed in this section of the CFRs;

- ❏ the results of any test of the injection well conducted by the owner or operator during the reported quarter if required by the Director; and

- ❏ any well work over performed during the reported quarter.

For Class II wells:

- ❏ An annual report to the Director summarizing the results of all monitoring, as required in this section of the CFRs. Such summary shall include monthly records of injected fluids, and any major changes in characteristics or sources of injtected fluids. Previously submitted information may be included by reference.

- ❏ The owner or operator of hydrocarbon storage and enhanced recovery projects may report on a field or project basis rather than on an individual well basis where manifold monitoring is used.

For Class III wells:

- ❏ Quarterly reporting on all monitoring, as required in this section of the CFRs;

- ❏ Quarterly reporting of the results of any periodic tests required by the Director that are performed during the reported quarter;

- ❏ Monitoring may be reported on a project or field basis rather than an individual well basis where manifold monitoring is used.

22.20.1 Retention of Records

The owner or operator shall retain records of all monitoring information, including the following:

❑ calibration and maintenance records and all original strip chart recordings for continuous monitoring instrumentation, and copies of all reports required by this section, for a period of at least three years from the date of the sample, measurement, or report. This period may be extended by request of the Director at any time; and

❑ the nature and composition of all injected fluids until three years after the completion of any plugging and abandonment procedures specified under 144.52(l)(6). The Director may require the owner or operator to deliver the records to the Director at the conclusion of the retention period. For EPA administered programs, the owner or operator shall continue to retain the records after the three-year retention period unless he delivers the records to the Regional Administrator or obtains written approval from the Regional Administrator to discard the records.

22.21 Notice of Abandonment

The owner or operator shall notify the Director, according to a time period required by the Director, before conversion or abandonment of the well.

For EPA administered programs, the owner or operator shall notify the Regional Administrator at least 45 days before plugging and abandonment. The Regional Administrator, at his discretion, may allow a shorter notice period.

22.21.1 Plugging and Abandonment Report

For EPA administered programs, within 60 days after plugging a well or at the time of the next quarterly report (whichever is less) the owner or operator shall submit a report to the Regional Administrator. If the quarterly report is due less than 15 days before completion of plugging, then the report shall be submitted within 60 days. The report shall be certified as accurate by the person who performed the plugging operation. Such report shall consist of either:

❑ a statement that the well was plugged in accordance with the plan previously submitted to the Regional Administrator; or

❑ where actual plugging differed from the plan previously submitted, an updated version of the plan, on the form supplied by the Regional Administrator, specifying the different procedures used.

Change of ownership or operational control. For EPA administered programs:

❑ The transferor of a Class I, II or III well authorized by rule shall notify the Regional Administrator of a transfer of ownership or operational control of the well at least 30 days in advance of the proposed transfer.

❑ The notice shall include a written agreement between the transferor and the transferee containing a specific date for transfer of ownership or operational control of the well; and a specific date when the financial responsibility demonstration of 144.28(d) will be met by the transferee.

❑ The transferee is authorized to inject unless he receives notification from the Director that the transferee has not demonstrated financial responsibility pursuant to 144.28(d).

22.22 Requirements for Class I Hazardous Waste Wells

The owner or operator of any Class I well injecting hazardous waste shall comply with 144.14(c). In addition, for EPA administered programs the owner or operator shall properly dispose of, or decontaminate by removing all hazardous waste residues, all injection well equipment.

22.22.1 Authorization by Permit

Unless an underground injection well is authorized by rule under subpart C of this part, all injection activities including construction of an injection well are prohibited until the owner or operator is authorized by permit. An owner or operator of a well currently authorized by rule must apply for a permit under this section unless well authorization by rule was for the life of the well or project. Authorization by rule for a well or project for which a permit application has been submitted terminates for the well or project upon the effective date of the permit. Procedures for applications, issuance and administration of emergency permits are found exclusively in 144.34. A RCRA permit applying the standards of part 264, subpart C of this chapter will constitute a UIC permit for hazardous waste injection wells for which the technical standards in part 146 of this chapter are not generally appropriate.

All applicants for permits shall provide the following information to the Director, using the application form provided by the Director:

❑ the activities conducted by the applicant which require it to obtain permits under RCRA, UIC, the National Pollution Discharge Elimination system (NPDES) program under the Clean Water Act, or the Prevention of Significant Deterioration (PSD) program under the Clean Air Act;

❑ name, mailing address, and location of the facility for which the application is submitted;

❑ up to four SIC codes which best reflect the principal products or services provided by the facility;

❑ the operator's name, address, telephone number, ownership status, and status as federal, state, private, public, or other entity;

❏ whether the facility is located on Indian lands; and

❏ a listing of all permits or construction approvals received or applied for under any of the following programs:

- Hazardous Waste Management program under RCRA

- UIC program under SDWA

- NPDES program under CWA

- Prevention of Significant Deterioration (PSD) program under the Clean Air Act

- Nonattainment program under the Clean Air Act

- National Emission Standards for Hazardous Pollutants (NESHAPS) preconstruction approval under the Clean Air Act

- ocean dumping permits under the Marine Protection Research and Sanctuaries Act

- dredge and fill permits under section 404 of CWA

- other relevant environmental permits, including state permits

Additional information such as the following is also required:

❏ A topographic map (or other map if a topographic map is unavailable) extending one mile beyond the property boundaries of the source depicting the facility and each of its intake and discharge structures; each of its hazardous waste treatment, storage, or disposal facilities; each well where fluids from the facility are injected underground; and those wells, springs, and other surface water bodies, and drinking water wells listed in public records or otherwise known to the applicant within a quarter mile of the facility property boundary.

❏ A brief description of the nature of the business.

❏ For EPA administered programs, the applicant shall identify and submit on a list with the permit application the names and addresses of all owners of record of land within one-quarter mile of the facility boundary. This requirement may be waived by the Regional Administrator where the site is located in a populous area and the Regional Administrator determines that the requirement would be impracticable.

❏ A plugging and abandonment plan that meets the requirements of 146.10 of this chapter and is acceptable to the Director.

Applicants shall keep records of all data used to complete permit applications and any supplemental information submitted under 144.31 for a period of at least three years from the date the application is signed.

22.22.2 Area Permits

The Director may issue a permit on an area basis, rather than for each well individually, provided that the permit is for injection wells:

- ❑ described and identified by location in permit application(s) if they are existing wells, except that the Director may accept a single description of wells with substantially the same characteristics;

- ❑ within the same well field, facility site, reservoir, project, or similar unit in the same state;

- ❑ operated by a single owner or operator; and

- ❑ used to inject other than hazardous waste.

Area permits shall specify:

- ❑ the area within which underground injections are authorized, and

- ❑ the requirements for construction, monitoring, reporting, operation, and abandonment, for all wells authorized by the permit.

The area permit may authorize the permittee to construct and operate, convert, or plug and abandon wells within the permit area provided:

- ❑ the permittee notifies the Director at such time as the permit requires;

- ❑ the additional well satisfies the criteria in this section of the CFRs and meets the requirements specified in the permit under this section of the CFRs; and

- ❑ the cumulative effects of drilling and operation of additional injection wells are considered by the Director during evaluation of the area permit application and are acceptable to the Director.

If the Director determines that any well constructed pursuant to this section of the CFRs does not satisfy any of the requirements of paragraphs (c) (1) and (2) of this section the Director may modify the permit under 144.39, terminate under 144.40, or take enforcement action. If the Director determines that cumulative effects are unacceptable, the permit may be modified under 144.39.

22.22.3 Emergency Permits

Coverage. Notwithstanding any other provision of this part or part 124, the Director may temporarily permit a specific underground injection if:

- ❑ an imminent and substantial endangerment to the health of persons will result unless a temporary emergency permit is granted; or

- ❑ a substantial and irretrievable loss of oil or gas resources will occur unless a temporary emergency permit is granted to a Class II well, and timely application for a permit could not practicably have been made, and the injection will not result in the movement of fluids into underground sources of drinking water; or

❑ a substantial delay in production of oil or gas resources will occur unless a temporary emergency permit is granted to a new Class II well and the temporary authorization will not result in the movement of fluids into an underground source of drinking water.

Any temporary permit under this section of the CFRs shall be for no longer term than required to prevent the hazard.

Any temporary permit under this section of the CFRs shall be for no longer than 90 days, except that if a permit application has been submitted prior to the expiration of the 90 day period, the Director may extend the temporary permit until final action on the application.

Any temporary permit under this section of the CFRs shall be issued only after a complete permit application has been submitted and shall be effective until final action on the application.

Notice of any temporary permit under this paragraph shall be published in accordance with 124.11 within 10 days of the issuance of the permit.

The temporary permit under this section may be either oral or written. If oral, it must be followed within five calendar days by a written temporary emergency permit.

The Director shall condition the temporary permit in any manner he or she determines is necessary to ensure that the injection will not result in the movement of fluids into an underground source of drinking water.

22.22.4 Permit Effect and Duration

Except for Class II and III wells, compliance with a permit during its term constitutes compliance, for purposes of enforcement, with Part C of the SDWA. However, a permit may be modified, revoked and reissued, or terminated during its term for cause as set forth in 144.39 and 144.40. The issuance of a permit does not convey any property rights of any sort, or any exclusive privilege.

The issuance of a permit does not authorize any injury to persons or property or invasion of other private rights, or any infringement of state or local law or regulations.

Permits for Class I and Class V wells shall be effective for a fixed term not to exceed 10 years. UIC permits for Class II and III wells shall be issued for a period up to the operating life of the facility. The Director shall review each issued Class II or III well UIC permit at least once every five years to determine whether it should be modified, revoked and reissued, terminated, or a minor modification made as provided in 144.39, 144.40, and 144.41.

Except as provided in 144.37, the term of a permit shall not be extended by modification beyond the maximum duration specified in this section. The Director may issue any permit for a duration that is less than the full allowable term under this section.

22.23 Continuation of Expiring Permits

When EPA is the permit issuing authority, the conditions of an expired permit continue in force under 5 U.S.C. 558(c) until the effective date of a new permit if:

❏ The permittee has submitted a timely application which is a complete application for a new permit; and

❏ The Regional Administrator, through no fault of the permittee does not issue a new permit with an effective date on or before the expiration date of the previous permit (for example, when issuance is impracticable due to time or resource constraints).

Permits continued under this section remain fully effective and enforceable. When the permittee is not in compliance with the conditions of the expiring or expired permit the Regional Administrator may choose to do any or all of the following:

❏ Initiate enforcement action based upon the permit which has been continued;

❏ Issue a notice of intent to deny the new permit. If the permit is denied, the owner or operator would then be required to cease the activities authorized by the continued permit or be subject to enforcement action for operating without a permit;

❏ Issue a new permit under part 124 with appropriate conditions; or

❏ Take other actions authorized by these regulations.

An EPA issued permit does not continue in force beyond its time expiration date under federal law if at that time a state is the permitting authority. A state authorized to administer the UIC program may continue either EPA or state issued permits until the effective date of the new permits, if state law allows. Otherwise, the facility or activity is operating without a permit from the time of expiration of the old permit to the effective date of the state issued new permit.

22.24 Transfer of Permits

Transfers by modification. Except as provided in this section of the CFRs, a permit may be transferred by the permittee to a new owner or operator only if the permit has been modified or revoked and reissued (under 144.39(b)(2)), or a minor modification made (under 144.41(d)), to identify the new permittee and incorporate such other requirements as may be necessary under the Safe Drinking Water Act.

As an alternative to transfers under this section of the CFRs, any UIC permit for a well not injecting hazardous waste may be automatically transferred to a new permittee if:

☐ the current permittee notifies the Director at least 30 days in advance of the proposed transfer date referred to in this section of the CFRs;

☐ the notice includes a written agreement between the existing and new permittees containing a specific date for transfer or permit responsibility, coverage, and liability between them, and the notice demonstrates that the financial responsibility requirements of 144.52(a)(7) will be met by the new permittee; and

☐ the Director does not notify the existing permittee and the proposed new permittee of his or her intent to modify or revoke and reissue the permit. A modification under this paragraph may also be a minor modification under 144.41. If this notice is not received, the transfer is effective on the date specified in the agreement mentioned in this section of the CFRs.

22.25 Causes for Modification

The following are causes for modification. For Class I hazardous waste injection wells, Class II, or Class III wells the following may be causes for revocation and reissuance as well as modification; and for all other wells the following may be cause for revocation or reissuance as well as modification when the permittee requests or agrees.

Alterations - There are material and substantial alterations or additions to the permitted facility or activity which occurred after permit issuance which justify the application of permit conditions that are different or absent in the existing permit.

Information - The Director has received information. Permits other than for Class II and III wells may be modified during their terms for this cause only if the information was not available at the time of permit issuance (other than revised regulations, guidance, or test methods) and would have justified the application of different permit conditions at the time of issuance. For UIC area permits (144.33), this cause shall include any information indicating that cumulative effects on the environment are unacceptable.

New Regulations - The standards or regulations on which the permit was based have been changed by promulgation of new or amended standards or regulations or by judicial decision after the permit was issued. Permits other than for Class I hazardous waste injection wells, Class II, or Class III wells may be modified during their terms for this cause only as follows—-

For promulgation of amended standards or regulations, when:

☐ the permit condition requested to be modified was based on a promulgated part 146 regulation; and

☐ EPA has revised, withdrawn, or modified that portion of the regulation on which the permit condition was based; and

☐ a permittee requests modification in accordance with 124.5 within ninety (90) days after Federal Register notice of the action on which the request is based.

For judicial decisions, a court of competent jurisdiction has remanded and stayed EPA promulgated regulations if the remand and stay concern that portion of the regulations on which the permit condition was based and a request is filed by the permittee in accordance with 124.5 within ninety (90) days of judicial remand.

The following are causes to modify or, alternatively, revoke and reissue a permit:

❑ cause exists for termination under 144.40, and the Director determines that modification or revocation and reissuance is appropriate;

❑ the Director has received notification (as required in the permit, see 144.41(d)) of a proposed transfer of the permit. A permit also may be modified to reflect a transfer after the effective date of an automatic transfer (144.38(b)) but will not be revoked and reissued after the effective date of the transfer except upon the request of the new permittee; or

❑ a determination that the waste being injected is a hazardous waste as defined in 261.3 either because the definition has been revised, or because a previous determination has been changed.

Suitability of the facility location will not be considered at the time of permit modification or revocation and reissuance unless new information or standards indicate that a threat to human health or the environment exists which was unknown at the time of permit issuance.

22.25.1 Minor Modifications

Minor modifications may only:

❑ correct typographical errors;

❑ require more frequent monitoring or reporting by the permittee;

❑ change an interim compliance date in a schedule of compliance, provided the new date is not more than 120 days after the date specified in the existing permit and does not interfere with attainment of the final compliance date requirement;

❑ allow for a change in ownership or operational control of a facility where the Director determines that no other change in the permit is necessary, provided that a written agreement containing a specific date for transfer of permit responsibility, coverage, and liability between the current and new permittees has been submitted to the Director; or

❑ amend a plugging and abandonment plan which has been updated under 144.52(a)(6).

Change quantities or types of fluids injected which are within the capacity of the facility as permitted and, in the judgment of the Director, would not interfere with the operation of the facility or its ability to meet conditions described in the permit and would not change its classification.

Change construction requirements approved by the Director pursuant to 144.52(a)(1) (establishing UIC permit conditions), provided that any such alteration shall comply with the requirements of this part and part 146.

22.26 Termination of Permits

The Director may terminate a permit during its term, or deny a permit renewal application for the following causes:

- ☐ noncompliance by the permittee with any condition of the permit;

- ☐ the permittee's failure in the application or during the permit issuance process to disclose fully all relevant facts, or the permittee's misrepresentation of any relevant facts at any time; or

- ☐ a determination that the permitted activity endangers human health or the environment and can only be regulated to acceptable levels by permit modification or termination.

The Director shall follow the applicable procedures in part 124 in terminating any permit under this section.

Upon the consent of the permittee, the Director may modify a permit to make the corrections or allowances for changes in the permitted activity listed in this section, without following the procedures of part 124. Any permit modification not processed as a minor modification under this section must be made for cause and with part 124 draft permit and public notice as required in 144.39.

Water Quality Planning and Management

> *This subpart applies to all state, eligible indian tribe, interstate, areawide and regional and local CWA water quality planning and management activities including all updates and continuing certifications for approved Water Quality Management (WQM) plans developed under sections 208 and 303 of the Act.*

23.1 Overview

A water quality standard (WQS) defines the water quality goals of a water body, or portion thereof, by designating the use or uses to be made of the water and by setting criteria necessary to protect the uses. A WQS should, wherever attainable, provide water quality for the protection and propagation of fish, shellfish and wildlife and for recreation in and on the water and take into consideration their use and value for public water supplies, propagation of fish, shellfish, wildlife, recreation in and on the water, and agricultural, industrial and other purposes including navigation.

A water quality standard (WQS) defines the water quality goals of a water body, or portion thereof, by designating the use or uses to be made of the water and by setting criteria necessary to protect the uses. States and EPA adopt WQS to protect public health or welfare, enhance the quality of water and serve the purposes of the Clean Water Act (CWA).

Such standards serve the dual purposes of establishing the water quality goals for a specific water body and serving as the regulatory basis for establishment of water quality–based treatment controls and strategies beyond the technology–based level of treatment required by sections 301(b) and 306 of the Act. States shall review and revise WQS in accordance with applicable regulations and, as appropriate, update their Water Quality Management (WQM) plans to reflect such revisions. Specific WQS requirements are found in 40 CFR Part 131.837.

Section 303 of the CWA gives the authority for promulgation of water quality standards (WQS) by states. Here is where the policies are established for water quality planning, management, and implementations of 303. The Water Quality Management process from the CWA provides the authority for a "consistent national approach for maintaining, improving and protecting water quality while allowing states to implement the most effective individual programs." After WQS are set by each state, implementation of the standards may be achieved by issuing permits, building publicly owned treatment works, or instituting Best Management Practices (BMP) through a water quality management plan. Total maximum daily loads (TMDL) and individual water quality-based effluent limitations are discussed in 130.7. States are required to submit water quality reports to the Regional Administrator in accordance with 305(b) of the CWA (130.8). Final points of the regulation cover state submittals to EPA and program management.

23.2 Water Quality Monitoring

In accordance with section 106(e)(1), states must establish appropriate monitoring methods and procedures (including biological monitoring) necessary to compile and analyze data on the quality of waters of the United States and, to the extent practicable, groundwaters. This requirement need not be met by indian tribes. However, any monitoring and/or analysis activities undertaken by a Tribe must be performed in accordance with EPA's quality assurance/quality control guidance.

The State's water monitoring program shall include collection and analysis of physical, chemical and biological data and quality assurance and control programs to assure scientifically valid data. The uses of these data include determining abatement and control priorities; developing and reviewing water quality standards, total maximum daily loads, wasteload allocations and load allocations; assessing compliance with National Pollutant Discharge Elimination System (NPDES) permits by dischargers; reporting information to the public through the section 305(b) report and reviewing site specific monitoring efforts.

23.3 Continuing Planning Process

Each state shall establish and maintain a continuing planning process (CPP) as described under section 303(e)(3)(A)–(H) of the Act. Each state is responsible for managing its water quality program to implement the processes specified in the continuing planning process. EPA is responsible for periodically reviewing the adequacy of the state's CPP.

23.3.1 Planning Processes

The state may determine the format of its CPP as long as the minimum requirements of the CWA and this regulation are met. The following processes must be described in each state CPP, and the state may include other processes at its discretion:

- ☐ the process for developing effluent limitations and schedules of compliance at least as stringent as those required by sections 301(b) (1) and (2), 306 and 307, and at least stringent as any requirements contained in applicable water quality standards in effect under authority of section 303 of the Act;

- ☐ the process for incorporating elements of any applicable areawide waste treatment plans under section 208, and applicable basin plans under section 209 of the Act;

- ☐ the process for developing total maximum daily loads (TMDLs) and individual water quality based effluent limitations for pollutants in accordance with section 303(d) of the Act and 130.7(a) of this regulation;

- ☐ the process for updating and maintaining Water Quality Management (WQM) plans, including schedules for revision;

- ☐ the process for assuring adequate authority for intergovernmental cooperation in the implementation of the State WQM program;

❑ the process for establishing and assuring adequate implementation of new or revised water quality standards, including schedules of compliance, under section 303(c) of the Act;

❑ the process for assuring adequate controls over the disposition of all residual waste from any water treatment processing;

❑ the process for developing an inventory and ranking, in order of priority of needs for construction of waste treatment works required to meet the applicable requirements of sections 301 and 302 of the Act; and

❑ the process for determining the priority of permit issuance.

The Regional Administrator shall review approved state CPPs from time to time to ensure that the planning processes are consistent with the Act and this regulation. The Regional Administrator shall not approve any permit program under Title IV of the Act for any state which does not have an approved continuing planning process.

23.4 Water Quality Management (WQM) Plans

WQM plans consist of initial plans produced in accordance with sections 208 and 303(e) of the Act and certified and approved updates to those plans. Continuing water quality planning shall be based upon WQM plans and water quality problems identified in the latest 305(b) reports. State water quality planning should focus annually on priority issues and geographic areas and on the development of water quality controls leading to implementation measures. Water quality planning directed at the removal of conditions placed on previously certified and approved WQM plans should focus on removal of conditions which will lead to control decisions.

Use of WQM plans

WQM plans are used to direct implementation. WQM plans draw upon the water quality assessments to identify priority point and nonpoint water quality problems, consider alternative solutions and recommend control measures, including the financial and institutional measures necessary for implementing recommended solutions. State annual work programs shall be based upon the priority issues identified in the State WQM plan.

23.4.1 WQM Plan Elements

Sections 205(j), 208 and 303 of the Act specify water quality planning requirements. The following plan elements shall be included in the WQM plan or referenced as part of the WQM plan if contained in separate documents when they are needed to address water quality problems:

❑ Total maximum daily loads

TMDLs in accordance with sections 303(d) and (e)(3)(C) of the Act and 130.7 of this part.

❑ Effluent limitations

263

Effluent limitations including water quality based effluent limitations and schedules of compliance in accordance with section 303(e)(3)(A) of the Act and 130.5 of this part.

❏ Municipal and industrial waste treatment

Identification of anticipated municipal and industrial waste treatment works, including facilities for treatment of stormwater induced combined sewer overflows; programs to provide necessary financial arrangements for such works; establishment of construction priorities and schedules for initiation and completion of such treatment works including an identification of open space and recreation opportunities from improved water quality in accordance with section 208(b)(2) (A) and (B) of the Act.

❏ Nonpoint source management and control

The plan shall describe the regulatory and non-regulatory programs, activities and Best Management Practices (BMPs) which the agency has selected as the means to control nonpoint source pollution where necessary to protect or achieve approved water uses. Economic, institutional, and technical factors shall be considered in a continuing process of identifying control needs and evaluating and modifying the BMPs as necessary to achieve water quality goals.

Regulatory programs shall be identified where they are determined to be necessary by the state to attain or maintain an approved water use or where non-regulatory approaches are inappropriate in accomplishing that objective.

23.4.2 BMPs

BMPs shall be identified for the nonpoint sources identified in section 208(b)(2)(F)–(K) of the Act and other nonpoint sources as follows:

❏ residual waste

Identification of a process to control the disposition of all residual waste in the area which could affect water quality in accordance with section 208(b)(2)(J) of the Act.

❏ land disposal

Identification of a process to control the disposal of pollutants on land or in subsurface excavations to protect ground and surface water quality in accordance with section 208(b)(2)(K) of the Act.

❏ agricultural and silvicultural

Identification of procedures to control agricultural and silvicultural sources of pollution in accordance with section 208(b)(2)(F) of the Act.

❏ Mines

Identification of procedures to control mine related sources of pollution in accordance with section 208(b)(2)(G) of the Act.

❑ Construction

Identification of procedures to control construction related sources of pollution in accordance with section 208(b)(2)(H) of the Act.

❑ Saltwater intrusion

Identification of procedures to control saltwater intrusion in accordance with section 208(b)(2)(I) of the Act.

❑ Urban stormwater

Identification of BMPs for urban stormwater control to achieve water quality goals and fiscal analysis of the necessary capital and operations and maintenance expenditures in accordance with section 208(b)(2)(A) of the Act.

The nonpoint source plan elements outlined in 130.6(c) (4)(iii)(A)(G) of this regulation shall be the basis of water quality activities implemented through agreements or memoranda of understanding between EPA and other departments, agencies or instrumentalities of the United States in accordance with section 304(k) of the Act.

❑ Management agencies

Identification of agencies necessary to carry out the plan and provision for adequate authority for intergovernmental cooperation in accordance with sections 208(b)(2)(D) and 303(e)(3)(E) of the Act. Management agencies must demonstrate the legal, institutional, managerial and financial capability and specific activities necessary to carry out their responsibilities in accordance with section 208(c)(2)(A) through (I) of the Act.

❑ Implementation measures

Identification of implementation measures necessary to carry out the plan, including financing, the time needed to carry out the plan, and the economic, social and environmental impact of carrying out the plan in accordance with section 208(b)(2)(E).

❑ Dredge or fill program

Identification and development of programs for the control of dredge or fill material in accordance with section 208(b)(4)(B) of the Act.

❑ Basin plans

Identification of any relationship to applicable basin plans developed under section 209 of the Act.

❑ Groundwater

Identification and development of programs for control of groundwater pollution including the provisions of section 208(b)(2)(K) of the Act. States are not required to develop groundwater WQM plan elements beyond the requirements of section 208(b)(2)(K) of the Act, but may develop a groundwater plan element if they determine it is necessary to address a groundwater quality problem.

If a state chooses to develop a groundwater plan element, it should describe the essentials of a state program and should include, but is not limited to:

- overall goals, policies and legislative authorities for protection of groundwater;

- monitoring and resource assessment programs in accordance with section 106(e)(1) of the Act;

- programs to control sources of contamination of groundwater including federal programs delegated to the state and additional programs authorized in state statutes;

- procedures for coordination of groundwater protection programs among state agencies and with local and federal agencies; and

- procedures for program management and administration including provision of program financing, training and technical assistance, public participation, and emergency management.

An indian tribe is eligible for the purposes of this rule and the Clean Water Act assistance programs under 40 CFR Part 35, subparts A and H if:

- ❑ the indian tribe has a governing body carrying out substantial governmental duties and powers;

- ❑ the functions to be exercised by the indian tribe pertain to the management and protection of water resources which are held by an indian tribe, held by the United States in trust for Indians, held by a member of an indian tribe if such property interest is subject to a trust restriction on alienation, or otherwise within the borders of an Indian reservation; and

- ❑ the indian tribe is reasonably expected to be capable, in the Regional Administrator's judgment, of carrying out the functions to be exercised in a manner consistent with the terms and purposes of the Clean Water Act and applicable regulations.

23.4.3 Update and Certification

State and/or areawide agency WQM plans shall be updated as needed to reflect changing water quality conditions, results of implementation actions, new requirements or to remove conditions in prior conditional or partial plan approvals. Regional Administrators may require that state WQM plans be updated as needed. State Continuing Planning Processes (CPPs) shall specify the process and schedule used to revise WQM plans. The state shall ensure that state and areawide WQM plans together include all necessary plan elements and that such plans are consistent with one another.

The Governor or the Governor's designee shall certify by letter to the Regional Administrator for EPA approval that WQM plan updates are consistent with all other Parts of the plan. The certification may be contained in the annual state work program.

Construction grant and permit decisions must be made in accordance with certified and approved WQM plans as described in 130.12(a) and 130.12(b).

23.5 Total Maximum Daily Loads (TMDL) and Water Quality-Based Effluent Limitations

As an integral part of a States Continuing Planning Process (CPP) processes and methodologies to be used must be clearly described for the following:

- ☐ identifying water quality limited segments still requiring wasteload allocations, load allocations and total maximum daily loads (WLAs/LAs and TMDLs), and setting priorities for developing these loads;

- ☐ establishing these loads for segments identified, including water quality monitoring, modeling, data analysis, calculation methods, and list of pollutants to be regulated;

- ☐ submitting the state's list of segments identified, priority ranking, and loads established (WLAs/LAs/TMDLs) to EPA for approval;

- ☐ incorporating the approved loads into the state's WQM plans and NPDES permits; and

- ☐ involving the public, affected dischargers, designated areawide agencies, and local governments in this process.

Each state must also identify those water quality limited segments still requiring TMDLs within its boundaries for which:

- ☐ Technology based effluent limitations required by sections 301(b), 306, 307, or other sections of the Act;

- ☐ more stringent effluent limitations (including prohibitions) required by either state or local authority preserved by section 510 of the Act, or federal authority (law, regulation, or treaty); and

- ☐ other pollution control requirements (e.g., best management practices) required by local, state, or federal authority are not stringent enough to implement any water quality standards (WQS) applicable to such waters.

Each state shall also identify on the same list developed in this section those water quality limited segments still requiring TMDLs or parts thereof within its boundaries for which controls on thermal discharges under section 301 or state or local requirements are not stringent enough to assure protection and propagation of a balanced indigenous population of shellfish, fish and wildlife.

The list required under 130.7(b)(1) and 130.7(b)(2) of this section shall include a priority ranking for all listed water quality limited segments still requiring TMDLs, taking into account the severity of the pollution and the uses to be made of such waters and shall identify the pollutants causing or expected to cause violations of the applicable water quality standards. The priority ranking shall specifically include the identification of waters targeted for TMDL development in the next two years.

Each state shall assemble and evaluate all existing and readily available water quality related data and information to develop the list required by 130.7(b)(1) and 130.7(b)(2). At a minimum "all existing and readily available water quality related data and information" includes but is not limited to all of the existing and readily available data and information about the following categories of waters:

❑ waters identified by the state in its most recent section 305(b) report as "partially meeting" or "not meeting" designated uses or as "threatened";

❑ waters for which dilution calculations or predictive models indicate nonattainment of applicable water quality standards;

❑ waters for which water quality problems have been reported by local, state, or federal agencies; members of the public; or academic institutions. These organizations and groups should be actively solicited for research they may be conducting or reporting. For example, university researchers, the United States Department of Agriculture, the National Oceanic and Atmospheric Administration, the United States Geological Survey, and the United States Fish and Wildlife Service are good sources of field data; and

❑ waters identified by the state as impaired or threatened in a nonpoint assessment submitted to EPA under section 319 of the CWA or in any updates of the assessment.

Each state shall provide documentation to the Regional Administrator to support the state's determination to list or not to list its waters as required by 130.7(b)(1) and 130.7(b)(2). This documentation shall be submitted to the Regional Administrator together with the list required by 130.7(b)(1) and 130.7(b)(2) and shall include at a minimum:

❑ a description of the methodology used to develop the list; and

❑ a description of the data and information used to identify waters, including a description of the data and information used by the state as required by 130.7(b)(5);

❑ a rationale for any decision to not use any existing and readily available data and information for any one of the categories of waters as described in 130.7(b)(5); and

❑ any other reasonable information requested by the Regional Administrator. Upon request by the Regional Administrator, each state must demonstrate good cause for not including a water or waters on the list. Good cause includes, but is not limited to, more recent or accurate data; more sophisticated water quality modeling; flaws in the original analysis that led to the water being listed in the categories in 130.7(b)(5); or changes in conditions, e.g., new control equipment, or elimination of discharges.

Each state shall establish TMDLs for the water quality limited segments identified in this section of the CFRs, and in accordance with the priority ranking. For pollutants other than heat, TMDLs shall be established at levels necessary to attain and maintain the applicable narrative and numerical WQS with seasonal variations and a margin of safety which takes into account any lack of knowledge concerning the relationship between effluent limitations and water quality. Determinations of TMDLs shall take into account critical conditions for stream flow, loading, and water quality parameters.

☐ TMDLs may be established using a pollutant by pollutant or biomonitoring approach. In many cases both techniques may be needed. Site specific information should be used wherever possible.

☐ TMDLs shall be established for all pollutants preventing or expected to prevent attainment of water quality standards as identified pursuant to this section of the CFRs. Calculations to establish TMDLs shall be subject to public review as defined in the State CPP.

Each state shall estimate for the water quality limited segments still requiring TMDLs identified in this section of the CFRs, the total maximum daily thermal load which cannot be exceeded in order to assure protection and propagation of a balanced, indigenous population of shellfish, fish and wildlife. Such estimates shall take into account the normal water temperatures, flow rates, seasonal variations, existing sources of heat input, and the dissipative capacity of the identified waters or parts thereof. Such estimates shall include a calculation of the maximum heat input that can be made into each such part and shall include a margin of safety which takes into account any lack of knowledge concerning the development of thermal water quality criteria for protection and propagation of a balanced, indigenous population of shellfish, fish and wildlife in the identified waters or parts thereof.

Each state shall submit biennially to the Regional Administrator the list of waters, pollutants causing impairment, and the priority ranking including waters targeted for TMDL development within the next two years as required under this section of the CFRs. For the 1992 biennial submission, these lists are due no later than October 22, 1992. Thereafter, each state shall submit to EPA lists required under this section of the CFRs on April 1 of every even-numbered year. The list of waters may be submitted as part of the state's biennial water quality report required by 130.8 of this part and section 305(b) of the CWA or submitted separately. All WLAs/LAs and TMDLs established under paragraph (c) for water quality limited segments shall continue to be submitted to EPA for review and approval. Schedules for submission of TMDLs shall be determined by the Regional Administrator and the state.

The Regional Administrator shall either approve or disapprove such listing and loadings not later than 30 days after the date of submission. The Regional Administrator shall approve a list developed under 130.7(b) that is submitted after the effective date of this rule only if it meets the requirements of 130.7(b). If the Regional Administrator approves such listing and loadings, the state shall incorporate them into its current WQM plan. If the Regional Administrator disapproves such listing and loadings, he shall, not later than 30 days after the date of such disapproval, identify such waters in such state and establish such loads for such waters as determined necessary to implement applicable WQS. The Regional Administrator shall promptly issue a public notice seeking comment on such listing and loadings. After considering public comment and making any revisions he deems appropriate, the Regional Administrator shall transmit the listing and loads to the state, which shall incorporate them into its current WQM plan.

For the specific purpose of developing information and as resources allow, each state shall identify all segments within its boundaries which it has not identified under this section of the CFRs and estimate for such waters the TMDLs with seasonal variations and margins of safety, for those pollutants which the Regional Administrator identifies under section 304(a)(2) as suitable for such calculation and for thermal discharges, at a level that would assure protection and propagation of a balanced indigenous population of fish, shellfish and wildlife. However, there is no requirement for such loads to be submitted to EPA for approval, and establishing TMDLs for those waters identified in this section of the CFRs shall be given higher priority.

23.6 Water Quality Report

Each state shall prepare and submit biennially to the Regional Administrator a water quality report in accordance with section 305(b) of the Act. The water quality report serves as the primary assessment of state water quality. Based upon the water quality data and problems identified in the 305(b) report, states develop water quality management (WQM) plan elements to help direct all subsequent control activities. Water quality problems identified in the 305(b) report should be analyzed through water quality management planning leading to the development of alternative controls and procedures for problems identified in the latest 305(b) report. States may also use the 305(b) report to describe groundwater quality and to guide development of groundwater plans and programs. Water quality problems identified in the 305(b) report should be emphasized and reflected in the state's WQM plan and annual work program under sections 106 and 205(j) of the Clean Water Act.

Each such report shall include but is not limited to the following:

- ❏ a description of the water quality of all waters of the United States and the extent to which the quality of waters provides for the protection and propagation of a balanced population of shellfish, fish, and wildlife and allows recreational activities in and on the water;

- ❏ an estimate of the extent to which CWA control programs have improved water quality or will improve water quality for the purposes of this section of the CFRs, and recommendations for future actions necessary and identifications of waters needing action;

- ❏ an estimate of the environmental, economic and social costs and benefits needed to achieve the objectives of the CWA and an estimate of the date of such achievement;

- ❏ a description of the nature and extent of nonpoint source pollution and recommendations of programs needed to control each category of nonpoint sources, including an estimate of implementation costs;

❑ an assessment of the water quality of all publicly owned lakes, including the status and trends of such water quality as specified in section 314(a)(1) of the Clean Water Act.

States may include a description of the nature and extent of groundwater pollution and recommendations of state plans or programs needed to maintain or improve groundwater quality.

In the years in which it is prepared the biennial section 305(b) report satisfies the requirement for the annual water quality report under section 205(j). In years when the 305(b) report is not required, the state may satisfy the annual section 205(j) report requirement by certifying that the most recently submitted section 305(b) report is current or by supplying an update of the sections of the most recently submitted section 305(b) report which require updating.

23.7 Program Management

State agencies may apply for grants under sections 106, 205(j) and 205(g) to carry out water quality planning and management activities. Interstate agencies may apply for grants under section 106 to carry out water quality planning and management activities. Local or regional planning organizations may request 106 and 205(j) funds from a state for planning and management activities. Grant administrative requirements for these funds appear in 40 CFR Parts 25, 29, 30, 33 and 35, subparts A and J.

Grants under section 106 may be used to fund a wide range of activities, including but not limited to assessments of water quality, revision of water quality standards (WQS), development of alternative approaches to control pollution, implementation and enforcement of control measures and development or implementation of ground water programs. Grants under section 205(j) may be used to fund water quality management (WQM) planning activities but may not be used to fund implementation of control measures (see part 35, subpart A). Section 205(g) funds are used primarily to manage the wastewater treatment works construction grants program pursuant to the provisions of 40 CFR Part 35, subpart J. A state may also use part of the 205(g) funds to administer approved permit programs under sections 402 and 404, to administer a statewide waste treatment management program under section 208(b)(4) and to manage waste treatment construction grants for small communities.

A state's 305(b) Report, WQM plan and other water quality assessments shall identify the state's priority water quality problems and areas. The WQM plan shall contain an analysis of alternative control measures and recommendations to control specific problems. Work programs shall specify:

❑ the activities to be carried out during the period of the grant;

❑ the cost of specific activities;

❑ the outputs, for example, permits issued, intensive surveys, wasteload allocations, to be produced by each activity; and

❑ where applicable, schedules indicating when activities are to be completed.

Water Quality Planning and Management

States shall also describe how the activities funded by these grants are used in a coordinated manner to address the priority water quality problems identified in the state's water quality assessment under section 305(b).

EPA, states, areawide agencies, interstate agencies, local and regional governments, and designated management agencies (DMAs) are joint participants in the water pollution control program. States may enter into contractual arrangements or intergovernmental agreements with other agencies concerning the performance of water quality planning and management tasks. Such arrangements shall reflect the capabilities of the respective agencies and shall efficiently utilize available funds and funding eligibilities to meet federal requirements commensurate with state and local priorities. State work programs under section 205(j) shall be developed jointly with local, regional and other comprehensive planning organizations.

Relationship to the National Pollutant Discharge Elimination System (NPDES) program. In accordance with section 208(e) of the Act, no NPDES permit may be issued which is in conflict with an approved Water Quality Management (WQM) plan. Where a state has assumed responsibility for the administration of the permit program under section 402, it shall assure consistency with the WQM plan.

Water Quality Guidance for the Great Lakes System

> *The Guidance in this part of the CFRs identifies minimum water quality standards, antidegradation policies, and implementation procedures for the Great Lakes System to protect human health, aquatic life, and wildlife.*

24.1 Overview

This part constitutes the Water Quality Guidance for the Great Lakes System (Guidance) required by section 118(c)(2) of the Clean Water Act (33 U.S.C. 1251 et seq.) as amended by the Great Lakes Critical Programs Act of 1990 (Pub. L. 101–596, 104 Stat. 3000 et seq.).

The Great Lakes includes Lake Ontario, Lake Erie, Lake Huron (including Lake St. Clair), Lake Michigan, and Lake Superior; and the connecting channels (Saint Mary's River, Saint Clair River, Detroit River, Niagara River, and Saint Lawrence River to the Canadian Border). These regulations apply to the states of Illinois, Indiana, Michigan, Minnesota, New York, Ohio, Pennsylvania, and Wisconsin, and any indian tribe which is located (in whole or in part) within the drainage basin of the Great Lakes, and for which EPA has approved water quality standards under section 303 of the Clean Water Act or which EPA has authorized to administer an NPDES program under section 402 of the Clean Water Act.

The U.S. Environmental Protection Agency, Great Lakes States, and Great Lakes Tribes will use the Guidance in this part to evaluate the water quality programs of the states and tribes to assure that they are protective of water quality. The Great Lakes States and Tribes must adopt provisions consistent with the Guidance in this part applicable to waters in the Great Lakes System or be subject to EPA promulgation of its terms pursuant to this part.

Certain documents referenced in the appendixes to this part with a designation of NTIS and/or ERIC are available for a fee upon request from:

> National Technical Information Center (NTIS)
> U.S. Department of Commerce
> 5285 Port Royal Road
> Springfield, VA 22161

Alternatively, copies may be obtained for a fee upon request to the:

Educational Resources Information Center/Clearinghouse (ERIC/CSMEE)

1200 Chambers Road, Room 310

Columbus, Ohio 43212

24.2 Adoption of Criteria

The Great Lakes States and Tribes shall adopt numeric water quality criteria for the purposes of section 303(c) of the Clean Water Act applicable to waters of the Great Lakes System in accordance with 132.4(d) that are consistent with:

❑ the acute water quality criteria for protection of aquatic life in Table 1 of this part, or a site specific modification thereof in accordance with procedure 1 of appendix F of this part;

❑ the chronic water quality criteria for protection of aquatic life in Table 2 of this part, or a site specific modification thereof in accordance with procedure 1 of appendix F of this part;

❑ the water quality criteria for protection of human health in Table 3 of this part, or a site specific modification thereof in accordance with procedure 1 of appendix F of this part; and

❑ the water quality criteria for protection of wildlife in Table 4 of this part, or a site specific modification thereof in accordance with procedure 1 of appendix F of this part.

24.2.1 State Adoption and Application of Methodologies

The Great Lakes States and Tribes shall adopt requirements applicable to waters of the Great Lakes System for the purposes of sections 118, 301, 303, and 402 of the Clean Water Act that are consistent with the:

❑ Methodologies for Development of Aquatic Life Criteria and Values in appendix A of this part of the CFRs;

❑ Methodology for Development of Bioaccumulation Factors in appendix B of this part of the CFRs;

❑ Methodologies for Development of Human Health Criteria and Values in appendix C of this part of the CFRs;

❑ Methodology for Development of Wildlife Criteria in appendix D of this part;

❑ Antidegradation Policy in appendix E of this part of the CFRs; and

❑ Implementation Procedures in appendix F of this part of the CFRs.

24.3 Other Information

24.3.1 Tables to Part 132

Tables 1 and 2 of this section in the CFRs presents Acute Water Quality Criteria for Protection of Aquatic Life in Ambient Water, and Chronic Water Quality Criteria for Protection of Aquatic Life in Ambient Water, respectively. EPA recommends that metals criteria be expressed as dissolved concentrations (see appendix A, I.A.4 for more information regarding metals criteria). Table 3 presents Water Quality Criteria for Protection of Human Health.

The Great Lakes Water Quality Initiative includes fairly extensive tables/lists of various types of pollutants of concern, including pollutants that are bioaccumulative chemicals of concern (BCCs), and pollutants that are not bioaccumulative chemicals of concern.

24.3.2 Appendices to Part 132

A wealth of information is contained in the six appendices to 40 CFR Part 132. Those directly affected by compliance issues in the Great Lakes area should refer to the following table for site specific water quality information:

Methodologies for Development of Aquatic Life Criteria and Values	Appendix A
Great Lakes Water Quality Initiative	Appendix B
Methodology for Development of Human Health Criteria and Values	Appendix C
Methodology for the Development of Wildlife Criteria	Appendix D
Antidegradation Policy	Appendix E
Implementation Procedures	Appendix F

Water Quality Standards (WQS)

> *A WQS defines the water quality goals of a water body by designating the uses to be made of the water and by setting criteria necessary to protect the uses. This section contains procedures for developing, reviewing, revising and approving WQS by the states and EPA. States are required to develop statewide antidegradation policies, that should be reviewed at least every three years.*

25.1 Overview

A water quality standard defines the water quality goals of a water body, or portion thereof, by designating the use or uses to be made of the water and by setting criteria necessary to protect the uses. States adopt water quality standards to protect public health or welfare, enhance the quality of water and serve the purposes of the Clean Water Act (the Act). "Serve the purposes of the Act" (as defined in sections 101(a)(2) and 303(c) of the Act) means that water quality standards should, wherever attainable, provide water quality for the protection and propagation of fish, shellfish and wildlife and for recreation in and on the water and take into consideration their use and value of public water supplies, propagation of fish, shellfish, and wildlife, recreation in and on the water, and agricultural, industrial, and other purposes including navigation.

Such standards serve the dual purposes of establishing the water quality goals for a specific water body and serve as the regulatory basis for the establishment of water quality based treatment controls and strategies beyond the technology based levels of treatment required by sections 301(b) and 306 of the Act.

25.1.1 State Authority

States are responsible for reviewing, establishing, and revising water quality standards. As recognized by section 510 of the Clean Water Act, states may develop water quality standards more stringent than required by this regulation. Consistent with section 101(g) and 518(a) of the Clean Water Act, water quality standards shall not be construed to supersede or abrogate rights to quantities of water.

States may issue certifications pursuant to the requirements of Clean Water Act section 401. Revisions adopted by states shall be applicable for use in issuing state certifications consistent with the provisions of 131.21(c).

Where EPA determines that a Tribe is eligible to the same extent as a state for purposes of water quality standards, the Tribe likewise is eligible to the same extent as a state for purposes of certifications conducted under Clean Water Act section 401.

25.1.2 EPA authority

Under section 303(c) of the Act, EPA is to review and to approve or disapprove state adopted water quality standards. The review involves a determination of:

- ❑ whether the state has adopted water uses which are consistent with the requirements of the Clean Water Act;

- ❑ whether the state has adopted criteria that protect the designated water uses;

- ❑ whether the state has followed its legal procedures for revising or adopting standards;

- ❑ whether the state standards which do not include the uses specified in section 101(a)(2) of the Act are based upon appropriate technical and scientific data and analyses, and

- ❑ whether the state submission meets the requirements included in 131.6 of this part and, for Great Lakes states or Great Lakes tribes (as defined in 40 CFR 132.2) to conform to section 118 of the Act, the requirements of 40 CFR Part 132.

If EPA determines that the state's or tribe's water quality standards are consistent with the factors listed in paragraphs (a)(1) through (a)(5) of this section of the CFRs, EPA approves the standards. EPA must disapprove the state's or tribe's water quality standards and promulgate federal standards under section 303(c)(4), and for Great Lakes States or Great Lakes Tribes under section 118(c)(2)(C) of the Act, if state or tribal adopted standards are not consistent with the factors listed in this section. EPA may also promulgate a new or revised standard when necessary to meet the requirements of the Act.

Section 401 of the Clean Water Act authorizes EPA to issue certifications pursuant to the requirements of section 401 in any case where a state or interstate agency has no authority for issuing such certifications.

25.2 Minimum Requirements for Water Quality Standards Submission

The following elements must be included in each state's water quality standards submitted to EPA for review:

- ❑ use designations consistent with the provisions of sections 101(a)(2) and 303(c)(2) of the Act;

- ❑ methods used and analyses conducted to support water quality standards revisions;

- ❑ water quality criteria sufficient to protect the designated uses;

- ❑ an antidegradation policy consistent with 131.12; and

❑ certification by the State Attorney General or other appropriate legal authority within the state that the water quality standards were duly adopted pursuant to state law.

25.3 Dispute Resolution Mechanism

Where disputes between states and indian tribes arise as a result of differing water quality standards on common bodies of water, the lead EPA Regional Administrator, as determined based upon OMB circular A–105, shall be responsible for acting in accordance with the provisions of this section of the CFRs. The Regional Administrator shall attempt to resolve such disputes where:

❑ the difference in water quality standards results in unreasonable consequences;

❑ the dispute is between a state (as defined in 131.3(j) but exclusive of all indian tribes) and a Tribe which EPA has determined is eligible to the same extent as a state for purposes of water quality standards;

❑ a reasonable effort to resolve the dispute without EPA involvement has been made;

❑ the requested relief is consistent with the provisions of the Clean Water Act and other relevant law;

❑ the differing state and tribal water quality standards have been adopted pursuant to state and tribal law and approved by EPA; and

❑ A valid written request has been submitted by either the tribe or the state.

Either a state or a tribe may request EPA to resolve any dispute which satisfies the criteria of this section of the CFRs.

If in accordance with applicable state and tribal law an indian tribe and state have entered into an agreement that resolves the dispute or establishes a mechanism for resolving a dispute, EPA shall defer to this agreement where it is consistent with the Clean Water Act and where it has been approved by EPA. EPA dispute resolution actions shall be consistent with one or a combination of the following options—

25.3.1 Mediation

The Regional Administrator may appoint a mediator to mediate the dispute. Mediators shall be EPA employees, employees from other federal agencies, or other individuals with appropriate qualifications.

❑ Where the state and tribe agree to participate in the dispute resolution process, mediation with the intent to establish tribal–state agreements, consistent with Clean Water Act section 518(d), shall normally be pursued as a first effort.

❑ Mediators shall act as neutral facilitators whose function is to encourage communication and negotiation between all parties to the dispute.

❑ Mediators may establish advisory panels, to consist in part of representatives from the affected parties, to study the problem and recommend an appropriate solution.

❑ The procedure and schedule for mediation of individual disputes shall be determined by the mediator in consultation with the parties.

❑ If formal public hearings are held in connection with the actions taken under this paragraph, Agency requirements at 40 CFR 25.5 shall be followed.

25.3.2 Arbitration

Where the parties to the dispute agree to participate in the dispute resolution process, the Regional Administrator may appoint an arbitrator or arbitration panel to arbitrate the dispute. Arbitrators and panel members shall be EPA employees, employees from other federal agencies, or other individuals with appropriate qualifications. The Regional administrator shall select as arbitrators and arbitration panel members individuals who are agreeable to all parties, are knowledgeable concerning the requirements of the water quality standards program, have a basic understanding of the political and economic interests of tribes and states involved, and are expected to fulfill the duties fairly and impartially.

The arbitrator or arbitration panel shall conduct one or more private or public meetings with the parties and actively solicit information pertaining to the effects of differing water quality permit requirements on upstream and downstream dischargers, comparative risks to public health and the environment, economic impacts, present and historical water uses, the quality of the waters subject to such standards, and other factors relevant to the dispute, such as whether proposed water quality criteria are more stringent than necessary to support designated uses, more stringent than natural background water quality or whether designated uses are reasonable given natural background water quality.

Following consideration of relevant factors as defined in this section of the CFRs, the arbitrator or arbitration panel shall have the authority and responsibility to provide all parties and the Regional Administrator with a written recommendation for resolution of the dispute. Arbitration panel recommendations shall, in general, be reached by majority vote. However, where the parties agree to binding arbitration, or where required by the Regional Administrator, recommendations of such arbitration panels may be unanimous decisions. Where binding or non-binding arbitration panels cannot reach a unanimous recommendation after a reasonable period of time, the Regional Administrator may direct the panel to issue a non-binding decision by majority vote.

The arbitrator or arbitration panel members may consult with EPA's Office of General Counsel on legal issues, but otherwise shall have no ex parte communications pertaining to the dispute. Federal employees who are arbitrators or arbitration panel members shall be neutral and shall not be predisposed for or against the position of any disputing party based on any federal trust responsibilities which their employers may have with respect to the tribe. In addition, arbitrators or arbitration panel members who are federal employees shall act independently from the normal hierarchy within their agency.

The parties are not obligated to abide by the arbitrator's or arbitration panel's recommendation unless they voluntarily entered into a binding agreement to do so.

If a party to the dispute believes that the arbitrator or arbitration panel has recommended an action contrary to or inconsistent with the Clean Water Act, the party may appeal the arbitrator's recommendation to the Regional Administrator. The request for appeal must be in writing and must include a description of the statutory basis for altering the arbitrator's recommendation.

The procedure and schedule for arbitration of individual disputes shall be determined by the arbitrator or arbitration panel in consultation with parties.

If formal public hearings are held in connection with the actions taken under this paragraph, Agency requirements at 40 CFR 25.5 shall be followed.

Where one or more parties refuse to participate in either the mediation or arbitration dispute resolution processes, the Regional Administrator may appoint a single official or panel to review available information pertaining to the dispute and to issue a written recommendation for resolving the dispute. Review officials shall be EPA employees, employees from other federal agencies, or other individuals with appropriate qualifications. Review panels shall include appropriate members to be selected by the Regional Administrator in consultation with the participating parties. Recommendations of such review officials or panels shall, to the extent possible given the lack of participation by one or more parties, be reached in a manner identical to that for arbitration of disputes specified in paragraphs (f)(2)(i) through (f)(2)(vii) of this section of the CFRs.

25.4 Establishment of Water Quality Standards

Each state must specify appropriate water uses to be achieved and protected. The classification of the waters of the state must take into consideration the use and value of water for public water supplies, protection and propagation of fish, shellfish and wildlife, recreation in and on the water, agricultural, industrial, and other purposes including navigation. In no case shall a state adopt waste transport or waste assimilation as a designated use for any waters of the United States.

In designating uses of a water body and the appropriate criteria for those uses, the state shall take into consideration the water quality standards of downstream waters and shall ensure that its water quality standards provide for the attainment and maintenance of the water quality standards of downstream waters.

States may adopt subcategories of a use and set the appropriate criteria to reflect varying needs of such subcategories of uses, for instance, to differentiate between cold water and warm water fisheries.

At a minimum, uses are deemed attainable if they can be achieved by the imposition of effluent limits required under sections 301(b) and 306 of the Act and cost effective and reasonable best management practices for nonpoint source control.

Prior to adding or removing any use, or establishing subcategories of a use, the state shall provide notice and an opportunity for a public hearing under 131.20(b) of this regulation.

States may adopt seasonal uses as an alternative to reclassifying a water body or segment thereof to uses requiring less stringent water quality criteria. If seasonal uses are adopted, water quality criteria should be adjusted to reflect the seasonal uses, however, such criteria shall not preclude the attainment and maintenance of a more protective use in another season.

States may remove a designated use which is not an existing use, as defined in 131.3, or establish subcategories of a use if the state can demonstrate that attaining the designated use is not feasible because:

- naturally occurring pollutant concentrations prevent the attainment of the use; or
- natural, ephemeral, intermittent or low flow conditions or water levels prevent the attainment of the use, unless these conditions may be compensated for by the discharge of sufficient volume of effluent discharges without violating state water conservation requirements to enable uses to be met; or
- human caused conditions or sources of pollution prevent the attainment of the use and cannot be remedied or would cause more environmental damage to correct than to leave in place; or
- dams, diversions or other types of hydrologic modifications preclude the attainment of the use, and it is not feasible to restore the water body to its original condition or to operate such modification in a way that would result in the attainment of the use; or
- physical conditions related to the natural features of the water body, such as the lack of a proper substrate, cover, flow, depth, pools, riffles, and the like, unrelated to water quality, preclude attainment of aquatic life protection uses; or
- controls more stringent than those required by sections 301(b) and 306 of the Act would result in substantial and widespread economic and social impact.

States may not remove designated uses if: they are existing uses, as defined in 131.3, unless a use requiring more stringent criteria is added; or such uses will be attained by implementing effluent limits required under sections 301(b) and 306 of the Act and by implementing cost effective and reasonable best management practices for nonpoint source control.

25.4.1 Attainability Analysis

Where existing water quality standards specify designated uses less than those which are presently being attained, the state shall revise its standards to reflect the uses actually being attained.

A state must conduct a use attainability analysis as described in 131.3(g) whenever:

❏ the state designates or has designated uses that do not include the uses specified in section 101(a)(2) of the Act, or

❏ the state wishes to remove a designated use that is specified in section 101(a)(2) of the Act or to adopt subcategories of uses specified in section 101(a)(2) of the Act which require less stringent criteria.

A state is not required to conduct a use attainability analysis under this regulation whenever designating uses which include those specified in section 101(a)(2) of the Act.

25.4.2 Criteria for Inclusion of Pollutants

States must adopt those water quality criteria that protect the designated use. Such criteria must be based on sound scientific rationale and must contain sufficient parameters or constituents to protect the designated use. For waters with multiple use designations, the criteria shall support the most sensitive use.

States must review water quality data and information on discharges to identify specific water bodies where toxic pollutants may be adversely affecting water quality or the attainment of the designated water use or where the levels of toxic pollutants are at a level to warrant concern and must adopt criteria for such toxic pollutants applicable to the water body sufficient to protect the designated use. Where a state adopts narrative criteria for toxic pollutants to protect designated uses, the state must provide information identifying the method by which the state intends to regulate point source discharges of toxic pollutants on water quality limited segments based on such narrative criteria. Such information may be included as part of the standards or may be included in documents generated by the state in response to the Water Quality Planning and Management Regulations (40 CFR Part 35).

In establishing criteria, states should base numerical values on:

❏ 304(a) Guidance; or

❏ 304(a) Guidance modified to reflect site specific conditions; or

❏ other scientifically defensible methods.

States should establish narrative criteria or criteria based upon biomonitoring methods where numerical criteria cannot be established or to supplement numerical criteria.

25.4.3 Antidegradation Policy

The state shall develop and adopt a statewide antidegradation policy and identify the methods for implementing such policy pursuant to this subpart. The antidegradation policy and implementation methods shall, at a minimum, be consistent with the following:

❏ existing instream water uses and the level of water quality necessary to protect the existing uses shall be maintained and protected;

❑ where the quality of the waters exceed levels necessary to support propagation of fish, shellfish, and wildlife and recreation in and on the water, that quality shall be maintained and protected unless the state finds, after full satisfaction of the intergovernmental coordination and public participation provisions of the state's continuing planning process, that allowing lower water quality is necessary to accommodate important economic or social development in the area in which the waters are located;

❑ when allowing degradation or lower water quality, the state shall assure water quality adequate to protect existing uses fully, and the state shall assure all cost-effective and reasonable best management practices for nonpoint source controls are used;

❑ where high quality waters constitute an outstanding national resource, such as waters of national and state parks and wildlife refuges and waters of exceptional recreational or ecological significance, that water quality shall be maintained and protected; and

❑ in those cases where potential water quality impairment associated with a thermal discharge is involved, the antidegradation policy and implementing method shall be consistent with section 316 of the Act.

States may, at their discretion, include in their state standards, policies generally affecting their application and implementation, such as mixing zones, low flows and variances. Important subparts in this section include:

❑ Subpart C-Procedures for Review and Revision of Water Quality Standards

❑ Subpart D-Federally Promulgated Water Quality Standards

Appendix A
EPA Office of Water, Regional, and State Web Site Listings

Appendix A
EPA Office of Water, Regional, and State Web Site Listings

EPA and EPA Office of Water

Homepage	www.epa.gov/
Office of Water (OW)	www.epa.gov/OW/
OW Hotlines	www.epa.gov/ow/info.html
OW Search	www.epa.gov/ow/search.html
OW Email	OW–General@epamail.epa.gov

EPA Regional Offices of Water		
region	*state*	*URL for OW Pages*
EPA Region 1		www.epa.gov/region01/water.htm
	Connecticut	www.epa.gov/ow/states/CT
	Maine	www.epa.gov/ow/states/ME
	Massachusetts	www.epa.gov/ow/states/MA
	New Hampshire	www.epa.gov/ow/states/NH
	Rhode Island	www.epa.gov/ow/states/RI
	Vermont	www.epa.gov/ow/states/VT
EPA Region 2		www.epa.gov/region02/water.htm
	New Jersey	www.epa.gov/ow/states/NJ
	New York	www.epa.gov/ow/states/NY
	Puerto Rico	www.epa.gov/ow/states/PR
	U.S. Virgin Islands	
EPA Region 3		www.epa.gov/reg3wapd/
	Delaware	www.epa.gov/ow/states/DE
	Maryland	www.epa.gov/ow/states/MD
	Pennsylvania	www.epa.gov/ow/states/PA
	Virginia	www.epa.gov/ow/states/VA
	West Virginia	www.epa.gov/ow/states/WV

EPA Regional Offices of Water		
region	*state*	*URL for OW Pages*
	District of Columbia	www.epa.gov/ow/states/DC
EPA Region 4		www.epa.gov/region4/waterpgs/wtr.html
	Alabama	www.epa.gov/ow/states/AL
	Florida	www.epa.gov/ow/states/FL
	Georgia	www.epa.gov/ow/states/GA
	Kentucky	www.epa.gov/ow/states/KY
	Mississippi	www.epa.gov/ow/states/MS
	North Carolina	www.epa.gov/ow/states/NC
	South Carolina	www.epa.gov/ow/states/SC
	Tennessee	www.epa.gov/ow/states/TN
EPA Region 5		www.epa.gov/r5water
	Illinois	www.epa.gov/ow/states/IL
	Indiana	www.epa.gov/ow/states/IN
	Michigan	www.epa.gov/ow/states/MI
	Minnesota	www.epa.gov/ow/states/MN
	Ohio	www.epa.gov/ow/states/OH
	Wisconsin	www.epa.gov/ow/states/WI
EPA Region 6		www.epa.gov/earth1r6/6wq/6wq.htm
	Arkansas	www.epa.gov/ow/states/AR
	Louisiana	www.epa.gov/ow/states/LA
	New Mexico	www.epa.gov/ow/states/NM
	Oklahoma	www.epa.gov/ow/states/OK
	Texas	www.epa.gov/ow/states/TX
EPA Region 7		www.epa.gov/region07/programs/wwpd/wwp.html
	Iowa	www.epa.gov/ow/states/IA
	Kansas	www.epa.gov/ow/states/KS
	Missouri	www.epa.gov/ow/states/MO
	Nebraska	www.epa.gov/ow/states/NE
EPA Region 8		www.epa.gov/region08/water/water.html
	Colorado	www.epa.gov/ow/states/CO
	Montana	www.epa.gov/ow/states/MT
	North Dakota	www.epa.gov/ow/states/ND
	South Dakota	www.epa.gov/ow/states/SD

EPA Regional Offices of Water		
region	*state*	*URL for OW Pages*
	Utah	www.epa.gov/ow/states/UT
	Wyoming	www.epa.gov/ow/states/WY
EPA Region 9		www.epa.gov/region09/water/
	Arizona	www.epa.gov/ow/states/AZ
	California	www.epa.gov/ow/states/CA
	Hawaii	www.epa.gov/ow/states/HI
	Nevada	www.epa.gov/ow/states/NV
	Guam and American Samoa	
EPA Region 10		www.epa.gov/region10/water.htm
	Alaska	www.epa.gov/ow/states/AK
	Idaho	www.epa.gov/ow/states/ID
	Oregon	www.epa.gov/ow/states/OR
	Washington	www.epa.gov/ow/states/WA

State Agencies*		
state	*URL*	*department/division*
Alabama	www.adem.state.al.us/h2owebpg.html	Department of Environmental Management
	www.adem.state.al.us/h2owebpg.html	Water Division
Alaska	www.state.ak.us/dec/home.htm	Department of Environmental Conservation
Arizona	www.adeq.state.az.us	Department of Environmental Quality
Arkansas	www.adeq.state.ar.us/water/main.htm	Department of Pollution Control and Ecology
	www.adeq.state.ar.us/water/main.htm	Water Division
California	www.dwr.water.ca.gov	Department of Water Resources
Colorado	www.state.co.us/gov_dir/cdphe_dir/wq/wqhom.html	Department of Public Health and Environment
	www.state.co.us/gov_dir/cdphe_dir/wq/wqhom.html	Water Quality Control Division
Connecticut	http://dep.state.ct.us/wtr/index.htm	Department of Environmental Protection
	http://dep.state.ct.us/wtr/index.htm	Bureau of Water Management
Delaware	www.dnrec.state.de.us/water.htm	Department of Natural Resources
	www.dnrec.state.de.us/water.htm	Division of Water Resources
Florida	www2.dep.state.fl.us/water	Department of Environmental Protection

State Agencies*		
	www2.dep.state.fl.us/water	Water Facilities Online
Georgia	www.Georgianet.org/dnr/environ	Department of Natural Resources
	www.Georgianet.org/dnr/environ	Environmental Protection
Hawaii	www.hawaii.gov/health/index.html	Hawaii Department of Health
Idaho	www2.state.id.us/deq/water/water.htm	Division of Environmental Quality
	www2.state.id.us/deq/water/water.htm	Water Quality
Illinois	www.epa.state.il.us/water/index.html	Environmental Protection Agency
	www.epa.state.il.us/water/index.html	Water Pollution Information
Indiana	www.ai.org/idem/owm/index.html	Department of Environmental Management
	www.ai.org/idem/owm/index.html	Office of Water Management
Iowa	www.state.ia.us/government/dnr/organiza/epd/wtrq/wtrqbur.htm	Department of Natural Resources
	www.state.ia.us/government/dnr/organiza/epd/wtrq/wtrqbur.htm	Environmental Protection Division
	www.state.ia.us/government/dnr/organiza/epd/wtrq/wtrqbur.htm	Water Quality Bureau
Kansas	www.kdhe.state.ks.us/water	Department of Health and Environment
	www.kdhe.state.ks.us/water	Division of Environment
	www.kdhe.state.ks.us/water	Bureau of Water
Kentucky	www.state.ky.us/agencies/nrepc/dow/dwhome.htm	Department for Environmental Protection
	www.state.ky.us/agencies/nrepc/dow/dwhome.htm	Division of Water
Louisiana	www.deq.state.la.us/owr/owr.htm	Department of Environmental Quality
	www.deq.state.la.us/owr/owr.htm	Office of Water Resources
	www.dnr.state.la.us/index.ssi	Department of Natural Resources
Maine	www.state.me.us/dep/blwq/index.htm	Department of Environmental Protection
	www.state.me.us/dep/blwq/index.htm	Bureau of Land & Water Quality
Maryland	www.mde.state.md.us	Department of the Environment
Massachusetts	www.magnet.state.ma.us/dep/brp	Department of Environmental Protection
	www.magnet.state.ma.us/dep/brp	Bureau of Resource Protection
Michigan	www.deq.state.mi.us	Department of Environmental Quality
Minnesota	www.pca.state.mn.us/water	Pollution Control Agency
	www.pca.state.mn.us/water	Water
Mississippi	www.deq.state.ms.us/domino/deqweb.nsf	Department of Environmental Quality

State Agencies*		
Missouri	www.dnr.state.mo.us/water.htm	Department of Natural Resources
	www.dnr.state.mo.us/water.htm	Water Issues
Montana	www.deq.mt.gov	Department of Environmental Quality
	www.dnrc.state.mt.us	Department of Natural Resources and Conservation
Nebraska	www.deq.state.ne.us/programs.nsf/pages/wqd	Department of Environmental Quality
	www.deq.state.ne.us/programs.nsf/pages/wqd	Water Quality Division
Nevada	www.state.nv.us/cnr/ndwp/home.htm	Department of Conservation and Natural Resources
	www.state.nv.us/health/bhps/sdwp.htm	Bureau of Health Protection Services
	www.state.nv.us/health/bhps/sdwp.htm	Safe Drinking Water Program
New Mexico	www.nmenv.state.nm.us	Environment Department
New York	www.dec.state.ny.us/website/dow/index.html	Department of Environmental Conservation
	www.dec.state.ny.us/website/dow/index.html	Division of Water
	www.nysefc.org	Environmental Facilities Corporation
New Jersey	www.state.nj.us/dep/dwq	Department of Environmental Protection
	www.state.nj.us/dep/dwq	Division of Water Quality
New Hampshire	www.state.nh.us/des/descover.htm	Department of Environmental Services
North Carolina	www.ehnr.state.nc.us/EHNR	Department of Environment and Natural Resources
North Dakota	www.health.state.nd.us/ndhd/environ	Department of Health, Environmental Health Section
Ohio	www.epa.ohio.gov/new/divs.html	Environmental Protection Agency
Oklahoma	www.deq.state.ok.us/Water1/home/index.html	Department of Environmental Quality
	www.deq.state.ok.us/Water1/home/index.html	Water Quality Division
Oregon	http://waterquality.deq.state.or.us/wq	Department of Environmental Quality
	http://waterquality.deq.state.or.us/wq	Water Quality Program
Pennsylvania	www.dep.state.pa.us/dep/deputate/watermgt/watermgt.htm	Department of Environmental Protection
	www.dep.state.pa.us/dep/deputate/watermgt/watermgt.htm	Office of Water Management
Rhode Island	www.health.state.ri.us/environment/dwq.htm	Department of Health
	www.health.state.ri.us/environment/dwq.htm	Office of Drinking Water Quality
	www.state.ri.us/dem	Department of Environmental Management

State Agencies*		
South Dakota	www.state.sd.us/state/executive/denr/denr.html	Department of Environment and Natural Resources
South Carolina	www.state.sc.us/dhec/water	Department of Health and Environmental Control
	www.state.sc.us/dhec/water	Bureau of Water
Tennessee	www.state.tn.us/environment/water.htm	Department of Environment and Conservation
	www.state.tn.us/environment/water.htm	Water
Texas	www.tnrcc.state.tx.us/water/index.html	Natural Resource Conservation Commission
	www.tnrcc.state.tx.us/water/index.html	Water Resource Management
	www.twdb.state.tx.us	Water Development Board
Utah	www.deq.state.ut.us/eqoas/wtr_new.htm	Department of Environmental Quality
	www.deq.state.ut.us/eqoas/wtr_new.htm	Water
Vermont	www.anr.state.vt.us	Agency of Natural Resources
Virginia	www.deq.state.us/water	Department of Environmental Quality – Water Program
Washington	www.wa.gov/ecology	Department of Ecology
West Virginia	www.dep.state.wv.us/wr/index.html	Division of Environmental Protection
	www.dep.state.wv.us/wr/index.html	Office of Water Resources
Wisconsin	www.dnr.state.wi.us/environmentprotect/water.html	Department of Natural Resources
	www.dnr.state.wi.us/environmentprotect/water.html	Water
Wyoming	http://deq.state.wy.us/wqd.htm	Department of Environmental Quality
	http://deq.state.wy.us/wqd.htm	Water Quality Division

*Disclaimer - This reflects only that information available on Region and State web pages. EPA does not guarantee the validity or the timeliness of the information.

Appendix B - Major CWA Provisions by Section

Appendix B - Major CWA Provisions

Section 201-209 (33 U.S.C. 1281-1289)	
Grants for construction of treatment works	These sections originally provided federal grants for the construction of wastewater treatment plants. The program has been phased out by the 1987 amendments in favor of a revolving loan fund.
Section 301 (33 U.S.C. 1311)	
Effluent limitations	The discharge of any pollutant into the nation's waters except for discharges in compliance with the CWA is prohibited, according to this section. Limitations are placed on existing sources which vary according to the nature of the pollutant discharged and to where the outfall is directed.
Section 302 (33 U.S.C. 1312)	
Water quality related effluent limitations	Point sources which interfere with the attainment or maintenance of desired water quality are subject to the imposition of more stringent effluent limitations.
Section 303 (33 U.S.C. 1313)	
Water quality standards and implementation plans	Water quality-based regulatory controls on dischargers known as Water Quality Standards (WQS) are required by states to protect designated uses of water bodies. Technological capability is not a consideration in setting WQS.
Section 304 (33 U.S.C. 1314)	
Information and guidelines	This section requires the EPA to develop water quality criteria and guidelines for effluent limitations, pretreatment programs, and administration of the National Pollutant Discharge Elimination System (NPDES) program.
Section 306 (33 U.S.C. 1316)	
National standards of performance	A list of categories of effluent sources is presented which specifies that each of the industries listed must conform to technology-based new source performance standards. The standards are to demonstrate the best demonstrated control technology.
Section 307 (33 U.S.C. 1317)	
Toxic and pretreatment effluent standards	This requires that industries discharging toxic pollutants meet effluent limits that employ the best available technology economically achievable. Part (b) mandates the establishment of pretreatment standards while part {c} looks at new sources of pollutants into publicly owned treatment works (POTWs).
Section 309 (33 U.S.C. 1319)	
Enforcement	Enforcement by the states, as well as compliance orders, and administrative, civil, and criminal penalties are authorized.
Section 311 (33 U.S.C. 1321)	

Oil and hazardous substance liability	The Congressional declaration of policy against discharges of oil or hazardous substances in harmful quantities into waters and adjoining shorelines is presented. A spill prevention, control, and countermeasure plan is to be developed by all facilities that handle, transport, and store oil. Any spill or discharge of a harmful quantity of oil must be reported to the National Response Center.
Section 319 (33 U.S.C. 1329)	
Nonpoint source management programs	This section requires that states identify waters that are not able to meet WQS because of nonpoint sources. The activities responsible for the pollution are to be identified and a management plan is to be created to help correct the nonpoint source problem.
Section 401 (33 U.S.C. 1341)	
Certification	Any applicant for a Federal license or permit to conduct any activity which may result in any discharge into the navigable waters, shall provide the licensing or permitting agency a certification from the State in which the discharge will originate.
Section 402 (33 U.S.C. 1342)	
National pollutant discharge elimination system	One of the most critical parts of the CWA is the establishment of the National Pollutant Discharge Elimination System which translates standards into enforceable limitations. This program may be administered by the EPA or states under EPA-delegated authority. After an opportunity for public hearing, a permit may be issued for the point source discharge of any pollutant, or combination of pollutants.
Section 404 (33 U.S.C. 1344)	
Permits for dredged or fill material	This is the major wetlands provision of the CWA, and largely, in environmental law. The basic gist of this section is that a permit is required from the U.S. Army Corps of Engineers for the disposal of dredged or filled materials into navigable waters , notably wetlands, with EPA concurrence, and notice and opportunity for public hearings.
Section 505 (33 U.S.C. 1365)	
Citizen suits	Any citizen is given the right to file suit against any person in violation of an effluent standard or against EPA for failure to perform nondiscretionary duties.

Appendix C - Related Acts, Executive Orders and Related References

Appendix C - Related Acts, Executive Orders and Related References

Applicable Statutes

- ☐ Estuary Protection Act (PL 90-454; 16 U.S.C. 1221-1226)
- ☐ Wild and Scenic Rivers Act of 1968 (PL 90-542; 16 U.S.C. 1271-1287)
- ☐ National Marine Sanctuaries Act (PL 92-532; 16 U.S.C. 1431-1445a)
- ☐ Coastal Zone Management Act of 1972, as amended (PL 92-583; 16 U.S.C. 1451 et seq.)
- ☐ Marine Protection, Research, and Sanctuaries Act of 1972 (PL 92-532; 33 U.S.C. 1401-1445)
- ☐ Outer Continental Shelf Lands Act, as amended (PL 95-372; 43 U.S.C. 1331-1356)
- ☐ Clean Water Act (section 404) (PL 92-500; 33 U.S.C. 1251 et seq.)

Summaries

Estuary Protection Act (PL 90-454; 16 U.S.C. 1221-1226)
The purpose of the Estuary Protection Act is to strike a balance between the national need of conserving the beauty of the nations estuaries and the need to develop these estuaries to further growth and development. States are given much of the responsibility of protecting, conserving, and restoring estuary areas.

Wild and Scenic Rivers Act of 1968 (PL 90-542; 16 U.S.C. 1271-1287)
The Wild and Scenic Rivers Act provides for the preservation of selected rivers due to their remarkable scenic, recreational, geologic, fish and wildlife, historic, or cultural values. The free-flowing state of rivers, and their adjacent lands, is intended to be protected for the benefit and enjoyment of present and future generations. The Act institutes a National Wild and Scenic River System, designates the components of that System, and prescribes the methods by which additional components might be added to the System in order to carry out this goal.

National Marine Sanctuaries Act (PL 92-532; 16 U.S.C. 1431-1445a)
The National Marine Sanctuaries Act designates "marine areas of special national significance" as national marine sanctuaries and provides for the conservation and management of these areas. The Act also supports research of marine sanctuaries and related resources.

Coastal Zone Management Act (CZMA) of 1972, as amended (PL 92-583; 16 U.S.C. 1451 et seq.)
The purpose of the CZMA is to preserve, protect, develop, and restore or enhance

coastal zones. The CZMA encourages states to implement coastal zone management programs by both authorizing suspension of its allocated federal funding when a coastal state fails to adhere to its management program and by mandating that federal activities in any states coastal zone be consistent with the states plan. Another intention of the act is to respond to changing circumstances of coastal environments. Nonpoint sources of coastal water pollution are targeted by the amendments of 1990.

Marine Protection, Research, and Sanctuaries Act (MPRSA) of 1972 (PL 92-532; 33 U.S.C. 1401-1445)
Known as the Ocean Dumping Act, the MPRSA was enacted to regulate the dumping of all types of materials into ocean waters and to prevent or strictly limit the dumping into ocean waters of any material which would adversely affect human health, welfare, or amenities, or the marine environment, ecological systems, or economic potentialities.

Outer Continental Shelf Lands Act (OCSLA) (PL 95-372; 43 U.S.C. 1331-1356)
The Outer Continental Shelf (OCS) Lands Act provides for the expeditious and orderly development of the shelf while providing environmental safeguards. The Act takes measures to include state and local governments in the policy and planning decisions made by the Federal government relating to OCS actions.

Other Provisions

30 CFR Part 251
Geological and Geophysical (G & G) Explorations of the Outer Continental Shelf, Minerals Management Service. The purpose of this regulation is stated as to prescribe policies, procedures, and requirements for conducting geological and geophysical activities associated with exploration for oil, gas, or sulphur not authorized under a lease in the Outer Continental Shelf.

30 CFR Part 252
Outer Continental Shelf (OCS) Oil and Gas Information Program, Minerals Management Service. The procedures and requirements are presented for the submission of oil and gas data and information resulting from exploration, development, and production operations on the Outer Continental Shelf.

30 CFR Part 250.34
Development and Production Plan, Minerals Management Service. Describes, among other things, the requirements for compliance with §307(c)(3)(B) of the CZMA which governs the consistency of Outer Continental Shelf Lands Act plans with approved State coastal management programs.

33 CFR Part 140
Outer Continental Shelf Activities-Part 140 falls under Subchapter N of CFR Title 33. It is written to promote safety of life and property on Outer Continental Shelf facilities, vessels, and other units engaged in OCS activities, protect the marine environment, and implement the Outer Continental Shelf Lands Act. The provisions apply to OCS facilities and vessels and includes inspections by the Coast Guard.

Administration of leasing (43 U.S.C. 1334)
Rules and regulations concerning leasing of the Outer Continental Shelf by the Secretary of the Interior.

Environmental studies (43 U.S.C. 1346)
The Secretary of the Interior's guidelines for conducting studies of any areas included in oil and gas lease sales to predict impacts on the marine biota from pollution or large spills.

Geological and geophysical explorations (43 U.S.C. 1340)
Federal agency guidelines and rights to conduct non-conflicting geological and geophysical explorations in the outer Continental Shelf. Explanation of plan approvals, state concurrence, and drilling permits that may be required by approved plans.

Grants of leases by Secretary (43 U.S.C. 1337)
Information concerning oil and gas leases, including bidding guidelines and terms and provisions for exploration, development, and production of minerals.

Oil and gas development and production (43 U.S.C. 1351)
Lessee requirements to submit a development and production plan to the Secretary of the Interior prior to development pursuant to an oil and gas lease for outer Continental Shelf areas.

Outer Continental Shelf leasing program (43 U.S.C. 1344)
This section presents a schedule of proposed oil and gas lease sales and other information for the establishment of a outer Continental Shelf leasing program.

Selected Executive Orders, Public Laws, etc.

516 DM 2 Appendix 2(2.2) & (2.9), Department of Interior
Environmental documents (EA, EIS, FONSI) must be prepared for actions which may adversely affect the unique geographic characteristics of floodplains and wetlands or which threaten to violate E.O.s 11988 and 11990.

520 DM 1- Floodplain Management and Wetlands Protection Procedures, DOI
Generally adopts the Water Resources Council (WRC) guidelines for floodplain management. Requires bureaus to prepare written compliance procedures and provides criteria for evaluation of bureau procedures. Summarizes the WRC procedural steps.

Executive Order (E.O.) 11988
Floodplain Management Issued by the President to avoid adverse impacts associated with the occupancy and modification of floodplains and to avoid direct or indirect support of floodplain development.

Executive Order (E.O.) 11990
Protection of Wetlands Issued by the President to avoid adverse impacts associated with the destruction or modification of wetlands and to avoid direct or indirect support of new construction in wetlands.

Floodplain Management Guidelines, Water Resources Council (WRC)
Provides explanation of key terms and floodplain management concepts along with a section-by-section analyses of E.O. 11988. Further procedures are given in the form of a decision making process leading from the determination that a proposed action is or is not located in the base floodplain, through the implementation of agency actions.

Advice on EO 11988 Floodplain Management, Federal Emergency Management Agency (FEMA) and the Interagency Task Force on Floodplain Management
Emphasizes the requirement for agencies to select alternative sites for projects outside of the floodplain and for preparation of mitigation measures for unavoidable impacts.

PL 101-233 16 U.S.C. 4408
Restoration, management, and protection of wetlands and habitat for migratory birds on Federal lands. The head of each Federal agency responsible for acquiring, managing, or disposing of Federal lands and waters shall, to the extent consistent with the mission of such agency and existing statutory authorities, cooperate with the Director of the United States Fish and Wildlife Service to restore, protect, and enhance the wetland ecosystems and other habitats for migratory birds, fish, and wildlife within the lands and waters of each such agency.

Selected Reference Documents

"Annotated Publication List," Office of Ground Water Protection, U.S. Environmental Protection Agency, Washington, D.C.

"Clean Water Act Section 401: Background and Current Issues," CRS Report 95–2 ENR.

"Developing a State Wellhead Protection Program: A User's Guide To Assist State Agencies Under the Safe Drinking Water Act," 1988. Office of Ground Water Protection, U.S. Environmental Protection Agency, Washington, D.C.

"Handbook of Chemical Hazard Analysis Procedures." U.S. DOT, FEMA and U.S. EPA.

"Hazardous Materials Emergency Planning Guide." National Response Team, 1987, Washington, DC.

"Methodologies for Hazard Analysis and Risk Assessment in the Petroleum Refining and Storage Industry." CONCAWE's Risk Assessment Ad–hoc Group, CONCAWE, 1982.

"National Potential Incident of Noncompliance (PINC) List." Minerals Management Service, Offshore Inspection and Enforcement Division, 1988, Reston, VA.

"Oil Spill Contingency Planning, National Status: A Report to the President." National Response Team, 1990, Washington, DC., U.S. Government Printing Office.

"Risk and Cost–Benefit: Comparison of Provisions in the 104th Congress," CRS Report 95-376 ENR. Public Law 104-4

"Siting of HUD–Assisted Projects Near Hazardous Facilities: Acceptable Separation Distances from Explosive and Flammable Hazards." Office of Environment and Energy, Environmental Planning Division, Department of Housing and Urban Development, 1987. Washington, DC.

"Stormwater Permits: Status of EPA's Regulatory Program," CRS Report 94–811 ENR.

"Technical Guidance for Hazards Analysis: Emergency Planning for Extremely Hazardous Substances." U.S. DOT, FEMA and U.S. EPA.

"USGS Guide to Law and Regulations"; USGS Water Resources, http://water.usgs.gov/public/eap/env_guide/h2o_quality.html

"Wellhead Protection Program: Tools for Local Governments," 1989. Office of Ground Water Protection, U.S. Environmental Protection Agency, Washington, D.C.

"18th edition of Standard Methods for the Examination of Water and Wastewater," 1992 American Public Health Association, 1015 Fifteenth Street NW., Washington, DC 20005

"Annual Book of ASTM Standards," American Society for Testing and Materials, 1916 Race Street, Philadelphia, PA 19103

Appendix D - Glossary of Selected CFR Water Terms

Appendix D - Glossary of Selected CFR Water Terms

ACP - Area Contingency Plan

Act - the Federal Water Pollution Control Act, as amended by the Federal Water Pollution Control Act Amendments of 1972 (Pub. L. 92–500), and as further amended by the Clean Water Act of 1977 (Pub. L. 95–217), 33 U.S.C. 1251 et seq.; and as further amended by the Clean Water Act Amendments of 1978 (Pub. L. 95–676).

Air emissions - the release or discharge of a toxic pollutant by an owner or operator into the ambient air either (1) by means of a stack or (2) as a fugitive dust, mist or vapor as a result inherent to the manufacturing or formulating process.

Ambient water criterion - that concentration of a toxic pollutant in a navigable water that, based upon available data, will not result in adverse impact on important aquatic life, or on consumers of such aquatic life, after exposure of that aquatic life for periods of time exceeding 96 hours and continuing at least through one reproductive cycle; and will not result in a significant risk of adverse health effects in a large human population based on available information such as mammalian laboratory toxicity data, epidemiological studies of human occupational exposures, or human exposure data, or any other relevant data.

Aquatic animals - appropriately sensitive wholly aquatic animals which carry out respiration by means of a gill structure permitting gaseous exchange between the water and the circulatory system.

Aquatic flora - plant life associated with the aquatic eco–system including, but not limited to, algae and higher plants.

Aquifer - a geological formation, group of formations, or part of a formation that is capable of yielding a significant amount of water to a well or spring.

ASTM - American Society of Testing Materials

bbls - Barrels

Best Management Practices (BMP) - schedules of activities, prohibitions of practices, maintenance procedures, and other management practices to prevent or reduce the pollution of "waters of the United States". (40 CFR Part 122.2)

bpd - Barrels per Day

bph - Barrels per Hour

CHRIS - Chemical Hazards Response Information System

Coastal zone - the coastal waters strongly influenced by each other and in proximity to the shorelines of the several coastal states, and includes islands, transitional and intertidal areas, salt marshes, wetlands, and beaches. (CZMA, 304(1))

Construction - any placement, assembly, or installation of facilities or equipment (including contractual obligations to purchase such facilities or equipment) at the premises where such equipment will be used, including preparation work at such premises.

Contaminant - any physical, chemical, biological, or radiological substance or matter in water (SDWA, 1401(6)).

Contiguous zone - the entire zone established or to be established by the United States under article 24 of the Convention of the Territorial Sea and the Contiguous Zone.

CWA - Clean Water Act

Designated river - study areas rivers, or river segments, which have been designated by Congress to be studied for possible inclusion in the System. During the study period these areas are granted the same protection as rivers in the System.

Discharge of a pollutant - any addition of any pollutant to navigable waters from any point source (CWA, 502(12)(A)). Discharge includes, but is not limited to, any spilling, leaking, pumping, pouring, emitting, emptying or dumping, but excludes (A) discharges in compliance with a permit under section 402 of this Act, (B) discharges resulting from circumstances identified and reviewed and made a part of the public record with respect to a permit issued or modified under section 402 of this Act, and subject to a condition in such permit, and (C) continuous or anticipated intermittent discharges from a point source, identified in a permit or permit application under section 402 of this Act, which are caused by events occurring within the scope of relevant operating or treatment systems.

DOC - Department of Commerce

DOI - Department of Interior

DOT - Department of Transportation

Effluent standard - for purposes of section 307, the equivalent of effluent limitation as that term is defined in section 502(11) of the Act with the exception that it does not include a schedule of compliance.

EPA - Environmental Protection Agency

Estuarine reserve - a research area which may include any part or all of an estuary, adjoining transitional areas, and adjacent uplands, constituting to the extent feasible a natural unit, set aside to provide scientists and students the opportunity to examine over a period of time the ecological relationships within the area.

Estuary - that part of a river or stream or other body of water having unimpaired connection with the open sea, where the sea water is measurably diluted with fresh water derived from land drainage. (15 CFR Part 921.2)

Exemption - a document for water systems having technical and financial difficulty meeting national primary drinking water regulations effective for one year granted by EPA "due to compelling factors".

FEMA - Federal Emergency Management Agency

FR - Federal Register

Fugitive dust, mist or vapor - dust, mist or vapor containing a toxic pollutant regulated under this part which is emitted from any source other than through a stack.

HAZMAT - Hazardous Materials

LC50 - that concentration of material which is lethal to one–half of the test population of aquatic animals upon continuous exposure for 96 hours or less.

LEPC - Local Emergency Planning Committee

Manufacturer - any establishment engaged in the mechanical or chemical transformation of materials or substances into new products including but not limited to the blending of materials such as pesticidal products, resins, or liquors.

Marine environment - those areas of coastal and ocean waters, the Great Lakes and their connecting waters, and submerged lands over which the United States exercises jurisdiction, including the exclusive economic zone, consistent with international law. (NMSA, 1432(3))

Maximum Contaminant Level (MCL) - the maximum permissible level of a contaminant in water which is delivered to any user of a public water system. (SDWA, 1401(3))

Maximum Contaminant Level Goal (MCLG) - the level at which no known or anticipated adverse effects on the health of persons occur and which allows an adequate margin of safety.

Mixture - any combination of two or more elements and/or compounds in solid, liquid, or gaseous form except where such substances have undergone a chemical reaction so as to become inseparable by physical means.

MMS - Minerals Management Service (part of DOI)

National Pollutant Discharge Elimination System (NPDES) - the national program for issuing, modifying, revoking and reissuing, terminating, monitoring and enforcing permits, and imposing and enforcing pretreatment requirements, under sections 307, 402, 318, and 405 of CWA. (40 CFR Part 122.2)

Nationwide Rivers Inventory (NRI) - a candidate list, compiled with input from Federal land managing agencies, of rivers and river segments designated as having potential to become part of the System.

Navigable waters - waters of the United States, including the territorial seas (CWA, 502(7)).

Navigable waters is defined in section 502(7) of the Act to mean "waters of the United States, including the territorial seas," and includes, but is not limited to: (1) All waters which are presently used, or were used in the past, or may be susceptible to use as a means to transport interstate or foreign commerce, including all waters which are subject to the ebb and flow of the tide, and including adjacent wetlands; the term wetlands as used in this regulation shall include those areas that are inundated or saturated by surface or ground water at a frequency and duration sufficient to support, and that under normal circumstances do support, a prevelance of vegetation typically adapted for life in saturated soil conditions. Wetlands generally include swamps, marshes, bogs and similar areas; the term adjacent means bordering, contiguous or neighboring; (2) Tributaries of navigable waters of the United States, including adjacent wetlands; (3) Interstate waters, including wetlands; and (4) All other waters of the United States such as intrastate lakes, rivers, streams, mudflats, sandflats and wetlands, the use, degradation or destruction of which affect interstate commerce including, but not limited to: (i) Intrastate lakes, rivers, streams, and wetlands which are utilized by interstate travelers for recreational or other purposes; and (ii) Intrastate lakes, rivers, streams, and wetlands from which fish or shellfish are or could be taken and sold in interstate commerce; and (iii) Intrastate lakes, rivers, streams, and wetlands which are utilized for industrial purposes by industries in interstate commerce.

NCP - National Oil and Hazardous Substances Pollution Contingency Plan

New source - any source discharging a toxic pollutant, the construction of which is commenced after proposal of an effluent standard or prohibition applicable to such source if such effluent standard or prohibition is thereafter promulgated in accordance with section 307.

NOAA - National Oceanic and Atmospheric Administration (part of DOC)

NRC - National Response Center

NRT - National Response Team

Ocean waters - those waters of the open seas lying seaward of the base line from which the territorial sea is measured, as provided for in the Convention on the Territorial Sea and the Contiguous Zone. (MPRSA, 3(b))

OPA - Oil Pollution Act of 1990

OSC - On–Scene Coordinator

Outer Continental Shelf (OCS) - all submerged lands which lie seaward and outside the area of lands beneath navigable waters and of which the subsoil and seabed appertain to the United States and are subject to its jurisdiction and control (OCSLA, 1331(a)).

Point source - any discernible, confined and discrete conveyance, including but not limited to any pipe, ditch, channel, tunnel, conduit, well, discrete fissure, container, rolling stock, concentrated animal feeding operation, or vessel, or other floating craft, from which pollutants are or may be discharged. This term does not include agricultural stormwater discharges and return flows from irrigated agriculture. (CWA, 502(14))

Pollutant - dredged spoil, solid waste, incinerator residue, filter backwash, sewage, garbage, sewage sludge, munitions, chemical wastes, biological materials, radioactive materials (except those regulated under the Atomic Energy Act of 1954), heat, wrecked or discarded equipment, rock, sand, cellar dirt and industrial, municipal, and agricultural waste discharged into water. It does not mean: (a) sewage from vessels; or (b) water, gas, or other material which is injected into a well to facilitate production of oil or gas, or water derived in association with oil and gas production and disposed of in a well, if the well used either to facilitate production or for disposal purposes is approved by authority of the State in which the well is located, and if the State determines that the injection or disposal will not result in the degradation of ground or surface water sources. (CWA, 502(6))

PREP - National Preparedness for Response Exercise Program

Process wastes - any designated toxic pollutant, whether in wastewater or otherwise present, which is inherent to or unavoidably resulting from any manufacturing process, including that which comes into direct contact with or results from the production or use of any raw material, intermediate product, finished product, by–product or waste product and is discharged into the navigable waters.

Public water system - a system for the provision to the public of piped water for human consumption, if such system has at least fifteen service connections or regularly serves at least twenty-five individuals. (SDWA, 1401(4))

Public vessel - a vessel owned or bareboat–chartered and operated by the United States, or a State or political subdivision thereof, or by a foreign nation, except when such vessel is engaged in commerce.

Publicly owned treatment works (POTW) - any device or system used in the treatment of municipal sewage or industrial wastes of a liquid nature which is owned by a "State" or "municipality". This definition includes sewer, pipes, or other conveyances only if they convey wastewater to a POTW providing treatment. (40 CFR Part 122.2)

RA - Regional Administrator

RCRA - Resource Conservation and Recovery Act

Recharge - a process, natural or artificial, by which water is added to the saturated zone of an aquifer.

Recharge zone - the area through which water enters a sole or principal source aquifer.

Recharge Area - an area in which water reaches the zone of saturation (ground water) by surface infiltration; in addition, a major recharge area is an area where a major part of the recharge to an aquifer occurs.

Recreational river areas - those rivers or sections of rivers that are readily accessible by road or railroad, that may have some development along their shorelines, and that may have undergone some impoundment or diversion in the past.

RRC - Regional Response Centers

RRT - Regional Response Team

RSPA - Research and Special Programs Administration

SARA - Superfund Amendments and Reauthorization Act

Scenic river areas - those rivers or sections of rivers that are free of impoundments, with shorelines or watersheds still largely primitive and shorelines largely undeveloped, but accessible in places by roads.

Significant hazard to public health - any level of contaminant which causes or may cause the aquifer to exceed any maximum contaminant level set forth in any promulgated National Primary Drinking Water Standard at any point where the water may be used for drinking purposes or which may otherwise adversely affect the health of persons, or which may require a public water system to install additional treatment to prevent such adverse effect.

SDWA - Safe Drinking Water Act of 1986

SERC - State Emergency Response Commission

SI - Surface Impoundment

SIC - Standard Industrial Classification

Sole or Principal Source Aquifer (SSA) - an aquifer which supplies 50 percent or more of the drinking water for an area.

Source - any building, structure, facility, or installation from which there is or may be the discharge of toxic pollutants designated as such by the Administration under section 307(a)(1) of the Act.

SPCC - Spill Prevention, Control, and Countermeasures

State Director - the chief administrative officer of a State or interstate water pollution control agency operating an approved NPDES permit program. In the event responsibility for water pollution control and enforcement is divided among two or more State or interstate agencies, the term State Director means the administrative officer authorized to perform the particular procedure to which reference is made.

State program agency - the state agency designated in the approved state program as the sole contact with Federal agencies on matters relating to consistency determination.

Streamflow source zone - the upstream headwaters area which drains into an aquifer recharge zone.

Ten year 24–hour rainfall event - the maximum precipitation event with a probable recurrence interval of once in 10 years as defined by the National Weather Service in Technical Paper No. 40, Rainfall Frequency Atlas of the United States, May 1961, and subsequent amendments or equivalent regional or State rainfall probability information developed therefrom.

Territorial seas - the belt of the seas measured from the line of ordinary low water along that portion of the coast which is in direct contact with the open sea and the line marking the seaward limit of inland waters, and extending seaward a distance of 3 miles.

Toxic pollutants - those pollutants...which after discharge and upon exposure, ingestion, inhalation or assimilation into any organism...,will, on the basis of the information available to the Administrator, cause death, disease, behavioral abnormalities, cancer, genetic mutations, physiological malfunctions or physical deformations, in such organisms or their offspring. (CWA, 502(13))

USCG - United States Coast Guard

Variance - a document for water systems having technical and financial difficulty meeting national primary drinking water regulations which postpones compliance when the issuing of which "will not result in an unreasonable risk to health."

Vessel - every description of watercraft or other artificial contrivance used, or capable of being used, as a means of transportation on water other than a public vessel.

Water resources project - any dam, water conduit, resevoir, powerhouse, transmission line, or other project works under the Federal Power Act as amended, or other construction of developments which would affect the free-flowing characteristics of a Wild and Scenic River or Study River (36 CFR Part 297.3).

Waters of the United States - a) all waters which are currently used, were used in the past, or may be susceptible to use in interstate or foreign commerce, including all waters which are subject to the ebb and flow of the tide; b) all interstate waters, including interstate "wetlands"; c) all other waters such as interstate lakes, rivers, streams..., mudflats, sandflats, "wetlands", sloughs, prarie potholes, wet meadows, playa lakes, or natural ponds the use, degradation, or destruction of which would affect...interstate or foreign commerce.

Wetlands - those areas that are inundated or saturated by surface or groundwater at a frequency and duration sufficient to support...a prevalence of vegetation typically adapted for life in saturated soil conditions. Wetlands generally include swamps, marshes, bogs, and similar areas. (40 CFR Part 122.2)

Wild and scenic river - a river and the adjacent area within the boundaries of a component of the Wild and Scenic Rivers System pursuant to section 3(a) or 2(a)(ii) of the Act (36 CFR Part 297.3).

Wild river areas - those rivers or sections of rivers that are free of impoundments and generally inaccessible except by trail, with watersheds or shorelines essentially primitive and waters unpolluted. These represent vestiges of primitive America.

Appendix E - Other References and Contacts

Appendix E - Other References and Contacts

Average slopes of rivers may be obtained from topographic maps:

> U.S. Geological Survey
> Map Distribution
> Federal Center, Bldg. 41, Box 25286
> Denver, Colorado 80225

Charts of Upper Mississippi River and Illinois Waterway to Lake Michigan:

> U.S. Army Corps of Engineers
> Rock Island District, P.O. Box 2004
> Rock Island, Illinois 61204
> Phone: (309) 794–5552

Charts of Canadian Coastal and Great Lakes Waters:

> Canadian Hydrographic Service
> Department of Fisheries and Oceans Institute
> P.O. Box 8080, 1675 Russell Road
> Ottawa, Ontario KIG 3H6, Canada
> Phone: (613) 998–4931

Charts of Ohio River:

> U.S. Army Corps of Engineers
> Ohio River Division
> P.O. Box 1159, Cincinnati, Ohio 45201
> Phone: (513) 684–3002

Charts of Tennessee Valley Authority Reservoirs, Tennessee River and Tributaries:

> Tennessee Valley Authority
> Maps and Engineering Section
> 416 Union Avenue, Knoxville, Tennessee 37902
> Phone: (615) 632–2921

Charts and Maps of Lower Mississippi River (Gulf of Mexico to Ohio River and St. Francis, White, Big Sunflower, Atchafalaya, and other rivers):

U.S. Army Corps of Engineers

Vicksburg District, P.O. Box 60

Vicksburg, Mississippi 39180

Phone: (601) 634–5000

Charts and related publications for navigational waters may be ordered from:

Distribution Branch (N/CG33)

National Ocean Service, Riverdale

Maryland 20737–1199

Phone: (301) 436–6990

Charts of Black Warrior River, Alabama River, Tombigbee River, Apalachicola River and Pearl River:

U.S. Army Corps of Engineers

Mobile District

P.O. Box 2288, Mobile, Alabama 36628–0001

Phone: (205) 690–2511

Charts of Missouri River:

U.S. Army Corps of Engineers

Omaha District

6014 U.S. Post Office and Courthouse

Omaha, Nebraska 68102

Phone: (402) 221–3900

Coastal zone management - Specific procedures for Federal agency compliance with state requirements for consistency determination are provided 15 CFR Part 930 and in the various approved state coastal management program documents. For additional information contact:

Chief, Coastal Programs Division

1305 East-West Highway

Silver Spring, MD 20910

Tel: 301-713-3102 Fax: 301-713-4367, or

EPA's Drinking Water Docket

401 M Street, SW.

Washington, DC 20460

Estuarine areas - If an estuarine sanctuary is in an area that may be affected by your proposed action, establish consultation with the Sanctuary and Reserves Program Office, NOAA at the following address:

Sanctuary and Reserves Program Office
Office of Coastal Zone Management
1305 East West Hwy. Building 4
Silver Spring, MD 20910
Tel: (301) 713-3145

Marine Sanctuaries - If any marine sanctuary is in an area that may be affected by your proposed action, establish consultation with the Sanctuary Programs Office, NOAA, at the following address:

Director, Sanctuary Programs Office
Office of Coastal Zone Management
3300 Whitehaven St., N.W.
Washington, DC 20235
Tel: (202) 634-4236

Office of the Federal Register

800 North Capitol Street, NW., Suite 700
Washington, DC

U.S. Geological Survey

Federal Center, Box 25425
Denver, CO 80225–0425

Wild and scenic rivers - The Wild and Scenic River Act as amended contains lists for designated rivers and study areas. To determine whether there is a river listed in the Nationwide Rivers Inventory (NRI) which has potential to be impacted by your project, contact the:

Recreation Resources Assistance Division
National Park Service
Washington, DC 20013-7123
Tel: (202) 343-3780.

Appendix F - List of Conventional and Hazardous Substances

Appendix F - List of Conventional and Hazardous Substances

Designation of Hazardous Substances

The elements and compounds appearing in Tables 116.4 A and B of this section of the CFRsare designated as hazardous substances in accordance with section 311(b)(2)(A) of the Act. This designation includes any isomers and hydrates, as well as any solutions and mixtures containing these substances. Synonyms and Chemical Abstract System (CAS) numbers have been added for convenience of the user only. In case of any disparity the common names shall be considered the designated substance.

Table 116.4B—List of Hazardous Substances by CAS Number	
CAS#	common name
50000	Formaldehyde
50293	DDT
51285	2,4–Dinitrophenol
52686	Trichlorfon
56382	Parathion
56724	Coumaphos
57249	Strychnine
57749	Chlordane
58899	Lindane
60004	Ethylenediaminetetraacetic acid (EDTA)
60571	Dieldrin
62533	Aniline
62737	Dichlorvos
63252	Carbaryl
64186	Formic acid
64197	Acetic acid
65850	Benzoic acid
67663	Chloroform
71432	Benzene
72208	Endrin

Table 116.4B—List of Hazardous Substances by CAS Number

CAS#	common name
72435	Methoxychlor
72548	TDE
74895	Monomethylamine
74908	Hydrogen cyanide
74931	Methyl mercaptan
75047	Monoethylamine
75070	Acetaldehyde
75150	Carbon disulfide
75207	Calcium carbide
75445	Phosgene
75503	Trimethylamine
75649	tert–Butylamine
75865	Acetone cyanohydrin
75990	2,2–Dichloropropionic acid
76448	Heptachlor
78002	Tetraethyl lead
78795	Isoprene
78819	iso–Butylamine
79094	Propionic acid
79312	iso–Butyric acid
79367	Acetyl chloride
80626	Methyl methacrylate
85007	Diquat
86500	Guthion
87865	Pentachlorophenol
88755	o–Nitrophenol
91203	Naphthalene
91225	Quinoline
93765	2,4,5 – T acid
93798	2,4,5–T ester
94111	2,4 – D ester
94757	2,4 – D acid

Table 116.4B—List of Hazardous Substances by CAS Number	
CAS#	common name
94791	2,4 – D ester
94804	2,4 – D Butyl ester
95476	o–Xylene
95487	o – Cresol
98011	Furfural
98884	Benzoyl chloride
98953	Nitrobenzene
99650	m–Dinitrobenzene
100027	p–Nitrophenol
100254	p–Dinitrobenzene
100414	Ethylbenzene
100425	Styrene
100447	Benzyl chloride
100470	Benzonitrile
105464	sec–Butyl acetate
106423	p–Xylene
106445	p–Cresol
107028	Acrolein
107051	Allyl chloride
107131	Acrylonitrile
107153	Ethylenediamine
107186	Allyl alcohol
107493	Tetraethyl pyrophosphate
107926	n–Butyric acid
108054	Vinyl acetate
108247	Acetic anhydride
108316	Maleic anhydride
108383	m–Xylene
108394	m–Cresol
108463	Resorcinol
108883	Toluene
108907	Chlorobenzene

Table 116.4B—List of Hazardous Substances by CAS Number

CAS#	common name
108952	Phenol(618–
109739	n–Butylamine
109897	Diethylamine
110167	Maleic acid
110178	Fumaric acid
110190	iso–Butyl acetate
110827	Cyclohexane
115297	Endosulfan
115322	Dicofol
117806	Dichlone
121211	Pyrethrin
121299	Pyrethrin
121448	Triethylamine
121755	Malathion
123626	Propionic anhydride
123864	n–Butyl acetate
123922	iso–Amyl acetate
124403	Dimethylamine
124414	Sodium methylate
127822	Zinc phenolsulfonate
133062	Captan
142712	Cupric acetate
143339	Sodium cyanide
151508	Potassium cyanide
298000	Methyl parathion
298044	Disulfoton
300765	Naled
301042	Lead acetate
309002	Aldrin
315184	Mexacarbate
329715	2,5–Dinitrophenol
330541	Diuron

Table 116.4B—List of Hazardous Substances by CAS Number	
CAS#	common name
333415	Diazinon
506774	Cyanogen chloride
506876	Ammonium carbonate
506967	Acetyl bromide
513495	sec–Butylamine
528290	o–Dinitrobenzene
540885	tert–Butyl acetate
541093	Uranyl acetate
542621	Barium cyanide
543908	Cadmium acetate
544183	Cobaltous formate
554847	m–Nitrophenol
557211	Zinc cyanide
557346	Zinc acetate
557415	Zinc formate
563122	Ethion
573568	2,6–Dinitrophenol
592018	Calcium cyanide
592041	Mercuric cyanide
592858	Mercuric thiocyanate
592870	Lead thiocyanate
625161	tert–Amyl acetate
626380	sec–Amyl acetate
628637	n–Amyl acetate
631618	Ammonium acetate
815827	Cupric tartrate
1066304	Chromic acetate
1066337	Ammonium bicarbonate
1072351	Lead stearate
1111780	Ammonium carbamate
1185575	Ferric ammonium citrate
1194656	Dichlobenil

Table 116.4B—List of Hazardous Substances by CAS Number

CAS#	common name
1300716	Xylenol
1303282	Arsenic pentoxide
1303328	Arsenic disulfide
1303339	Arsenic trisulfide
1309644	Antimony trioxide
1310583	Potassium hydroxide
1310732	Sodium hydroxide
1314621	Vanadium pentoxide
1314803	Phosphorus pentasulfide
1314847	Zinc phosphide
1314870	Lead sulfide
1319773	Cresol (mixed)
1320189	2,4–D ester
1327533	Arsenic trioxide
1330207	Xylene
1332076	Zinc borate
1333831	Sodium bifluoride
1336216	Ammonium hydroxide
1336363	Polychlorinated biphenyls
1338245	Naphthenic acid
1341497	Ammonium bifluoride
1762954	Ammonium thiocyanate
1863634	Ammonium benzoate
1918009	Dicamba
1928387	2,4–D esters
1928478	2,4,5–T ester
1928616	2,4–D ester
1929733	2,4–D ester
2545597	2,4,5–T ester
2764729	Diquat
2921882	Chlorpyrifos
2944674	Ferric ammonium oxalate

Table 116.4B—List of Hazardous Substances by CAS Number

CAS#	common name
2971382	2,4–D ester
3012655	Ammonium citrate, dibasic
3164292	Ammonium tartrate
3251238	Cupric nitrate
3486359	Zinc carbonate
5893663	Cupric oxalate
5972736	Ammonium oxalate
6009707	Ammonium oxalate
6369966	2,4,5–T ester
7428480	Lead stearate
7440235	Sodium
7446084	Selenium oxide
7446142	Lead sulfate
7447394	Cupric chloride
7558794	Sodium phosphate, dibasic
7601549	Sodium phosphate, tribasic
7631892	Sodium arsenate
7631905	Sodium bisulfite
7632000	Sodium nitrite
7645252	Lead arsenate
7646857	Zinc chloride
7647010	Hydrochloric acid
7647189	Antimony pentachloride
7664382	Phosphoric acid
7664393	Hydrofluoric acid
7664417	Ammonia
7664939	Sulfuric acid
7681494	Sodium fluoride
7681529	Sodium hypochlorite
7697372	Nitric acid
7699458	Zinc bromide
7705080	Ferric chloride

Table 116.4B—List of Hazardous Substances by CAS Number

CAS#	common name
7718549	Nickel chloride
7719122	Phosphorus trichloride
7720787	Ferrous sulfate
7722647	Potassium permanganate
7723140	Phosphorus
7733020	Zinc sulfate
7758294	Sodium phosphate, tribasic
7758943	Ferrous chloride
7758954	Lead chloride
7758987	Cupric sulfate
7773060	Ammonium sulfamate
7775113	Sodium chromate
7778441	Calcium arsenate
7778509	Potassium bichromate
7778543	Calcium hypochlorite
7779864	Zinc hydrosulfite
7779886	Zinc nitrate
7782505	Chlorine
7782630	Ferrous sulfate
7782823	Sodium selenite
7782867	Mercurous nitrate
7783359	Mercuric sulfate
7783462	Lead fluoride
7783495	Zinc fluoride
7783508	Ferric fluoride
7783564	Antimony trifluoride
7784341	Arsenic trichloride
7784409	Lead arsenate
7784410	Potassium arsenate
7784465	Sodium arsenite
7785844	Sodium phosphate, tribasic
7786347	Mevinphos

Table 116.4B—List of Hazardous Substances by CAS Number

CAS#	common name
7786814	Nickel sulfate
7787475	Beryllium chloride
7787497	Beryllium fluoride
7787555	Beryllium nitrate
7788989	Ammonium chromate
7789006	Potassium chromate
7789062	Strontium chromate
7789095	Ammonium bichromate
7789426	Cadmium bromide
7789437	Cobaltous bromide
7789619	Antimony tribromide
7790945	Chlorosulfonic acid
8001352	Toxaphene
10022705	Sodium hypochlorite
10025873	Phosphorus oxychloride
10025919	Antimony trichloride
10026116	Zirconium tetrachloride
10028225	Ferric sulfate
10028247	Sodium phosphate, dibasic
10039324	Sodium phosphate, dibasic
10043013	Aluminum sulfate
10045893	Ferrous ammonium sulfate
10045940	Mercuric nitrate
10049055	Chromous chloride
10099748	Lead nitrate
10101538	Chromic sulfate
10101630	Lead iodide
10101890	Sodium phosphate, tribasic
10102064	Uranyl nitrate
10102188	Sodium selenite
10102440	Nitrogen dioxide
10102484	Lead arsenate

Table 116.4B—List of Hazardous Substances by CAS Number

CAS#	common name
10108642	Cadmium chloride
10124502	Potassium arsenite
10124568	Sodium phosphate, tribasic
10140655	Sodium phosphate, dibasic
10192300	Ammonium bisulfite
10196040	Ammonium sulfite
10361894	Sodium phosphate, tribasic
10380297	Cupric sulfate, ammoniated
10415755	Mercurous nitrate
10421484	Ferric nitrate
10588019	Sodium bichromate
11115745	Chromic acid
12002038	Cupric acetoarsenite
12054487	Nickel hydroxide
12125018	Ammonium fluoride
12125029	Ammonium chloride
12135761	Ammonium sulfide
12771083	Sulfur chloride
13597994	Beryllium nitrate
13746899	Zirconium nitrate
13765190	Calcium chromate
13814965	Lead fluoborate
13826830	Ammonium fluoborate
13952846	sec–Butylamine
14017415	Cobaltous sulfamate
14216752	Nickel nitrate
14258492	Ammonium oxalate
14307358	Lithium chromate
14307438	Ammonium tartrate
14639975	Zinc ammonium chloride
14639986	Zinc ammonium chloride
14644612	Zirconium sulfate

Table 116.4B—List of Hazardous Substances by CAS Number

CAS#	common name
15699180	Nickel ammonium sulfate
16721805	Sodium hydrosulfide
16871719	Zinc silicofluoride
16919190	Ammonium silicofluoride
16923958	Zirconium potassium fluoride
25154545	Dinitrobenzene
25154556	Nitrophenol
25155300	Sodium dodecylbenzenesulfonate
25167822	Trichlorophenol
25168154	2,4,5–T ester
25168267	2,4–D ester
26264062	Calcium dodecylbenzenesulfonate
27176870	Dodecylbenzenesulfonic acid
27323417	Triethanolamine dodecylbenzenesulfonate
27774136	Vanadyl sulfate
28300745	Antimony potassium tartrate
30525894	Paraformaldehyde
36478769	Uranyl nitrate
37211055	Nickel chloride
42504461	Dodecylbenzenesulfonate isopropanolamine
52628258	Zinc ammonium chloride
52740166	Calcium arsenite
53467111	2,4–D ester
55488874	Ferric ammonium oxalate
61792072	2,4,5–T ester

Appendix G - Determination of Reportable Quantities

Appendix G - Determination of Reportable Quantities

Each substance in Table 117.3 that is listed in Table 302.4, 40 CFR Part 302, is assigned the reportable quantity listed in Table 302.4 for that substance. Table 117.3–Reportable Quantities of Hazardous Substances Designated Pursuant to Section 311 of the Clean Water Act is included below. The first number under the column headed "RQ" is the reportable quantity in pounds. The number in parentheses is the metric equivalent in kilograms. For convenience, the table contains a column headed "Category" which lists the code letters "X", "A", "B", "C", and "D" associated with reportable quantities of 1, 10, 100, 1000, and 5000 pounds, respectively.

Reportable Quantities of Hazardous Substances		
Material	Category	RQ in pounds(kilograms)
Acetaldehyde	C	1,000 (454)
Acetic acid	D	5,000 (2,270)
Acetic anhydride	D	5,000 (2,270)
Acetone cyanohydrin	A	10 (4.54)
Acetyl bromide	D	5,000 (2,270)
Acetyl chloride	D	5,000 (2,270)
Acrolein	X	1 (0.454)
Acrylonitrile	B	100 (45.4)
Adipic acid	D	5,000 (2,270)
Aldrin	X	1 (0.454)
Allyl alcohol	B	100 (45.4)
Allyl chloride	C	1,000 (454)
Aluminum sulfate	D	5,000 (2,270)
Ammonia	B	100 (45.4)
Ammonium acetate	D	5,000 (2,270)
Ammonium benzoate	D	5,000 (2,270)
Ammonium bicarbonate	D	5,000 (2,270)
Ammonium bichromate	A	10 (4.54)
Ammonium bifluoride	B	100 (45.4)
Ammonium bisulfite	D	5,000 (2,270)
Ammonium carbamate	D	5,000 (2,270)

Reportable Quantities of Hazardous Substances		
Material	Category	RQ in pounds(kilograms)
Ammonium carbonate	D	5,000 (2,270)
Ammonium chloride	D	5,000 (2,270)
Ammonium chromate	A	10 (4.54)
Ammonium citrate dibasic	D	5,000 (2,270)
Ammonium fluoborate	D	5,000 (2,270)
Ammonium fluoride	B	100 (45.4)
Ammonium hydroxide	C	1,000 (454)
Ammonium oxalate	D	5,000 (2,270)
Ammonium silicofluoride	C	1,000 (454)
Ammonium sulfamate	D	5,000 (2,270)
Ammonium sulfide	B	100 (45.4)
Ammonium sulfite	D	5,000 (2,270)
Ammonium tartrate	D	5,000 (2,270)
Ammonium thiocyanate	D	5,000 (2,270)
Amyl acetate	D	5,000 (2,270)
Aniline	D	5,000 (2,270)
Antimony pentachloride	C	1,000 (454)
Antimony potassium tartrate	B	100 (45.4)
Antimony tribromide	C	1,000 (454)
Antimony trichloride	C	1,000 (454)
Antimony trifluoride	C	1,000 (454)
Antimony trioxide	C	1,000 (454)
Arsenic disulfide	X	1 (0.454)
Arsenic pentoxide	X	1 (0.454)
Arsenic trichloride	X	1 (0.454)
Arsenic trioxide	X	1 (0.454)
Arsenic trisulfide	X	1 (0.454)
Barium cyanide	A	10 (4.54)
Benzene	A	10 (4.54)
Benzoic acid	D	5,000 (2,270)
Benzonitrile	D	5,000 (2,270)
Benzoyl chloride	C	1,000 (454)
Benzyl chloride	B	100 (45.4)

Reportable Quantities of Hazardous Substances

Material	Category	RQ in pounds(kilograms)
Beryllium chloride	X	1 (0.454)
Beryllium fluoride	X	1 (0.454)
Beryllium nitrate	X	1 (0.454)
Butyl acetate	D	5,000 (2,270)
Butylamine	C	1,000 (454)
n–Butyl phthalate	A	10 (4.54)
Butyric acid	D	5,000 (2,270)
Cadmium acetate	A	10 (4.54)
Cadmium bromide	A	10 (4.54)
Cadmium chloride	A	10 (4.54)
Calcium arsenate	X	1 (0.454)
Calcium arsenite	X	1 (0.454)
Calcium carbide	A	10 (4.54)
Calcium chromate	A	10 (4.54)
Calcium cyanide	A	10 (4.54)
Calcium dodecylbenzenesulfonate	C	1,000 (454)
Calcium hypochlorite	A	10 (4.54)
Captan	A	10 (4.54)
Carbaryl	B	100 (45.4)
Carbofuran	A	10 (4.54)
Carbon disulfide	B	100 (45.4)
Carbon tetrachloride	A	10 (4.54)
Chlordane	X	1 (0.454)
Chlorine	A	10 (4.54)
Chlorobenzene	B	100 (45.4)
Chloroform	A	10 (4.54)
Chlorosulfonic acid	C	1,000 (454)
Chlorpyrifos	X	1 (0.454)
Chromic acetate	C	1,000 (454)
Chromic acid	A	10 (4.54)
Chromic sulfate	C	1,000 (454)
Chromous chloride	C	1,000 (454)
Cobaltous bromide	C	1,000 (454)

Reportable Quantities of Hazardous Substances		
Material	Category	RQ in pounds(kilograms)
Cobaltous formate	C	1,000 (454)
Cobaltous sulfamate	C	1,000 (454)
Coumaphos	A	10 (4.54)
Cresol	B	100 (45.4)
Crotonaldehyde	B	100 (45.4)
Cupric acetate	B	100 (45.4)
Cupric acetoarsenite	X	1 (0.454)
Cupric chloride	A	10 (4.54)
Cupric nitrate	B	100 (45.4)
Cupric oxalate	B	100 (45.4)
Cupric sulfate	A	10 (4.54)
Cupric sulfate, ammoniated	B	100 (45.4)
Cupric tartrate	B	100 (45.4)
Cyanogen chloride	A	10 (4.54)
Cyclohexane	C	1,000 (454)
2,4–D Acid	B	100 (45.4)
2,4–D Esters	B	100 (45.4)
DDT	X	1 (0.454)
Diazinon	X	1 (0.454)
Dicamba	C	1,000 (454)
Dichlobenil	B	100 (45.4)
Dichlone	X	1 (0.454)
Dichlorobenzene	B	100 (45.4)
Dichloropropane	C	1,000 (454)
Dichloropropene	B	100 (45.4)
Dichloropropene–Dichloropropane (mix)	B	100 (45.4)
2,2–Dichloropropionic acid	D	5,000 (2,270)
Dichlorvos	A	10 (4.54)
Dicofol	A	10 (4.54)
Dieldrin	X	1 (0.454)
Diethylamine	B	100 (45.4)
Dimethylamine	C	1,000 (454)

Reportable Quantities of Hazardous Substances

Material	Category	RQ in pounds(kilograms)
Dinitrobenzene (mixed)	B	100 (45.4)
Dinitrophenol	A	10 (45.4)
Dinitrotoluene	A	10 (4.54)
Diquat	C	1,000 (454)
Disulfoton	X	1 (0.454)
Diuron	B	100 (45.4)
Dodecylbenzenesulfonic acid	C	1,000 (454)
Endosulfan	X	1 (0.454)
Endrin	X	1 (0.454)
Epichlorohydrin	B	100 (45.4)
Ethion	A	10 (4.54)
Ethylbenzene	C	1,000 (454)
Ethylenediamine	D	5,000 (2,270)
Ethylenediamine–tetraacetic acid (EDTA)	D	5,000 (2,270)
Ethylene dibromide	X	1 (0.454)
Ethylene dichloride	B	100 (45.4)
Ferric ammonium citrate	C	1,000 (454)
Ferric ammonium oxalate	C	1,000 (454)
Ferric chloride	C	1,000 (454)
Ferric fluoride	B	100 (45.4)
Ferric nitrate	C	1,000 (454)
Ferric sulfate	C	1,000 (454)
Ferrous ammonium sulfate	C	1,000 (454)
Ferrous chloride	B	100 (45.4)
Ferrous sulfate	C	1,000 (454)
Formaldehyde	B	100 (45.4)
Formic acid	D	5,000 (2,270)
Fumaric acid	D	5,000 (2,270)
Furfural	D	5,000 (2,270)
Guthion	X	1 (0.454)
Heptachlor	X	1 (0.454)
Hexachlorocyclopentadiene	A	10 (4.54)

Reportable Quantities of Hazardous Substances		
Material	Category	RQ in pounds(kilograms)
Hydrochloric acid	D	5,000 (2,270)
Hydrofluoric acid	B	100 (45.4)
Hydrogen cyanide	A	10 (4.54)
Hydrogen sulfide	B	100 (45.4)
Isoprene	B	100 (45.4)
Isopropanolamine dodecylbenzenesulfonate	C	1,000 (454)
Kepone	X	1 (0.454)
Lead acetate	A	10 (4.54)
Lead arsenate	X	1 (0.454)
Lead chloride	A	10 (4.54)
Lead fluoborate	A	10 (4.54)
Lead fluoride	A	10 (4.54)
Lead iodide	A	10 (4.54)
Lead nitrate	A	10 (4.54)
Lead stearate	A	10 (4.54)
Lead sulfate	A	10 (4.54)
Lead sulfide	A	10 (4.54)
Lead thiocyanate	A	10 (4.54)
Lindane	X	1 (0.454)
Lithium chromate	A	10 (4.54)
Malathion	B	100 (45.4)
Maleic acid	D	5,000 (2,270)
Maleic anhydride	D	5,000 (2,270)
Mercaptodimethur	A	10 (4.54)
Mercuric cyanide	X	1 (0.454)
Mercuric nitrate	A	10 (4.54)
Mercuric sulfate	A	10 (4.54)
Mercuric thiocyanate	A	10 (4.54)
Mercurous nitrate	A	10 (4.54)
Methoxychlor	X	1 (0.454)
Methyl mercaptan	B	100 (45.4)
Methyl methacrylate	C	1,000 (454)

Reportable Quantities of Hazardous Substances		
Material	Category	RQ in pounds(kilograms)
Methyl parathion	B	100 (45.4)
Mevinphos	A	10 (4.54)
Mexacarbate	C	1,000 (454)
Monoethylamine	B	100 (45.4)
Monomethylamine	B	100 (45.4)
Naled	A	10 (4.54)
Naphthalene	B	100 (45.4)
Naphthenic acid	B	100 (45.4)
Nickel ammonium sulfate	B	100 (45.4)
Nickel chloride	B	100 (45.4)
Nickel hydroxide	A	10 (4.54)
Nickel nitrate	B	100 (45.4)
Nickel sulfate	B	100 (45.4)
Nitric acid	C	1,000 (454)
Nitrobenzene	C	1,000 (454)
Nitrogen dioxide	A	10 (4.54)
Nitrophenol (mixed)	B	100 (45.4)
Nitrotoluene	C	1,000 (454)
Paraformaldehyde	C	1,000 (454)
Parathion	A	10 (4.54)
Pentachlorophenol	A	10 (4.54)
Phenol	C	1,000 (454)
Phosgene	A	10 (4.54)
Phosphoric acid	D	5,000 (2,270)
Phosphorus	X	1 (0.454)
Phosphorus oxychloride	C	1,000 (454)
Phosphorus pentasulfide	B	100 (45.4)
Phosphorus trichloride	C	1,000 (454)
Polychlorinated biphenyls	X	1 (0.454)
Potassium arsenate	X	1 (0.454)
Potassium arsenite	X	1 (0.454)
Potassium bichromate	A	10 (4.54)
Potassium chromate	A	10 (4.54)

Reportable Quantities of Hazardous Substances		
Material	Category	RQ in pounds(kilograms)
Potassium cyanide	A	10 (4.54)
Potassium hydroxide	C	1,000 (454)
Potassium permanganate	B	100 (45.4)
Propargite	A	10 (4.54)
Propionic acid	D	5,000 (2,270)
Propionic anhydride	D	5,000 (2,270)
Propylene oxide	B	100 (45.4)
Pyrethrins	X	1 (0.454)
Quinoline	D	5,000 (2,270)
Resorcinol	D	5,000 (2,270)
Selenium oxide	A	10 (4.54)
Silver nitrate	X	1 (0.454)
Sodium	A	10 (4.54)
Sodium arsenate	X	1 (0.454)
Sodium arsenite	X	1 (0.454)
Sodium bichromate	A	10 (4.54)
Sodium bifluoride	B	100 (45.4)
Sodium bisulfite	D	5,000 (2,270)
Sodium chromate	A	10 (4.54)
Sodium cyanide	A	10 (4.54)
Sodium dodecylbenzenesulfonate	C	1,000 (454)
Sodium fluoride	C	1,000 (454)
Sodium hydrosulfide	D	5,000 (2,270)
Sodium hydroxide	C	1,000 (454)
Sodium hypochlorite	B	100 (45.4)
Sodium methylate	C	1,000 (454)
Sodium nitrite	B	100 (45.4)
Sodium phosphate, dibasic	D	5,000 (2,270)
Sodium phosphate, tribasic	D	5,000 (2,270)
Sodium selenite	B	100 (45.4)
Strontium chromate	A	10 (4.54)
Strychnine	A	10 (4.54)
Styrene	C	1,000 (454)

Reportable Quantities of Hazardous Substances		
Material	Category	RQ in pounds(kilograms)
Sulfuric acid	C	1,000 (454)
Sulfur monochloride	C	1,000 (454)
2,4,5–T acid	C	1,000 (454)
2,4,5–T amines	D	5,000 (2,270)
2,4,5–T esters	C	1,000 (454)
2,4,5–T salts	C	1,000 (454)
TDE	X	1 (0.454)
2,4,5–TP acid	B	100 (45.4)
2,4,5–TP acid esters	B	100 (45.4)
Tetraethyl lead	A	10 (4.54)
Tetraethyl pyrophosphate	A	10 (4.54)
Thallium sulfate	B	100 (45.4)
Toluene	C	1,000 (454)
Toxaphene	X	1 (0.454)
Trichlorfon	B	100 (45.4)
Trichloroethylene	B	100 (45.4)
Trichlorophenol	A	10 (4.54)
Triethanolamine dodecylbenzenesulfonate	C	1,000 (454)
Triethylamine	D	5,000 (2,270)
Trimethylamine	B	100 (45.4)
Uranyl acetate	B	100 (45.4)
Uranyl nitrate	B	100 (45.4)
Vanadium pentoxide	C	1,000 (454)
Vanadyl sulfate	C	1,000 (454)
Vinyl acetate	D	5,000 (2,270)
Vinylidene chloride	B	100 (45.4)
Xylene (mixed)	B	100 (45.4)
Xylenol	C	1,000 (454)
Zinc acetate	C	1,000 (454)
Zinc ammonium chloride	C	1,000 (454)
Zinc borate	C	1,000 (454)
Zinc bromide	C	1,000 (454)

Reportable Quantities of Hazardous Substances		
Material	Category	RQ in pounds(kilograms)
Zinc carbonate	C	1,000 (454)
Zinc chloride	C	1,000 (454)
Zinc cyanide	A	10 (4.54)
Zinc fluoride	C	1,000 (454)
Zinc formate	C	1,000 (454)
Zinc hydrosulfite	C	1,000 (454)
Zinc nitrate	C	1,000 (454)
Zinc phenolsulfonate	D	5,000 (2,270)
Zinc phosphide	B	100 (45.4)
Zinc silicofluoride	D	5,000 (2,270)
Zinc sulfate	C	1,000 (454)
Zirconium nitrate	D	5,000 (2,270)
Zirconium potassium fluoride	C	1,000 (454)
Zirconium sulfate	D	5,000 (2,270)
Zirconium tetrachloride	D	5,000 (2,270)

Index to 40 CFRs Water Regulations by Subject and Topic

Index to 40 CFR Water Regulations by Subject and Topic

subject/topic	section	title	part
Acrolein and Acrylonitrile – Method 603	Appendix A	Guidelines Establishing Test Procedures for the Analysis of Pollutants	136
Action after Hearing	142.45	National Primary Drinking Water Regulations Implementation	142
Adjustment of Effluent Standard for Presence of Toxic Pollutant in the Intake Water	129.6	Toxic Pollutant Effluent Standards	129
Administrator's Rescission	142.24	National Primary Drinking Water Regulations Implementation	142
Administrator's Review of State Decisions That Implement Criteria under Which Filtration Is Required	Subpart I	National Primary Drinking Water Regulations Implementation	142
Admission of Evidence	104.9	Public Hearings on Effluent Standards for Toxic Pollutants	104
Adoption of New Water Quality Standards	121.25	State Certification of Activities Requiring a Federal License or Permit	121
Alabama	Subpart B	State Underground Injection Control Programs	147
Alaska	Subpart C	State Underground Injection Control Programs	147
Aldrin/Dieldrin	129.101	Toxic Pollutant Effluent Standards	129
Alternate Analytical Techniques	141.27	National Primary Drinking Water Regulations	141
Alternative Treatment Techniques	142.46	National Primary Drinking Water Regulations Implementation	142
American Samoa	Subpart DDD	State Underground Injection Control Programs	147
Analysis of the Potential for an Oil Spill	Appendix F (1.4.3)	Oil Pollution Prevention	112
Analytical and Monitoring Requirements	141.75	National Primary Drinking Water Regulations	141
Analytical Methods	141.90	National Primary Drinking Water Regulations	141
Analytical Methods for Radioactivity	141.25	National Primary Drinking Water Regulations	141
Analytical Procedures	140.6	Marine Sanitation Device Standard	140
"Application for a Permit (State Programs, See º12325)"	122.21	EPA Administered Permit Programs: the National Pollutant Discharge Elimination System	122
Application for Alternate Test Procedures	136.5	Guidelines Establishing Test Procedures for the Analysis of Pollutants	136
Applications	121.22	State Certification of Activities Requiring a Federal License or Permit	121

Index to 40 CFR Water Regulations by Subject and Topic

subject/topic	section	title	part
Approval of Alternate Test Procedures	136.6	Guidelines Establishing Test Procedures for the Analysis of Pollutants	136
Approval Process	123.61	State Program Requirements	123
Approval Process	145.31	State UIC Program Requirements	145
"Aquaculture Projects (State NPDES Programs, See °12325)"	122.25	EPA Administered Permit Programs: the National Pollutant Discharge Elimination System	122
Area of Review	146.6–146.63	Underground Injection Control Program: Criteria and Standards	146
Area Permits	144.33	Underground Injection Control Program	144
Arizona	Subpart D	State Underground Injection Control Programs	147
Arkansas	Subpart E	State Underground Injection Control Programs	147
Attorney General's Statement	123.23	State Program Requirements	123
Attorney General's Statement	145.24	State UIC Program Requirements	145
Authorization by Permit	Subpart D	Underground Injection Control Program	144
"Authorization by Permit, Application for a Permit"	144.31	Underground Injection Control Program	144
Authorization of Underground Injection by Rule	Subpart C	Underground Injection Control Program	144
Automated Discharge Detection	Appendix F (1.6.2)	Oil Pollution Prevention	112
Base/Neutrals and Acids – Method 625	Appendix A	Guidelines Establishing Test Procedures for the Analysis of Pollutants	136
Benzidine	129.105	Toxic Pollutant Effluent Standards	129
Benzidines – Method 605	Appendix A	Guidelines Establishing Test Procedures for the Analysis of Pollutants	136
Bottled Water, Point–of–use, and Point–of–entry Devices"	142.57	National Primary Drinking Water Regulations Implementation	142
Bottled Water, Use of	141.102	National Primary Drinking Water Regulations	141
Briefs and Findings of Fact	104.11	Public Hearings on Effluent Standards for Toxic Pollutants	104
Calculating Npdes Permit Conditions (State NPDES Programs	122.45	EPA Administered Permit Programs: the National Pollutant Discharge Elimination System	122
Calculating Planning Volumes for a Worst Case Discharge	Appendix E (7.0)	Oil Pollution Prevention	112

Index to 40 CFR Water Regulations by Subject and Topic

subject/topic	section	title	part
Calculation of the Planning Distance	Attachment C–III	Oil Pollution Prevention	112
California	Subpart F	State Underground Injection Control Programs	147
California List Wastes, Waste Specific Prohibitions	148.12	Hazardous Waste Injection Restrictions	148
case by case Extensions to an Effective Date	148.4	Hazardous Waste Injection Restrictions	148
Certification	121.24	State Certification of Activities Requiring a Federal License or Permit	121
Certification by the Administrator	Subpart C	State Certification of Activities Requiring a Federal License or Permit	121
Certification for Facilities That Do Not Pose Substantial Harm	Appendix C (3.0)	Oil Pollution Prevention	112
Certification of Record	104.12	Public Hearings on Effluent Standards for Toxic Pollutants	104
Certification of the Applicability of the Substantial Harm Criteria	Attachment C–II	Oil Pollution Prevention	112
Certified Laboratories	141.28	National Primary Drinking Water Regulations	141
Chlorinated Hydrocarbons – Method 612	Appendix A	Guidelines Establishing Test Procedures for the Analysis of Pollutants	136
Civil Penalty for Violation of Administrative Compliance Order, Administrative Assessment of	142.208	National Primary Drinking Water Regulations Implementation	142
Class I Hazardous Waste Injection Wells, Criteria and Standards Applicable to	Subpart G	Underground Injection Control Program: Criteria and Standards	146
Class I Nonhazardous Wells, Criteria and Standards Applicable to	146.11	Underground Injection Control Program: Criteria and Standards	146
Class I Wells, Criteria and Standards Applicable to	Subpart B	Underground Injection Control Program: Criteria and Standards	146
Class II Wells, Criteria and Standards Applicable to	Subpart C	Underground Injection Control Program: Criteria and Standards	146
Class III Wells, Criteria and Standards Applicable to	Subpart D	Underground Injection Control Program: Criteria and Standards	146
Class IV Wells	144.23	Underground Injection Control Program	144
Class V Injection Wells, Criteria and Standards Applicable to	Subpart F	Underground Injection Control Program: Criteria and Standards	146
Class V Wells	144.24	Underground Injection Control Program	144

Index to 40 CFR Water Regulations by Subject and Topic

subject/topic	section	title	part
Classification of Injection Wells	146.5	Underground Injection Control Program: Criteria and Standards	146
Classification of Wells	144.6	Underground Injection Control Program	144
Closure	146.72	Underground Injection Control Program: Criteria and Standards	146
Coliform Sampling	141.21	National Primary Drinking Water Regulations	141
Colorado	Subpart G & H	State Underground Injection Control Programs	147
Commonwealth of the Northern Mariana Islands	Subpart EEE	State Underground Injection Control Programs	147
Compliance	129.5	Toxic Pollutant Effluent Standards	129
Compliance Date	129.8	Toxic Pollutant Effluent Standards	129
Compliance Evaluation Programs	123.26	State Program Requirements	123
Compliance with Secondary Maximum Contaminant Level and Public Notification for Fluoride	143.6	National Secondary Drinking Water Regulations	143
Concentrated Animal Feeding Operation	Appendix B	EPA Administered Permit Programs: the National Pollutant Discharge Elimination System	122
Concentrated Animal Feeding Operations	122.23, 122.24	EPA Administered Permit Programs: the National Pollutant Discharge Elimination System	122
Concentrated Aquatic Animal Production Facility	Appendix C	EPA Administered Permit Programs: the National Pollutant Discharge Elimination System	122
Conditions All Permits	144.51	Underground Injection Control Program	144
Conditions All Permits	122.41	EPA Administered Permit Programs: the National Pollutant Discharge Elimination System	122
Conditions Specified Categories of NPDES Permits	122.42	EPA Administered Permit Programs: the National Pollutant Discharge Elimination System	122
Conduct of Public Hearings	142.206	National Primary Drinking Water Regulations Implementation	142
Confidentiality of Information	122.7	EPA Administered Permit Programs: the National Pollutant Discharge Elimination System	122
Confidentiality of Information	144.5	Underground Injection Control Program	144

Index to 40 CFR Water Regulations by Subject and Topic

subject/topic	section	title	part
Considerations under Federal Law	122.49	EPA Administered Permit Programs: the National Pollutant Discharge Elimination System	122
Considerations under Federal Law	144.4	Underground Injection Control Program	144
Construction Requirements	146.12–146.65	Underground Injection Control Program: Criteria and Standards	146
Consultations	Subpart D	State Certification of Activities Requiring a Federal License or Permit	121
Containment and Drainage Planning	Appendix F (1.7.3)	Oil Pollution Prevention	112
Contents of Application	121.3	State Certification of Activities Requiring a Federal License or Permit	121
Contents of Certification	121.2	State Certification of Activities Requiring a Federal License or Permit	121
Contents of Notice	135.13, 135.4	Prior Notice of Citizen Suits	135
Continuation of Expiring Permits	122.6	EPA Administered Permit Programs: the National Pollutant Discharge Elimination System	122
Continuation of Expiring Permits	144.37	Underground Injection Control Program	144
Control of Disposal of Pollutants into Wells	123.28	State Program Requirements	123
Control of Lead and Copper	Subpart I	National Primary Drinking Water Regulations	141
Coordination with Other Programs	123.3	State Program Requirements	123
Copies of Documents	121.11	State Certification of Activities Requiring a Federal License or Permit	121
Corrective Action	144.55	Underground Injection Control Program	144
Corrective Action	146.7	Underground Injection Control Program: Criteria and Standards	146
Corrective Action for Wells in the Area of Review	146.64	Underground Injection Control Program: Criteria and Standards	146
Corrosion Control Treatment Steps to Small, Medium–size and Large Water Systems, Applicability of"	141.82	National Primary Drinking Water Regulations	141
Corrosivity Characteristics, Special Monitoring for	141.43	National Primary Drinking Water Regulations	141
Cost Estimate for Plugging and Abandonment	144.62	Underground Injection Control Program	144

Index to 40 CFR Water Regulations by Subject and Topic

subject/topic	section	title	part
Counties with Unincorporated Urbanized Areas between 100,000 and 250,000	Appendix I	EPA Administered Permit Programs: the National Pollutant Discharge Elimination System	122
Counties with Unincorporated Urbanized Areas with a Population of 250,000 or More	Appendix H	EPA Administered Permit Programs: the National Pollutant Discharge Elimination System	122
Coverage	141.4	National Primary Drinking Water Regulations	141
Criteria for Avoiding Filtration	141.72	National Primary Drinking Water Regulations	141
Criteria for Establishing Permitting Priorities	146.9	Underground Injection Control Program: Criteria and Standards	146
Critical Aquifer Protection Areas	149.4	Sole Source Aquifers	149
Critical Aquifer Protection Areas, Criteria for Identifying	Subpart A	Sole Source Aquifers	149
DDT, DDD and DDE	129.101	Toxic Pollutant Effluent Standards	129
Definition and Procedure for the Determination of the Method Detection Limit	Appendix B	Guidelines Establishing Test Procedures for the Analysis of Pollutants	136
Definition and Procedure for the Determination of the Method Detection Limit–revision 111	Appendix B	Guidelines Establishing Test Procedures for the Analysis of Pollutants	136
Delaware	Subpart I	State Underground Injection Control Programs	147
Demonstration Projects	117.14	Determination of Reportable Quantities for Hazardous Substances	117
Description of Corrosion Control Treatment Requirements	141.83	National Primary Drinking Water Regulations	141
Description of Methods	Appendix D	Oil Pollution Prevention	112
Designation of Hazardous Substances	116.4	Designation of Hazardous Substances	116
Designation of Presiding Officer	104.6	Public Hearings on Effluent Standards for Toxic Pollutants	104
Determination and Evaluation of Required Response Resources for Facility Response Plans	Appendix E	Oil Pollution Prevention	112
Determination of Effect on Other States	Subpart B	State Certification of Activities Requiring a Federal License or Permit	121
Determination of Primary Enforcement Responsibility	142.11	National Primary Drinking Water Regulations Implementation	142

Index to 40 CFR Water Regulations by Subject and Topic

subject/topic	section	title	part
Determining Effective Daily Recovery Capacity for Oil Recovery Devices	Appendix E (6.0)	Oil Pollution Prevention	112
Determining the Availability of Alternative Response Methods	Appendix E (8.0)	Oil Pollution Prevention	112
"Development and Implementation Criteria for State, Local and Regional Oil Removal Contingency Plans"	109.5	"Criteria for State, Local and Regional Oil Removal Contingency Plans"	109
Diagrams	Appendix F (1.9)	Oil Pollution Prevention	112
Dilution Prohibited as a Substitute for Treatment	148.3	Hazardous Waste Injection Restrictions	148
Dioxin–Containing Wastes, Waste Specific Prohibitions	148.11	Hazardous Waste Injection Restrictions	148
Discharge Detection by Personnel	Appendix F (1.6.1)	Oil Pollution Prevention	112
Discharge Detection Systems	Appendix F (1.6)	Oil Pollution Prevention	112
Discharge Notice	110.6	Discharge of Oil	110
Discharge of Oil in Such Quantities as May Be Harmful Pursuant to Section 311(b)(4) of the Act	110.3	Discharge of Oil	110
Discharge Prevention Meeting Logs	Appendix F (1.8.3.2)	Oil Pollution Prevention	112
Discharge Scenarios	Appendix F (1.5)	Oil Pollution Prevention	112
"Discharges from Facilities with NPDES Permits, Applicability to "	117.12	Determination of Reportable Quantities for Hazardous Substances	117
Discharges from Publicly Owned Treatment Works and Their Users, Applicability to	117.13	Determination of Reportable Quantities for Hazardous Substances	117
Discharges of Oil Not Determined As May Be Harmful Pursuant to Section 311(b)(3) of the Act	110.5	Discharge of Oil	110
Disinfection	141.73	National Primary Drinking Water Regulations	141
Disinfection Byproduct and Related Monitoring	141.143	National Primary Drinking Water Regulations	141

353

Index to 40 CFR Water Regulations by Subject and Topic			
subject/topic	section	title	part
Disinfection Byproduct Precursor Removal Studies	141.145	National Primary Drinking Water Regulations	141
Dispersants	110.4	Discharge of Oil	110
"Disposal of Pollutants into Wells, into Publicly Owned Treatment Works or by Land Application (State NPDES Programs, See °12325)"	122.5	EPA Administered Permit Programs: the National Pollutant Discharge Elimination System	122
Disposal Plans	Appendix F (1.7.2)	Oil Pollution Prevention	112
Disposition of a Variance Request	142.43	National Primary Drinking Water Regulations Implementation	142
Disposition of an Exemption Request	142.53	National Primary Drinking Water Regulations Implementation	142
District of Columbia	Subpart J	State Underground Injection Control Programs	147
Docket and Record	104.5	Public Hearings on Effluent Standards for Toxic Pollutants	104
Duration of Permits	144.36	Underground Injection Control Program	144
Duration of Permits	122.46	EPA Administered Permit Programs: the National Pollutant Discharge Elimination System	122
Effect of a Permit	122.5	EPA Administered Permit Programs: the National Pollutant Discharge Elimination System	122
Effect on Other Laws	113.6	Liability Limits for Small Onshore Storage Facilities	113
Effective Dates	141.6	National Primary Drinking Water Regulations	141
Effluent Standards and Prohibitions for Toxic Pollutants	Subpart A	Toxic Pollutant Effluent Standards	129
Elements of a Program Submission	123.21	State Program Requirements	123
Elements of a Program Submission	145.22	State UIC Program Requirements	145
Emergency Permits	144.34	Underground Injection Control Program	144
Emergency Response Action Plan	Appendix F	Oil Pollution Prevention	112
Emulsification Factors for Petroleum Oil Groups	Table 3 to Appendix E	Oil Pollution Prevention	112
Endrin	129.103	Toxic Pollutant Effluent Standards	129
Enforcement Authority Requirements	123.27	State Program Requirements	123

Index to 40 CFR Water Regulations by Subject and Topic

subject/topic	section	title	part
Entry and Inspection of Public Water Systems	142.34	National Primary Drinking Water Regulations Implementation	142
EPA Review of and Objections to State Permits	123.44	State Program Requirements	123
EPA Review of State Implementation of National Primary Drinking Water Regulations for Lead and Copper	142.19	National Primary Drinking Water Regulations Implementation	142
EPA Review of State Monitoring Determinations	142.18	National Primary Drinking Water Regulations Implementation	142
Equipment Necessary to Sustain Response Operations	Appendix E (9.0)	Oil Pollution Prevention	112
Equipment Operability and Readiness	Appendix E (2.0)	Oil Pollution Prevention	112
"Establishing Limitations, Standards and Other Permit Conditions (State NPDES Programs, See °12325)"	122.44	EPA Administered Permit Programs: the National Pollutant Discharge Elimination System	122
Establishing Permit Conditions	144.52	Underground Injection Control Program	144
Establishing Permit Conditions	122.43	EPA Administered Permit Programs: the National Pollutant Discharge Elimination System	122
Evacuation Plans	Appendix F	Oil Pollution Prevention	112
Exempted Aquifers in New Mexico	Appendix A to Subpart HHH	State Underground Injection Control Programs	147
Exempted Aquifers, Criteria for	146.4	Underground Injection Control Program: Criteria and Standards	146
Exemption Request	142.51	National Primary Drinking Water Regulations Implementation	142
Exemption Request, Consideration of an	142.52	National Primary Drinking Water Regulations Implementation	142
Exemption Schedules, Public Hearings	142.54	National Primary Drinking Water Regulations Implementation	142
Exemptions	142.51	National Primary Drinking Water Regulations Implementation	142
Exemptions Issued by the Administrator	Subpart F	National Primary Drinking Water Regulations Implementation	142
Existing Class I, II and III Wells	144.21	Underground Injection Control Program	144

Index to 40 CFR Water Regulations by Subject and Topic

subject/topic	section	title	part
Existing Class II Enhanced Recovery and Hydrocarbon Storage Wells	144.22	Underground Injection Control Program	144
Extension of Date for Compliance	142.56	National Primary Drinking Water Regulations Implementation	142
Facilities That Have Experienced Reportable Oil Spills > 10,000 Gallons	Appendix C (2.5)	Oil Pollution Prevention	112
Facility Information	Appendix F (1.2)	Oil Pollution Prevention	112
Facility Reportable Oil Spill History	Appendix F (1.4.4)	Oil Pollution Prevention	112
Facility Response Plans	112.2	Oil Pollution Prevention	112
Facility Response Training and Drills/exercises	112.21	Oil Pollution Prevention	112
Facility Self–inspection	Appendix F (1.8.1)	Oil Pollution Prevention	112
Facility–specific Response Plan	Appendix F	Oil Pollution Prevention	112
Failure by State to Assure Enforcement	142.31	National Primary Drinking Water Regulations Implementation	142
Federal Enforcement	Subpart D	National Primary Drinking Water Regulations Implementation	142
Filing and Time	104.16	Public Hearings on Effluent Standards for Toxic Pollutants	104
Filtration	141.74	National Primary Drinking Water Regulations	141
Filtration and Disinfection	Subpart H	National Primary Drinking Water Regulations	141
Filtration and Disinfection, Variances and Exemptions	142.64	National Primary Drinking Water Regulations Implementation	142
Final Schedule	142.55	National Primary Drinking Water Regulations Implementation	142
Financial Assurance for Plugging and Abandonment	144.63	Underground Injection Control Program	144
Financial Responsibility for Post–closure Care	146.74	Underground Injection Control Program: Criteria and Standards	146
Financial Responsibility: Class I Hazardous Waste Injection Wells	Subpart F	Underground Injection Control Program	144
First Third Wastes, Waste Specific Prohibitions	148.14	Hazardous Waste Injection Restrictions	148

Index to 40 CFR Water Regulations by Subject and Topic

subject/topic	section	title	part
Florida	Subpart K	State Underground Injection Control Programs	147
Fluoride, Variances from the Maximum Contaminant Level	142.61	National Primary Drinking Water Regulations Implementation	142
Forwarding to Affected State	121.14	State Certification of Activities Requiring a Federal License or Permit	121
General Permits (State NPDES Programs, See 123.25)	122.28	EPA Administered Permit Programs: the National Pollutant Discharge Elimination System	122
General Requirements for Program Approvals	145.21	State UIC Program Requirements	145
General Requirements, Applicability, and Information Collection	141.142	National Primary Drinking Water Regulations	141
Georgia	Subpart L	State Underground Injection Control Programs	147
Guam	Subpart AAA	State Underground Injection Control Programs	147
Guidelines for Spill Prevention Control and Countermeasure Plans	112.7	Oil Pollution Prevention	112
Haloethers – Method 611	Appendix A	Guidelines Establishing Test Procedures for the Analysis of Pollutants	136
Hawaii	Subpart M	State Underground Injection Control Programs	147
Hazard Evaluation and Identification	Appendix F	Oil Pollution Prevention	112
Hearing Before Administrator	108.7	Employee Protection Hearings	108
Hearing Procedures	104.1	Public Hearings on Effluent Standards for Toxic Pollutants	104
Hearings, Objection of Affected State	121.15	State Certification of Activities Requiring a Federal License or Permit	121
Idaho	Subpart N	State Underground Injection Control Programs	147
Identification of Best Technology, Treatment Techniques	Subpart G	National Primary Drinking Water Regulations Implementation	142
Identification of Test Procedures	136.4	Guidelines Establishing Test Procedures for the Analysis of Pollutants	136
Identification of Underground Sources of Drinking Water and Aquifers	144.7	Underground Injection Control Program	144
Illinois	Subpart O	State Underground Injection Control Programs	147
Incapacity of Owners or Operators, Guarantors, or Financial Institutions	144.64	Underground Injection Control Program	144

Index to 40 CFR Water Regulations by Subject and Topic

subject/topic	section	title	part
Incorporated Places with Populations Greater than 250,000	Appendix F	EPA Administered Permit Programs: the National Pollutant Discharge Elimination System	122
Indian Tribe Request for a Determination of Eligibility	123.32	State Program Requirements	123
Indian Tribes	Subpart H	National Primary Drinking Water Regulations Implementation	142
Indian Tribes	Subpart E	State UIC Program Requirements	145
Indiana	Subpart P	State Underground Injection Control Programs	147
Individual Control Strategies	123.46	State Program Requirements	123
Inductively Coupled Plasma–atomic Emission Spectrometric Method for Trace Element Analysis of Water and Wastes – Method 2007	Appendix C	Guidelines Establishing Test Procedures for the Analysis of Pollutants	136
Information Collection Requirements (ICR) for Public Water Systems	Subpart M	National Primary Drinking Water Regulations	141
Information to Be Evaluated by the Director	146.71, 146.14, 146.24, 146.34	Underground Injection Control Program: Criteria and Standards	146
Information to Be Submitted in Support of Petitions	148.21	Hazardous Waste Injection Restrictions	148
Initial Determination of Primary Enforcement Responsibility	142.11	National Primary Drinking Water Regulations Implementation	142
Inorganic and Organic Contaminants, Special Monitoring	141.41	National Primary Drinking Water Regulations	141
Inorganic Chemical Sampling and Analytical Requirements	141.23	National Primary Drinking Water Regulations	141
Inspection of Facility or Activity Before Operation	121.26	State Certification of Activities Requiring a Federal License or Permit	121
Interlocutory and Post–hearing Review of Rulings of the Presiding Officer; Motions	104.13	Public Hearings on Effluent Standards for Toxic Pollutants	104
Inventory Requirements	144.26	Underground Injection Control Program	144
Investigation by Regional Administrator	108.4	Employee Protection Hearings	108
Iowa	Subpart Q	State Underground Injection Control Programs	147

Index to 40 CFR Water Regulations by Subject and Topic

subject/topic	section	title	part
Issuance, Amendment or Withdrawal of Administrative Compliance Order	142.207	National Primary Drinking Water Regulations Implementation	142
Judicial Review of Approval or Denial of Permits	123.3	State Program Requirements	123
Kansas	Subpart R	State Underground Injection Control Programs	147
Kentucky	Subpart S	State Underground Injection Control Programs	147
Lack of Adequate Secondary Containment at Facilities w/Oil Storage Capacity > 1 Million Gallons	Appendix C (2.2)	Oil Pollution Prevention	112
Lead and Copper in Source Water Monitoring Requirements	141.89	National Primary Drinking Water Regulations	141
Lead Service Line Replacement Requirements	141.85	National Primary Drinking Water Regulations	141
Liabilities for Removal	117.23	Determination of Reportable Quantities for Hazardous Substances	117
Logging, Sampling, and Testing Prior to New Well Operation	146.66	Underground Injection Control Program: Criteria and Standards	146
Louisiana	Subpart T	State Underground Injection Control Programs	147
Maine	Subpart U	State Underground Injection Control Programs	147
Maryland	Subpart V	State Underground Injection Control Programs	147
Massachusetts	Subpart W	State Underground Injection Control Programs	147
Maximum Contaminant Level Goals	Subpart F	National Primary Drinking Water Regulations	141
Maximum Contaminant Level Goals for Inorganic Contaminants	141.52	National Primary Drinking Water Regulations	141
Maximum Contaminant Level Goals for Microbiological Contaminants	141.53	National Primary Drinking Water Regulations	141
Maximum Contaminant Level Goals for Organic Contaminants	141.51	National Primary Drinking Water Regulations	141
Maximum Contaminant Levels	Subpart B	National Primary Drinking Water Regulations	141
Maximum Contaminant Levels (MCLs) for Microbiological Contaminants	141.64	National Primary Drinking Water Regulations	141
Maximum Contaminant Levels for Beta Particle and Photon Radioactivity from Radionuclides	141.16	National Primary Drinking Water Regulations	141
Maximum Contaminant Levels for Inorganic Chemicals	141.11	National Primary Drinking Water Regulations	141

Index to 40 CFR Water Regulations by Subject and Topic

subject/topic	section	title	part
Maximum Contaminant Levels for Inorganic Contaminants	141.63	National Primary Drinking Water Regulations	141
Maximum Contaminant Levels for Organic Chemicals	141.12	National Primary Drinking Water Regulations	141
Maximum Contaminant Levels for Organic Contaminants	141.62	National Primary Drinking Water Regulations	141
Maximum Contaminant Levels for Radium–226, Radium–228, and Gross Alpha Particle Radioactivity	141.15	National Primary Drinking Water Regulations	141
Maximum Contaminant Levels for Turbidity	141.13	National Primary Drinking Water Regulations	141
Mechanical Integrity	146.8	Underground Injection Control Program: Criteria and Standards	146
Medium Discharges, Determining Response Resources Required for	Appendix E (4.0)	Oil Pollution Prevention	112
Memorandum of Agreement with the Regional Administrator	123.24	State Program Requirements	123
Memorandum of Agreement with the Regional Administrator	145.25	State UIC Program Requirements	145
Memorandum of Understanding among the DOI, DOT and EPA	Appendix B	Oil Pollution Prevention	112
Methods for Organic Chemical Analysis of Municipal and Industrial Wastewater	Appendix A	Guidelines Establishing Test Procedures for the Analysis of Pollutants	136
Methods to Calculate Production Volumes for Facilities Producing under Pressure	Appendix D – Attachment D	Oil Pollution Prevention	112
Michigan	Subpart X	State Underground Injection Control Programs	147
Microbial Monitoring	141.144	National Primary Drinking Water Regulations	141
Minimum Criteria for Siting	146.62	Underground Injection Control Program: Criteria and Standards	146
Minnesota	Subpart Y	State Underground Injection Control Programs	147
Minor Modifications of Permits	122.63	EPA Administered Permit Programs: the National Pollutant Discharge Elimination System	122
Minor Modifications of Permits	144.41	Underground Injection Control Program	144
Mississippi	Subpart Z	State Underground Injection Control Programs	147
Missouri	Subpart AA	State Underground Injection Control Programs	147

Index to 40 CFR Water Regulations by Subject and Topic

subject/topic	section	title	part
Model Facility–specific Response Plan	Appendix F (1.0)	Oil Pollution Prevention	112
Modification or Revocation and Reissuance of Permits	144.39	Underground Injection Control Program	144
Modification or Revocation and Reissuance of Permits	122.62	EPA Administered Permit Programs: the National Pollutant Discharge Elimination System	122
Monitoring	143.5	National Secondary Drinking Water Regulations	143
Monitoring and Analytical Requirements	Subpart C	National Primary Drinking Water Regulations	141
Monitoring Frequency for Radioactivity in Community Water Systems	141.26	National Primary Drinking Water Regulations	141
Monitoring of Consecutive Public Water Systems	141.29	National Primary Drinking Water Regulations	141
Monitoring Requirements for Lead and Copper in Tap Water	141.87	National Primary Drinking Water Regulations	141
Monitoring Requirements for Water Quality Parameters	141.88	National Primary Drinking Water Regulations	141
Montana	Subpart BB	State Underground Injection Control Programs	147
National Revised Primary Drinking Water Regulations: MCLs	Subpart G	National Primary Drinking Water Regulations	141
Nebraska	Subpart CC	State Underground Injection Control Programs	147
Nevada	Subpart DD	State Underground Injection Control Programs	147
New Hampshire	Subpart EE	State Underground Injection Control Programs	147
New Jersey	Subpart FF	State Underground Injection Control Programs	147
New Mexico	Subpart GG	State Underground Injection Control Programs	147
New Sources and New Dischargers	122.29	EPA Administered Permit Programs: the National Pollutant Discharge Elimination System	122
New York	Subpart HH	State Underground Injection Control Programs	147
Nitroaromatics and Isophorone – Method 609	Appendix A	Guidelines Establishing Test Procedures for the Analysis of Pollutants	136
Nitrosamines – Method 607	Appendix A	Guidelines Establishing Test Procedures for the Analysis of Pollutants	136
Non-Centralized Treatment Devices	Subpart J	National Primary Drinking Water Regulations	141

Index to 40 CFR Water Regulations by Subject and Topic			
subject/topic	*section*	*title*	*part*
Noncompliance and Program Reporting by the Director	123.45	State Program Requirements	123
Noncompliance and Program Reporting by the Director	144.8	Underground Injection Control Program	144
Non–persistent Oils or Group 1 Oils Include	Appendix E	Oil Pollution Prevention	112
Non-transportation-related Facilities w/Oil Storage Capacity >42,000 gals	Appendix C (2.1)	Oil Pollution Prevention	112
North Carolina	Subpart II	State Underground Injection Control Programs	147
North Dakota	Subpart JJ	State Underground Injection Control Programs	147
Notice and Hearing	121.23	State Certification of Activities Requiring a Federal License or Permit	121
Notice of Discharge of a Reportable Quantity	Subpart C	Determination of Reportable Quantities for Hazardous Substances	117
Notice of Hearing; Objection; Public Comment	104.3	Public Hearings on Effluent Standards for Toxic Pollutants	104
Notice of Proposed Administrative Compliance Orders	142.204	National Primary Drinking Water Regulations Implementation	142
Notice to State	142.23, 142.81	National Primary Drinking Water Regulations Implementation	142
Notification	Appendix F (1.3.1)	Oil Pollution Prevention	112
Notification to Licensing or Permitting Agency	121.27	State Certification of Activities Requiring a Federal License or Permit	121
NPDES Permit Application Testing Requirements	Appendix D	EPA Administered Permit Programs: the National Pollutant Discharge Elimination System	122
NPDES Primary Industry Categories	Appendix A	EPA Administered Permit Programs: the National Pollutant Discharge Elimination System	122
Ohio	Subpart KK	State Underground Injection Control Programs	147
Oil Storage Facilities	Subpart A	Liability Limits for Small Onshore Storage Facilities	113
Oil Transport	Attachment C	Oil Pollution Prevention	112
Oklahoma	Subpart LL	State Underground Injection Control Programs	147
On-water Oil Recovery Resource Mobilization Factors	Table 4 to Appendix E	Oil Pollution Prevention	112

Index to 40 CFR Water Regulations by Subject and Topic

subject/topic	section	title	part
Operating Requirements	146.67	Underground Injection Control Program: Criteria and Standards	146
Operating, Monitoring and Reporting Requirements	146.13–146.33	Underground Injection Control Program: Criteria and Standards	146
Opportunity for Public Hearings; Opportunity for State Conferences	142.205	National Primary Drinking Water Regulations Implementation	142
Oregon	Subpart MM	State Underground Injection Control Programs	147
Organic and Inorganic Chemicals, Variances and Exemptions from MCLs	142.62	National Primary Drinking Water Regulations Implementation	142
Organic Chemical Analysis of Municipal and Industrial Wastewater– Method 601	Appendix A	Guidelines Establishing Test Procedures for the Analysis of Pollutants	136
Organic Chemicals, Sampling and Analytical Reqs	141.24	National Primary Drinking Water Regulations	141
Organochlorine Pesticides and PCBs- Method 608	Appendix A	Guidelines Establishing Test Procedures for the Analysis of Pollutants	136
Osage Mineral Reserve–Class II Well	Subpart GGG	State Underground Injection Control Programs	147
Pennsylvania	Subpart NN	State Underground Injection Control Programs	147
Permit Application and Special NPDES Program Requirements	Subpart B	EPA Administered Permit Programs: the National Pollutant Discharge Elimination System	122
Permit Conditions	Subpart C	EPA Administered Permit Programs: the National Pollutant Discharge Elimination System	122
Permit Conditions	Subpart E	Underground Injection Control Program	144
Permitting Requirements	123.25	State Program Requirements	123
Persistent Oils	Appendix E	Oil Pollution Prevention	112
Personnel	Appendix F (1.3.4)	Oil Pollution Prevention	112
Personnel Response Training Logs	Appendix F (1.8.3.1)	Oil Pollution Prevention	112
Petition for Public Hearing	142.32	National Primary Drinking Water Regulations Implementation	142
Petition Standards and Procedures	Subpart C	Hazardous Waste Injection Restrictions	148
Petitions to Allow Injection of a Waste Prohibited under Subpart B	148.21	Hazardous Waste Injection Restrictions	148

Index to 40 CFR Water Regulations by Subject and Topic

subject/topic	section	title	part
Phenols - Method 604	Appendix A	Guidelines Establishing Test Procedures for the Analysis of Pollutants	136
Phthalate Esters – Method 606	Appendix A	Guidelines Establishing Test Procedures for the Analysis of Pollutants	136
Places with Populations between 100,000 and 250,000	Appendix G	EPA Administered Permit Programs: the National Pollutant Discharge Elimination System	122
Plan Implementation	Appendix F (1.7)	Oil Pollution Prevention	112
Planning Distance Calculation for Oil Transport on Water	Attachment C-III	Oil Pollution Prevention	112
Plugging and Abandoning Class I-III Wells	146.11	Underground Injection Control Program: Criteria and Standards	146
Polychlorinated Biphenyls (PCBs)	129.106	Toxic Pollutant Effluent Standards	129
Polynuclear Aromatic Hydrocarbons (PAH) - Method 610	Appendix A	Guidelines Establishing Test Procedures for the Analysis of Pollutants	136
Post-closure Care	146.73	Underground Injection Control Program: Criteria and Standards	146
Powers of Presiding Officer	104.7	Public Hearings on Effluent Standards for Toxic Pollutants	104
Precision and Recovery Statements for Methods for Measuring Metals	Appendix D	Guidelines Establishing Test Procedures for the Analysis of Pollutants	136
Prehearing Conferences	104.8	Public Hearings on Effluent Standards for Toxic Pollutants	104
Preparation of Spill Prevention Control and Countermeasure Plans	112.3	Oil Pollution Prevention	112
Primary Enforcement Responsibility	Subpart B	National Primary Drinking Water Regulations Implementation	142
Prior Notice under the Clean Water Act	Subpart A	Prior Notice of Citizen Suits	135
Prior Notice under the Safe Drinking Water Act	Subpart B	Prior Notice of Citizen Suits	135
Procedure for Processing an Indian Tribe's Application	145.59	State UIC Program Requirements	145
Procedures for Establishing a More Stringent Effluent Limitation	129.7	Toxic Pollutant Effluent Standards	129
Procedures for Revision of State Programs	123.62	State Program Requirements	123

Index to 40 CFR Water Regulations by Subject and Topic

subject/topic	section	title	part
Procedures for Revision of State Programs	145.32	State UIC Program Requirements	145
Procedures for Withdrawal of State Programs	123.64	State Program Requirements	123
Procedures for Withdrawal of State Programs	145.34	State UIC Program Requirements	145
Processing an Indian Tribe's Application	142.78	National Primary Drinking Water Regulations Implementation	142
Processing an Indian Tribe's Application	123.33	State Program Requirements	123
Prohibition	123.29	State Program Requirements	123
Prohibition of Class IV Wells	144.13	Underground Injection Control Program	144
Prohibition of Movement of Fluid into Underground Sources of Drinking Water	144.12	Underground Injection Control Program	144
Prohibition of Unauthorized Injection	144.11	Underground Injection Control Program	144
Prohibition on Use of Lead Pipes, Solder and Flux	141.44	National Primary Drinking Water Regulations	141
Prohibitions (State NPDES Programs, See 123.25)	122.4	EPA Administered Permit Programs: the National Pollutant Discharge Elimination System	122
Prohibitions on Injection	Subpart B	Hazardous Waste Injection Restrictions	148
Promulgation of Class II Programs for Indian Lands	144.3	Underground Injection Control Program	144
Promulgation of Standards	104.15	Public Hearings on Effluent Standards for Toxic Pollutants	104
Proposed Administrative Compliance Orders	142.203	National Primary Drinking Water Regulations Implementation	142
Provisions for Tribal Criminal Enforcement Authority710	123.34	State Program Requirements	123
Proximity to Sensitive Environments	Appendix C (2.3)	Oil Pollution Prevention	112
Proximity to Public Drinking Water Intakes	Appendix C (2.4)	Oil Pollution Prevention	112
Public Education and Supplemental Monitoring Requirements	141.86	National Primary Drinking Water Regulations	141
Public Hearing	"142.13, 142.33"	National Primary Drinking Water Regulations Implementation	142

Index to 40 CFR Water Regulations by Subject and Topic

subject/topic	section	title	part
Public Hearings on Variances and Schedules	142.44	National Primary Drinking Water Regulations Implementation	142
Public Notification	141.32	National Primary Drinking Water Regulations	141
Public Water Systems Using Point-of-Entry Devices, Criteria for	141.101	National Primary Drinking Water Regulations	141
Puerto Rico	Subpart BBB	State Underground Injection Control Programs	147
Purgeable Aromatics – Method 602	Appendix A	Guidelines Establishing Test Procedures for the Analysis of Pollutants	136
Purgeable Halocarbons – Method 601	Appendix A	Guidelines Establishing Test Procedures for the Analysis of Pollutants	136
Purgeable Organics – Method 624	Appendix A	Guidelines Establishing Test Procedures for the Analysis of Pollutants	136
PWS Compliance Orders	Subpart J	National Primary Drinking Water Regulations Implementation	142
Qualified Individual's Duties	Appendix F	Oil Pollution Prevention	112
Rainfall Zones of the United States	Appendix E	EPA Administered Permit Programs: the National Pollutant Discharge Elimination System	122
Receipt and Use of Federal Information	123.42	State Program Requirements	123
Recommendations	108.6	Employee Protection Hearings	108
Record Maintenance	141.33	National Primary Drinking Water Regulations	141
Recording and Reporting of Monitoring Results	144.54	Underground Injection Control Program	144
Recording and Reporting of Monitoring Results	122.48	EPA Administered Permit Programs: the National Pollutant Discharge Elimination System	122
Recordkeeping Requirements	141.92	National Primary Drinking Water Regulations	141
Records	144.17	Underground Injection Control Program	144
Records Kept by States	142.14	National Primary Drinking Water Regulations Implementation	142
Relationship to Federal Response Actions	109.4	Criteria for State, Local and Regional Oil Removal Contingency Plans	109
Removal Capacity Planning Table	Table 2 to Appendix E	Oil Pollution Prevention	112
Reportable Quantities Notice	117.21	Determination of Reportable Quantities for Hazardous Substances	117

Index to 40 CFR Water Regulations by Subject and Topic

subject/topic	section	title	part
Reportable Quantities, Determining	117.3	Determination of Reportable Quantities for Hazardous Substances	117
Reporting and Public Notification for Certain Unregulated Contaminants	141.35	National Primary Drinking Water Regulations	141
Reporting and Recordkeeping Requirements	141.76	National Primary Drinking Water Regulations	141
Reporting Requirements	141.91, 141.31	National Primary Drinking Water Regulations	141
Reporting Requirements	146.70	Underground Injection Control Program: Criteria and Standards	146
Reporting, Public Notification and Recordkeeping	Subpart D	National Primary Drinking Water Regulations	141
Reports by States	142.15	National Primary Drinking Water Regulations Implementation	142
Request by an Indian Tribe for Eligibility	142.76	National Primary Drinking Water Regulations Implementation	142
Request by an Indian Tribe Eligibility	145.56	State UIC Program Requirements	145
Request for Investigation	108.3	Employee Protection Hearings	108
Requirements for Class I, II and III Wells	144.28	Underground Injection Control Program	144
Requirements for Compliance Evaluation Programs	145.12	State UIC Program Requirements	145
Requirements for Eligibility of Indian Tribes	123.31	State Program Requirements	123
Requirements for Enforcement Authority	145.13	State UIC Program Requirements	145
Requirements for Permitting	145.11	State UIC Program Requirements	145
Requirements for Petition Submission, Review and Approval or Denial	148.22	Hazardous Waste Injection Restrictions	148
Requirements for Wells Injecting Hazardous Waste	144.14	Underground Injection Control Program	144
Requiring a Permit	144.25	Underground Injection Control Program	144
Requiring Other Information	144.27	Underground Injection Control Program	144
Response Capability Caps	Table 5 to Appendix E	Oil Pollution Prevention	112
Response Equipment Inspection	Appendix F (1.8.1.2)	Oil Pollution Prevention	112

Index to 40 CFR Water Regulations by Subject and Topic

subject/topic	section	title	part
Response Equipment Listing, Testing/deployment	Appendix F	Oil Pollution Prevention	112
Response Plan Cover Sheet	Appendix F (2.0)	Oil Pollution Prevention	112
Response Resource Operating Criteria	Table 1 to Appendix E	Oil Pollution Prevention	112
Response Resources for Small, Medium and Worst Case Spills	Appendix F (1.7.1)	Oil Pollution Prevention	112
Review and Advice	121.3	State Certification of Activities Requiring a Federal License or Permit	121
Review by Regional Administrator and Notification	121.13	State Certification of Activities Requiring a Federal License or Permit	121
Review of Exemptions Granted Pursuant to a Petition	148.23	Hazardous Waste Injection Restrictions	148
Review of Projects Affecting the Edwards Underground Reservoir	Subpart B	Sole Source Aquifers	149
Review of State Programs and Withdrawal of Primacy Programs	142.17	National Primary Drinking Water Regulations Implementation	142
Review of State Variances, Exemptions and Schedules	142.22	National Primary Drinking Water Regulations Implementation	142
Review of State issued Variances and Exemptions	Subpart C	National Primary Drinking Water Regulations Implementation	142
Review Procedures	142.81	National Primary Drinking Water Regulations Implementation	142
Revision of State Programs	142.12	National Primary Drinking Water Regulations Implementation	142
Rhode Island	Subpart OO	State Underground Injection Control Programs	147
Schedule of Compliance	144.53	Underground Injection Control Program	144
Schedules of Compliance	122.47	EPA Administered Permit Programs: the National Pollutant Discharge Elimination System	122
Screening Criteria for the Substantial Harm Flowchart, Description of	Appendix C (2.0)	Oil Pollution Prevention	112
Secondary Containment Inspection	Appendix F (1.8.1.3)	Oil Pollution Prevention	112
Secondary Maximum Contaminant Levels	143.4	National Secondary Drinking Water Regulations	143

Index to 40 CFR Water Regulations by Subject and Topic

subject/topic	section	title	part
Security	Appendix F (1.10)	Oil Pollution Prevention	112
Semivolatile Organic Compounds by Isotope Dilution, Method 1625 Rev. B	Appendix A	Guidelines Establishing Test Procedures for the Analysis of Pollutants	136
Service of Complaint	135.5	Prior Notice of Citizen Suits	135
Service of Notice	135.12, 135.3	Prior Notice of Citizen Suits	135
Service of Proposed Consent Judgment	135.6	Prior Notice of Citizen Suits	135
Sharing of Information	123.41	State Program Requirements	123
Sharing of Information	145.14	State UIC Program Requirements	145
Signatories to Permit Applications and Reports	144.32	Underground Injection Control Program	144
Signatories to Permit Applications and Reports (State Programs, See 123.25)	122.22	EPA Administered Permit Programs: the National Pollutant Discharge Elimination System	122
Silvicultural Activities	122.27	EPA Administered Permit Programs: the National Pollutant Discharge Elimination System	122
Siting Requirements	141.5	National Primary Drinking Water Regulations	141
Size Classes and Liability Limits for Oil Storage Facilities <1,000 Barrels	113.4	Liability Limits for Small Onshore Storage Facilities	113
Small and Medium Discharges	Appendix F (1.5.1)	Oil Pollution Prevention	112
Small Discharges, Determining Response Resources Required for	Appendix E (3.0)	Oil Pollution Prevention	112
Sodium, Special Monitoring for	141.42	National Primary Drinking Water Regulations	141
Solvent Wastes, Waste Specific Prohibitions	148.11	Hazardous Waste Injection Restrictions	148
Source Water Treatment Requirements	141.84	National Primary Drinking Water Regulations	141
South Carolina	Subpart PP	State Underground Injection Control Programs	147
South Dakota	Subpart QQ	State Underground Injection Control Programs	147
SPCC Plan Amendments by Regional Administrator	112.4	Oil Pollution Prevention	112
Special Primacy Requirements	142.16	National Primary Drinking Water Regulations Implementation	142

Index to 40 CFR Water Regulations by Subject and Topic

subject/topic	section	title	part
Special Regulations, Monitoring Regulations and Prohibition on Lead	Subpart E	National Primary Drinking Water Regulations	141
Spill Management Team Tabletop Exercise Logs	Appendix F (1.8.2.2)	Oil Pollution Prevention	112
Spill Prevention Control and Countermeasure Plan Amendments	112.5	Oil Pollution Prevention	112
State Assumption of Responsibility	144.66	Underground Injection Control Program	144
State Consideration of a Variance or Exemption Request	142.21	National Primary Drinking Water Regulations Implementation	142
State Program Approval, Revision and Withdrawal	Subpart D	State Program Requirements	123
State Program Description	123.22	State Program Requirements	123
State Program Submissions	Subpart B	State Program Requirements	123
State Program Submissions	Subpart C	State UIC Program Requirements	145
State Programs, Criteria for Withdrawal of	123.63	State Program Requirements	123
State UIC Programs, Criteria for Withdrawal of	145.33	State UIC Program Requirements	145
State issued Variances and Exemptions	142.21	National Primary Drinking Water Regulations Implementation	142
State-Required Mechanisms, Use of	144.65	Underground Injection Control Program	144
Storm Water Discharges (for State NPDES, See 123.25)	122.26	EPA Administered Permit Programs: the National Pollutant Discharge Elimination System	122
Substantial Harm Criteria	Appendix C	Oil Pollution Prevention	112
Substantial Harm Criteria, Applicability	Appendix F	Oil Pollution Prevention	112
Supplemental Information	121.12	State Certification of Activities Requiring a Federal License or Permit	121
Tank Inspection	Appendix F (1.8.1.1)	Oil Pollution Prevention	112
Tennessee	Subpart RR	State Underground Injection Control Programs	147
Tentative and Final Decision by the Administrator	104.14	Public Hearings on Effluent Standards for Toxic Pollutants	104
Termination of Approved Petition	148.24	Hazardous Waste Injection Restrictions	148
Termination of Permits	144.41	Underground Injection Control Program	144

subject/topic	section	title	part
Termination of Permits (State Programs, See 123.25)	122.64	EPA Administered Permit Programs: the National Pollutant Discharge Elimination System	122
Termination of Suspension	121.28	State Certification of Activities Requiring a Federal License or Permit	121
Testing and Monitoring Requirements	146.68	Underground Injection Control Program: Criteria and Standards	146
Texas	Subpart SS	State Underground Injection Control Programs	147
Timing of Notice	135.14	Prior Notice of Citizen Suits	135
Total Coliforms, Variances and Exemptions from the MCL	142.63	National Primary Drinking Water Regulations Implementation	142
Total Trihalomethanes Sampling, Analytical and Other Requirements	141.3	National Primary Drinking Water Regulations	141
Total Trihalomethanes, Variances from the MCL	142.61	National Primary Drinking Water Regulations Implementation	142
Toxaphene	129.104	Toxic Pollutant Effluent Standards	129
Toxic Pollutants	129.4	Toxic Pollutant Effluent Standards	129
Transfer of Information and Permit Review	Subpart C	State Program Requirements	123
Transfer of Permits	144.38	Underground Injection Control Program	144
Transfer of Permits	122.61	EPA Administered Permit Programs: the National Pollutant Discharge Elimination System	122
Transfer, Modification, Revocation, Reissuance, Termination of Permits	Subpart D	EPA Administered Permit Programs: the National Pollutant Discharge Elimination System	122
Transmission of Information to EPA	123.43	State Program Requirements	123
Treatment Techniques	Subpart K	National Primary Drinking Water Regulations	141
Treatment Techniques for Acrylamide and Epichlorohydrin	141.112	National Primary Drinking Water Regulations	141
Tribal Eligibility Requirements	142.72	National Primary Drinking Water Regulations Implementation	142
Trust Territory of the Pacific Islands	Subpart FFF	State Underground Injection Control Programs	147
Turbidity Sampling and Analytical Reqs	141.22	National Primary Drinking Water Regulations	141
UIC Permit Effect	144.35	Underground Injection Control Program	144

**Index to 40 CFR Water Regulations by Subject and Topic**

Index to 40 CFR Water Regulations by Subject and Topic

subject/topic	section	title	part
UIC Program Approval, Revision and Withdrawal	Subpart D	State UIC Program Requirements	145
UIC Program Description	145.23	State UIC Program Requirements	145
Utah	Subpart TT	State Underground Injection Control Programs	147
Variance Request	142.41	National Primary Drinking Water Regulations Implementation	142
Variances	142.41	National Primary Drinking Water Regulations Implementation	142
Variances and Exemptions	141.4	National Primary Drinking Water Regulations	141
Variances Issued by the Administrator	Subpart E	National Primary Drinking Water Regulations Implementation	142
Vermont	Subpart UU	State Underground Injection Control Programs	147
Virgin Islands	Subpart CCC	State Underground Injection Control Programs	147
Virginia	Subpart VV	State Underground Injection Control Programs	147
Volatile Organic Compounds	Appendix A	Guidelines Establishing Test Procedures for the Analysis of Pollutants	136
Vulnerability Analysis	Appendix F (1.4.2)	Oil Pollution Prevention	112
Waiver	121.16	State Certification of Activities Requiring a Federal License or Permit	121
Waiver of Requirement by Director	144.16	Underground Injection Control Program	144
Washington	Subpart WW	State Underground Injection Control Programs	147
Waste Analysis	148.5	Hazardous Waste Injection Restrictions	148
West Virginia	Subpart XX	State Underground Injection Control Programs	147
Wisconsin	Subpart YY	State Underground Injection Control Programs	147
Wording of the Instruments	144.71	Underground Injection Control Program	144
Worst Case Discharge	Appendix F (1.5.2)	Oil Pollution Prevention	112
Worst Case Discharge Planning Volume, Determination of	Appendix D	Oil Pollution Prevention	112
Wyoming	Subpart ZZ	State Underground Injection Control Programs	147

Government Institutes Mini-Catalog

PC #		ENVIRONMENTAL TITLES	Pub Date	Price
629		ABCs of Environmental Regulation: Understanding the Fed Regs	1998	$49
627		ABCs of Environmental Science	1998	$39
672		Book of Lists for Regulated Hazardous Substances, 9th Edition	1999	$79
579		Brownfields Redevelopment	1998	$79
4100	◙	CFR Chemical Lists on CD ROM, 1998 Edition	1997	$125
4089	🖫	Chemical Data for Workplace Sampling & Analysis, Single User Disk	1997	$125
512		Clean Water Handbook, 2nd Edition	1996	$89
581		EH&S Auditing Made Easy	1997	$79
673		E H & S CFR Training Requirements, 4th Edition	1999	$89
4082	◙	EMMI-Envl Monitoring Methods Index for Windows-Network	1997	$537
4082	◙	EMMI-Envl Monitoring Methods Index for Windows-Single User	1997	$179
525		Environmental Audits, 7th Edition	1996	$79
548		Environmental Engineering and Science: An Introduction	1997	$79
643		Environmental Guide to the Internet, 4rd Edition	1998	$59
650		Environmental Law Handbook, 15th Edition	1999	$89
353		Environmental Regulatory Glossary, 6th Edition	1993	$79
652		Environmental Statutes, 1999 Edition	1999	$79
4097	◙	OSHA CFRs Made Easy (29 CFRs)/CD ROM	1998	$129
4102	◙	1999 Title 21 Food & Drug CFRs on CD ROM-Single User	1999	$325
4099	◙	Environmental Statutes on CD ROM for Windows-Single User	1999	$139
570		Environmentalism at the Crossroads	1995	$39
536		ESAs Made Easy	1996	$59
515		Industrial Environmental Management: A Practical Approach	1996	$79
510		ISO 14000: Understanding Environmental Standards	1996	$69
551		ISO 14001: An Executive Report	1996	$55
588		International Environmental Auditing	1998	$149
518		Lead Regulation Handbook	1996	$79
554		Property Rights: Understanding Government Takings	1997	$79
582		Recycling & Waste Mgmt Guide to the Internet	1997	$49
615		Risk Management Planning Handbook	1998	$89
603		Superfund Manual, 6th Edition	1997	$115
566		TSCA Handbook, 3rd Edition	1997	$95
534		Wetland Mitigation: Mitigation Banking and Other Strategies	1997	$75

PC #	SAFETY and HEALTH TITLES	Pub Date	Price
547	Construction Safety Handbook	1996	$79
553	Cumulative Trauma Disorders	1997	$59
663	Forklift Safety, 2nd Edition	1999	$69
539	Fundamentals of Occupational Safety & Health	1996	$49
612	HAZWOPER Incident Command	1998	$59
535	Making Sense of OSHA Compliance	1997	$59
589	Managing Fatigue in Transportation, *ATA Conference*	1997	$75
558	PPE Made Easy	1998	$79
598	Project Mgmt for E H & S Professionals	1997	$59
552	Safety & Health in Agriculture, Forestry and Fisheries	1997	$125
669	Safety & Health on the Internet, 4th Edition	1999	$59
597	Safety Is A People Business	1997	$49
668	Safety Made Easy, 2nd	1999	$59
590	Your Company Safety and Health Manual	1997	$79

Government Institutes

4 Research Place, Suite 200 • Rockville, MD 20850-3226
Tel. (301) 921-2323 • FAX (301) 921-0264
Email: giinfo@govinst.com • Internet: http://www.govinst.com

Please call our customer service
department at (301) 921-2323
for a free publications catalog.

CFRs now available online.
Call (301) 921-2355 for info.

Government Institutes Order Form

4 Research Place, Suite 200 • Rockville, MD 20850-3226
Tel (301) 921-2323 • Fax (301) 921-0264
Internet: http://www.govinst.com • E-mail: giinfo@govinst.com

4 EASY WAYS TO ORDER

1. Tel: **(301) 921-2323**
Have your credit card ready when you call.

2. Fax: **(301) 921-0264**
Fax this completed order form with your company purchase order or credit card information.

3. Mail: **Government Institutes Division**
ABS Group Inc.
P.O. Box 846304
Dallas, TX 75284-6304   USA

Mail this completed order form with a check, company purchase order, or credit card information.

4. Online: Visit http://www.govinst.com

PAYMENT OPTIONS

❑ **Check** *(payable in US dollars to **ABS Group Inc. Government Institutes Division**)*

❑ **Purchase Order** *(This order form must be attached to your company P.O. Note: All International orders must be prepaid.)*

❑ **Credit Card**   ❑ VISA   ❑ MasterCard   ❑ AMERICAN EXPRESS

Exp. ____ /____

Credit Card No. _____

Signature _____

(Government Institutes' Federal I.D.# is 13-2695912)

CUSTOMER INFORMATION

Ship To: (Please attach your purchase order)

Name _____

GI Account # *(7 digits on mailing label)* _____

Company/Institution _____

Address _____
(Please supply street address for UPS shipping)

City _____ State/Province _____

Zip/Postal Code _____ Country _____

Tel ( ) _____

Fax ( ) _____

Email Address _____

Bill To: (if different from ship-to address)

Name _____

Title/Position _____

Company/Institution _____

Address _____
(Please supply street address for UPS shipping)

City _____ State/Province _____

Zip/Postal Code _____ Country _____

Tel ( ) _____

Fax ( ) _____

Email Address _____

Qty.	Product Code	Title	Price

❑ **New Edition No Obligation Standing Order Program**
Please enroll me in this program for the products I have ordered. Government Institutes will notify me of new editions by sending me an invoice. I understand that there is no obligation to purchase the product. This invoice is simply my reminder that a new edition has been released.

Subtotal _____
MD Residents add 5% Sales Tax _____
Shipping and Handling (see box below) _____
Total Payment Enclosed _____

15 DAY MONEY-BACK GUARANTEE
If you're not completely satisfied with any product, return it undamaged within 15 days for a full and immediate refund on the price of the product.

SOURCE CODE: BP01

Shipping and Handling	Sales Tax
Within U.S:	Maryland 5%
1-4 products: $6/product	Tennessee 6%
5 or more: $4/product	Texas 8.25%
Outside U.S:	Virginia 4.5%
Add $15 for each item (Global)	